RED VIRGIN SOIL

First published, Cornell Paperbacks, 1987.

The W. Averell Harriman Institute for Advanced Study of the Soviet Union, Columbia University, sponsors the *Studies of the Harriman Institute* in the belief that their publication contributes to scholarly research and public understanding. In this way the Institute, while not necessarily endorsing their conclusions, is pleased to make available the results of some of the research conducted under its auspices. A list of the *Studies* appears at the back of this book.

Printed in the United States of America
Librarians: Library of Congress cataloging information appears on the last page of the book

The paper in this book is acid-free and meets the guidelines for permanence and durability of the Committee on Production Guidelines for Book Longevity of the Council on Library Resources.

For

R. P. and F.W.M.

CONTENTS

PREFACE

WITH this book I hope to contribute to the knowledge of one of the richest and liveliest periods in Russian literature —the 1920's—through a study of what seems to me its most distinguished body of writing: the belles lettres, theory, and criticism that centered in the "thick" journal *Red Virgin Soil* (*Krasnaya nov'*). Founded in 1921, *Red Virgin Soil* represented the first serious attempt in nearly half a century to create and shape an entire generation of writers, readers, and critics through the energy and authority of a journal. The ways in which it successfully did so form the main lines of my investigation.

I believe that we deal here with a "school" or "movement" in the sense of a like-minded—though not always consciously held—view of the purposes and techniques of art. It is my hope, therefore, to demonstrate that *Red Virgin Soil* forms a genuine unity, not just one imposed by a title, and that each of the components, while retaining its individuality, worked together with the others to create the journal's physiognomy. Because the thick journal once again became the focus of literary activity in the twenties, I think that a study of its most important representative— *Red Virgin Soil*—is a valid, fruitful, and convenient way of studying an age. That age ended in 1928; so did the effective life of this journal (even though publication went on for another fourteen years). One of my aims is to show that this coincidence is no coincidence at all.

Until recently, this period has been little known to the general reader and little investigated by scholars. In the Soviet Union the purposes of literature in the two decades following the twenties left no place for many of the best writers, critics, and theorists who had been active then. They were considered not merely anachronistic, but positively dangerous, and were consigned to an oblivion so engulfing that not even their names remained behind. The history of those first exciting years in the development of a new literature, when not suppressed outright, was rewritten in such a way as to take in only a small and highly selected area of reality. *Red Virgin Soil* did not fall within that area: since it epitomized practically everything that Stalinists found abhorrent about the twenties, it did not merit even invective, but was simply ignored for two decades. So was its editor, Aleksandr Konstantinovich Voronskii. His writings were banned, and every reference to him was excised from the memoirs, diaries, and letters of the writers who had worked with him but had not shared his fate.

In the last ten years, efforts have been made in the Soviet Union to rewrite the history of the 1920's, but with a much greater concern for accuracy. Readers are now making the acquaintance of new and strange books, ideas, and writers that are in fact forty years old. Voronskii, like many of his contemporaries, has been "rehabilitated" and is being acclaimed as a major critic. The importance of *Red Virgin Soil* as a "school" is at least being acknowledged. This long look backward is one of the most striking features of the so-called "thaw," and perhaps the most important: for it is no less true in Soviet Russia that a literature draws vitality from its own past. The boundaries of that past, which for Soviet literature lie preeminently in the twenties, are gradually being extended. Yet exploration is on the whole still timid and tentative, as if it feared to discover too much. The only reasonably extensive account of *Red Virgin Soil* so far covers a mere thirty-five pages in a book entitled *Sketches of the History of Soviet Russian Journalism, 1917-1932 (Ocherki istorii russkoi sovetskoi zhurnalistiki* [Moscow, 1966]; devotes more than half of its discussion to the uninteresting period after the twenties; and amounts to little more than a gloss on the tables of contents. So far there has been no real study of Voronskii: the brief appreciations which have appeared ignore two-thirds of his work and seriously distort the rest. In a society where a literary act is still a political act, caution restrains enthusiasm and crimps originality—particularly when a period as varied, experimental, and rich as the twenties is involved.

In Western Europe and America we would expect to find a different picture. In many ways the twenties speak more eloquently to us than to today's Soviet reader, and we have had the opportunity to look at those years with a clearer and sharper eye. The studies that do exist are for the most part models of balanced judgment and scholarly detective work. They have tended to concentrate on two or three large areas of literary theory and criticism—notably Formalism and the various proletarian movements. But many others await investigation. Furthermore, virtually no book-length monographs exist on most of the major writers; much of their work remains untranslated; and much which has been translated needs to be redone. In poetics, the investigations made by the Russian Formalists forty years ago are still standard. The economics of publishing and writing, the life of salons and circles, and what Schücking has called the "sociology of literary taste"[1]—these, and countless other topics, remain untouched.

As for *Red Virgin Soil*, scholars outside the Soviet Union have generally acknowledged its importance as a journal, but have accorded it virtually no recognition as a "school," and, until this present book, no detailed study. Voronskii has fared better: there have been at least one good article on his literary theory and criticism,[2] brief treatments of him in various histories, and in 1964 the first attempt at a real investigation, in Gabriela Porębina's *Aleksander Woronski. Poglądy estetyczne i krytycznoliterackie (1921–1928)*. This short monograph, a publication of the Polish Academy of

[1] Cf. Levin L. Schücking, *Sociology of Literary Taste* (London, 1941).

[2] Hugh McLean, Jr., "Voronskij and VAPP," *The American Slavic and East European Review*, VIII, No. 3 (October 1949), 188-200.

Sciences, has several merits, among them clear exposition and a mention of all Voronskii's major work. But serious omissions of fact and distortions of perspective compromise its value. For example, it came out too early to make use of the archival materials that have recently been published (primarily the Voronskii-Gor'kii correspondence); it neglects Voronskii's editorial activities, which provided much of the impetus for his criticism and theory; it interprets his work from the standpoint of a naïve Marxism which regards itself as a finished and perfect system, and therefore gives little indication, beyond expressions of disapproval, of what he contributed himself to that "system"; it evaluates strengths and weaknesses in a way disappointingly repetitive of recent Soviet accounts. Nonetheless, I am grateful to Miss Porębina for helping me make some of my own formulations more precise.

My study, then, aims to fill what I regard as a serious gap in our understanding of modern Russian literature. It must, of course, speak for itself. But I should like to mention some of the techniques and approaches involved, and some of the limitations I have had to observe, particularly with regard to the four traditional areas of literary study I cut across.

So FAR most studies of the twenties have concentrated on literary theory and criticism; but as yet there has been no investigation of the unique contribution made by *Red Virgin Soil*. In comparison with Formalism it looks pale; held up against Futurism and the various proletarian movements of the period it seems unspectacular. But I contend that it has been the most serious and most developed of all the literary versions of Marxism so far and, therefore, probably the most decisive single influence on the subsequent course of Russian literature. In studying it, my overall aim is to throw some light on problems that remain ungrasped in the Marxist accounting of art, and to suggest an answer to the question that is being asked with ever-greater insistence: does Marxism really have any future in the theory, criticism, and practice of literature?

Often when I say "Voronskii" in this study I am merely using a shorthand for all the journal's contributors. Voronskii did make the largest single contribution, but his ideas were not synonymous with *Red Virgin Soil*. Other men and women left a substantial legacy as well—for example, A. Lezhnev, V. Pravdukhin, Fyodor Zhits, Valentina Dynnik, and Lyubov' Aksel'rod (Ortodoks). Each had a strongly individual approach, and often a substantial reputation in his own right. The important thing, for my purpose, is the way in which their ideas meshed, within *Red Virgin Soil*, to form a consistent and unified body of thought (and criticism) which is not reducible to any one of them.

ALTHOUGH it is generally agreed that the thick journals occupy an important position in the Russian literature of the last forty years, no one has yet asked why this is so, what the nature of that position is, and why such a traditional form should have taken such firm hold in a "new" society. As far as I know, mine is the first extensive treatment of the genre for the Soviet period. It is my contention that the thick journal, like any other literary genre, develops largely by its own laws; and I hope, through a detailed study of the structure and function of *Red Virgin Soil*, to help illuminate what those laws are. I concentrate mainly on the literature sections—that is, belles lettres, criticism, theory, and book reviews—with only glancing reference to the others. I believe this restriction is legitimate; for in these sections throbs the engine of any real thick journal. I make no attempt, however, to account for every story, every review, every article; that kind of completeness has been the curse of many journal studies. Rather, I am concerned with patterns and trends; and I therefore do not hesitate to be selective.

The one serious drawback to an internal study of *Red*

Virgin Soil—indeed, of any Soviet journal—has been the in-accessibility of its files. It seems unlikely that they were "destroyed in the war," as I was told in Moscow. Some of the gap has been filled by the recent publication of the Voronskii-Gor'kii correspondence, of which I make extensive use. Otherwise I must rely almost wholly on the evidence of the printed page. Still, that is how any literature must ultimately be judged.

THE preeminence of *Red Virgin Soil* assured it of rich and tangled external affairs. In particular, it was the focus of the noisiest and most consequential literary quarrel of the decade—between the defenders of the so-called "fellow travelers" and the proletarians. This quarrel has been better documented and studied by Western scholars than any other aspect of literature in the twenties, and I frequently send the reader to them for fuller treatment of certain matters that I touch only briefly. Having restudied the major documents myself, I believe that my accounting is new in the following respects: it describes the quarrel from the standpoint of *Red Virgin Soil*, with special reference to the effects on the journal's internal life; and it makes use of new materials which illuminate some of the hitherto mysterious maneuverings and shiftings in literary politics from 1924 to 1928.

My treatment of the imaginative literature in *Red Virgin Soil* involves me with the best and most characteristic work of the important writers of the twenties. Since I emphasize their participation in a movement, my approach to them is quite different from what it would be if I were making monographs on them. But I hope that my observations may help stimulate some much-needed monographic studies.

I also try to give some attention to two extrinsic areas of literature in the twenties: the function of the literary group, particularly in relation to the thick journal; and the situation of the writer in the literary "market." Here I only scratch the surface; but it is a deeper scratch than has so far been made, at least outside Russia. My chief sources are memoirs by writers active at the time, and the extensive statistical material that is scattered throughout various publications in the twenties, particularly *The Journalist* (*Zhurnalist*). But I owe my heaviest debt to two outstanding studies which also date from that period: *Literature and Commerce* (*Slovesnost' i kommertsiya*) by Grits, Trenin, and Nikitin (Moscow, 1929), which deals with the eighteenth and nineteenth centuries but raises problems that are relevant to the twenties; and Boris Eikhenbaum's article "Literature and the Writer" ("Literatura i pisatel'," *Zvezda*, No. 5 [1927]), whose riches are disproportionate to its modest size.

THROUGHOUT the book, I try to make a framework rather than a frame: my main emphasis falls on the points at which these special approaches intersect to form the unity that made the journal, defined the school, and, to a large extent, shaped the "personality" of the age. And I hope that I may also raise some problems whose solutions (if any there are) lie outside the scope of this book.

MY SYSTEM of transliteration follows the British Standard (1958), with some small modifications, the most important of which is the substitution of "yo" for "ë." All translations from the Russian are my own.

MANY PEOPLE have assisted in the preparation of this study. Ernest J. Simmons suggested the topic, in a somewhat different form. Robert L. Belknap, Robert Gorham Davis, Maurice Friedberg, William E. Harkins, and Frederick Maguire read the manuscript in an earlier version and made valuable suggestions for revision. Mrs. Galina Stilman brought her masterful command of Russian and English to bear on many a sticky problem in translation. Miss

Lalor Cadley of Princeton University Press has been a most patient and helpful editor. To the Periodicals Division of the Saltykov-Shchedrin Library in Leningrad and to the Microfilm Division of the Lenin Library in Moscow I am grateful for courteous and efficient help in securing materials unavailable in the United States and Western Europe. Grants from the Ford Foundation and the Inter-University Committee on Travel Grants made preliminary research possible. I owe a special debt of gratitude to Rufus W. Mathewson, Jr., for generous encouragement throughout. Finally, my heartfelt thanks go to Albert E. Anderson, Ruth C. Anderson, and Cecilia H. Hecht for support in a variety of ways.

ROBERT A. MAGUIRE

January 1967
New York, N.Y.

RED VIRGIN SOIL

CHAPTER I

Beginnings

THE FIRST ISSUE OF *Red Virgin Soil*, a "literary and scientific-publicistic journal,"[1] rolled off the presses in June 1921. This was no ordinary undertaking. For one thing, it represented a deliberate attempt to revive a form of literature that had been virtually extinct in Russia for half a century—the "thick" journal. In addition, it had the backing of three of the most important people of the time—Lenin, his wife Krupskaya, and Maksim Gor'kii. Finally, it flouted common sense, for 1921 was the least promising time imaginable to start any new publication.

Russia had been at war for seven years—with Germany, Austria, and Poland, with foreign interventionists, and with itself. The Bolsheviks had defeated their rivals and clung precariously to power in the cities, while an exhausted populace looked on. Factories had shut down. Villages had reverted to savagery. Demobilized soldiers, hungry and jobless, roamed the countryside. Inflation had destroyed money and created a barter economy. Pilfering, graft, and highjacking had replaced commerce. Society and nationhood had crumbled. The life of the mind had withered.

For most men of the old society, the turning point had come two years earlier. Until 1919 it had been possible to suppose that the hardships, uncertainties, and disruptions of this strange new life were subject to some control and would soon pass. In many ways, the cultural world had looked almost as lively as ever, and the government had even seemed interested in trying to guarantee the minimal physical conditions essential to the survival of that world. The State Publishing House (Gosizdat) had been set up

[1] Hereafter abbreviated as *RVS* in the text and *KN* in the notes. The quotation appears on the title page.

4 BEGINNINGS

specially to provide employment for penurious intellectuals, as translators, editors, and copyreaders. The new mass education programs and the burgeoning bureaucracy required an army of teachers, counsellors and quill drivers. Wide publicity had been given to officially-sponsored writing contests, which paid off in generous prizes. Censorship had been kept lax enough to permit the survival of many old journals and publishing enterprises, and to encourage the founding of new ones. But during the winter of 1919-1920, the war finally reached into the capital cities. People encountered hunger, cold, misery, and deprivation of an intensity they had never imagined possible. Probably the members of the old intelligentsia suffered the most; for now they saw clearly, where before they had been able to doubt, that the old values they had cherished and the new ones they had hoped to create bore no relation to actuality. Many interpreted the death of Aleksandr Blok (from what popular opinion diagnosed as disillusionment) as a sign of their own death. They could find no place in Russia, either as it was or as it now seemed likely to become.[2] By 1920 they had begun to leave in large numbers, transferring their ideals and their work in science, philosophy,

[2] The history of intellectual (particularly literary) life in Russia during the Civil War remains to be written, even though sources abound. To recommend just a few that seem relevant here: Vl. Khodasevich, *Literaturnye stat'i i vospominaniya* (New York, 1954); for government policy toward the press, the appropriate documents reproduced in *O partiinoi i sovetskoi pechati. Sbornik dokumentov* (Moscow, 1954); for an enumeration and sketchy description of literary journals, A. A. Maksimov, "Pervye sovetskie literaturno-khudozhestvennye zhurnaly," *Voprosy pechati* (*Uchonye zapiski L.G.U.* [Leningradskogo gosudarstvennogo universiteta]), No. 257, Seriya filologicheskikh nauk, No. 47 (Leningrad, 1959), pp. 65-92; N. I. Dikushina, "Literaturnye zhurnaly 1917-1929 gg.," *Istoriya russkoi sovetskoi literatury*, i, 1917-1929 (Moscow, 1958), 490-527; and *Ocherki istorii russkoi sovetskoi zhurnalistiki, 1917-1932*, ed. A. G. Dement'ev (Moscow, 1966); for the attitudes of a large and vocal part of the "old" intelligentsia, the complete run of the newspaper *Vestnik literatury* (Petrograd, 1919-1921).

politics, and the arts to Berlin, Prague, Belgrade, Sofia, Constantinople, Paris. Among the writers, Bunin, Kuprin, Aleksei Tolstoi, Merezhkovskii, Gippius, Aldanov, and nearly fifty others who had won reputations before the Revolution were living abroad by 1921.[3] Their ranks grew the following year when the Bolsheviks expelled over 160 intellectuals for "oppositional" attitudes, and again in 1923, with the arrival of Tsvetaeva, Khodasevich, Vyacheslav Ivanov, Remizov, Shmelyov, Zaitsev, and many more. To all appearances, no promising young talents were coming forth to replace the old.

The outward signs of cultural life were fading away as well. Not one of the dozens of journals that had come out during the Civil War survived beyond 1921. Lithography and photo-lithography had been introduced on a large scale after the Revolution; but with paper production down to one-eighth of what it had been before the war, and with as many as 75 per cent of the printing presses immobilized for repairs, nothing could halt the relentless diminution in the number of printed pages.[4] The *Herald of Literature* reported that printed books were "being replaced by the manuscript, and the printer by the scribe," and went on— not wholly facetiously—to forecast a time when books might be copied en masse at the dictation of a single reader and the shortages of paper might make it necessary to write on rocks with a nail.[5] The rising cost of goods and services (such as a 120 per cent increase in the printing rates in 1920) pushed the retail price of books up to a prohibitively high level and threatened to ruin the private publishers who were being forced to charge anywhere from three to

[3] Gleb Struve, *Russkaya literatura v izgnanii* (New York, 1956), pp. 16-17.
[4] Cf. N. I. Buzlyakov, *Voprosy planirovaniya pechati v SSSR* (Moscow, 1957); A. I. Nazarov, *Ocherki istorii sovetskogo knigoizdatel'stva* (Moscow, 1952), p. 104.
[5] "Ot nabornoi mashiny k rukopisnoi knige," *Vestnik literatury*, No. 8 (1920), p. 1.

five times more than the state for their products.[6] A black market in paper flourished, also at the expense of the private publishers, who were said to pay 150 roubles and more a pound in Petrograd, as compared with the ten-to-fifteen rouble price prevailing in the Main Administration of Paper Industry Establishments (Glavbum).[7] The system of cost accounting (*khozraschot*) that was introduced in 1921 piled still another burden on the publishing industry and put an end to many periodicals.[8] By 1921, only 66 journals were coming out in Moscow—a decline of 85 per cent from 1918—and a mere 116 in all of Russia.[9] The production of

[6] "Nachalo kontsa," *Vestnik literatury*, No. 11 (1921), p. 12.

[7] "Nakanune katastrofy v izdatel'skom dele," *Vestnik literatury*, No. 6 (1920), p. 1.

[8] Though cost accounting for the press was not introduced officially until 1922, it had been in effect for most state publishing houses since mid-1921, and they were responsible for putting out most of the journals.

[9] D. Lebedev, "Zhurnaly SSSR," *Zhurnalist*, No. 7 (1923), pp. 34-35. The figures include journals in the "national" languages, but there were few of those.

Notorious indeed are the difficulties involved in handling Soviet statistics in any field. Publishing is no exception. For one thing, it is not always clear what the Soviets mean by "journal" (*zhurnal*). The term may also cover collections or miscellanies (*sborniki*), agitators' notebooks, and the transactions of scholarly organizations. V. Narbut writes, for instance, that in 1922 some 944 journals were registered in all of Soviet Russia, and the following year, some 1,054. His figures cover "periodical press organs," and, though he says he is limiting them to journals, it is obvious, by contrast with D. Lebedev's more modest figures, that he includes more than journals in the usual sense of the word ("Knizhnozhurnal'noe delo," *Zhurnalist*, No. 5 [1925], p. 15). Variations in the number of copies printed (*tirazh*) tend to be even greater. N. I. Buzlyakov writes, for instance, that the circulation of journals reached a peak of 418 million in 1931 (*Voprosy planirovaniya pechati v SSSR* [Moscow, 1957], p. 105). Another source gives 170 million as the figure for 1933 (*Pechat' strany sotsializma*, Vsesoyuznyi Nauchno-Izdatel'skii Institut Izobrazitel'noi Statistiki TsUNKhU Gosplana SSSR [1939], p. 74). To be sure, Buzlyakov does say that circulation dropped after 1931, but one finds it hard to believe that it fell as much as the other source indicates. In most cases, we have taken the more modest figures, whenever there are discrepancies, as probably being closer to the facts for journals

books followed a similar curve: from over 26,000 titles in 1913, it declined to 4,500 between 1920 and 1921.[10] In an open letter to the Eighth Congress of Soviets, Gor'kii reported that textbooks were so scarce that students were banding together in groups of fifteen or twenty to buy a single volume, which was then passed around or recopied. With masterful understatement, he suggested that such conditions turned the government's mass-literacy program into a farce.[11]

To an observer from abroad, Russia presented a grim picture in 1920:

> there is no paper, no ink, no machines, no transportation or telegraph, no productive labor, *there is no living Russia*. Whole generations are dying out. Not only are whole categories of people dying off, but things, institutions, science, culture as well. All movement natural to life is coming to a standstill in literature and ideas. Alas, one must make a survey not so much of life in Russia as of death, the processes of quick and slow death. . . .[12]

AN ATTEMPT to establish a new journal under such circumstances must have appeared ludicrously misguided. Yet it was a decision not lightly taken. The question of a thick journal, according to *Pravda*, had more than once been "put on the agenda of Party congresses and conferences," but "until now, all decisions and desires have remained only on paper."[13] It was one man—Aleksandr Konstantinovich

---

proper. As it is, the trends revealed by the statistics are more important than the figures themselves.

[10] A. I. Nazarov, *ibid.*, p. 103. These figures may include journals and almanacs as well.

[11] "O vol'nykh izdatel'stvakh," *Vestnik literatury*, No. 3 (1921), p. 11.

[12] M. Vishnyak, "Na Rodine," *Sovremennyya zapiski*, No. 1 (Paris, 1920), p. 206.

[13] K. T., review of *RVS*, No. 1 (1921), *Pravda*, July 6, 1921, p. 2.

Voronskii—who converted intentions into actualities. On February 3, 1921, he took up his new assignment as editor-in-chief of the publishing division of Glavpolitprosvet.[14] Two days later he presented the directing board with a detailed proposal for a thick monthly journal, to be called *Red Virgin Soil* (*Krasnaya nov'*). His plan, obviously made well in advance, was quickly approved. The head of Glavpolitprosvet was Lenin's wife N. K. Krupskaya, who later that month accompanied Voronskii to the Politburo, where the proposal was again set forth and swiftly endorsed. All that now remained was to interest Lenin in the project and secure the blessing of Gor'kii. Several years later Voronskii described the occasion:

> The first organizational meeting of the editors of *Red Virgin Soil* took place in the Kremlin, in the office of Vladimir Il'ich Lenin. Present at the meeting, besides him, were Nadezhda Konstantinovna Krupskaya, Aleksei Maksimovich Peshkov (Gor'kii), and myself. Vladimir Il'ich arrived at this meeting during an interval between two others. I made a brief report on the need for publishing a thick literary-artistic journal. Vladimir Il'ich agreed with my opinions. And here too it was planned that the journal would be published by Glavpolitprosvet,

[14] Glavpolitprosvet stands for Glavnyi politiko-prosvetitel'nyi komitet—the Central Political Enlightenment Committee. It was established in 1920 as an agency of the People's Commissariat of Education (Narkompros) and had the responsibility of organizing and carrying out—largely through an active publishing house of the same name—the political education of adults in the various provinces of Russia. See N. Krupskaya, "Glavpolitprosvet i iskusstvo," *Pravda*, February 13, 1921, p. 1; "O Glavpolitprosvete i agitatsionno-propagandistskikh zadachakh partii," Resolution of Tenth Party Congress, Moscow, March 8-16, 1921, reproduced in *O partiinoi i sovetskoi pechati. Sbornik dokumentov* (Moscow, 1954), p. 230.

The details that follow concerning the early proposals for *RVS* are based on unpublished archival materials as summarized by I. Smirnov, "Pis'mo A. K. Voronskogo V. I. Leninu," *Novyi mir*, No. 12 (1964), pp. 213-15. The text of the proposal to the Politburo is given on p. 215.

that I would be chief editor, and that Aleksei Maksimovich would edit the belles lettres section of this journal.[15]

With permission granted, matters moved swiftly. By mid-March Voronskii was frantically trying to put the first issue together. The articles on science and politics, he reported, "in part are already coming in, in part are being finished"; but the problems with belles lettres looked insurmountable. A promised contribution from I. Vol'nov had literally gone up in smoke when the Cheka in Oryol burned everything he had written. And Gor'kii, who was entrusted with editing all the prose fiction, had so far sent in virtually nothing, despite Voronskii's desperate urgings.[16] But somehow things pulled together, a volume took shape, and a scant five months after Voronskii had appeared before the Politburo, his proposal became a reality.

CERTAINLY there was nothing modest about this first issue. Here were three hundred pages,[17] densely set in a large format roughly seven by ten inches, printed in 15,000 copies and graced with a title which, however clumsy it may sound in English, was both poetic and bold. Dignity and

[15] "Iz proshlogo," *Prozhektor*, No. 6 (1927), p. 19.

[16] Letter to Gor'kii, March 24, 1921, in *M. Gor'kii i sovetskaya pechat'. Arkhiv A. M. Gor'kogo*, x, Book 2 (Moscow, 1965), 9. All the letters between Voronskii and Gor'kii that have so far been published are in this volume, which hereafter is referred to as *Arkhiv*.

[17] Theoretically, the number of pages could have been almost tripled. According to N. Meshcheryakov, the chief editor of the State Publishing House, all the journals published by Gosizdat (*RVS, LEF, October,* and *The Workers' Journal*) were allotted exactly the same amount of paper, fifty signatures (*listy*) per issue a month. One signature is sixteen printed pages. (Speech at meeting of Press Section of Central Committee, May 9-10, 1924, in *K voprosu o politike RKP (b) v khudozhestvennoi literature* [Moscow, 1924], pp. 83-84.) In fact, the journals rarely exceeded 300 pages an issue; and there was a serious paper shortage in Russia throughout the twenties, which kept down the number of copies printed, and even made it impossible for most journals, *RVS* included, to publish a full twelve issues a year.

solidity lay heavy on it: with departments of literature, bibliography, criticism, popular science, politics, and economics, it called to mind a typical nineteenth-century thick journal. However, the contents of this issue, and the following one, presented a curiously flawed picture. The non-literary departments were brilliant. Voronskii, obviously taking no chances, had stocked them with contributions from prominent specialists: Preobrazhenskii and Varga wrote on economics; Timiryazev on popular science; V. Friche on literature; and M. Pavlovich on political science. But the real plums were the aristocrats of Bolshevism, beginning with Lenin and Krupskaya, followed by Radek, Lunacharskii, Bukharin, Pyatakov, Frunze, Ol'minskii, and the late Rosa Luxemburg. They wrote not the polite testimonials one might expect of busy politicians, but substantial and thoughtful articles. Their participation, if nothing else, gave evidence of the value which the Party attached to this new enterprise. At the other extreme stood the literature section. It was filled with unfamiliar names and, with one exception, seemed dedicated to the service of mediocrity. Of the three poets featured in the first issue and the four in the second, only Boris Pasternak had any kind of a national reputation, and he was not a new writer; the others could scarcely have been expected to jog the memory of the average reader. The same was true for the prose writers. Semyon Pod''yachev, Ol'ga Forsh, and Pavel Nizovoi had started publishing before the Revolution, but had made no real reputations; and the quality of their contributions here suggested that they probably never would. Only Vsevolod Ivanov's *The Guerrillas* (*Partizany*) and A. Arosev's *Torment* (*Strada*) had the double merit of coming from young, unknown writers and displaying a genuine, if somewhat tentative talent.

This distance separating the two parts of the journal is not difficult to explain. In literature, Voronskii was forced to print anything he could get, as his letter to Gor'kii in

March indicates. What is surprising is that Gor'kii himself contributed nothing to the first two issues. Of the older men of letters sympathetic to Bolshevism, he was the only one with a name comparable to those that graced the other sections of the journal. But his absence did make possible a kind of literary illusion. Although only about half the writers who appeared in these first two issues were novices, all except Pasternak were virtual strangers to the public and therefore might well have passed for "new writers." It would have been easy for the reader, who knew nothing about the desperate shortage of things to print, to form the impression that the "revival" of literature showed far more vigor than it actually possessed, particularly with the distinguished and familiar names in the other departments lending luster and, in the case of the Bolshevik dignitaries, virtually an official endorsement as well.

The pull of some such illusion is suggested by the enthusiasm with which the public received *RVS*. It was an enthusiasm which to us seems extravagant, especially since it was lavished on the literature. *Pravda* raved; Polonskii spoke of "a major victory on our literary front"; Anna Karavaeva reported that "in the libraries people were gulping down [the first issue], and you even had to put your name on a waiting list to read it."[18] The printing run was increased to 25,000 for the remaining issues that year. As for the response of the writers, Voronskii wrote Lenin that "Vsevolod Ivanov is only the first bomb to burst among the Zaitsevs and the Zamyatins ['old' anti-Bolshevik writers]. I am sure there will be others as well."[19] He was right. Slowly the manuscripts began to come in—some from established pro-

[18] K. T., review of *RVS*, No. 1, *Pravda*, July 6, 1921, p. 2; V. Polonskii, review of *RVS*, Nos. 1 and 2, *Pechat' i revolyutsiya*, No. 2 (1921), p. 228; A. Karavaeva, "Iz vospominanii starogo 'Ognelyuba,'" *Po dorogam zhizni. Dnevniki, ocherki, vospominaniya* (Moscow, 1957), p. 707.

[19] Letter to Lenin, April 21, 1922, quoted in I. Smirnov, "Pis'mo . . . ," p. 216.

fessionals, but most from writers, young and old, whose existence no one had suspected. Slowly the literary section of *RVS* grew in size and quality. The gamble had paid off. New talents throughout Russia were, as Voronskii put it, "really pushing up from below,"[20] and they were coming to *RVS* on its own terms. The appearance of this new journal gave them the assurance that literature had revived, and that literary ambitions had every chance of finding fulfillment. "Don't think," wrote one of them, "that publishing in *RVS* was an ordinary, everyday thing at the time. It was a serious and perhaps to some extent a political step in one's life. In fact, on the 'Petersburg Parnassus' people began to say that the young writers were going over to the Bolsheviks. . . ."[21] Lidiya Seifullina, who was living in Siberia at the time, described the impact of *RVS* on herself and on the other young writers in her town who were hoping to put out a journal of their own, *Siberian Lights*:

> [M. M. Basov] brought the first issues of the journal *Red Virgin Soil* into the library. For five evenings or so after that we talked about Vs. Ivanov's *The Guerrillas*, about Arosev's *Torment*, about the poems published in this issue. We discovered that a literature of our times had appeared in the R.S.F.S.R. We began to dream of having Vs. Ivanov as a possible contributor. He was a Siberian. In fact, the whole writers' world of *Red Virgin Soil*, without any false pathos, seemed then to be a special, sacred world. Its existence was both an encouragement and an obligation. I would give five years of my life, even though it is already in decline, to experience once again that feeling of love for a writer which I experienced then. It evoked a real response, it made one want to grow up so that one might

[20] *Ibid.*

[21] N. Nikitin, *Izbrannoe v dvukh tomakh*, i (Moscow-Leningrad, 1959), 17-18, as cited in A. G. Dement'ev, "A. Voronskii—kritik," *A. Voronskii. Literaturno-kriticheskie stat'i*, compiled by G. A. Voronskaya and A. G. Dement'ev, ed. by L. A. Shubin (Moscow, 1963), p. 8.

become as worthy of the name of writer as, for example, Vsevolod Ivanov.[22]

Certainly the reviewer in *Pravda* had not foreseen anything like this: he tempered his excitement over the first issue with gloomy doubts that the new journal could survive, the times being what they were.[23] Voronskii himself must have had serious misgivings more than once during the next two years. Apparently he had no help in running day-to-day business. And even though he had edited a newspaper, he felt utterly ignorant about the technical operations of a journal, as he later revealed in a story about himself:

> Once I went to see Aleksei Maksimovich [Gor'kii] on some editorial business. I told him that the first issue was being set up and that things were going well. Gor'kii asked me: "How many signatures will there be in the issue?" I thought that by signatures were meant two journal pages. According to my rough estimate, there were to be 320 pages in the journal. I answered Gor'kii: "160 signatures [2,560 pages]." Gor'kii looked at me in such a way that I hastened to end the conversation and get out of his room. At the State Publishing House they explained to me what was meant by the "signature" of a journal [one signature equals 16 pages]. For a week I was afraid to go and see Gor'kii.[24]

Eagerness, intelligence, and enthusiasm soon overcame his inexperience; but there were other formidable obstacles

[22] "Pamyatnoe pyatiletie," *O literature* (Moscow, 1958), p. 277.
[23] K. T., review of *RVS*.
[24] "Iz proshlogo," p. 20. A further observation on the "signature" is in order. There are three different kinds of signatures, but only two need concern us here: the printer's signature, or sheet (*pechatnyi list*), which equals sixteen printed pages, and the author's signature (*avtorskii list*), which equals 40,000 characters (individual letters, punctuation marks, numerals, and the spaces between words), or, in poetry, 700 lines. It is not always clear which of these two is meant (cf., e.g., Ch. IX, nn. 29 and 30).

over which he had no control. The paper shortage, for one, seemed chronic. In his proposal to the Politburo, Voronskii stated that the journal would appear every month and a half or two months. Since it was impossible for him to know then whether he could assemble enough material for a single issue, even this was an optimistic prediction. No doubt Voronskii did look forward to producing eventually a regular monthly publication on the pattern of the old thick journals. While the inflow of material soon made this necessary, it was not until 1926 that he managed to put out a full twelve issues a year. It seems safe to blame the shortages of supplies that dogged all editors throughout the twenties.

Then there was the problem of money. To be a so-called "literary worker" in the spring of 1921 was in effect to commit suicide by starvation, for the pay scales had fallen far behind the inflation in one of the hungriest times in Russian history; and *RVS*, as the official publication of a government organization, paid according to the scales. It was immediately obvious to Voronskii that emergency measures had to be taken if there was to be any journal at all. The printers, as independent a breed in Russia as anywhere, flatly refused to set the second issue unless he came up with a sizable supplement. Voronskii therefore went to the Secretariat of the Central Committee where he was received by Emel'yan Yaroslavskii:

> I requested several million roubles, and when he asked me what I needed the money for, I replied: "For bribes. To sweeten up the printers." Comrade Yaroslavskii was horrified and said: "Such conversations are unthinkable in the Secretariat of the Central Committee." I then corrected myself. I said that I needed the money not for bribes but to give bonuses to the workers. Comrade Yaroslavskii grimly signed a piece of paper for me. I got the money. This was precisely at the time the famine was

beginning. And so, we managed to put out the first issue of RVS.[25]

His writers, paid not by salary but according to what they produced, were far worse off. Voronskii badgered, hectored, and scrounged for them; and when money was not to be had, he sometimes came up with things that money could not buy. "I can boast of the fact," he wrote Gor'kii, "that I got [for Pod' 'yachev] some shoes, underwear, and a suit."[26] On one occasion he hauled two enormous sacks of extra food rations into his tiny office and doled out the contents himself.[27] Even when the government increased the rate of payment fivefold, he still was not satisfied. His writers, he insisted, deserved even more; and somehow he managed to get it. By 1922 he could report that he was "paying excellently."[28]

Probably none of this maneuvering would have been possible if Voronskii had not had constant access to the highest levels of the Party. Friends at court were essential in those years if one hoped to get anything done, for the regular channels of administration were often hopelessly clogged with people who seemed to be running the government out of a do-it-yourself manual. From his editorial office—a single room the size of a closet tucked away in a building on Chistoprudnyi Boulevard—Voronskii could easily visit Krupskaya, who worked across the hall. To Lenin he sent each new issue of RVS; and Lenin in turn gave careful attention to at least the articles on politics and economics, frequently offered "advice and instructions," occasionally handed on literary manuscripts that had come in unsolicited, and asked to be kept apprised of developments in emigré literature, on which he considered Voronskii an

[25] Ibid.
[26] Letter to Gor'kii, March 24, 1921, Arkhiv, p. 9.
[27] "Iz proshlogo," p. 20.
[28] Letter to Gor'kii, April 27, 1922, Arkhiv, p. 10.

expert.[29] Voronskii did not hesitate to exploit these connections at least to the extent of dropping Lenin's name
wherever it might open doors. "I would arrive at our
Soviet institutions," he recalled, "and when I ran into difficulties—and there were many—I would let it be understood
unequivocally that Vladimir Il'ich was very much interested
in *RVS*, and that would help me."[30]

BY THE spring of 1922 Voronskii could report to Gor'kii that
"the work is hard but the journal is 'settling down.' "[31] He
now felt confident enough to declare himself "firmly convinced that in a year or two this young spring greenery
will grow up strong and will take the place of the Chirikovs
and gentlemen of like ilk [i.e., 'decadents']—and with
honor too. I'm organizing youth against the 'old men.' "[32]
He did not exaggerate. By 1923 it was obvious that *RVS*
had more than justified the high hopes raised two years
earlier: a wholly new Russian literature, rich in theme and
reach, had appeared, most of it within this one journal. And
it had a large and steady audience.

The press runs of 25,000 in 1921 had not lasted. The
paper famine, the natural erosion of reader interest once
the novelty wore off, and the competing claims of other

[29] The quote is from Voronskii, "Iz proshlogo," p. 19. Lenin's
respect for Voronskii as a student of emigré literature is mentioned
by S. Vinogradskaya, "Esli podoidyot," *Ogonyok*, No. 18 (1962),
p. 7. (Voronskii had published in *Pravda* the first substantial Soviet
survey of that literature.) Voronskii as a reader of manuscripts for
Lenin is briefly discussed by I. Smirnov, "Pis'mo . . . ," p. 215. He
gives by way of example a play of D. S. Kovalenko, *The Bolsheviks*
(*Bol'sheviki*), and observes: "It was characteristic that Vladimir
Il'ich should rely on Voronskii . . ." (p. 215). He suggests that there
are other such cases on record in the Central Party Archives.
[30] "Iz proshlogo," p. 19. Cf. also Voronskii, "Zaklyuchitel'noe slovo,"
K voprosu o politike RKP (b) v khudozhestvennoi literature (Moscow,
1924), p. 100.
[31] Letter to Gor'kii, April 27, 1922, *Arkhiv*, p. 10.
[32] Letter to Lenin, April 21, 1922, quoted in I. Smirnov, "Pis'mo
. . . ," p. 215.

new journals that began to appear—all these factors pulled the figures down to an average of 8,000 in 1922 and 7,000 in 1923. But after that, they began to climb again, and finally they leveled off at around 11,000, which was very respectable for the twenties. Although mere figures cannot tell us how many people actually read the journal, we do know that in 1925 some 83 per cent of the sales were by subscription (where one could save 10 per cent off the regular price of two to three roubles a copy), and the rest through retail outlets.[33] This suggests that the journal reached more people through reading rooms, libraries, and hand-to-hand circulation than it would have if its sales had been largely over the counter. It is not possible to say just who these readers were. According to Voronskii's original proposal, the journal was "aimed at the new reader: those taking courses in workers' faculties, those in courses for military commanders, in Soviet courses, in Soviet and Party schools"—in other words, the new Soviet intelligentsia.[34] Certainly RVS was not a "mass" publication in the American sense of the word. There was never any obvious attempt to write down to the reader, or any of the usual devices for building circulation, or any of the advertisements for toothpaste, cameras, and perfume that other Soviet publications continued to carry during the NEP period. As in the nineteenth-century thick journals, the range of departments and the level of writing presupposed a rather well-educated reader—one who had gone through at least the equivalent of the secondary school curriculum.

Not until the middle of 1923 did the various departments in RVS become fixed and take on permanent names. But the basic structure was laid down from the outset. Belles lettres occupied the most prominent place: approximately the first third of every issue was given to the latest works

---

[33] V. Narbut, "Khudozhestvennaya literatura v 1924 i 1925 gg.," *Zhurnalist*, No. 1 (1926), p. 15.

[34] As quoted in I. Smirnov, "Pis'mo . . . ," p. 215.

of fiction and poetry. Practically no plays were published. And it was the policy, to which we find very few exceptions, to offer only original Russian works, not translations.[35] Next in importance were theory and criticism, usually combined under the heading "Literary Regions" (Literaturnye kraya); then came book reviews, under the unimaginative rubric of "Criticism and Bibliography" (Kritika i Bibliografiya). As befits a typical thick journal, the emphasis fell on literature; the other arts, for reasons we shall suggest later, never got any comprehensive or systematic treatment. And it was the writing of the younger talents of contemporary Russia, especially the so-called "fellow travelers," which received by far the most attention. Relatively scanty notice was given the emigrants: there were no studies of individual writers, only a few desultory attempts, usually couched in invective, at surveying that literature as a whole. The older "bourgeois" writers who had remained in Russia fared somewhat better: Belyi, Blok, and Zamyatin were each given a monograph, albeit unflattering. As for the foreign literature of the time, anyone reading only *RVS* formed a curiously lopsided picture. Naturally the favorites were "exposers" of the evils of bourgeois civilization (like Anatole France and Upton Sinclair), friends of the Soviet Union (like Romain Rolland), out-and-out Communists (like Henri Barbusse), and in a class by himself as an apostle of the machine age, H. G. Wells. But Mann, Proust, Joyce, Hemingway, Lawrence, Malraux, Eliot, Fitzgerald—they might as well not have been. Still, in restricting itself to the new Soviet writing, *RVS* was only following the purpose it had set itself from the start. And herein, as we shall see, lay its strength.

[35] This was a policy of which Voronskii was proud. He wrote Lenin: ". . . my task is immensely difficult: it's very easy to translate [H. G.] Wells from the original and give [the journal] a 'name,' but very hard to produce one's own brood" (letter of April 21, 1922, as quoted in I. Smirnov, "Pis'mo . . . ," p. 216).

"Politics and Economics" (Politika i Ekonomika) featured surveys and studies in depth on a wide range of subjects, from urgent topics of the day like mass literacy and
juvenile delinquency to more abstruse problems of theory.
Occasionally an article on popular science appeared here
too. This department, as a whole, was far more interesting
in *RVS* than it had been in the nineteenth-century journals,
mainly because the subject matter, once all but taboo, was
now respectable and attracted some of the best Marxist
minds. Among them in *RVS* were Preobrazhenskii and
Varga (economics); Karl Radek (the foreign scene from
a Komintern slant); Nikolai Bukharin (economic theory
and general culture); Lyubov' Aksel'rod (Ortodoks) (political and esthetic theory); and Nikolai Timiryazev (popular science).

Documentary and ethnographical writing occupied a
prominent place. It was organized in a department called
"From the Soil and the Towns" (Iz zemli i gorodov), which
took its name from the title of a sketch by Mikhail Prishvin,
and suggested the idea of the unity of rural and urban life—
a burning issue at the time—and the journal's hope of representing both in its literature. The foreign scene—mainly
Europe—was covered in a section entitled "Abroad"
(Za rubezhom). It specialized in reportorial rather than
analytic accounts of specific events, such as the Ruhr crisis
and the Moroccan rebellion, though it also included some
specimens of the artistic travel memoir, notably Mayakovskii's "America" (No. 2, 1926) and "Mexico" (No. 1, 1926).
Late in 1927, a department entitled "Art" (Iskusstvo) was
added. Sections were sometimes created for special occasions, such as newly discovered archival materials or
memoirs; but with few variations, the departmental structure remained unchanged throughout Voronskii's tenure
as editor. And this was the structure of the typical nineteenth-century thick journal as well.

· I I ·

Why had the Party so long considered publishing a journal, and why at this inauspicious time did Voronskii try to put flesh on the idea?

Many students of Soviet literature have insisted that the Party had no policy toward literature in those early years. This is not quite true. Although there was no *program* for literature at the time, a policy did exist from the moment the Bolsheviks seized power. That policy, generally speaking, was to create a situation which would persuade writers to lend enthusiastic support to the new regime or at least not to oppose it. They were permitted to write in any way they pleased, and to express almost any sentiment they wished, provided they were not blatantly counter-revolutionary. An important corollary was the principle of "free competition," which meant that all literary groups had an equal right to existence, and that none would be allowed to presume to speak for the Party, lest it frighten off the others. This principle represented a logical extension of the Bolshevik belief that the written word has political power and is a weapon in the class struggle; but it also answered to the very practical need of giving the Revolution prestige and tone.

These same considerations held even more firmly in 1921. The number of writers who could then be assembled in support of the Revolution had dwindled to a handful. Nonetheless, it seemed evident to anyone who thought in terms of bases and superstructures that somewhere a new literature must be taking shape in response to the events that had overturned Russian society. As a matter of fact, there were stirrings which might well have suggested new life. In the provincial town of Ivanovo-Voznesensk the proletarian culture movement had yielded up a few young poets. On the shores of the Pacific a group of enthusiastic young writers and critics had given notice of itself under the name of "Creative Work" (Tvorchestvo). In Petrograd the so-called Serapion Brothers were beginning to produce short stories about contemporary Russia. From Siberia Gor'kii had received the manuscript of an unknown writer named Vsevolod Ivanov. "Gor'kii liked *The Guerrillas*," Ivanov reported later. "He took the story to Moscow and promised to get it published and even to bring some money back. But instead he brought the story back. The newspaper could print stories half a signature in length [*The Guerrillas* was much longer], the wretched little journals, which came out irregularly anyway, couldn't manage more than a signature. . . ." Clearly this was a story made for a thick journal; but as Ivanov noted, "there wasn't a single thick journal in all the length and breadth of the land."[36] Might there not be other writers with promising manuscripts, in the cities as well as the provinces, who could find no outlet for their work?

Assuming that there were, it mattered a great deal to the Party which way their loyalties turned. The bourgeoisie, though defeated on the battlefields of the Civil War, operated publishing houses and journals in Russia under the protection of the NEP, and showed keen interest in new talent. The emigration had established several thick journals of high quality which boasted some of the noblest names in Russian literature. The most eminent and, from the Bolshevik point of view, the most dangerous of them all was *Contemporary Notes* (*Sovremennyya zapiski*). If ambitious young writers like Vsevolod Ivanov could find no chance for recognition within Russia, was it impossible that they might send their work abroad, where it could conceivably appear in print beside the work of Bunin, Tolstoi, Remizov, and Merezhkovskii? Despite the absence of diplomatic relations between Soviet Russia and all the major European countries, writers found it relatively easy to make

[36] Vs. Ivanov, "Vstrechi s Maksimom Gor'kim," *Povesti, rasskazy, vospominaniya* (Moscow, 1952), p. 381.

more than casual contacts with the West. Berlin, one of the most spirited centers of emigré culture, received a steady flow of visitors from the East. Indeed it was sometimes hard to tell who was in emigration and who was not: a few writers, like Andrei Belyi and Viktor Shklovskii, practically commuted between Russia and Germany.[37] Such lively literary commerce, as far as the Bolsheviks were concerned, held great ideological dangers for those writers who, for the time being, had elected to retain Soviet citizenship.

There was no need to worry much about the writers who descended from the proletariat or belonged to the Communist Party: their allegiances provided a built-in protection. But there were other young writers who, while supporting the aims of the Revolution in a general way, were themselves neither proletarians nor Communists, and took no active part in political life—writers whom Trotskii later dubbed "fellow travelers" (poputchiki). Because they lacked a firm faith buttressed by Bolshevik truth and the unerring instincts rooted in proletarian parentage, they might easily be led astray. Yet these writers, to all appearances, made up the majority of the new literary talents that had come forth so far. The Bolsheviks felt they had to win them. Voronskii put it succinctly: "at a time when petty-bourgeois, philistinish literature, hostile to us, is flourishing luxuriantly, it is essential to rally the writers who are on our side because only in this way will we be able to wage the war of ideas in the book market."[38]

The plan in short was to form a "center" that would attract the best writers, new and old, who were sympathetic, or at least not openly hostile to the Revolution; to bring them together under Party auspices, carefully blunted in

[37] Cf. Gleb Struve, ibid., pp. 26-27.

[38] At a conference organized by the Agitation-Propaganda Department of the Central Committee in February 1922, to discuss what was to be done with private publishing houses. As quoted in A. G. Dement'ev, "A. Voronskii—kritik," p. 6.

order to avoid any suggestion of coercion; and gradually, through example and patient persuasion, to win them over completely. At the same time, such a center would presumably hasten the "decomposition" of the literature of the bourgeoisie by cutting off transfusions of new blood, and, at the other extreme, reduce the dangers of left-wing opposition by stealing thunder from groups like the Proletkul't and the Futurists, whose radical programs for literature carried an implication—at least to many Bolshevik leaders—of a competing political activism. Finally, the lie would be given to the emigré taunts that the Bolsheviks ruled a cultural desert. A united front of new literature would form under Communist patronage, riding the crest of history and therefore dazzling the world. The center for this ambitious program was to be *RVS*.

CONSIDERING the importance Party leaders attached to this new journal, it is surprising that they did not appoint someone more prominent than Aleksandr Konstantinovich Voronskii as editor. He was a faithful old Bolshevik, but a relatively obscure one. Born at Tambov in August 1884, he descended from a family of provincial priests, as did many Russian revolutionaries. *Vita* and *gesta* merged early. His formal education came to a premature end in 1904, when he was expelled from the Tambov Seminary for unruly behavior. After languishing in the town for a few months, giving lessons and playing at conspiracy in the sluggish local revolutionary movement, he set off for St. Petersburg. As soon as he arrived, in the momentous year of 1905, he tried to join the Social Democrats: he had decided on revolution as a career. To his surprise, they were not impressed. "They" in this case were two people who later occupied high positions in the Party: Sergei Malyshev and Lenin's sister, Mar'ya Il'inichna Ul'yanova. In their eyes Voronskii was a typical seminary student—over-imaginative, hyper-romantic, and likely, if arrested, to blab everything he knew. They urged him to return to Tambov.[39] But Voronskii would not be dissuaded. He demanded an immediate assignment, not to routine work, but to something dangerous and challenging. They finally relented. It is hard to imagine anything more routine than the job of messenger, which is where novices, including Voronskii, traditionally began; but it certainly had its dangers, and Voronskii was satisfied. Indeed he soon discovered that for a young man without conventional work mere existence in the capital was challenging enough. For a long time he lived virtually in solitude, ate irregularly, and rarely slept twice on the same floor. Soon, however, he was promoted to running a printing press, carrying on propaganda in factories and workshops, and even writing up dispatches for the Bolsheviks' official newspaper, *The Social Democrat,* which was published abroad. Eventually he began receiving a small stipend from the Party: he had become a professional.

For the next decade he led the harried and dull life of the typical revolutionary: doing propaganda work in Helsingfors, Moscow, Saratov, Odessa, and Nikolaevsk, serving two stretches in prison and three years in exile in sub-Arctic Yarensk.[40] As careers in the Party apparatus went, his was relatively successful. In 1912 he traveled to Prague as the delegate of the Saratov Organization to the Sixth Congress of the Social Democrats; for a year after the Revolution he served as chairman of the Odessa Soviet; in 1920 he was elected to the Provincial Committee (Gubkom) of the

[39] S. Malyshev, "Stranichki o bor'be 1905 goda," *Prozhektor,* No. 2 (1925), p. 24.

[40] Cf. A. Voronskii, *Za zhivoi i myortvoi vodoi,* I (Moscow, 1927), II (Moscow, 1929). Translated by L. Zarine as *Waters of Life and Death* (London, 1936). These memoirs are semi-fictional in some details, but not in spirit. They are all we have on Voronskii's early years, except for Malyshev's brief memoir. Among other things, they treat in greater detail than is possible here the vicissitudes of Voronskii's initiation into Party work.

Party in Ivanovo-Voznesensk; and during the Civil War he was appointed to the All-Russian Central Executive Committee.

BUT VORONSKII was not cut out to be a professional bureaucrat. His real interest lay in writing. Exile for him, as for many Russian revolutionaries, was a university where he read voraciously and began to turn note-taking into original expression. In 1911, under the pseudonym "Nurmin," which he used occasionally in the twenties as well, he published his first attempts at literary criticism, with a few feuilletons and articles on Gor'kii, Averchenko, and Andreev in *Clear Dawn* (*Yasnaya zarya*), the Odessa newspaper edited by V. V. Vorovskii.

Several years later he himself became an editor, when the Party sent him to the textile town of Ivanovo-Voznesensk, 145 miles northeast of Moscow, to run the newspaper *Workers' Region* (*Rabochii krai*). This was no exile, but a major assignment. Ivanovo-Voznesensk, one of Russia's largest industrial centers with a population of over one hundred thousand, had been a stronghold of the labor movement since the 1880's. One of the first Soviets of Workers' Deputies had been established there in 1905, and the Bolsheviks could always count on its loyal support. Voronskii plunged into his new job with characteristic energy. Of necessity he had to write voluminously on a wide variety of topics; but he concentrated on literature, publishing his first serious critical articles here.[41] Voronskii lost no time in introducing the town's young proletar-

---

[41] *Rabochii krai* has been unavailable; but in the interests of a fuller bibliography of Voronskii's work we list these articles as A. G. Dement'ev gives them (*ibid.*, p. 4): "Maksim Gor'kii i sovetskaya vlast'," No. 154 (1918); "Klassiki i upadochnaya literatura," No. 166 (1919); "Obrechonnye" (concerning Andreev and other "decadents"), No. 79 (1920); "Doloi razum" (about Gershenzon's "Mudrost' Pushkina"), No. 184 (1920); "Bez dorogi" (about Remizov and others), No. 265 (1920).

ian poets to the readers of his newspaper. The best of them—D. Semyonovskii, M. Artamonov, and I. Zhizhin—he later brought to national fame through publication in *RVS*. The partisans of proletarian culture had always insisted that a workers' literature would follow naturally from a well-developed class consciousness; and Ivanovo-Voznesensk gave their case eloquent support.

Voronskii's transfer to Moscow early in 1921 followed a new policy of moving important Party workers "from place to place in order to give them the opportunity of studying in greater breadth the Soviet and Party apparatus, and to lighten their task of struggling with routine."[42] In Voronskii's case, strings may also have been pulled. He had written at least two letters to Lenin between 1919 and 1920. As far as one can tell—for only paraphrases are available—they did not touch on literary matters, but reported on local conditions and Party activities in Ivanovo-Voznesensk and Tambov. Still, from them Lenin obviously knew that Voronskii was an editor, and the latter's remark, in the second of the letters, that he was "still sitting in Ivanovo" looks like a very broad hint.[43]

By then Voronskii had also caught the eye of the country's most influential literary figure, Maksim Gor'kii. The older man had always been a hero to the younger, both as a writer and as a sympathizer with radical causes. Voronskii had seen him driving in the streets of Helsingfors in

[42] Resolution of the Ninth All-Russian Congress of the RKP(b), as quoted by I. Smirnov, "Pis'mo . . . ," p. 214. The organization responsible for carrying out this policy was the Registration and Distribution Section of the Central Committee (Uchotno-raspredelitel'nyi otdel—Uchraspred).

[43] These letters, still unpublished, repose in the Central Party Archives of the Institute of Marxism-Leninism. They are summarized by I. Smirnov, "Pis'mo . . . ," pp. 213-14. The quotation is on p. 214. Smirnov does not make it clear exactly how many letters in all exist. Probably there are three—the two mentioned, and the one that Voronskii wrote in 1922 on literary matters, to which reference has already been made.

1905; he had devoted one of his earliest essays in criticism
to him; under the pseudonym "A. Klimskii" he had sent him
two articles for publication in the Bolshevik journal *Enlightenment* (*Prosveshchenie*), of which Gor'kii was the
literary editor;[44] he had met him fleetingly in St. Petersburg just before the war. But it was not until *Workers'
Region* that he made any impression on his idol. Gor'kii,
always a champion of working-class culture, was impressed
by the young poets whom Voronskii had been publishing
in his newspaper—poets whose accents sounded authen-
tically proletarian to him, even though they derived much
of their effect from a nostalgic contrast between machine
civilization and a dying rural way of life. Gor'kii mentioned
his discovery to Lenin, who thereupon sent the following
memorandum to his secretary:

> Please get *Workers' Region* (the full set) from Ivanovo-
> Voznesensk. (There's a group of real proletarian poets
> there.) Gor'kii praises: Zhizhin, Artamonov, Semyonov-
> skii.)[45]

Whether Gor'kii actually recommended Voronskii for the
chief editorial post in a projected journal that eventually
became *RVS*, we do not know. In any event, Voronskii arrived in Moscow in 1921 to find him a colleague.

Gor'kii edited the literature department of *RVS* until he
left Russia late in 1921. It had been agreed that nothing
would go to the print shop which had not first passed under

[44] *Prosveshchenie*, a monthly "social-political and literary journal,"
edited by Lenin, was a legal publication of the Bolsheviks and
came out in St. Petersburg from the end of 1911 to June 1914. One
of Voronskii's articles was accepted, though the journal closed before
it could be published; of the second there is no trace. Voronskii wrote
to Gor'kii in 1915 inquiring about the fate of his manuscripts (March
4, *Arkhiv*, pp. 8-9); Gor'kii's reply was later confiscated by the
police, and has been lost.
[45] Sh. Manchur'yants, *Vospominaniya o V. I. Lenine*, Part 2 (Moscow, 1957), pp. 674-75, as quoted in A. G. Dement'ev, "V. I. Lenin i
sovetskaya zhurnalistika," *Voprosy literatury*, No. 6 (1962), pp. 10-11.

his blue pencil, and from all we know, that pencil was used lavishly.[46] Even after he had settled in Italy, he still remained "in effect the editor of the literary part of the journal,"[47] as far as Voronskii was concerned. Even if this was not strictly true, at least in an administrative sense, Gor'kii did continue to read the journal carefully during his residence abroad, offered advice freely, and recommended new writers to Voronskii.[48] It was obviously useful for Voronskii to be able to link Gor'kii publicly with *RVS*, and reassuring for him to feel that he could count on his support in the savage literary wars that raged at the time. As a working editor, he never forgot that he was dealing with a working writer: letter after letter contained pleas for contributions, and reproaches when none were made.[49] He also performed certain useful services for Gor'kii, such as sending on new materials, apprising him of the latest

[46] Letter, Voronskii to Gor'kii, March 24, 1921, *Arkhiv*, p. 9.

[47] "Iz proshlogo," p. 20. This exaggeration is characteristic of Soviet accounts of the Gor'kii-Voronskii relationship, and follows the pattern of making Gor'kii responsible for virtually everything in Soviet literature. Cf., e.g., A. G. Dement'ev, "A. Voronskii—kritik," p. 8.

[48] The correspondence between 1922 and 1928 consists of twenty-seven letters from Voronskii and twenty-one from Gor'kii. There are no letters from 1928 or 1929, the years when Voronskii was in disgrace, having been (as we shall see in Chapter v) removed from *RVS* and expelled from the Party; but his temporary restoration to favor is marked by five letters to Gor'kii and four from Gor'kii, in 1930 and 1931. The last letter in the correspondence was written by Voronskii on April 2, 1931, after which he again fell into disfavor. Before 1921, there are but two letters, both from Voronskii: one in 1915 and one in 1921. The correspondence is published in *Arkhiv*, pp. 7-79. Apparently it is complete: nothing is said one way or the other in the notes, but there are a few editorial omissions in the letters, which are indicated by dots and brackets, but not explained.

[49] Gor'kii actually contributed a great deal to *RVS* (see Chapters iii and viii). But one problem any Soviet editor had to contend with was his government's failure to sign the international copyright agreement. This meant, among other things, that in order not to lose his author's rights in Europe, Gor'kii had to publish his works there first. (Cf., e.g., letter to Voronskii, June 18, 1925, *Arkhiv*, pp. 20-21.)

literary gossip, arranging generous advances for works as yet unwritten,[50] and, on one occasion, taking the steps necessary to clear his name in a criminal case.[51] But Voronskii was no sycophant. He could retort quickly and pointedly to slights and unkindnesses from a busy and sometimes impatient correspondent.[52] In the two large articles he wrote on Gor'kii in the 1920's, he could make many unfavorable observations about "world-view" that were not

[50] Gor'kii was chronically in need of money throughout the twenties. (Cf. e.g., Gor'kii to Voronskii, March 23, 1926, *Arkhiv*, pp. 29-30; and Voronskii to Gor'kii, March 1926, *Arkhiv*, pp. 28-29.)

[51] The case in question was briefly: an elaborate swindle, involving foreign currency for the purchase of some scythes in Czechoslovakia, had been perpetrated by one Shatil' in collusion with some high officials of GUM. Gor'kii allegedly recommended Shatil'—a friend of a good friend—to the Czech mission as a reliable go-between. This fact came out in the trial, and the impression given, in the account by *Izvestiya*, was that more was at stake for Gor'kii than mere friendship ("V Verkhovnom sude. Delo GUMa," *Izvestiya*, December 19, 1923, p. 7). Gor'kii, most upset, withdrew his *Notes from a Diary* (*Zametki iz dnevnika*) from *RVS*, explaining to Voronskii that he meant nothing personal, but was obliged, as a "Russian man of letters and a revolutionary, to react as I am able and know how" to such "slander" (letter of February 20, 1924, *Arkhiv*, p. 13). Voronskii reported to Gor'kii, after a visit to Bukharin, that the Central Control Committee of the Party had looked into the matter and arranged for a retraction to be published (letter of February 28, 1924, *Arkhiv*, p. 14; see also his letter of February 19, 1924, *Arkhiv*, pp. 11-12). That was done on April 25, 1924 ("Ot redaktsii," p. 7). Gor'kii, in turn, retracted his withdrawal, and *Notes* was published in Nos. 1 and 2 of *RVS* for 1924.

[52] Voronskii had snubbed Vsevolod Ivanov (who apparently had been drinking heavily and neglecting his writing), and Ivanov complained to Gor'kii, who replied that Voronskii was becoming conceited and had turned into a "venerable critic." Ivanov spread the word, and people began to say that Gor'kii had repudiated Voronskii. This happened at a time when Voronskii had been ousted from his job and plans were being made to throw him out of the Party (see Chapter v). Gor'kii admitted to Voronskii that he had made the remark, but insisted he meant it ironically, and that his respect for Voronskii was undiminished (letter of December 4, 1927, *Arkhiv*, p. 61, in reply to Voronskii's letter of November 26, 1927, *Arkhiv*, p. 60).

at all to the subject's liking.[53] His expressions of admiration for Gor'kii seem genuine, and as disinterested as possible under the circumstances. The hero-worship of the earlier years gradually ripened into a warm, if not intimate friendship. As his position in Russian letters grew more precarious, he seemed to look on Gor'kii as the only person, outside his immediate family, to whom he could unburden his fears and disappointments with the assurance that he had a sympathetic ear.

It took Gor'kii until 1926 to drop the abrupt "Voronskii" or "Comrade Voronskii" with which he began his letters, and start addressing him by first name and patronymic.[54] But he always gave respectful encouragement to the younger man's work as an editor, a critic, and, from 1927 on, a promising writer of belles lettres. As he wrote to Voronskii in 1924: "generally speaking I know how to value a man's work, and you can be assured that I can well imagine what labor it has cost you to set up a journal the way you have and to keep it on such a high level." On reading the first part of *Waters of Life and Death* he observed to Voronskii: "if you could forget, at least for a time, that you are a critic, a very good and very interesting imaginative writer would develop out of you." In 1929 he returned a manuscript that needed fixing to one of his correspondents with the remark that "among the editors around today I don't see anyone

---

[53] A. Voronskii, "O Gor'kom"; and, under the pseudonym "L. Anisimov," "Voprosy khudozhestvennogo tvorchestva," *Sibirskie ogni*, No. 1 (1928), pp. 176-98. Gor'kii's replies were detailed and generous: see his letters to Voronskii of April 17, 1926, *Arkhiv*, pp. 31-33, and March 17, 1928, *Arkhiv*, pp. 62-66; this last one was published in *Sibirskie ogni* under the title "O sebe," No. 2 (1928), pp. 186-89.

[54] Voronskii called Gor'kii "Aleksei Maksimovich" practically from the beginning, the proper Russian manner for a younger man to address an older one. It was after Voronskii's article on Gor'kii ("O Gor'kom," *KN*, No. 4 [1926]) that Gor'kii asked for his name and patronymic, and addressed him accordingly from then on (letter of April 17, 1926, *Arkhiv*, p. 33).

who could evaluate your novel on its merits. A. K. Voronskii could do it, but, as you know, he's 'out of circulation' [Voronskii had been purged by then]."[55] There is no reason to doubt the sincerity of such remarks: Gor'kii repeated them to other correspondents; and, as we shall see, he was probably Voronskii's most steadfast and outspoken supporter throughout the twenties, even when Voronskii had fallen into disgrace.[56]

STRANGE TO SAY, Voronskii's relative obscurity and lack of experience may have been just what the Party needed. The task of attracting the best writers required an editor with taste, perception, and tact. At the same time, he had to be a man who would not be identified, a priori, with a particular school or a particular set of ideas about literature. The all-important job of political education could be entrusted only to a Bolshevik; but he had to be a man whose position in the Party apparatus was sufficiently inconspicuous to spare him the scorn that men of letters reserve for professional politicians who dabble in literature. Certainly he would have to be someone not so prominent as to be mainly concerned with protecting his reputation, yet well enough known to command the respect of Party functionaries. Ideally, he would be a man ambitious enough to take risks, yet modest enough to subordinate personal ambition to the larger needs of a literary journal.

Voronskii met all these qualifications; and the success of

[55] The first quote is from a letter to Voronskii, February 20, 1924, *Arkhiv*, pp. 12-13; the second, from a letter to Voronskii of February 23, 1927, *Arkhiv*, p. 50; and the third from a letter to A. P. Platonov, September 18, 1929, *Gor'kii i sovetskie pisateli. Literaturnoe nasledstvo*, LXX (Moscow, 1963), 313.

[56] Except for the incident with Ivanov, which he made light of and promised to rectify by making it known that "I have no reason to alter my feeling of sympathy for you" (letter to Voronskii, December 4, 1927, *Arkhiv*, p. 61). Cf. Chapter V for more details of Gor'kii's support of Voronskii.

RVS proved that the choice had been a good one. He had no desire to serve as merely the docile instrument of Party policy; and the Party had no intention of so limiting his role. He was given a chance to grow, and he took it. Despite his inexperience, his foundations were basically sound: *Workers' Region* had given him a valuable three-year course in writing quick, clear prose, in developing a critical idiom, and in handling young writers. Within two years he had achieved not only fame, but such a mastery of his new job that he had energies to spare. Running a journal would have been a good day's work for most men, and Voronskii always gave it his first loyalty and his keenest talents. But it did not satisfy him completely. Before long he had become co-editor, with Bukharin, of *The Searchlight* (*Prozhektor*), a popular version of *RVS*. Four of the distinguished literary miscellanies of the time received his editorial guidance: *Our Days* (*Nashi dni*), *The Circle* (*Krug*), *The Red Virgin Soil Miscellany* (*Al'manakh Krasnoi novi*), and, for a time, *The Pass* (*Pereval*). He founded and ran the "Circle" Publishing House, which was a kind of hard-cover version of the literary section of *RVS*; had a hand in the operations of the "Red Virgin Soil" Publishing House; edited the literary series of Glavpolitprosvet; and worked as an editor in the belles lettres section of the State Publishing House. Though he disapproved of formal literary organizations, he served on the board of directors and the presidium of the Union of Writers (vsp), which was made up chiefly of fellow travelers, and later represented that organization in the Federation of Organizations of Soviet Writers (fosp).

But Voronskii was not merely a literary bureaucrat. In addition to the prodigious reading that any good editor must do, he wrote extensively, and became a major critic and theorist. Though his work appeared in many different journals, the bulk of it is to be found in *RVS*. In his seven years as editor, he produced nearly forty full-length articles in a variety of genres: surveys, feuilletons, polemical pieces, theoretical disquisitions, "silhouettes" of individual writers, and review articles. Many of these were collected in books, the most important of which are: *At the Junction* (*Na styke*, 1923), *Art and Life* (*Iskusstvo i zhizn'*, 1924), *Concerning Art* (*Ob iskusstve*, 1925), *Literary Notes* (*Literaturnye zapisi*, 1926), and *Literary Types* (*Literaturnye tipy*, 1927).

VORONSKII's association with *RVS* ended abruptly in 1927 when he was removed from his post as editor and expelled from the Communist Party for alleged "Trotskiite" activities. We shall consider the details of his purge in the last chapter of this study. For now it is enough to say that thereafter his life see-sawed between repression and freedom. He continued to write prolifically and managed to have nearly all of his work published, but he took practically no active part in literary politics. Though eventually readmitted to the Party, he never, as far as we know, made a public recantation of the "errors" with which he had been charged. His final arrest probably came in 1937 during the great purges, and he died in 1943. Concerning the place and the circumstances of his death no word has been said publicly; but such reticence, in an age otherwise eager to produce evidence of Stalinist "excesses" and "misunderstandings," usually points straight to the labor camp.[57]

Of Voronskii's private life, little is known beyond the fact that he had a wife and daughter. Diaries, if they exist, have not been made public; the files of his journal lie buried deep in the archives that are sealed off to foreigners; and only a small part of what must have been a voluminous correspondence has been published (the letters to Gor'kii). In one sense these gaps are unimportant; for Voronskii, a thorough professional, would have insisted on being judged

[57] Cf. A. G. Dement'ev, "A Voronskii—kritik," pp. 3-46.

by what he published. From the spirit of his own writings, the testimony of his associates, and the correspondence with Gor'kii we can see a man generously endowed with qualities that predispose toward ruthlessness—energy, drive, ambition—yet possessing a certain sweetness, even naïveté. This interesting combination of traits is found in many old Bolsheviks. Voronskii was a sentimental man, even when writing about his hardships; his stories of political exiles are all autobiographical, lyrical, and nostalgic. Yet deep within him lay a firm faith in the rightness of his actions, which sustained him through adversity, even though it ill prepared him to meet the cynical pragmatism of Stalin. Nowhere do we find a trace of evidence that he was motivated by a desire for self-advancement. He considered his journal more important than himself, and the welfare of Soviet literature more important than any position he might occupy in it. While generally liked by the young writers, Voronskii had his enemies too—bitter, dedicated ones— but even they tended to accord him respect. Pyotr Kogan, one of the most hostile and articulate of them, wrote: "More than any of the other critics of the time he was able to take on himself the immense task of switching our literature onto new tracks, inasmuch as he combined in himself, together with the stamp of the hardened revolutionary, an intuitive esthetic sensibility and a deep love of literature."[58]

Voronskii's tenure as editor of RVS lasted a mere six years. But in that time this mousy little man in the pince-nez and the black peasant blouse who wore the look of a perpetual seminary student became one of the most important men of twentieth-century Russian letters. His prodigious energy, his selflessness, his conviction that literature must serve social betterment, his versatility as a polemicist, critic, theorist, and administrator—all these qualities established his kinship with the great editors and

[58] *Nashi literaturnye spory* (Moscow, 1927), p. 7.

critics of the nineteenth century, like Nekrasov, Belinskii, Panaev, and Druzhinin.

WHY did the Party choose to make a journal, rather than a publishing house or a literary organization, the instrument of its policy for the new literature? And why a journal that looked back over a span of fifty years or more to a tradition which many people considered inappropriate to an age that cherished innovation? These questions are fundamental to any discussion of the shape that Russian literature took in the twenties. It is essential to understand what this tradition was, what it meant to a Bolshevik in 1921, and why it was chosen as a model for a journal and a whole literature that were meant to display the highest ideals of a new society.

CHAPTER II

The Tradition

IN A LETTER to his close friend V. P. Botkin, Belinskii wrote:

for our society the [thick] journal is everything, and . . . nowhere else in the world does it have such an important and great significance as in our country. . . . The journal has now swallowed up all our literature—the public doesn't want books—they want journals—and plays and novels are printed in full in the journals, and each issue weighs a *pood*.[1]

He did not know the half of what was to come. In 1840, when he made these observations, the thick journal was in its infancy; a decade later it had become the most authoritative literary and (some said) social force in Russia. Every moderately well-educated Russian certainly knew by name *The Contemporary* (*Sovremennik*, 1836-1866), *Notes of the Fatherland* (*Otechestvennye zapiski*, 1839-1884), *The Russian Herald* (*Russkii vestnik*, 1856-1906), *The Herald of Europe* (*Vestnik Evropy*, 1866-1918), *Russian Wealth* (*Russkoe bogatstvo*, 1876-1918), *Russian Thought* (*Russkaya mysl'*, 1880-1918), and many others. More likely than not, he read at least one of them regularly. By today's standards, their circulation was small,[2] but their impor-

[1] Letter to V. P. Botkin, October 31, 1840, *Polnoe sobranie sochinenii*, XI (Moscow, 1956), 566.

[2] In the early 1860's, for example, the leading journals had the following circulations: *The Contemporary*, 6,658; *Notes of the Fatherland*, 4,500; *Russian Herald*, 6,100; *Library for Reading*, 3,500. Of a total of 137 journals at that time, fifteen were thick. The number of journals and their circulation rose steadily throughout the rest of the century. By the 1890's, for example, *Russian Thought* had approximately 10,000 subscribers and the total number of journals had nearly doubled. Figures are according to M. Mazaev, "Zhurnal," *Entsiklopedicheskii slovar'*, eds. A. F. Brokgauz and I. A. Efron, XII (St. Petersburg, 1894), 64-65.

A useful survey of Russian literary journals may be found in

tance was disproportionate to their size. As Belinskii remarked: "No more than five [individual] works have circulated in 5,000 copies during the past hundred years— yet here's a journal with 5,000 subscribers."[3] In a country where newspapers were impotent, universities often infirm, and well over 90 per cent of the population illiterate, the thick journals formed the oases wherein a culture developed. There the new novels, stories, and poems made their first appearance. There literary criticism grew up vigorous and sturdy. There the vague rhythms of society swelled into the steady throb of great issues.

The journals resembled universities in their attempt to take account of all the activities of the mind in a variety of departments organized according to specialties. And, just as universities do not merely preserve and pass on knowledge but create and shape it as well, so the thick journals did not merely record society, but helped give it definition, direction, and flavor. In these respects, they carried proportionately more weight than their illustrious counterparts in other countries, such as *The Edinburgh Review*, the *Nouvelle Revue Française*, or the *North American Review*. In Russia, they fulfilled a good many functions that elsewhere devolved on society as a whole. For one thing, they provided an arena of action for the most creative and energetic men of their time—men who were eager to change things, but who could find no effective way of doing so within the normal round of Russian life. In England, America, or France these men might have become politicians, business entrepreneurs, or social workers; in Russia, such professions were illegal, underdeveloped, or closed to all but a select few. The range of meaningful pro-

---

William E. Harkins, "Journals," *Dictionary of Russian Literature* (New York, 1956), pp. 163-70. Mazaev (*ibid.*) gives an alphabetical listing of the journals in all fields in the nineteenth century.

[3] Letter to Botkin, *ibid.*

fessions was particularly limited for young men of humble circumstances who were convinced of the value of the life of the mind. In the thick journals, however, such men found a place where talent counted more than social provenience, and intellect more than rank. And, since culture in Russia had always found its highest expression in the written word, the act of writing, for these young men, took on a profound social significance.

THE HISTORY of the thick journal is a relatively short one, coinciding roughly with the fifty-year span of *Notes of the Fatherland,* from 1839 to 1884. Its roots strike deep into the past—to songs of the folk, which beat to the pulse of events from one generation to the next; to the old Russian chronicles, which recorded happenings, and sometimes even commented on them from a point of view that resembled an editorial policy; to the so-called *kuranty,* handwritten extracts of reports by seventeenth-century ambassadors that were made to keep the Tsar informed of developments abroad. By the middle of the eighteenth century, the term "journal" was being used to describe any publication other than a book or a newspaper which came out periodically and did more than simply record current events. The first was the *Monthly Compositions Serving for Usefulness and Diversion* (*Ezhemesyachnye sochineniya, k pol'ze i uveseleniyu sluzhashchie*). Published irregularly in St. Petersburg between 1755 and 1764 by the Academy of Sciences and edited by Gerhard Friedrich Miller, it offered the reader scholarly and scientific articles on a variety of topics, a bibliography of books from home and abroad, and some belles lettres, both Russian and foreign. In itself this venture merits little attention. But it marked a beginning. For the next 150 years, the journal remained the chief form of periodical literature in Russia; the newspaper, though

dating back to 1702, offered no real competition until late
in the nineteenth century.[4]

On the whole, the journals of the eighteenth century
were flimsy and ephemeral affairs. They were the work not
of professional journalists, but of amateurs, and offered
nothing to compare in reach or quality with the "review"
journals of contemporary Europe, such as England's *Monthly Review* (1749-1845) which, in addition to literature and
criticism, published articles on science and various fields of
scholarship. Nonetheless, it was mainly through journals
that the burgeoning urban civilization of Russia gave notice
of itself. Music, fashions, art, the drama, medicine, and economics—each had its own publication.[5] So did the major
literary movements: among the earliest were Sumarokov's
Industrious Bee (*Trudolyubivaya pchela*, 1756); the
Kheraskov circle's *Useful Diversion* (*Poleznoe uveselenie*,
1760-1762) and *Free Hours* (*Svobodnye chasy*, 1763); and
Bogdanovich's *Innocent Exercise* (*Nevinnoe uprazhnenie*,
1763). In fact, with these first literary journals began a tradition of author-editor that was firmly planted in the nineteenth century when Pushkin founded *The Contemporary*,
and has been honored ever since, by writers like Nekrasov,

[4] *The Journal* (*Yurnal*) of December 1702, ranks as the first, but
it was a one-shot affair, published specially to report on the siege
of Noteburg. In the following month a more substantial venture
was launched—the *News of Military and Other Matters Worthy of
Knowledge and Memory That Have Occurred in the State of Moscow
and in Other Neighboring Countries* (*Vedomosti o voennykh i inykh
delakh, dostoinykh znaniya i pamyati, sluchivshikhsya v Moskovskom
gosudarstve i v inykh okrestnykh stranakh)*—which lasted until 1728,
with a change of title in 1725 to *Russian News* (*Russkie vedomosti*).

[5] For example: *Musical Entertainment* (*Muzykal'noe uveselenie*,
1774); *The Monthly Fashion Publication* (*Modnoe ezhemesyachnoe
izdanie*, 1779); *Russia in Discovery* (*Otkryvaemaya Rossiya*, 1774),
an art periodical; *Russian Theater* (*Rossiiskii teatr*, 1776); *The St.
Petersburg Medical Register* (*Sanktpeterburgskie vrachebnye vedomosti*, 1793); *Proceedings of the Free Economic Society* (*Trudy
Vol'nogo Ekonomicheskogo Obshchestva*, 1765).

Mikhailovskii, and Shchedrin (*Notes of the Fatherland*), Dostoevskii (*Time* and *Age*), Korolenko (*Russian Conversation*), Gor'kii (*The Chronicle*), and, in our own times, Tvardovskii (*New World*).

Conspicuously lacking at that time, and in the first two decades of the nineteenth century, were journals of a general or "encyclopedic" cast. Even though Nikolai Karamzin's *Herald of Europe* (*Vestnik Evropy*, 1802-1830) and Nikolai Grech's *Son of the Fatherland* (*Syn otechestva*, 1812-1852) were larger and more ambitious than anything the eighteenth century had dreamed of, they were nonetheless very limited in scope: the first concentrated almost wholly on Russian history and archeology; the second on literature and history. Like all the journals before them, they shunned economics, politics, and social problems.

Quite apart from the general run stood the twelve or so "satirical" journals that began with Catherine the Great's *Omnium-Gatherum* (*Vsyakaya vsyachina*) in 1769 and continued through 1774.[6] Even though the satire was supposed to be of the so-called "smiling" kind, which aimed at individual, not institutional foibles, it was nonetheless read—and in most cases intended—as a commentary upon society and politics. That was one of the main reasons why none of these journals lasted long. But they have considerable importance in the history of journalism, literature, and the literary language. They were the first periodicals to venture a serious concern with society as a whole, not just the elite; the first to demonstrate that important issues could be discussed in the hitherto despised forms of narrative prose; and the first to show that the easy language of

---

[6] They were Novikov's *The Drone* (*Truten'*), *The Windbag* (*Pustomelya*), *The Painter* (*Zhivopisets*), and *The Purse* (*Koshelyok*); Emin's *Hellish Mail* (*Adskaya pochta*) and *Miscellany* (*Smes'*); Ruban's *Neither This Nor That* (*Ni to ni siyo*); Chulkov's *Both This and That* (*I to i siyo*) and *The Parnassian Trinket Dealer* (*Parnasskii shchepetil'nik*); Tuzov's *The Day's Labors* (*Podenshchina*) and *The Useful and The Pleasant* (*Poleznoe s priyatnym*).

personal letters and conversation possessed enough sup-
pleness to fit a variety of such forms, the commonest of
which, in these journals, were the anecdote, the dialogue,
the sketch, the letter to the editor, and the appeal to the
reader. Perhaps because they all touched on similar problems, looked at the world in similar ways, and suffered a
common fate, their appeal to later generations of journalists has been quite disproportionate to their longevity and
their size.

Most of these early journals were not designed as commercial ventures, and only rarely did they make money.
The pressruns, for one thing, were very low. Catherine's
Omnium-Gatherum started with 1,692 copies and Novikov's *Drone* averaged 1,240 for the year 1769; but once the
novelty faded, they declined by half. Rare indeed was the
journal that could count on running off 500 or 600 copies
an issue; most hovered between 250 and 300, and some
could not even manage a round 100. Krylov's *Spirits' Mail*
(*Pochta dukhov*), for example, counted a mere 80 subscribers in 1789. Just where the break-even point lay depended of course on the size of the journal and the selling
price. Perhaps we may take as representative of fairly large
and ambitious ventures Karamzin's *Moscow Journal* (*Mos-
kovskii zhurnal*), where the 256 subscriptions for 1791 and
the 294 for the following year did cover costs, though just
barely.[7] The subscribers to these early journals lived for
the most part in the capital cities; in the provinces, the
squires who could read preferred the homelier fare of chap
books, calendars, dream books, and song books.

[7] These figures are taken from T. Grits, V. Trenin, and M. Nikitin,
Slovenost' i kommertsiya (*Knizhnaya lavka A. F. Smirdina*), eds.
V. B. Shklovskii and B. M. Eikhenbaum (Moscow, 1929), p. 74; and
from M. Mazaev, "Zhurnal," pp. 56-69. There are many discrepancies in these and other sources as to the circulation of the eighteenth-
century journals. *Slovesnost' i kommertsiya*, for example, considers
600 the average for the period 1769-1774; Mazaev takes 200 to 300
as his average.

THE EIGHTEENTH-CENTURY mould began to crack in the 1820's, and it fell apart in the next decade, as journals expanded their coverage and aimed their appeals at what was then considered a mass audience. Bulgarin's *Northern Archive* (*Severnyi arkhiv*, 1822-1829) was the first of the new breed, with articles on Russian history, descriptions of all the important Russian explorations of the twenties, numerous "statistical" surveys, and a series of literary annexes containing moralistic and satirical commentaries on contemporary society. Other journals soon began reviewing a greater variety of books, and adding regular departments designed to deal with long-neglected economic questions such as the railroads, and with natural science, commerce, agriculture, and geography. A new kind of journal was taking shape—one that tried to serve not just literature and history, or the arts, or scholarship, but all the interests of society. This was the so-called "encyclopedic" journal. Perhaps the first was the *Moscow Telegraph*, which Nikolai Polevoi founded in 1825. Its slant was primarily literary: the best young writers of the time contributed—among them, Pushkin, Vyazemskii, and Odoevskii; the latest Russian and foreign books were reviewed; and portraits of the reigning romantic deities—Scott, Byron, Goethe, and Schiller—were reproduced on its pages. In addition, Polevoi published articles on history, mythology, archaeology, jurisprudence, economics, mathematics, and a host of other subjects. He even gave his readers reports on the latest fashions, and drawings of the modish furniture styles of the time.

In its range of interests, the encyclopedic journal prepared the way for the thick journal that arose in the late thirties and early forties. Yet the latter differed in several essential respects: its literature department was built principally on prose fiction and not on poetry; it featured a strong and vigorous literary criticism; and most important, it was no longer just a sponge to be exposed to the elements, but a structure carefully organized according to a "line" that reflected a specific ideology. This line found fullest expression in the literary criticism; but it penetrated and shaped every department and gave the journal a unity. It might be Slavophilism, as in Pogodin's *Muscovite* (*Moskvityanin*, 1841-1856), or Populism, as in *The Word* (*Slovo*, 1873-1881), or Westernism, as in the early years of *Notes of the Fatherland*, or Marxism, as in *The Beginning* (*Nachalo*, 1899), or Kadet, as in *Russian Thought*. As passions, issues, and editors changed, so too might the line; what mattered was not its content but its presence. Without it no journal could be truly thick. Whenever it weakened or disappeared, as in periods of severe censorship, the thick journal tended to disintegrate into merely a faceless assemblage or encyclopedia of materials.

The most famous thick journal of our century illustrates the operation of this law just as well as any journal of the past. *Contemporary Notes* (*Sovremennyya zapiski*) was founded in 1920 in Paris as a deliberate imitation of the thick journals of the nineteenth century, two of which echoed in the title—*The Contemporary* and *Notes of the Fatherland*. While many people considered it better than any of its predecessors, it seemed unable at first to make the impact that the editors hoped it would. One of them thought he knew why:

> The point was that all the Russian journals had been linked with a definite world outlook. A world outlook lay at the basis of every political line and every journal. Such was the Russian tradition. The Russian intellectual was not capable of living or acting without a world view. There was nothing one could do about it. . . .[8]

[8] I. O. Fondaminskii-Bunakov, as reported by M. Vishnyak, "Sovremennyya zapiski," *Vospominaniya redaktora* (Bloomington: Indiana University Publications, VII Graduate School, Slavic and East European Series, 1957), 302.

And so a "world outlook" had to be created. However, recognizing the necessity for one was far easier than formulating it. The editors themselves were Socialist Revolutionaries, yet they wished to appeal to all their fellow emigrants, regardless of opinions, convictions, or prejudices. What was the solution? Mark Vishnyak, the journal's chief editor, found the answer:

> just as in politics, the "front" here too has to be broad enough—but not entirely without boundary. Speaking concretely: idealism against materialism, meaning by the first all forms of idealism—from Kantianism to outright religiosity. Contributors of a non-idealistic bent were not to be excluded from participation in the journal —by no means! They were just to be switched onto different tracks; it was to be proposed to them—for instance, to Ivanovich—that they write on political, social, and economic subjects, and not on general ones pertaining to world view.[9]

A strong ideology, though essential, is not the only characteristic of a thick journal. It may, after all, be present in publications which cater to poetry, lack a vigorous literary criticism, or concentrate exclusively on literature—publications, in other words, which are not "thick." No, all the traits we have mentioned must be present: compendiousness, a definite ideology, a lively criticism, and a predominance of prose. Together, they define the genre.

The first Russian journal that met all these requirements was *Notes of the Fatherland*—not the one started by Svin'in in 1820 and terminated in 1831, but the fresh venture undertaken by Andrei Kraevskii in 1839. In an advertisement several months before the first issue, Kraevskii stated the purpose of his journal as follows:

[9] *Ibid.*

to promote, as far as possible, Russian enlightenment in all its branches, by conveying to the reading public of the fatherland everything remarkable, useful and pleasant that might be encountered in literature and life, everything that might enrich the mind with knowledge or attune the heart to an apprehension of what is refined, everything that might develop the taste.[10]

For such scope, he thought that nothing less than 320 to 400 pages a month would do. In other words this was to be "an *encyclopedic journal* in the full sense of the word, i.e., it will contain everything that merits the special attention of the Russian reader. . . ." But he immediately went on to say that such a journal could not be simply a compilation: on each of the topics it offered it must have "its own opinion, its own view," which would "not only be expressed in the selection of articles, but would also manifest itself in a positive way in judgments about contemporary scholarly, scientific and literary works—in criticism." At the same time, this "opinion" would not be reducible to any particular "literary party": the journal would function as an independent, self-contained unit.[11]

Kraevskii envisaged eight permanent departments and gave detailed descriptions of what each was intended to do. First came the "Contemporary Chronicle of Russia" (Sovremennaya Khronika Rossii), which would take account of the "remarkable and curious phenomena of Russian life"[12] in every conceivable field, including, as a unique feature, reports on governmental activities through the citation and summary of official documents. Here the old

[10] "Ob' 'yavlenie ob izdanii Otechestvennykh Zapisok v 1839 godu," *Literaturnye pribavleniya k Russkomu Invalidu na 1838 god* (St. Petersburg, 1838), p. 857.

[11] *Ibid.*, p. 858.

[12] "Sovremennaya Khronika Rossii," *Otechestvennye zapiski*, No. 1 (1839), Section 1, p. 5.

encyclopedic journal lived on; but even though Kraevskii considered it the most important section of *Notes of the Fatherland,* it made up but a small part of the whole. Next came "Science and Scholarship" (Nauki), which would contain articles on geography, mathematics, statistics, and literary theory, but would give special emphasis to Russian history and the history of Russian literature. "Belles Lettres" (Slovesnost') would contain both poetry and prose (they formed two separate divisions in the first issue), shun excerpts and abridgments in favor of complete works, and admit translations from foreign literatures. "The Arts" (Khudozhestva) would feature "articles on the theory and history of the four free arts: music, painting, sculpture, and architecture,"[13] and a chronicle of events, particularly exhibitions, in Russia and abroad. In "Domestic Science, Agriculture, and Industry in General" (Domovodstvo, Sel'skoe Khozyaistvo i Promyshlennost' voobshche) the last two topics carried on an old tradition of commentary on the more prosaic sides of the country's economy. But the first was an innovation that testified to the growth of Russia's material civilization in the higher sense: it hoped to promote good living, the amenities of daily life, sheer "comfort" in ways that would be "comprehensible and perhaps indispensable to every paterfamilias."[14] Featured in the inaugural issue was a long discussion of the preparation and enjoyment of truffles. "Criticism" (Kritika) would deal with important new works of literature at home and abroad: the first issue contained a long appraisal of a recent Russian translation of Goethe's *Faust.* In the "Contemporary Bibliographical Chronicle" (Sovremennaya Bibliograficheskaya Khronika) the reader would find notice, month by month, of all the new Russian books, and the

[13] Kraevskii, "Ob' 'yavleniye . . . ," p. 859.
[14] *Ibid.* There is a discussion of "comfort" in an introductory note to the "Domovodstvo" section, *Otechestvennye zapiski,* No. 1 (1839), Section 5, p. 43.

most important ones in German, French, and English. Finally, the "Miscellany" (Smes') would offer news on the lighter side.

The departments advertised by Kraevskii all appeared in the first issue, for January 1839, and remained, by and large, in the journal for many years thereafter. In fact, all thick journals were built on more or less the same structure. To be sure, special interests and special needs produced variations, such as the sermons published in *The Muscovite*'s department of "Clerical Eloquence," which reflected the editors' close connection with the Church in the 1840's. But no substantial modifications could be made without creating an entirely different genre of journal. In *Notes of the Fatherland*, as in most thick journals, literature and criticism occupied at least half of each issue and displayed far greater vigor than the other departments. From the outset, Belinskii was the leading critic: he established the "line" (practically everything he wrote between 1839 and his death in 1848 was published there), and the belles lettres were supposed to illustrate his theories of "national" literature—in other words, prose fiction of a "naturalistic" (realistic) cast. *Notes of the Fatherland* ushered in a new age of Russian journalism. It quickly swept the field, attracting all the best writers and most of the intelligent readers. The 1,200 subscribers to the first issue grew to 4,000 by 1847—a figure that was astronomical by contemporary standards. Its nearest rivals were completely outclassed: in that same year, for instance, *The Muscovite* had only 300 subscribers and *The Contemporary* could scratch up a mere 233. But in the wake of *Notes of the Fatherland*, new journals were formed and old ones were revamped. By the late forties, the thick journals had come to dominate cultural life. And they maintained that position for half a century.[15]

[15] A useful study of *Notes of the Fatherland* in the 1840's has been

· I I ·

Let us consider some of the main forces that worked to create the thick journals and bring them to their position of eminence.

One of these may be called the physical or quantitative. The growing complexity of Russian society made almost limitless material available to enterprising journalists, provided they redefined their concept of what a journal might properly treat. The appearance of the encyclopedic journals indicated that they had done so. Meanwhile, the potential market for journals was slowly expanding, as literacy and the rudiments of culture began to filter down into society. Anna Andreevna, the wife of the mayor in Gogol's *Inspector General*, represents the height of small-town sophistication in her enthusiasm for the novels of Baron Brambeus, the contemporary equivalent of pulp fiction. But she was well ahead of most provincial ladies a generation or two earlier; and, as the general level of education rose, her granddaughters would probably think nothing of subscribing to one of the new journals and probably even perusing it every month. These journals were aimed at minds garnished with a moderately good education. The possessors of such minds might devour books and perhaps subscribe to one of the specialized journals; but they would also require an easy and inexpensive way of keeping *au courant* with the latest fiction and with the intellectual fashions in the capitals; and for that, a thick journal was essential. Some of these new readers developed the itch to wield the pen themselves; and the journals held the lure of a ready outlet, a large audience, a way of acquiring intellectual and perhaps even social prestige if one's origins did not automatically provide them, and, often most

made by V. I. Kulsehov, *"Otechestvennye zapiski" i literatura 40-kh godov XIX veka* (Moscow, 1959).

important of all, the possibility of earning a living wage. The journals encountered no real competition from the newspapers for readers, for writing talent, or for material. To be sure, book publishing had surged after 1789, when the government granted permission for private publishers to operate in all the towns of Russia, and it had shown a steady increase ever since.[16] (In the 1830's and the 1840's A. F. Smirdin's inexpensive and attractive editions of the Russian writers created a mass market for books, not merely in the capitals, but in the provinces as well.) But books, being the product of a single author, could hardly hold out the same sort of appeal as a journal, which offered ten times the variety at a quarter of the price.

ANOTHER factor at work was economic. In the eighteenth century, if a young man wished to make a living from his pen, he could always take up translating: the thirst for foreign novels seemed insatiable. Or if, like Emin and Chulkov, he had a touch of originality, he could produce picaresque tales or adventure romances or love stories, and count on finding an eager audience among the merchants, the provincial landowners, and, if the truth be told, among many ladies of quality as well. (Matvei Komarov's *Tale of the English Lord George* [*Povest' o priklyucheniyakh angliiskogo milorda Georg*, 1782] went through thirty editions in all, seven of them during the author's lifetime.) In other words, the commercial literature which existed then was largely a literature of prose fiction; rare indeed was the toiler in the "higher" genres—poetry and drama—who could earn a livelihood from writing. And because commercial success depended so much upon gratifying the tastes of a distinctly lowbrow audience, or chaining oneself to the endlessly turning wheel of translations, the serious

[16] The government had given permission in 1771 to a foreigner, Hartung, to establish a private press provided his books were printed in a foreign language.

writers of means saw no reason to seek it. Here, for example, is how the poet Konstantin Batyushkov reacted to his brush with the world of commercial literature in Moscow at the beginning of the nineteenth century:

> Anyone who has not visited Moscow does not know that it is possible to deal in books exactly the way one deals in fish, furs, vegetables, etc., without taking literature into account at all; he does not know that here there exists a translation factory, a journal factory, and a novel factory, and that book tradesmen buy learned goods, that is, translations and [original] works, by weight, repeating over and over again to the poor authors: not quality but quantity, not style but the number of pages! I am afraid to glance into a shop, for, to our shame, I think that there is not a single nation that has or ever has had such a disgraceful literature.[17]

It was on this "disgraceful literature" and the people who read it that three of the most remarkable men of the early nineteenth century built their careers: Nikolai Grech, Osip Senkovskii, and Faddei Bulgarin. All of them wrote novels and tales in the way that Batyushkov found deplorable, and they became famous in the households of merchants, lower-grade civil servants, and country squires. ("Baron Brambeus," the one writer whom Gogol's Anna Andreevna *had* read, was Senkovskii's pen name.) In addition, they realized that this audience would be receptive to periodical publications, and lost no time in exploiting it. Grech described his *Son of the Fatherland* as "the first of the journals (if we exclude *The Herald of Europe*) which brings its publisher not a loss, but a profit, and which gives him the opportunity to devote himself entirely to his chosen profession. Until now, publishing a journal has meant go-

[17] "Progulka po Moskve," *Sochineniya*, ed. D. Blagoi (Moscow-Leningrad, 1934), pp. 301-02.

ing into debt with the print shop and the paper store."[18] Bulgarin's *Northern Bee* (*Severnaya pchela*), a journal in newspaper format, was built on the formula of information and entertainment: together with the latest news from Russia and from abroad, the reader was treated to tales and stories, articles on music and the theater, reviews, and a large "miscellaneous" section, all presented in a smooth, untaxing style. The *Library for Reading* (*Biblioteka dlya chteniya*), published by A. F. Smirdin and edited by Senkovskii, was aimed at readers in the provinces and, with a subscription list numbering between 5,000 and 7,000, was the most successful commercial undertaking in journalism up to that time. Senkovskii himself grew prosperous, receiving, in addition to a regular salary of 15,000 roubles a year, 6,000 roubles for every 3,000 copies of the journal he sold and 2,000 roubles for each additional thousand.[19] The old journals, which drew for the most part on poetry, went into a rapid decline with the shift toward a journalism based on prose. At the turn of 1830, for instance, Moscow alone had been able to boast of six journals: *The Herald of Europe*, *The Moscow Telegraph*, *The Ladies' Journal* (*Damskii zhurnal*), *The Moscow Messenger*, *Atheneum* (*Atenei*), and *Galatea* (*Galateya*). But three years later, only three remained in Moscow, three in St. Petersburg, and three in the provinces: nine journals, in other words, for a total population of fifty-two million and a reading public that must have numbered well over a million.

These three men demonstrated beyond a doubt that the literary life could also provide a comfortable income; and they saw no reason to be ashamed of it. Grech insisted that the money one made from writing was "income of exactly the same kind as from a house, or a village that have been acquired by one's own labor," a "salary received for unre-

---

[18] *Chteniya o russkom yazyke*, Part 2 (St. Petersburg, 1840), p. 392.

[19] Grits, Trenin, and Nikitin, *ibid.*, p. 167.

mitting, arduous, honest labors, and one that is in no way adequate recompense to a man for the many privations, the incessant vexations, grievances, and even insults."[20] Bulgarin, in a long review of the reasons why Russian literature was not more highly developed, pointed an accusing finger at society's emphasis on material achievement and the fascination with things French; but he felt that

> the most important obstacle to the success of literature . . . is the lack of sufficient remuneration for one's labors and time. More than one intelligent and educated man, who would be a splendid Author, has to stifle the noble passion within him and write petitions and resolutions, if he is to escape the poverty with which the pursuit of Literature threatens him. Think as you please, but the Man of Letters ought to be bound to literature soul and *body*. We have examples of the passion of rich and distinguished people for Authorship, a passion that has always ended in a few piddling little articles and drowned in a slough of pleasures and ambition. "It's no work for a rich man [they say]!"[21]

Such sentiments only hardened the prejudice that many "amateurs," like Batyushkov, felt toward any suggestion of "commercialism" in literature. Their prejudice extended to the journals as well, in the early part of the century; for the conspicuously successful ones were those citadels of commercialism defended by Bulgarin, Grech, and Senkovskii. Changes, however, were in the making. A few of the amateurs began to wonder, in effect, whether the sort of suc-

[20] Quoted from S. Vesin, *Ocherki istorii russkoi zhurnalistiki dvadtsatykh i tridtsatykh godov* (St. Petersburg, 1881), pp. 245-46.
[21] "Ob obshchepoleznom predpriyatii knigoprodavtsa A. F. Smirdina," *Severnaya pchela*, No. 299 (Dec. 29, 1833), p. 1,184; the article continues in No. 300 (Dec. 30), pp. 1,186-88. For an interesting reappraisal of the work of these three editors, see V. Kaverin, "Legenda o zhurnal'nom triumvirate," *Zvezda*, No. 1 (1929), pp. 160-92.

cess enjoyed by the men they despised necessarily depended on the kind of literature those men were exploiting; whether, in other words, good writing and a living
wage necessarily excluded one another. Respectable literature could, after all, count a few commercial successes
of its own—a good example was the almanac *Polar Star*
(*Polyarnaya zvezda*) which had netted the editors, Ryleev
and Bestuzhev, 2,000 roubles of clear profit in the twenties.
One of the distinguished journals of the time, *The Herald
of Europe*, was also a money-maker. Even Bulgarin, Grech,
and Senkovskii constantly made overtures to the very writers who spurned them. More than anyone else, Pushkin
was responsible for breaking down the hostility of his fellow writers toward money. His famous statement—"I write
for myself but I publish for money, and by no means for
a smile from the fair sex"[22]—announced his intention of being a professional in Bulgarin's sense of the term, and suggested how, at the same time, a writer could rationalize
himself into respectability. Pushkin was chronically short
of money. His letters brim with references to his work in
the language of the marketplace and the countinghouse.
For instance, he offered to sell a "piece" of his "Prisoner of
the Caucasus" to Grech at a discount price "so that the
goods won't go stale by lying around."[23] And he drove a
hard bargain. To his friends, like Vyazemskii, who professed shock at the idea of vending works of literature like
pretzels or cattle, Pushkin replied that he was no eighteenth-century writer who could afford to scribble for mere
pleasure:

> one should look on poetry, if you'll permit me to say so,
> as a craft. Rousseau didn't tell his first lie when he said
> *que c'est le plus vil des métiers. Pas plus vil qu'un autre.*

[22] Letter to P. A. Vyazemskii, March 8, 1824, *Polnoe sobranie
sochinenii v desyati tomakh*, x (2d ed.; Moscow, 1958), 83.
[23] Letter to N. I. Grech, September 21, 1821, *ibid.*, p. 31.

Aristocratic prejudices have clung to you, but not to me
—I look on a finished poem of mine the way a bootmaker
looks on a pair of his boots: I sell at a profit. The shop
foreman finds my jackboots don't fit; he trims a little off,
and spoils the goods. And at a loss. I go and complain to
the chief of police. All that's in the normal course of
things....[24]

Many passages in Pushkin's letters and poems seem to
suggest just the opposite: a protest against commercialism.
But, as Boris Eikhenbaum has pointed out, Pushkin was
protesting not against the principle of commercialism, but
against the kind of commercialism practiced by Bulgarin,
Grech, and Senkovskii, which to him was synonymous with
shameless pandering to depraved tastes. With *Poltava*, according to Eikhenbaum, Pushkin hoped to show that good
literature could have a mass appeal and still make money.[25]
Gradually, other writers came around to the point of view
that Pushkin, out of necessity, had adopted and advertised.
Perhaps we can date the decisive change from 1832, when
the bookshop and library of A. F. Smirdin opened on the
Nevskii Prospekt in St. Petersburg.

Smirdin by then had won a reputation as a shrewd literary entrepreneur. Though he had no literary pretensions
of his own, his commercial instincts were finely honed and,
in the language of the salesman he was, he worked both
sides of the street. His chief interest lay in what would sell,
regardless of whether it was "high" or "low" literature;
thus, it was only sound business practice to cultivate Bulgarin with one hand and Pushkin with the other. In 1829
he brought out Bulgarin's picaresque novel *Ivan Vyzhigin*,

[24] Letter to P. A. Vyazemskii, March 1823, *ibid.*, p. 57.
[25] "Literatura i pisatel'," *Zvezda*, No. 5 (1927), pp. 126-28. For
support of Eikhenbaum's interpretation, see the following letters of
Pushkin, all in *Polnoe sobranie sochinenii*, x: to M. P. Pogodin, July
1, 1828, 247; to P. A. Vyazemskii, May 2, 1830, 285; to P. A. Pletnyov, December 9, 1830, 324.

which was a best seller by the standards of the day. At
the same time, he was negotiating a contract with Pushkin,
according to which, in 1830, he obtained the rights to all of
Pushkin's new work for four years, agreeing in return to
pay him 600 paper roubles a month until the agreement expired.[26] By 1832, he was ready to launch his biggest venture: a series of inexpensive yet attractive editions of the
Russian writers, which would reward everyone concerned.
The gala dinner that marked the occasion was attended by
nearly all the important writers of the time. That in itself
gave evidence that the old "aristocratic prejudices," with
which Pushkin taxed Vyazemskii, had eroded. From that
moment on "commercialism" was an accepted and increasingly necessary attribute of the profession of letters. During his relatively brief career (he was ruined in the 1840's
largely because he overextended himself), Smirdin published more than seventy writers. His shop on the Nevskii
Prospekt, with its library and its convivial surroundings,
became a gathering place for all the writers of Petersburg.
Belinskii, the first great classifier in Russian literary history, assigned to the "Smirdin period" in Russian literature
an importance equal to the "Lomonosov," "Karamzin," and
"Pushkin" periods.[27] For Belinskii understood that the relationship between writer and public had changed forever. In his mind, as in the mind of nearly all the new writers and critics, there was no question but that "profession-
alism" and "commercialism" were the keys to a vigorous
national literature:

> Is it possible to assume the actual existence of literature
> in a place where the day-laborer and the peddler and the
> dealer in old rags and broken crockery and still more the
> clerk can make a living from their labor, but where a

[26] Grits, Trenin, and Nikitin, *ibid.*, p. 265. See esp. Ch. VIII.
[27] "Literaturnye mechtaniya," *Polnoe sobranie sochinenii*, I (Moscow, 1953), 98.

writer, a man of letters cannot make a living from his labor? No matter what people say, it is an undisputable axiom that you cannot be at one and the same time a civil servant and a good man of letters; the civil servant will be sure to interfere with the man of letters, and the man of letters with the civil servant. In order to be a scholar, a poet, or a man of letters in the full sense of the term, it is essential to see in scholarship, in art or in literature one's exclusive calling, one's trade, so to speak, one's branch of industry, speaking in the language of political economy.[28]

These sentiments, which had outraged writers when uttered by Bulgarin, were now commonplace.

We can trace a similar development in the attitude of the writers toward those journals that were considered mass publications. Again Pushkin pointed the way. He regarded almanacs—the characteristic outlets for poetry, and thus for "high" literature—as old-fashioned and ineffectual because they lacked a clearly defined direction.[29] Instead he envisaged forming a journal that would publish good literature, exert a beneficial influence on the taste of the public, and at the same time bring in a profit. Although he did not draw up any systematic plans for such a journal, recurring themes in his chance remarks suggest that he had in mind something very much like what eventually became the thick journal. He spoke of the need to build on prose fiction, not poetry: "A propos of tales (*povesti*)," he wrote in an advice-filled letter to M. P. Pogodin, "they should be

[28] "Sto russkikh literatorov," *Polnoe sobranie sochinenii*, IX (Moscow, 1955), 245.

[29] Letter to M. P. Pogodin, August 31, 1827, *Polnoe sobranie sochinenii*, p. 234. Pushkin at this time was trying to bring Pogodin, the editor of the *Moscow Herald*, around to his views on the role of journals in Russian society, and to persuade him to turn the *Moscow Herald* into a journal that would oppose Bulgarin, Grech, Senkovskii, and Polevoi's *Moscow Telegraph*.

absolutely the essential part of the journal, just as fashions are in the [Moscow] *Telegraph*. . . ."[30] He insisted that there must be a strong "direction," as in the *Edinburgh Review*, and a competent literary criticism that would establish a "canon of taste" and "take public opinion in its hands and give our literature a new, genuine direction."[31] But firmness must never trespass upon good taste and lofty purpose: the *Moscow Telegraph* had disappointed Pushkin's hopes by adopting a strong polemical stance, thereby lowering itself, in his opinion, to the level of the cheap journalism of Bulgarin and Grech. Pushkin's own attempts to establish a journal were inconclusive: the *Literary Gazette* (*Literaturnaya gazeta*), which began in 1829 in newspaper format, was aimed at the small community of writers, not at the general public, depended mainly on poetry, and quickly folded up for lack of material. *The Contemporary*, which he helped launch in 1836, nearly foundered at the start. None of the other journals of the time answered to his ideas of what a good journal should be, but those ideas in themselves portended change. Two years after Pushkin's death, *Notes of the Fatherland* was founded; within the next five years, the thick journals had won the respect of Russian men of letters and were taken for granted as the natural outlet for new works of literature.

Along with the gradual acceptance of commercialism in literature went the acceptance of the journal and, inevitably, of the one form of writing most closely associated with the journal: prose fiction. By the early 1840's, when the thick journals had become firmly entrenched, novels, stories, and tales had moved up to the position of authority vacated by poetry. While the new journals continued to publish some poetry, their mainstay was prose fiction. On the whole it was far more attractive and nourishing fare than Bulgarin and Senkovskii had offered their readers.

[30] *Ibid.*
[31] Letter to P. A. Katenin, first half of February 1826, *ibid.*, p. 200.

The first-rate talents of the time no longer considered it an inferior branch of literature, and were anxious to try their hand at it. The despised "triumvirate" of Bulgarin, Grech, and Senkovskii had actually done much to prepare the conditions that made prose fiction of quality possible. Perhaps more important, they had created an audience for it.[32]

Fiction, of course, appeals to a far greater public than does poetry; inevitably, therefore, it holds out a lure to the mass publications. Conversely, it cannot fit comfortably into the modest albums and almanacs that are poetry's natural media. For the reader, fiction goes more easily with the other forms of prose published in journals: on the face of it, there is less difference between a short story and an article on economics than between a story and a poem. And because all the forms of prose writing within a thick journal are contiguous and subordinated to a ruling point of view, they tend to take on a certain equality, perhaps even to resemble different genres of a single large prose literature. This is especially the case whenever the concept of literature is broad, whenever the lines between the traditional genres blur or disappear. So it was in the 1840's and in the 1920's. People began to find value in the smaller kinds of writing that lay on the margin of imaginative literature—sketches, feuilletons, ethnographical pieces, travel memoirs—which were thought to document the experiences and events of the age and, in this way, to provide raw material for the works of future geniuses.[33] (Perhaps this is what Pushkin meant when he wrote of *The Moscow Herald*: "we have a splendid poetry section; the prose can be still better, but

[32] For an interesting study of the rise of prose fiction in Russia, and Bulgarin's part in promoting it, see Jurij Striedter, *Der Schelmenroman in Russland. Ein Beitrag zur Geschichte des russischen Romans vor Gogol'* (Berlin, 1961), esp. pp. 212-75.

[33] See e.g., N. A. Nekrasov, "Vstuplenie," *Fiziologiya Peterburga*, I (St. Petersburg, 1845), 5-27.

here's the trouble: there's too little rubbish in it. . . .")[34]
From here it was but a step to regarding any kind of writing about problems of the time as fuel for the great machine
of fiction. As we shall see in the next chapter, the thick
journal provided an ideal environment for the development of this broader concept of literature.

THE ONE activity that conferred a unity on the thick journal was literary criticism. In the eighteenth century, when
the assumption was that writer and reader shared a common intellectual heritage, a common education, and common sensibilities, there was no need to "interpret" works
of literature. "Criticism" amounted, in the main, to polemic
within the small family of writers. Although Karamzin
went as far as to make summaries and descriptions of the
new writing that he considered interesting, he was merely
drawing the reader's attention, not telling him how to read.
Even Pushkin, who grumbled continually that Russia
lacked real criticism, tended in his own treatments of literature to deal in personalities, like a good eighteenth-
century writer, and not in the realities of the text. But all
that changed with the rise of the thick journals. There the
critic reigned supreme.

From about 1810 onward, the journals had gradually
grown to the point that the various functions of editor, publisher, writer, and critic, which had all fitted comfortably
in the hands of a single man during the eighteenth century, each came to require the attention of a specialist.
(Belinskii's entire career, for instance, unfolded in literary
journals—not all of them "thick," to be sure: in *The Telescope* between 1834 and 1836, in *The Moscow Observer*
and *Notes of the Fatherland* between 1838 and 1841, in
Notes of the Fatherland and *The Contemporary* between
1842 and 1847.) In particular, the growth of a mass reading

[34] Letter to M. P. Pogodin, August 31, 1927, *Polnoe sobranie
sochinenii*, p. 235.

public made necessary an interlocutor between reader and writer; and many a young man who, by reason of background and circumstance, could leave a mark nowhere else except in the profession of letters, discovered that he had a career. A respectable career it was too. The new critics came to maturity in an age dominated by Romanticism and by Hegel. The world was seen as a unity, all of whose parts reflected a ruling idea. Literature, for the Romantics, and philosophy, for the Hegelians, gave perfect expression to this unity. Was not criticism, as these young Russians conceived of it, a branch of both literature and philosophy— the two highest activities of man wherein all the others met? And were not the thick journals, in the variety and range of their departments and their strong unifying point of view, a splendid imitation of the idea of multiplicity in oneness? If the journal seemed to represent the body of the nation in miniature, then criticism seemed to represent its spirit.

It was not surprising then that in the minds of readers the "line" of the thick journal—and by extension, everything in the journal—turned so easily into commentary on specific social and economic situations, whether or not it was intended that way. To the authorities, such commentary was automatically suspect, and, in periods of social unrest, likely to be seditious. After the events of 1848 in Europe, the Tsar appointed a special commission with Prince Menshikov as chairman to study the thick journals, report on their contents, and draft recommendations about how the government should handle them. Predictably, the conservative *Northern Bee*, *Library for Reading*, and *Muscovite* got a clean bill. But the two most important journals, *Notes of the Fatherland* and *The Contemporary*, were pronounced dangerous. Their editors, Kraevskii and Nikitenko respectively, were summoned to the Third Section and forced to sign a statement attesting that the two journals had admitted, in their articles, thoughts criminal to the highest degree, capable of implanting in our fatherland the principles of communism, disrespect for secular and ecclesiastical institutions and for the services of people who are esteemed by all, for family obligations and even for religion; of impairing the national morals and in general of preparing the ground in our country for those baneful events that are at present shaking the states of the West.[35]

The statement went on to say that the editors deserved to be severely punished, but that the Tsar, in his mercy, was letting them off with a stiff warning, and charging them with personal responsibility for the contents of their journals in the future. They were required not only to refrain from publishing pernicious material, but also "to strive with every means to give their journals a direction quite compatible with the views of our government. . . ."[36] Both men were badly frightened by the incident. Nikitenko tried to put the blame on the other members of the editorial board of *The Contemporary*, and ultimately resigned; Kraevskii offered to become a government informer. A permanent body on matters of the press was established—the notorious Buturlin committee—which was to serve as a check on the censorship itself.

In the seventies and eighties, the censors tended to make the thick journals responsible for the mounting wave of overt revolutionary activity in Russia. Yuferov, for instance, wrote of *Notes of the Fatherland*:

The harmful aspirations of this publication are expressed primarily in sorrow for the poor folk and in general for all the lesser brotherhood, in ill will toward the upper classes of society, particularly the nobility, in the sys-

[35] Cited in A. G. Dement'ev, *Ocherki po istorii russkoi zhurnalistiki 1840-1850 gg.* (Moscow, 1951), pp. 95-96.
[36] *Ibid.*, p. 95.

tematic assemblage and selection of the gloomy features
of our life, in sympathy for false Western teachings and
for the nihilistic manifestations of the younger generation, and in particular, in pessimistic views toward our
state system and obvious hostility toward the government. In this last respect, the activity of Mr. Shchedrin is
especially harmful, inasmuch as it attracts public attention more than that of others.[37]

This censorship tightened and eased at various periods
in Russian history. Journals were sometimes shut down—
The Telescope for publishing Chaadaev's "Philosophical
Letter," for instance; *The Contemporary* and *Russian
Word* as a result of the Karakozov affair. Yet no Tsar dared
abolish them outright. Their position in Russian society
was too powerful.

· I I I ·

In the more relaxed political atmosphere of the late nineteenth century, a number of new thick journals were established. The best of them—*Russian Wealth, Russian
Thought,* and *The Herald of Europe*—yielded nothing in
vigor or quality to their predecessors. Some, as voices of
the newly formed and officially tolerated political parties,
went much further in defining a point of view and making it
specifically political. Such, for example, was *New Word*
(*Novoe slovo*), which began as a Populist journal in 1894
and three years later became the first legal Marxist journal
in Russia. But the center of literary and intellectual life had
shifted. For all their splendor, these new publications
stood outside the mainstream. The great age of the thick
journal had ended in 1884, with the closing of *Notes of the
Fatherland* by the censorship.

What caused this shift? No doubt there is something in
Eikhenbaum's theory that the focus of literature, in obedi-

[37] *Ibid.*

ence to immanent laws, moved back once again, as in Pushkin's time, into the salon and the circle where the characteristic forms of published utterance are the almanac and the
miscellany, not the journal.[38] No doubt profound changes
in society's structure were also at work—particularly the
enormous enlargement of the range of professions that ambitious and idealistic youths might enter. But we need not
look much beyond the world of the periodical press itself
to see that an important factor, perhaps the decisive one,
in the decline of the thick journals was the rise of
competition.

THE NEWSPAPERS, weak and despised throughout the eighteenth and nineteenth centuries, began to revive as the journals started to wane. The government, during one of its
fitful spells of generosity toward the press in the early six-
ties, had extended to all newspapers an important privilege
theretofore reserved to official publications: the privilege
of publishing advertisements and notices of a private
nature. At about the same time, the practice of
selling individual newspapers direct to the public grew
up beside the practice of selling by subscription. In
April 1865, the most important newspapers were freed
from preliminary censorship, i.e., from the obligation to
submit articles for review before publication. All these developments helped to boost the popularity and circulation
of the daily press. But it was the wars of the seventies—
especially the bitter one with Turkey in 1877-1878—that
really made the fortunes of the newspapers. Correspond-

---

[38] B. Eikhenbaum, "Literatura i pisatel'," pp. 121-23. The parallel
between the early and the late nineteenth century is taken by
Eikhenbaum as evidence of the cyclical nature of literary develop-
ment. For interesting studies of salons and circles, and their role in
Russian literature, cf. *Literaturnye salony i kruzhki. Pervaya polovina
XIX veka*, ed. N. L. Brodskii (Moscow-Leningrad, 1929), and M.
Aronson and S. Reiser, *Literaturnye kruzhki i salony*, edited and
with an introduction by B. M. Eikhenbaum (Leningrad, 1929).

ents were dispatched to the fronts and the telegraph sped their reports home to a news-hungry public. From that time on, newspapers showed a steady gain in circulation. In 1860 all of Russia was served by only seven dailies and about a hundred non-dailies. But by 1891, the dailies had grown tenfold, and the number of non-dailies had more than doubled. *New Times* (*Novoe vremya*) claimed a circulation of 25,000 a day; *The News* (*Novosti*) sold 20,000 copies in both its daily editions. Much of this growth was made possible only by rapid developments in communications and printing technology. Naturally the thick journals, which came out semi-monthly at most, were unable to compete with the newspapers for topical news. In addition, the newspapers cut deeply into the social, political, and economic questions that the thick journals had so long monopolized under the various disguises which censorship made necessary. Beginning with the reign of Nicholas II, such questions could be discussed more or less openly and treated, in effect, as current news.

Keen competition also came from the growing number of specialized publications in the sciences, in art, and in the professions. They tended to drain off the kind of material that once filled the nonliterary departments of the thick journals. There was one—M. P. Gershenzon's *Critical Survey* (*Kriticheskoe obozrenie*)—which even gave digests of important articles in the thick journals. Illustrated weekly journals, like *The Universal Illustrated* (*Vsemirnaya illyustratsiya*, 1869-1898), *The Grainfield* (*Niva*, 1870-1918), and *Around the World* (*Vokrug sveta*, 1885-1917) posed another threat. They had begun to appear in the 1860's, along foreign—primarily German—lines, and by the end of the century had grown into mass publications. *The Grainfield*, for example, printed 100,000 copies each run. Many of the eager, but badly educated new readers created by the spread of literacy—readers who in earlier decades would have subscribed to a thick journal only at the risk of wading in over their heads—now found their tastes and thirsts pleasantly serviced by this new kind of periodical. The thick journals were ill equipped by tradition or nature to operate in this mass literary market. Finally, book publishing began to make increasingly heavy inroads upon fiction. It was no longer axiomatic that new works appeared first in thick journals and only later between hard covers. New technical developments, the expansion of the mass market, improved methods of distribution, and a breed of aggressive entrepreneurs had seen to that.

The Symbolist journals that began to come out around the turn of the century—*The World of Art* (*Mir iskusstva*, 1898-1904), *The Golden Fleece* (*Zolotoe runo*, 1906-1909), *Apollo* (*Apollon*, 1909-1917), and *The Scales* (*Vesy*, 1904-1909)—provide a convenient illustration of the changes that had occurred in the relationship between literature and the periodical press. For one thing, these journals appealed to an elite audience and cared nothing about making money, in contrast to the thick journals, which aimed at the general, educated public and pursued commercial ends. In them, furthermore, that distinction between writer, critic, and editor which the thick journals had carefully maintained now tended to blur. More likely than not, these three functions merged in one man: a writer was sometimes the founder and editor of a publication that served mainly as an outlet for his own manuscripts, which he might then proceed to discuss as a critic. The most significant feature of these Symbolist publications, however, was their complete dedication to literature and the arts, with scarcely a nod in the direction of politics, sociology, or popular science. *Apollo*, for example, started with the following departments: belles lettres; literary theory and criticism; art theory and criticism; music; theater; satire ("*Apollo*'s Bees and Wasps"); chronicle; and a literary almanac (a supplement devoted to belles lettres). This structure reflects the Symbolist notion that the world of art is itself a microcosm, the "source and focus of the innumerable radiations of life,"[39] and therefore needs to take no special account of anything outside itself. In a way, this is the logical consequence of the tendency of the critics in the old thick journals to regard art as a commentary on every aspect of life.

THE REVOLUTION of 1917 dealt the final blow to the old thick journals. A few, such as *The Herald of Europe* and *Russian Wealth*, struggled on for several months; others, like Pyotr Struve's *Russian Thought*, began a new life abroad. But by the middle of 1918, not a single representative of the genre remained in the whole of Russia.

[39] "Vstuplenie," *Apollon*, No. 1 (December 1909), p. 4.

CHAPTER III

The Revival: Literature and the Journal, 1921 to 1923

HALF A CENTURY of history met defiance in the creation of a thick journal in 1921. Four years of failure in every similar attempt since the Revolution suggested that history was right. How was it, then, that the Party dared press on with a rash, even foolhardy project?

PERHAPS they felt they had nothing to lose. Failure was no stranger to them; their prestige abroad could have sunk no lower; Voronskii was not that prestigious a figure. But probably factors of a more positive nature also came into play. The thick journal was associated in the Bolshevik mind with that glorious period in Russian literature between 1840 and 1885, when the "realistic" novel rose to supremacy; and the decline of the journal toward the end of the century coincided with what was regarded as the decline of literature into "modernism." Some of the makers of the new society detected the symptoms of that decline in all the art of the past, and prepared a mass burial. Most, however—including Lenin, Voronskii, and Lunacharskii— saw modernism as a deviation from the essentially healthy tradition of social activism, personal idealism, and political radicalism that to them epitomized nineteenth-century "realistic" literature and was now supposedly reviving in Soviet society. Once the cancer had been extirpated, they thought, the body would recover its health. What could be more natural, then, than to expect that the thick journal, wherein the great tradition focused, would revive as well? It may be that they believed a new golden age of literature could actually be brought into being by re-creating the medium in which it had characteristically developed, by giving the logic of history a push. In any event might not the reappearance of something that recalled, even if only externally, the lambent days of *Notes of the Fatherland* and *The Contemporary* provide a stimulus to literary morale and productivity?

The Party's program for literature also made a journal inevitable. A publishing house would be too spacious, too impersonal for the benevolent, but purposeful Communist nudging that the uncommitted writers needed. Books were a scarce, and therefore impractical commodity in 1921; literature was running to short forms, like the sketch, the anecdote, and the story, no one of which by itself offered enough substance to justify hard covers. Perhaps, too, it was generally understood that a piece of writing makes a very different impression when it has company than when it stands alone. Much of the new writing was bound to be shaky in ideology, and likely, by itself, to produce an undesirable, even harmful impression on readers. If, however, it could be placed in a larger context, surrounded by proper interpretations of the same events and moods in the less ambiguous language of economics, sociology, and politics, then it could be qualified; in some cases, bad might even change to good. This would be a kind of censorship by association; and obviously, only a journal could make such association possible. Finally, a more controlled and enduring impact could be made on a reader by a single publication that came out at regular intervals than by hundreds of books that followed no schedule.

The old system of genres, which ranked the novel supreme and tried to set "literature" apart from mere "writing," had long been in decline. Now, in the twenties, it gave way entirely. People tended to regard everything written down as "literature," regardless of structure or purpose. Even the distinction between "poetic" and "nonpoetic" language, which for the Symbolists and Futurists had revolutionized the concept of genre, no longer meant much.

At a time when the claims of life seemed so urgent and exciting, the notebook, the diary, the travel memoir, and interpretive journalism became respected genres, wherein art and life seemed most readily to intermingle. The journal, particularly in its encyclopedic phase, provides a favorable environment for the development of this concept of literature; for it assembles a great variety of styles, manners, and subjects—both literary and nonliterary—without distinguishing them very carefully. To be sure, each of the several departments is normally devoted to a specific kind of writing; but very often the lines between the departments are arbitrary, particularly where fiction and reportage are concerned. In *RVS*, for example, pieces that to all appearances were travel memoirs could be found sometimes in the company of short stories, sometimes with articles on economics and politics, and sometimes in a section all their own. (*The Diary of Kostya Ryabtsev* [*Dnevnik Kosti Ryabtseva*]— Nikolai Ognyov's famous account of school life in the 1920's—even straddled two departments: the first installment was printed among the belles lettres, and the second in "From the Soil and the Towns.") Actually, a journal does not need departments, and some do get along without them. Although an editor naturally is concerned with the placement of his material so as to provide contrast, relief, and variety, it is the total effect which really matters: the journal is meant to stand as a unity.

The tradition of the thick journal also complemented Marxist ways of looking at literature and society. The old journal rested on the assumption that society had a personality which was mirrored in the several branches of culture and the various activities of the mind; and in its range of departments, the journal presumed to imitate that mind in its most striking and significant varieties. Now, this fact by itself conferred a certain equality on the different kinds of writing that appeared between the two covers of a journal. From here it was but a step to the Marxist assumption that the culture of any age, in all its manifestations, is subordinate to a dominant idea, and that the insights of sociologists can sharpen the pens of poets.

Finally, it may be that certain conditions must prevail in a society before thick journals can appear. At any rate, it is curious to note some striking parallels between the early years of Soviet rule and the Russian 1840's, two periods in which journals flourished. Both periods produced men who had an almost morbid sense of an alien and oppressive past, but believed that a new culture (called "Soviet" in the one case and "national" in the other) could be created to overcome that past. Both conceived of such a culture as resting primarily but no longer exclusively on literature, one that drew from all activities of the mind, with special respect accorded to science and philosophy. Both accelerated the breakdown of an old genre system, which appears to be characteristic of periods of vigorous literary renewal, and defined the purposes, scope, and nature of literature in broad terms, insisting that it must renounce its privileges as the plaything of an elite group, direct itself to a mass audience, move away from poetry and orient itself on prose fiction, and give recognition to third-rate writing as a kind of sub-soil from which stately trees might later grow. Both periods were characterized by a radical change in the economics and sociology of literature, with the collapse of the patronage system, the rise to predominance of fully professional writers, the formation of a mass reading public, and the appearance of professional critics. The parallels could be extended further, even into the kinds of literature produced.

WHATEVER factors may have been involved, it is clear that the decision to revive the thick journal in 1921 was a happy one. And once it was revived, it began to operate within the system of laws that seems to guide all thick journals, regardless of the special requirements of day-to-day operations. In fact, during the seven brief years of Voronskii's stewardship, *RVS* recapitulated, in much accelerated tempo, the main line of development of the thick journal throughout the nineteenth century. Its first phase, 1921-1923, corresponded to the 1830's when the encyclopedic journal took form. In both periods, quantity and diversity were the aims. But in 1923—as in the 1840's—it became clear that a merely general agreement on the purposes of literature, even among the "progressive" minds of society, was not enough: abundance brought diversity, diversity controversy, and controversy the need to take strong stands and make positions clear. *RVS*, like the journals of the 1840's, had to spell out the theory of literature that until then had been only hinted at, and develop a critical methodology. At this point it became a true thick journal, selecting writers according to a definite "line." But by 1927, *RVS* had moved into the third stage, which corresponded to the four decades beginning around 1880: that of a wholly literary journal. Prose and poetry swelled up and forced everything else out; personality withered as the "line" disappeared. The true thick journal came to an end.

The statement of purpose with which *RVS* opened in June 1921 was as ambitiously conceived as the programs of the encyclopedic journals in the late 1820's:

> The journal *Red Virgin Soil* is published with the co-operation of the most eminent representatives of Communist thought in Soviet Russia. The literary section is edited by M. Gor'kii. Because they attach great importance to questions of philosophy, physics, biology, and other branches of science, the editors are making it their task to attract as contributors, on as broad a basis as possible, representatives of scientific thought.[1]

Not a word was said about "fellow travelers," or "proletarians," or any other group of writers. The almost casual

[1] *KN*, No. 1 (1921).

mention of Gor'kii's name made it clear that all would be welcome; for the memory of his work on behalf of writers of all persuasions during the Civil War still bloomed in the public mind, and every young aspirant to literary fame knew that Gor'kii was a prodigious reader of unsolicited manuscripts and a generous dispenser of advice. At the same time, the word "Communist" served notice that an interest in contemporary themes and at least a rudimentary respect for the Bolsheviks were required.

"Contemporariness," indeed, proved to be the most important requirement for the new art during the first two years of the journal's life. From it everything else followed. Here all Marxists at the time found themselves in substantial agreement. Voronskii might have been speaking for any of them when he reminded his readers that "only an artist-prophet, an artist-leader, an artist-tribune can be a really great artist." Since everything the artist did in those days "falls on the scales of revolution or counter-revolution," he must in his work "say exactly and unambiguously whom he is with, what he intends to fight for in the very near future."[2] He must be for or against (*za ili protiv*); there was no middle way. The writers who fled Russia had made a clear choice, but it was a choice against history, and therefore against art, and it would be punished by artistic sterility and death. Those writers who remained had also made a choice. And they should have no doubts or hesitations about it: the artist who is in harmony with society creates best, as Plekhanov showed in *Art and Social Life*. The Revolution opened up the possibility for just such creative harmony, and writers now had an opportunity to do fully what even the best classical writers could do only partially—tell the whole truth about the world, undistorted by

[2] The first quote is from "Literaturnye siluety. B. Pil'nyak," *KN*, No. 4 (1922), pp. 267-69; the second from "Literaturnye siluety. Vsev. Ivanov," *KN*, No. 5 (1922), p. 254; the third from "Literaturnye otkliki," *KN*, No. 2 (1922), p. 274.

the fantasies of a doomed society. Naturally their point of view would be Bolshevik, but after all, that was history's verdict; and a choice in favor of history was the only one consistent with a desire for productivity.

"CONTEMPORARINESS," in these senses, fashioned the tools of criticism that Voronskii and his colleagues employed during the "encyclopedic" phase of the journal's history. One must say that these tools resembled the crude implements of a stone-age culture. Writers were treated less as individuals than as members of groups; and the groups, in turn, were defined according to their attitudes toward the Revolution. Thus, Voronskii clustered the fellow travelers around two poles: one, the "new intelligentsia," included writers like Tikhonov, Ivanov, and Seifullina, who had fought for the Soviets without themselves being Communists; the other, "remnants of the old intelligentsia," brought together two generations of writers who paraded a repertoire of prejudices against the Revolution, such as Gor'kii, Aleksei Tolstoi, Erenburg, Pil'nyak, and Nikitin.[3] The typical critical essay in 1921 and 1922 grew out of the assumption that the work of art was a picture or document of actual life. The critic would first decide what milieux, situations, or attitudes a given work described, and would treat them to the kind of analysis a Marxist sociologist or economist might make. Then he would go back to the work and juxtapose the relevant passages to the results of his analysis: the closer the correspondence, the better the art. In writing on Vsevolod Ivanov, for instance, Voronskii first decided that the characters actually existed in real life, and then cast an eye back to Ivanov's works and concluded that he "artistically, faithfully, precisely has grasped and communicated one of the most characteristic and remarkable processes in the countryside—the power of the earth over the peas-

[3] "Iskusstvo, kak poznanie zhizni, i sovremennost'" (K voprosu o nashikh literaturnykh raznoglasiyakh)," *KN*, No. 5 (1923), p. 369.

ants."[4] An analysis of Boris Pil'nyak's portrait of the Civil War village proceeded from what existed in real life back to what must have been necessary in order that it could exist, bypassing literature: the Red Army was a strong and disciplined force in the village; therefore its leaders had found common tongue with the "new young countryside" in its most "advanced" sector. When measured against this reality, Pil'nyak's work revealed a serious flaw: it faithfully portrayed the anarchy that seethed in the villages at certain periods, but made the mistake of assuming that such anarchy was "typical" of all sectors of the village in all periods of the Civil War. The small role that anarchistic ideas actually played in the Revolution could be seen by "what the countryside is becoming now."[5] The critic, in what we might call the time-lag method, could use his knowledge of the "now" in order to check the writer's depictions of the "then."

Similar techniques were employed to measure the all-important attitude of the writer toward contemporary reality. Esenin's "hooliganism"—the personal and poetic kind were not differentiated—was traced to hooliganistic tendencies in the peasantry from which he came. Though Voronskii considered it a deplorable aberration in a talented writer, he did credit Esenin with giving it accurate documentation.[6] Similarly, Voronskii discovered the key to Zamyatin's prose in the philosophy of "entropy" and "energy," and even went on to show how it influenced the structure of his works. But he did not really care whether or not this philosophy was valid within Zamyatin's literary world or how well it served his strategies; what mattered was the quality of the idea itself, regardless of its function in the work.[7] In other words, the mind of the writer was

[4] "Literaturnye siluety. Vsev. Ivanov," p. 263.
[5] "Literaturnye siluety. B. Pil'nyak," p. 259.
[6] "Literaturnye siluety. Sergei Esenin," *KN*, No. 1 (1924), p. 281.
[7] "Literaturnye siluety. Evg. Zamyatin," *KN*, No. 6 (1922), pp. 309-12.

considered interesting neither for itself nor for the way it shaped a work of art, but rather for what it told of realities extrinsic to it. If the predominant tone of Vsevolod Ivanov's fiction was "joyfulness" that mattered only insofar as it reflected the "joyfulness" that was presumed typical of Bolshevism. For that reason, Ivanov's works were cherished as "a marvelous artistic document of our age, which explained from the inner psychological angle why we Bolsheviks emerged victorious in the Civil War."[8]

These procedures followed the principles of Marxist criticism that Plekhanov outlines in the preface to *Twenty Years*. He sees two stages in the critic's work: the first, to determine the "sociological equivalent" and the second, to make an "esthetic" analysis. The first, which is the more important, involves "translating the idea of a given work of art *from the language of art* [images] *into the language of sociology*."[9] In Voronskii's paraphrase, which is clearer than the original, we thereby discover that "a given work has matured on the basis of such-and-such characteristics of class psychology; we determine to what degree this psychology, these feelings, thoughts, attitudes correspond to the interests of all society in the person of the most advanced and most viable class in a given creative period. In this way one perceives the place, the role, one determines the weight of a given teaching or artistic generalization in the current social struggle."[10] We must first decide, in effect, whether a given work should be handed a passport; then we may go on to consider the "essential complement" of this first act, and make "an analysis of *artistic merits*."[11] Yet what do these really amount to? Plekhanov tells us that "the attributes of the artistic creation of any age are

[8] "Literaturnye siluety. Vsev. Ivanov," p. 259.
[9] "Predislovie k tret'emu izdaniyu sbornika 'Za dvadtsat' let,'" *G. V. Plekhanov. Literatura i estetika*, I (Moscow, 1958), 123.
[10] "Iskusstvo, kak poznanie . . . ," *KN*, No. 5 (1923), p. 365.
[11] Plekhanov, "Predislovie . . . ," p. 129.

always in the most intimate causal connection with the social state of mind which is expressed in that creation"; and
this social state of mind, in turn, is "determined by the social relations peculiar to it."[12] In other words, the "esthetic"
act that Plekhanov deems so essential has meaning not for
itself (inasmuch as it lacks an independent existence and
does not merit any definition either by Plekhanov or Voronskii), but only because it is a social phenomenon as
well. The two "stages," at best, represent two phases of the
same operation.

Here were all the materials needed for fashioning a
blackjack. Since no one in *RVS* was then questioning the
"ideology" of the proletarian writers (as yet they had produced practically no writing to question), the bludgeon
blows would have fallen full force on the fellow travelers.
But *RVS* moved gently. It could not enforce the kind of
"contemporariness" that it expected writers to serve.

The fact was that most of the young fellow-traveler
writers seemed unconcerned with becoming "artist-proph-
ets," and it was often distressingly difficult to define their
views on the Revolution, apart from the obvious interest
they took in the event itself. Unlike their predecessors,
they were remarkably evasive about themselves. Consider
the four versions of Esenin's "autobiography": each is brief
and each presents a different, even contradictory man.
Esenin's purpose, of course, is not to compile a *curriculum
vitae*, but to show four sides of a poetic sensibility. Their
sum does not create a consistent personality and therefore
sidesteps the sort of question that men like Voronskii expected writers to answer in those years.[13] As far as we can
determine, however, the writer's image of himself had
changed. Voronskii's talk about the "artist-seer" and "artist-

---

[12] *Ibid.*

[13] S. Esenin, *Sobranie sochinenii,* v (Moscow, 1962): "Sergei
Esenin," 7-10; "Avtobiografiya," 11-14; "Avtobiografiya," 15-19; "O
sebe," 20-22.

prophet" better suited an earlier generation which began
by identifying the public good with the insights of their
art, and ended (in the hieratic posturings of the Symbolists) by turning the public good into art. Some of the
new writers—the Proletkul'tists, the Octobrists, and a few
of the Futurists—had done much the same by defining art's
purpose as social service and its strategies as agitation-
propaganda. But the great majority, particularly the so-
called "fellow travelers," cultivated reticence. While most
wrote on contemporary themes, they did so with a sense
of detachment, distance, often irony—attitudes which, in an
age that set talent against the stern measure of "for" or
"against," seemed to evade the proper responsibility of the
artist. The Serapion Brothers had even written into their
credo the artist's right *not* to involve himself in anything
outside his art, while leaving it to him to define the terms
of that art.

Perhaps the Revolution had taught these young writers a
hard lesson. Would Russian literature have disintegrated
if clear distinctions had been made between art and life,
writer and rhetorician, symbol and slogan? Would the
worthiest talents of the age now be sitting in Paris, Prague,
and Berlin? Would Blok have gone dry and withered
away? Would Gumilyov have been stood against a wall
and shot? Would Gor'kii, who, if anyone, epitomized an
activist art, have left Russia in 1921? The only writers now
who felt no pull between artist and ideologue were second-
raters, the Dem'yan Bednyis, the Libedinskiis, the Tarasov-
Rodionovs. Except Mayakovskii, of course: no one could
deny that he wrote powerful revolutionary verses, yet
many people suspected that power had been bought at the
price of a brighter and gentler lyrical side. The endless talk
about "art and ideology" throughout the twenties pointed
to a deep and uneasy awareness that the two could not
meet. Most of the new writers preferred not to have to
choose.

This attitude baffled and annoyed the Bolsheviks. Voronskii sympathized with it to some extent, but he sincerely
believed that a "contemporary" point of view, clearly expressed, made no incursions into that freedom to create
which young writers reserved for themselves. Did they
dare presume to set themselves above the Russian classics?
"If the old art," Voronskii reminded them, "had been passive, contemplative, devoid of will, it would not have compelled people to act and struggle." On the contrary: "Sobakevich and Manilov, Plyushkin and Nozdryov arouse
quite definite feelings, after which there also follows a very
definite action which by no means benefits these Gogol'
characters." Russian literature, he concluded, played an
"honorable, beneficial, noble role" in the "struggle against
Tsarist despotism."[14] Why, then, should the young Soviet
writer hesitate to take a stand on the side of truth? *Some*
point of view was better than none at all, for, even if dead
wrong, it could be corrected. Voronskii was merely rehears-
ing a cliché of the times when he reminded writers that
they could not go "floating along without a rudder or sail
[nurturing] a carefree attitude with regard to their world-
outlook, a conscious apoliticalness apotheosized and made
into a principle—that is death for a writer in our time, no
matter what gifts he might possess."[15] "Neutralism," "mask-
wearing," "objectivism"—three tags for writers who attempted to "dissolve" their personalities in their material,
thereby evading all commentary—were considered far more
pernicious than out-and-out hostility, for they gave equal
priority to all aspects of reality, and consequently implied
that all were of equal value. Accusing fingers pointed at
the Smithy poets, at much of Gor'kii's early work, and especially at the Serapion Brothers, with Nikolai Nikitin's
story "The Barge" (Barka) an admonishing example: by
depicting the White officer as sympathetically as the Red,

---

[14] "Iskusstvo, kak poznanie . . . ," p. 354.
[15] "Literaturnye otkliki," *KN*, No. 2 (1922), p. 274.

he had created the impression that both men had equally valid points of view.[16] Alone among the Serapions, Vsevolod Ivanov was highly prized because he seemed to write from an unmistakably pro-Bolshevik stand.

What, then, was to be done? Should these new writers be forced to register for courses in Bolshevism? Should they be drummed out of literature altogether? Consistency demanded as much; and Voronskii often talked as if he were prepared to defend it down to the last line of the agitation-propaganda manual. Art, lest anyone forget, was a "class weapon," and the task of the writer therefore lay "in the struggle with the new petty-bourgeoisie that is infecting the Soviet air. . . . a struggle in the name of the old, glorious precepts, in the name of the tried-and-true slogans of the Revolution. This is the basic thing: the rest will follow."[17] (One imagines the reader rushing to the barricades with a rifle in one hand and a copy of Vsevolod Ivanov's *The Guerrillas* in the other.) But when it came down to cases, such talk evaporated into rhetoric. An insistence on ideological purity would, after all, have excluded from *RVS* practically everyone who was putting pen to paper at the time. The Party's policy was to attract writers, not repel them; and, although no secret was made of the fact that converts were welcome, great care was taken lest there be any suggestion of coercion.

But how was it possible to keep one's purity while losing it? Voronskii's solution lay in insisting on Communist ideology as an ideal, admitting that the fellow travelers fell far short of it, and finding concrete signs of progress in their work. Their defects were easy enough to see: of the "remnants of the old intelligentsia," Gor'kii, for example, had complained of the "cruelty and Asiaticism" of Russian life, with scarcely a word about its liberating push;

---

[16] Yu. Sobolev, review of N. Nikitin, *Rvotnyi fort* and *Amerikanskoe schast'e*, KN, No. 1 (1923), p. 328.

[17] "Literaturnye otkliki," p. 275.

Pil'nyak "confuses leather jackets [his symbol of the Bolsheviks] and pre-Petrine Rus'."[18] Writers from the "new intelligentsia" were obsessed with the peasantry to the exclusion of the proletariat. Even so, they were basically sympathetic toward the urban workers and the Communists, and any flaws in their portraits of proletarian reality, according to Voronskii, came not from malevolence but from simple ignorance; the "old" writers, though miles away from the goal, nonetheless nourished a healthy hatred of bourgeois civilization, and knew, heart of hearts, that Bolshevism was the only way out. And by 1923, Voronskii had discovered positive evidence of progress: Gor'kii's reminiscences, which had just begun to appear, showed a resurgence of artistic power that probably reflected healthier political attitudes; Pil'nyak seemed to be throwing off his primitive, anarchistic view of the Revolution.[19] A year later, Voronskii found solid proof of fundamental change in a letter sent by a group of thirty-six prominent fellow travelers to a meeting of the Press Section of the Central Committee in May 1924. In it, they protested against harassment by proletarian critics, and reaffirmed their allegiance to Bolshevik ideals and their feeling of solidarity with the proletarian and peasant writers.[20] Voronskii, in flourishing this letter, reminded his readers that no fellow traveler had made such effusive attestations of political loyalty in 1921. What more, then, did people want? After all, Lenin had declared that there were different roads to Communism; and in that respect, Voronskii thought that the policy of tactful persuasion had proven its wisdom.[21]

The real measure of "contemporariness," the one which actually determined what went into the journal between

[18] "Iskusstvo, kak poznanie . . . ," *KN*, No. 5 (1923), p. 369.
[19] *Ibid.*
[20] The letter is reproduced in A. Voronskii, "Literatura i politika," *Prozhektor*, No. 15 (1924), p. 26.
[21] "O 'tekushchem momente' i zadachakh RKP v khudozhestvennoi literature," *Prozhektor*, No. 5 (1924), p. 25.

1921 and 1923, amounted to no more than this: literature should focus on the Russia of 1917-1921, depict it at best sympathetically, at least not inimically, and reflect the viewpoints of the "new" people—not necessarily Bolsheviks, but certainly those who had remained in Russia and had thereby accepted the fact of the Revolution, albeit with varying degrees of enthusiasm. Even this definition was subject to sudden erosion in the case of the older writers of proletarian backgrounds. Most of their work could by no stretch of the imagination qualify as "contemporary." Lyashko's "Thief's Mother" (Vorova mat', No. 4, 1921), which told of a woman whose heart was too pure for the world around her, and Nizovoi's "Replacement" (Smena, No. 4, 1921), which depicted the decay of a patriarchal peasant way of life, mined the lyrical-sentimental vein of nineteenth-century Populist writing. Prishvin specialized in the timeless world of nature. Kasatkin and Pod''yachev drew their themes exclusively from the pre-war village. Veresaev, the doctor turned writer, contributed graceful vignettes of Pushkin and Tolstoi. Gor'kii never set any of his work later than the Revolution. Only Neverov, of all the "old" writers whom RVS published, produced a major work on a contemporary theme: *Tashkent, the Bread City* (*Tashkent, gorod khlebnyi*), which quickly became a classic. But by a stroke of irony, it was not published in RVS. That the work submitted by these men was old-fashioned, or that it was generally not as well written as that of the younger writers did not seem to matter. They had symbolic importance.

It was unfortunate that Voronskii stated his case for "contemporariness" so baldly, without refining his implicit distinction between ideals or goals, and tactics. For he undoubtedly created the impression that he proposed to take a militantly purist stance in every dealing with the fellow travelers. The radical proletarians, who tolerated no dilution of principle even in the name of tactics, might well have assumed that anyone who talked such language—a language that seemed no different from theirs—would have to reject all but a handful of the fellow-traveler writers, and concentrate on the proletarian writers, whose styles might be rude but whose ideology presumably was impeccable. They could only interpret the constant influx into *RVS* of new nonproletarian writers—some of them, like Pil'nyak, even dubiously pro-Bolshevik—as a retreat from militancy, a slow surrender to the enemy. Voronskii later dropped the aggressive manner, but the damage had been done: for the rest of his life he was haunted by accusations that he had gone soft toward hostile ideologies. He had never been that militant—it was in fact a manner of speaking more than anything else—and he paid dearly for his failure to make his position clear to the literalists.

We can be sure that the writers themselves grasped the distinction that Voronskii groped for so ineptly. Their number and variety prove it. Although only seventeen new names appeared in *RVS* during those first two years, mere figures are misleading. The point is that they represented a sizable majority of the writers with talent and originality who started publishing in Russia in those years.[22] Most of them have become Soviet classics. As for those relatively few writers of promise who never appeared in *RVS*—Mikhail Bulgakov, Veniamin Kaverin, Mikhail Slonimskii, or, most surprisingly, Konstantin Fedin—we cannot determine whether it was their choice or Voronskii's until the files of the journal have been opened to researchers.[23]

[22] Cf., e.g., V. Lidin, *Pisateli. Avtobiografii i portrety sovremennykh russkikh prozaikov* (Moscow, 1926), and V. Tarsis, *Sovremennye russkie pisateli* (Leningrad, 1930).

[23] Voronskii and Fedin did know one another personally. Fedin served on the governing board of the "Circle" (Krug) Writers' Artel, which Voronskii headed. Recently four letters from Fedin to Voronskii were published (in *Tvorchestvo Konstantina Fedina* [Moscow, 1966], pp. 381-86). They deal mainly with publishing projects of the Artel; their tone is cordial and businesslike, but not warm. Fedin did promise excerpts from his novel *Cities and Years* (*Goroda i*

RVS did not cater exclusively to beginners. Voronskii considered it important to publish older writers—more or less his contemporaries in age—who would be to the young in literature what in politics the Bolsheviks were to the Young Communists: mentors, models, and living links with a revolutionary or progressive tradition. Only four of them— Vyacheslav Shishkov, Mikhail Prishvin, V. V. Veresaev, and Aleksei Tolstoi—descended from the intelligentsia. Most were of peasant stock, and, before the Revolution, had led that vagabond existence which Gor'kii made famous in his own life and writings. The majority had managed to get a few stories, sketches, or poems published in the provincial press; a few had reached the heights of big-city journals like *Russian Wealth*. Ordinarily they would have drifted into oblivion, but circumstance saved them: they had the kind of pasts that the times required. Many, though not Bolsheviks, had become sufficiently involved in anti-government activities under the old regime to qualify as "revolutionaries." Aleksei Chapygin, Nikolai Lyashko, Aleksandr Neverov, Pavel Nizovoi, Semyon Pod' 'yachev, Aleksandr Yakovlev, Ivan Kasatkin, and Nikolai Nikandrov— all have attained a modest place in the history of Russian literature largely because of their early association with *RVS*. Besides the entire literary emigration, the only obvious exceptions from among the older generation were Belyi, Sologub, and Zamyatin. Even if they had wanted to publish in *RVS*—which is doubtful—Voronskii could scarcely have relaxed his already flaccid standards enough to cover them, at least in this early period; for they summed up everything that Marxists found most abhorrent in the literature of the age just past. Sologub stood for pornography,

---

gody) for *RVS* (letter of April 12, 1923, p. 383), and he asked Voronskii to publish his *Caucasian Stories* (*Kavkazskie rasskazy*) in the journal (letter of August 2, 1925, p. 384). But they never appeared there, and nothing in Fedin's letters, or in the editorial commentary, suggests why. Parts of *Cities and Years* were, however, published in the almanac *Our Days* (*Nashi dni*), which Voronskii edited.

Belyi for a tortured style and a hopelessly reactionary philosophy of anthroposophy, and Zamyatin—despite his satirical treatment of the English bourgeoisie in earlier works —for querulous philistinism.

During these first two years, Voronskii gave both generations more or less equal space. But two of the older writers overshadowed everyone else: Gor'kii and Aleksei Tolstoi. Gor'kii, of course, was the showpiece. Although his own contributions to *RVS* and to literature generally were meager at the time, he had become an institution, not only surviving his departure from Russia in 1921, but even deriving a certain grandeur from it. Tolstoi moved in just the opposite direction. After military service with the Whites, he settled down in Paris in 1919, brought out the first volume of *Road to Calvary* (*Khozhdenie po mukam*) in 1921 to the cheers of the emigrés and the hisses of the Bolsheviks, and then, to everyone's surprise, returned to Russia shortly after Gor'kii left. Even before the prodigal set foot on native soil, *RVS*, which had rummaged the lexicon of invective as thoroughly as anyone, abruptly decided that he was a major writer after all, and undertook the serial publication of his latest novel, *Aelita*, in 1922 and 1923. This could scarcely qualify as a "contemporary" work even in Voronskii's loose sense of the term. To be sure, it was science fiction; but it owed far less to Communist vision than to the rocketship-to-Mars genre that Jules Verne and H. G. Wells had made so popular in Russia. Nonetheless, some forgiving gesture had to be made, and *RVS*, as the leading Soviet journal, was obviously the place to make it.

Yet we can trace no satisfactory pattern to the selection of works in this early period. Once again we see how typically "encyclopedic" the journal then was. In effect, it took what it could get, excluding, of course, out-and-out reactionaries. Quantity counted more than anything else—more, certainly, than consistency. (The belles lettres sections even offered a few writers, like Erenburg and Pil'nyak, on whom the criticism section usually cast a disapproving eye.) But the main thing was to get the writing down on paper. Quality would come later, as a strong "line" took shape.

THE ESSAYS on literature published in *RVS* during this period, while no worse than those being produced by other observers of Russian life, were neither distinguished criticism nor competent sociology. Voronskii, like his colleagues, meant well but he was the victim of an inferior literary education and, perhaps even more, of the several traditions within which he had to work. One of them was the Marxist. Even as late as 1923, no consistent Marxist theory of art existed, much less a set of workable critical tools. To be sure, many Marxists in the past had written about literature, but their utterances did not weigh enough to precipitate into a sediment of tradition. Few saw the need for such a tradition at the time anyway. For most Marxists, a separate "theory" of literature made no more sense than a separate theory of economics: both were functions of the Marxist world-view. If one grasped that, one grasped everything. It was common practice at the time to consider statements made by Marx and Engels about society, economics, or the workings of the dialectic as generally applicable to the arts as well. N. Chuzhak, for example, was practicing what passed as a perfectly sound technique when he lifted a passage from Marx on the dialectic in order to buttress his argument that art could not focus on what *is*, but on what will be.[24] Since literature was the result of social process, all

[24] The passage in question—which Chuzhak abridges without saying so, fails to identify, and misdates—is from Marx's preface to the second edition of *Capital* (1873), and runs as follows: "In the mystified form [the reference is to Hegel], dialectic became the fashion in Germany, because it seemed to transfigure and to glorify the existing state of things. In its rational form it is a scandal and abomination to bourgeoisdom and its doctrinaire professors, because it includes in its comprehension and affirmation recognition of the negation of that state, of its inevitable breaking up; because it regards every historically developed social form as in fluid movement, and therefore takes

the critic apparently could do was to link cause and effect, pointing out those specimens of the literary art that seemed most responsive to the pulsations of society. Programs for literature therefore were not considered necessary, provided literature opened itself fully to real life. Since Marxists agreed basically on what real life was, they could not help but agree on what literature ought to be: contemporary and pro-Bolshevik.

So the assumption went. The disagreements that had given rise to schools within Soviet literature were put down to tactical differences that left fundamentals untouched. (Even the rude and unsociable Octobrists attributed their formation as a group in 1922 to a disagreement with the Proletkul't over tactics.) Nowhere was this assumption more amply illustrated than in *RVS*. Between 1921 and 1923, critics of very diverse outlooks and talents met there: Arvatov, Bik, and Aseev—theoreticians of *LEF*; Pletnyov and Yarovoi—Proletkul'tists; Friche and Kogan—strict economic determinists; Yakubovskii—a Smith who had become intrigued with the possibilities of Pavlovian reflexology for literature. It was not until 1923 that Voronskii finally realized that a unified Marxism did not exist in literature any more than in politics. He then decided to acquire a literary education; from that point on, a marked change occurred in the tack of his journal's criticism.

LET US not be too quick, however, to dismiss this early criticism, despite its crudities. It served several important functions. For one, it introduced new writers to the public and bestowed a semi-official blessing on their efforts. For another, it was earnest, sincere, and on the whole benevolent

---

into account its transient nature not less than its momentary existence; because it lets nothing impose upon it, and is in essence critical and revolutionary" (*Capital*, trans. by Samuel Moore and Edward Aveling [Chicago, 1919], I, 25-26). Chuzhak's citation may be found in his article "Pod znakom zhiznestroeniya," *LEF*, No. 1 (1923), p. 14.

and charitable: it showed the writers, as no pronouncement or slogan could, that they had a friend at court who took their work seriously. In return, they were expected to attend to the criticism, and make every effort to improve. There is some evidence, as we shall see in the case of Ivanov and Pil'nyak, that many of them at least made a show of doing so. But even if they did not pay the critics any more heed than most writers do, such encouragement in difficult and uncertain times meant a great deal; without it the literary renaissance would probably have come much later, if at all. And fairness compels us to observe that Voronskii himself, for all his naïveté, did have an eye for quality. He made surprisingly few mistakes in the writers he chose for special encouragement. Beneath the fumbling for words, one often senses an insight at work.

Finally, this kind of criticism was indirectly responsible for the richly textured experiments in style and language that writers made in the early twenties within *RVS*. The variety is impressive. We see the enumerative, space-defying manner typical of "ornamentalist" writing:

In Nizhnii-Novgorod, in Kanavino, beyond the Makarii, where along the Makarii that same Moscow daytime Il'inka sprawled its enormous rump, in November, after the September millions of poods, barrels, pieces, francs, marks, sterling, dollars, liras and the rest, after October's debauch, which spilled over, just before curtain-fall, in a Volga of wines, icons, Venices—European, Tartar, Persian, Chinese—and litres of spermatozoa, in November, in Kanavino, in the snow, from the shuttered stands and the boarded-up stalls, from the emptiness—that same nocturnal China, Muscovite and concealed behind the Great Stone Wall—looks with soldiers' buttons instead of eyes. Dead silence. Riddle unsolved. Unbowlered. Soldiers' buttons for eyes.[25]

[25] B. Pil'nyak, *Golyi god* (Petersburg-Berlin, 1922), pp. 16-17.

And the straightforward, descriptive narrative that recalls nineteenth-century fiction:

> The master was sitting in the corner room and drinking wine. A lamp burned by the icon, candles had been lighted on the round antique table and on the window sills as well. Outside it was gloomy, but here it was warm and comfortable. An overcoat, hat and pistol lay on the chair beside, as if he had just come in or intended to go out. He was sitting in a black velvet shirt without a belt, with silver lace on the hem. Two glasses stood on the table, as if the master were waiting for someone to come visiting. Emptying the bottle, he placed it beneath the table, and from under the table he took a fresh one that had been opened. Up to the master, out of the darkness of the room, squinting at the light, came Petrukha Tsapai. The master glanced at him indifferently, poured some wine into the empty glass, and, thrusting the neck of the bottle into the filled glass, said:
> "Drink, you scoundrel!"[26]

And the *skaz* manner:

> So what oddball said living's lousy in Peter[sburg]? Living's great. No other place can hold a candle to Peter as far as liveliness goes. If only a guy had some of the green stuff on him. Without dough. . . . Yup, your goose is sure cooked without dough. And just when do you suppose that great day'll come when a guy'll get everything for free?[27]

And the ingenuously exotic:

> This, you see, is how it was.

RVS printed an abridged version of this passage in No. 1 (1922), p. 65.

[26] A. Chapygin, *Na lebyazh'ikh ozyorakh*, KN, No. 2 (1922), p. 11.
[27] M. Zoshchenko, "Lyal'ka Pyat'desyat," *KN*, No. 1 (1922), p. 31.

The maiden Kyzymil', a maiden fair (like a cherry tree in spring) fell in love with the good god Vuis. Rosy, juicy, and strong was he—like a cedar cone.

Very well.

She went out into the meadow, turned her face to the sun, let down her hair. She said:

"Vuis! Vuis! I love thee."

Up flew Vuis the joyful god.

He smiled and said:

"Thou art good. I love thee too. But the god Kutai is an old and angry god . . . I cannot love thee, Kutai will grow angry."

"I love Vuis," said Kyzymil', and her eyes shone like the eyes of a maral, beautiful eyes. . . .[28]

The point is that all these styles, and many others that we have not mentioned, were accepted as "realistic" by *RVS*. On the one hand, the commonest strategies of literature were simply overlooked in the ruthless focus on "content," "theme," and "idea." On the other hand, variety and experimentation were taken as "imitations" of the variety and experimentation that were supposed to exist in Soviet life. The colorful weft of Ivanov's prose seemed "entirely appropriate for the depiction of the feral, spiritually and physically healthy people" he specialized in.[29] Pil'nyak's elliptic manner mimicked the "style of our age" too: terse, definite, business-like, a style beside which even Chekhov seemed prolix.[30] If literature had an element of fantasy in it, that was because "in our life there is so much that is terrible, fantastic, uncertain, so much that does not fit into a

---

[28] Vsev. Ivanov, "Kyzymil'—zolotaya reka," in "Altaiskie skazki," *KN*, No. 2 (1922), p. 8.

[29] A. Voronskii, "Literaturnye siluety. Vsev. Ivanov," *KN*, No. 5 (1922), p. 272.

[30] A. Voronskii, "Literaturnye siluety. B. Pil'nyak," *KN*, No. 4 (1922), p. 268.

normal framework."[31] If the new prose struck some as loud, chaotic, mad, disconnected, nervous, broken, teetering, then that was a reflection of Russia itself. Under the circumstances of the time, after all, "the calm and placid attitude of those who once lived in quiet country estates and wrote works in the quiet of their studies is . . . physically impossible."[32]

Criticism's sheer incompetence, then, gave writers license to do virtually anything they wished. No program for literature, beyond the vaguest generalities, existed in this first period; permissiveness *was* the "style." Without it, Soviet literature would surely have been the poorer, since many writers might never have gone beyond their first halting steps.

NEVERTHELESS, this early literature was more than the sum of its individual works; it was like a society which has a personality of its own, irreducible to the achievements of even its most illustrious members, and shaped in some way by even its most humble. Because RVS bestowed its citizenship so lavishly, it offers one of the clearest pictures we have of what that literature was like.

· I I ·

All the new literature, in one way or another, took account of the Revolution and the Civil War. These were the dominant themes of the period, and writers explored them in a variety of settings: in the village (Artyom Vesyolyi) and the city (Mikhail Zoshchenko), among the intelligentsia (Marietta Shaginyan), White officers (A. Drozdov), Red officers (Sergei Semyonov), guerrillas (V. Tamarin), aristocrats (Boris Pil'nyak), and so on.[33] Even silence as-

[31] A. Voronskii, "Literaturnye otkliki," *KN*, No. 2 (1922), p. 271.
[32] *Ibid.*
[33] A. Vesyolyi, "V derevne na maslenitse," No. 4 (1921); Mikhail Zoshchenko, "Lyal'ka Pyat'desyat"; M. Shaginyan, *Peremena*, Nos. 6

sented to the event, or so people thought: the writer who shunned the times was nonetheless measured by them. Probably no event in modern European history has had a comparable impact on an entire literary generation. Certainly no event in recent times has so quickly passed into myth, and has continued so long to cast its spell.

Out of the turmoil, a new style was born—of hard surfaces that reflected brilliantly and refracted feebly. It moves between understatement and hyperbole, deceiving our expectations at every turn. High lyricism drenches what is ordinary, if not sordid; a matter-of-factness verging on boredom conveys what is extraordinary, if not heroic. The writer pursues paradox and fashions his world out of grotesquerie. And, because the reader's sensibilities are derouted, because he is denied the wonderment, pity, and fear which he normally reserves for those moments of passion, courage, and violence that inhere in war, he is persuaded that what he sees before him is somehow more "real" than mere fiction; and he is thus prepared to brand as "sensationalism" any obvious attempts at courting awe or compassion. Leonid Andreev's treatments of war would have been ridiculed by the new writers, not so much because they fail to understate, but because they overstate the obvious.

Since this new literature does shun the obvious, we are tempted to call it sophisticated. In fact, it is not. Considering the magnitude of its theme, it is a strangely small literature—small in reach, small in emotion. There are violence and death, but no tragedy; action, but no heroics; confrontation, but no exploration. Perhaps this is so because it lacks a firm ethical and moral center, and is therefore unable to raise, except by implication, the large human

(1922)—6 (1923); A. Drozdov, "Bes," No. 5 (1922); S. Semyonov, "Tif," No. 1 (1922); V. Tamarin, "Pustynya (iz istorii odnogo pokhoda)," No. 3 (1921); B. Pil'nyak, Golyi god. (All in KN.)

questions that superior fiction must raise. Thus the under-played treatment of war, which is so effective in the hands of the intensely moralistic Garshin and Tolstoi, turns decadent at the touch of the new writers, and the lyrical heightening of the trivial often travesties naturalism. This was not quite what Voronskii had in mind when he observed that much of the new literature was bloodless and morally neutral. He meant that it lacked an extractable message. Yet his observation was right, if for the wrong reason.

MUCH the same point can be made about the treatment of character. Although there is scarcely a profession or station in life that cannot be found in the work of these writers, man plays a strangely subdued role here. He may be given the opportunity for heroics, but he is robbed of his most human qualities: the capacity to reason, to question, to wonder, to choose. For the hero of romance, such deficiencies are all virtues; and much of the fiction of the time is nothing more than military romance, whose heroes provide strong hands to help events along and sharp eyes to record their progress. Such heroes are invariably proletarian, not merely because they exemplify that identity of will and action that underlies the proletarian myth, but because their effectiveness depends on service to the right set of events. Gornykh, the young Cheka agent in Libedin-skii's *A Week*, triumphs where all his sensitive Communist colleagues fail precisely because he is illiterate, has never developed the fateful habit of thought, operates strictly by instinct, and thus fingers the secret pulse of events.[34] Stupidity's survival value is high.

Only a few writers of the time, notably Vsevolod Ivanov, used such heroes as ironic commentaries on man's enslavement to a universe that was unworthy of his potentialities.

[34] *Nedelya* (Moscow, 1922). The work was not published in *RVS*.

Otherwise, this theme—the richest and commonest—normally centered in a hero who is incapable of any meaningful action at all. The trappings of society, family, and civilization have been torn from him by war, and he stands naked, the fig leaf out of reach. His repertoire of ready responses now finds no familiar stimuli. Situations elude him; he is at the beck of events which he can neither control nor understand; his flitting memories provide no clue to action. Such is Dondryukov, that "speck of dust" without ambitions or goals who is the hero of Nikolai Nikitin's *Fort Vomit* (*Rvotnyi fort*, No. 4, 1922). Although he is an army officer and supposedly a man of action, much of his life passes in dreams. Unmarried, he has learned to enjoy a vicarious sex life by recalling a single love affair far in the past, and by leafing through a cheap, romance novel which he has fondled to shreds over a period of twenty years. Such is the neurasthenic Bolshevik (a stock character in this early fiction, despite vigorous protests from Bolshevik critics that he was "untypical"), like Libedinskii's Martynov (*A Week*), for example, whose bourgeois past paralyzes his Bolshevik will; or Arosev's Terentii Zabytyi, whose tormented visions of unconsummated love induce narcosis.[35] Men of this kind drift between the distant shores of memory and action, aware that they can never touch land. Crushed by events, they nearly always perish. But their doom lacks real moral significance, because they are incapable of making the sort of questioning confrontation that would lend grandeur to their situation. Often they are but tawdry allegories of an old world, which is swept away on the ebb of history.

These empty men are suffering the ravages of a terminal disease that writers began to diagnose and chart some fifty years earlier: the disease of the rational mind. Dostoevskii

[35] *Ibid.*; A. Arosev, *Strada, KN*, No. 2 (1921). For an example of protest, see G. Lelevich, "Literaturnye ocherki (A. Fadeev)," *Molodaya gvardiya*, No. 4 (1926), p. 215.

undoubtedly created the most intelligent heroes in nine-teenth-century fiction—men capable of building the ideas of their age into stupendous, often brilliant intellectual structures. But there was always a cornerstone misplaced or a beam left out: the structures ultimately collapsed. Yet they went on building, all the while knowing that the flaw was there. Čapek's *Robots*, H. G. Wells's *The Time Machine*, E. M. Forster's "The Machine Stops," Valerii Bryusov's *Republic of the Southern Cross* were among the first in a long line of modern Utopias that man put up in quest of freedom only to discover that the price of freedom is enslavement.

Chekhov wrote of the impotent despair attendant on man's awareness that an indifferent universe mocks his insistence on purposefulness. Other writers created rebels—men touched with the power to make their own meanings in defiance of the universe. Belyi's *Petersburg* explores the paradox of the eternal impulse to create that drives the engine of the mind: every act of creation is at the same time an act of destruction; yet only through destruction is creation possible. The bomb, for instance, annihilates its creator but liberates him from the obsession that drove him to create it. Peredonov, the hero of Sologub's *Petty Demon* (*Melkii bes*) is not just a paranoid schizophrenic, although the novel is usually read as a case study in psychopathology. He is also an artist, the only character in that poisonous provincial town who has imagination and can give life to what is dead. Of course his creations parody artistry (they are nasty and noxious, the excrement of the mind), but they represent the world as it really exists there, and as only Peredonov can see it. Society esteems him as the highest representative of those sordid values it secretly cherishes but cannot and dares not express by itself. It fears him and persecutes him because he sees too clearly and exposes too much. That is why his visions are branded insane, even though they are the realest of realities, and why

his supreme creation—the dust demon, the *nedotykomka*—
remains a purely private vision. Because he cannot communicate, he avenges his vision through acts of destruction.
Leonid Andreev sees—far less imaginatively—the same
paradox of destructive creation in war, as a kind of new
democracy in which all are made equal through slaughter.
"Friends!" the doctor in *The Red Laugh* exclaims. "We
shall have a red moon and a red sun, and the animals will
have a merry red coat, and we will skin all those who are
too white."[36]

With the disintegration of the mind went all the splendid
values of nineteenth-century humanism. Beneath romantic
love lurked necrophilia (Andreev's "The Abyss"). Glory,
honor, and patriotism cloaked greed, hypocrisy, and savagery (Kuprin's *The Duel*). Death was the only reality,
violence the only meaningful act. Even the revolutionary
movements, with their promises of justice and their faith in
man's goodness, were assailed as delusions. Mikhail Artsybashev was one of the first writers to offer the revolutionary
as a hero in fiction. But this man is not the builder of a new
world; his function is to annihilate the old society and the
revolutionary ideal itself. Shevyryov, the hero of the story
by the same name, feels keenly the poverty, misery, and
injustice created and perpetuated by society, yet he also
believes that man is "vile by nature," and that love, compassion, and self-sacrifice—the qualities needed to perfect
society—do not inhere in human nature but are merely "the
product of ideas," a "cloak to cover unsightly nakedness
and a protection from the predatory instincts."[37] Shevyryov
turns revolutionary merely to square accounts with his de-
luding beliefs. The final act mocks his own idealism: as the
police close in, he flees into a crowded theater, and, from

[36] L. Andreev, "Krasnyi smekh," *Sobranie sochinenii*, v (St. Petersburg, 1911), 117.

[37] M. Artsybashev, "Shevyryov," *Sobranie sochinenii*, v (Moscow,
[1918]), 8-9.

a plush box, fires his pistol blindly into the crowd below.

In the literature of the early twenties, the mind has been utterly extinguished, reason abandoned, thought banished, conflict erased, conscience extirpated. The organizing principle of the new fiction is something other than man: a mood (Chaos, Terror), a passion (Greed, Envy), an idea (Asiaticism, Bolshevism). Personality is now a function of the thing, of the idea, of the event, which exist quite apart from any person. The irony comes not from the idea's or the thing's refusing to be grasped, but from the fact that no one tries to grasp it, or, more properly, that there is no one to grasp it. At best, the mind now serves merely to open a window on a mindless world. One of the most famous examples in the new fiction is the refugee train in Pil'nyak's *Bare Year*: a swaying, creaking boxcar packed with reeking, starving, typhus-raddled humanity going they know not where is described through the eyes of a delirious and dying man.

No writer of the time was capable of making great art out of these confrontations of character and event. A few did attempt to suggest a complexity of personality that in more skillful hands might well have opened onto significant human problems. Thus Klychkov, the political commissar in Furmanov's *Chapaev*, manages to assess his relationships to the situations he confronts and to reshape himself accordingly. Personality (a rigid ideologue's), event (the pressing demands of life in a guerrilla band), and situation (the need to give Chapaev a political education) interweave to create a fuller human being and to intimate a novelistic texture. But the achievement is only apparent. Actually Klychkov is an entrepreneur, whose growth is measured not by self-knowledge, but by the ease with which he seizes opportunities, resolves disharmonies, and contrives solutions. His stature as a man depends on his effectiveness as a political commissar. He is a slave to events, and the apparent complexity of his mind amounts to nothing more than problem-solving.[38] Like all the heroes of the literature of the early twenties, he lacks a true moral dimension.

IMPLICIT in the work of virtually all these young writers was a rebellion against the novel. We have mentioned the absence in the new literature of that sense of constant quest, inquiry, wonderment, and sensitivity to ethical questions that belong properly to the novel. Even the physical dimensions of this new literature were modest. The term "novel" sometimes attached itself to works, like Furmanov's *Chapaev* or Vsevolod Ivanov's *Azure Sands*, that were really only baggy assemblages of shorter materials. Of the better-known works of the time, probably only Aleksei Tolstoi's *Road to Calvary* could safely be called a novel, but it struck a very old-fashioned note. Even the classical short story was not much in evidence, except among the older writers, like Lyashko and Nizovoi. The characteristic forms of fiction now were the anecdote, the short tale, and the sketch, in addition to a variety of forms that fell somewhere between fiction and nonfiction, such as the diary, the letter, and the travel memoir. The closest thing to the classical short story in *RVS* during this early period was the mood study, the tale of a passion: Drozdov's "The Demon" (Bes, No. 5, 1922) tells of the erosion of old humanistic values by Sensuality and Fear; Shimkevich's "The Wolf" (Volk, No. 3, 1921) shows Bestiality as a human condition; Semyonov's "Typhus" (Tif, No. 1, 1922) has as its hero a mindless Will to Live.

The young writers also used narrative techniques that the novel normally shuns. The commonest of them resembles *skaz*, in that the narration is carried by someone who is himself a persona, but also serves as the eyes and ears for many events in which he himself does not participate. *Skaz*

[38] This work was not published in *RVS*.

was a useful vehicle for the new fiction, for the *skaz* narrator, traditionally, is limited in education, intellect, and imagination, and is therefore all but incapable of embroidering what he sees. He is thus a fine candidate for the sort of mindless character that writers favored in those days. And, because he is a literalist who is bound to report faithfully what he sees or what is told to him, he could be used to motivate a variety of narrative styles and voices. The possibilities for verbal play were thereby greatly enhanced, and reinforcement given to the predominant view of reality as a chance, unstructured, and unmediated series of experiences. We find, then, a return to the old pre-novel notion that someone must actually be telling a story, and a protest, usually unspoken but sometimes very explicit, against the well-tailored works of nineteenth-century fiction. Life, according to these new writers, is too unpredictable a thing to be cut to measure.

In their desire to be "honest," writers deliberately challenged literature's traditional pretense of imitating "real" life: instead of concealing craftsmanship they flaunted it, exposing all the joints and seams of their art, making it equivalent to the act of creation itself. Though we find interesting examples of this technique of "baring the device" (*obnazhenie priyoma*) in the work of many prerevolutionary writers, notably Rozanov and Bunin, it was the Symbolists who had made of it an esthetic. From them it passed over into Soviet literature, where it was perhaps most skillfully employed in Viktor Shklovskii's several accounts of the Civil War. Other writers defied what they regarded as the novel's proclivity for windy talk and endless analysis by cultivating pure story, usually in the form of adventure tales. Examples abound in the works of the Serapion Brothers, particularly Veniamin Kaverin, Nikolai Nikitin, and Vsevolod Ivanov, and contributors to the neo-Futurist journal *LEF*, notably Osip Brik: situation and event predominate, often at the expense of credulity; there is a ruthless focus on the

present, with little or no interpretation and virtually no attempt at character analysis; life is seen as a continual present that unfolds according to chance, and defeats those
who attempt to coax meaning out of it. Such fiction differs
sharply from the "ornamental" in emphasizing narrative
line, a chronological sense of time, and a more or less uniform level of language, but approximates it in the assumption that life is essentially purposeless and resistant to
interpretation.

If, as the quip has it, Marcel Proust made the writing of
novels impossible in France because he perfected the form,
then we may say that Andrei Belyi made the writing of
novels impossible in Russia because he destroyed the form.
Petersburg is an anti-novel. It parodies the standard novel
plots of the nineteenth century—and in a deadly way indeed, for Belyi uses these plots to move his own novel, and
at the same time to ridicule the novel tradition from which
they derive. There is the nihilist plot (strongly reminiscent
of Dostoevskii's *Possessed*) complete with double agents,
neurotic students, psychotic revolutionaries, secret rendez-
vous, purloined letters, and all the trappings of political
melodrama. There is the adulterous wife plot (from *Anna
Karenina?*), graced by an elopement with a mustachioed
Italian (the wish-fulfillment of *Family Happiness?*); the
fathers and sons plot, updated with an Oedipus complex;
and many others. At the end of the story, all are blown to
nothing by the explosion of an absurd bomb that has ticked
away in the sardine can. Thus the literary myths and associations that any educated Russian would know are assembled in a kind of synecdoche, and destroyed. No writer of the early twenties could rival Belyi's talent, but the
mood of his anti-novel suffused the air.

WE SEE, then, that many of the themes and moods of the
new writing had been the common currency of the literature before the Revolution: violence, death, the deceptions

of civilization, the breakdown of the mind, the relativism of moral values, the cult of primitivism, the search for freedom through sensualism, the vision of the world as a grotesque farce, even some of the philosophical and religious motifs, such as Russia's mission vis-à-vis East and West. The "ornamental" style that was considered so typical of the twenties derived for the most part from Belyi and Remizov. The reshaping of the genre system brought to logical completion a process that had been underway for at least forty years. The rebellion against the novel was certainly as old as Tolstoi's "renunciation" of literature.

The paradox was that by 1920, practically none of the important writers of the preceding generation could bring direct influence on the new literature, for they were discredited artistically or politically; yet they exerted a powerful and decisive pull on its course. To grasp this paradox, we must examine the work of two of the new writers, Boris Pil'nyak and Vsevolod Ivanov. Although both enjoyed great popularity among readers, they were writers' writers as well: for it was they, more than anyone else, who opened up the channels through which the stream of Russian literature flowed into the work of the young writers of the twenties. And it was *RVS* which played a decisive role in making their reputations and thereby determining their influence.

CHAPTER IV

The Pioneers: Pil'nyak and Ivanov

BORIS PIL'NYAK is one of those writers who miss greatness but who alter the literary history of their country in a decisive way. He lacked a real gift for fiction—an incandescent vision capable of fusing good intentions, prodigious reading, and keen powers of observation into compelling art. He was instead a borrower, an eclectic, the diligent pupil of Belyi, Remizov, and Bunin. Yet his lack of originality determined his importance, for he adapted the techniques and strategies of his teachers to the new themes of Revolution and Civil War. Through him, they took on a respectability that they could no longer command by themselves; and because he was extremely popular and widely imitated during the early twenties, they left a deep and lasting impression on the new literature.

He began around 1915 as an allegorist in the "primitive" vein, which writers had been mining since the turn of the century in rebellion against reason, humanism, and esthetics. The cult of violence and death (Andreev), of sex and instinctual will (Artsybashev), of children, savages, and outlaws (Sologub, Gumilyov, Gor'kii), the attempt to destroy beauty with nonsense, dissonance, ugliness, formlessness, or artlessness—these had been but a few of the ways in which the theme displayed itself. Pil'nyak's palette in the early stories was subdued by comparison, his vision on the whole lyrical and benevolent, and his technical resources ruthlessly conventional. All these stories proceeded from the idea that nature knows best. "An Entire Life" (Tselaya zhizn'), for example, tells of two birds who mate, release their young into the world without regrets, and finally separate when the male can no longer provide. Sentiment, loyalty, even habit—the bases of human marriage—have no place in this superior realm of sheer instinct.

"A Year of Their Life" (God ikh zhizni) unites the whole world in one vast procreative urge: the hunter Demid mates with Marina in the spring and fills her with child; a year later Makar, the bear who is Demid's constant companion, comes to maturity and goes off in search of a mate of his own. What is embarrassing in paraphrase does not come off at all badly in context. Pil'nyak works here in a quiet, subdued way with his animals and nature-men and does not overstate the simple and obvious moral of his tales—virtues that he unfortunately let atrophy as he went on.

But these excursions into exoticism were merely exercises; his ambitions reached higher. "The Snows" (Snega), another story from the same period, foreshadowed the direction they would take. Here the hero is an intellectual who has wearied of civilization and the deceptive importunings of the mind, and has finally unlocked the secret of life through a liaison with a simple peasant woman. "Yes," he muses, "a year closer to death, a year further away from birth"—that is all there is to it. His former mistress comes to understand this, even though she cannot accept it. "There have been hundreds of religions, hundreds of ethics, esthetics, sciences, philosophical systems; and everything has changed and is still changing, and only one thing does not change: that everything living—man, rye, a mouse—is born, breeds and dies. . . ."[1]

The conflict which is merely implied in most of the other early stories is here stated outright: instinct versus intellect, nature versus civilization, chaos versus logic. It remained Pil'nyak's characteristic theme, no matter how intricately he embroidered it. Usually, however, he grants his heroes no

[1] "Snega," *Rasplyosnutoe vremya. Rasskazy* (Moscow-Leningrad, 1927): first quotation on p. 121, second on p. 117. The story "God ikh zhizn" is also in this collection, pp. 99-101. "Tselaya zhizn'" can be found in *Prostye rasskazy. Sobranie sochinenii,* v (Moscow-Leningrad, 1929), 16-26.

such blissful repose in the arms of their discovery. He prefers to catch them at the moment when they have become aware of the conflict within them, and then watch it tear them apart. For man is both agent and victim, pulled by the competing claims of intellect, which wills toward consciousness and seeks it in a self-definition through system and order, and instinct, which is formless and timeless, and constitutes the ground of all being. Hence the paradox, which Pil'nyak contains in the recurring image of the caged wolf, that man builds higher and higher walls to shut out what he yearns after. Nearly always, man tries to jump the walls of his self-made prison, but the serene and ordered life behind them has sapped his vitality. Once outside, he can never return; he has left all illusion behind. This is the truth that those impassioned seekers, the men of science, discover in the story "Zavoloch'e." Their journey to the Arctic is a journey back into time in quest of man's primeval state. But they find there only an endless universe of cold and ice without dimension. Their minds shout out across the empty spaces that planlessness must have a plan; but only the gelid wind replies. This is the answer to their quest. They cannot accept it, but they know it is true.[2]

For his longer stories, Pil'nyak works this conflict into a whole cosmology. The aboriginal idyll now lodges in a vast and mysterious realm called "Asia," or "East," or "Mongol." Ranged against it is the world that man has created in order and symmetry, with urban machine civilization the pinnacle: this is called "Europe." There is nothing in the universe which does not serve one or the other. Each realm has agents carrying on ceaseless sabotage. Each has an army that wages tireless warfare with the other. Each also has its internal emigrés, men who look longingly at the other world, yet who do not really wish to leave their

---

[2] "Zavoloch'e," *Sobranie sochinenii*, IV (Moscow-Leningrad, 1929), 69-164. Excerpt in *KN*, as "Gibel' Sverdrupa," No. 3 (1925), pp. 113-24.

own; and it is on these divided and guilt-ridden souls that
Pil'nyak focuses his gaze, watching the emotional balance
tip now one way, now the other. It was when he began to
set the history of Russia, particularly the recent history,
into this cosmology that he found his true voice and won
his fame. The Revolution of 1917 became, in his works,
the decisive and final encounter in this vast cosmic struggle.
It is the subject of his first novel, *Bare Year* (*Golyi god*,
1922).

For Pil'nyak, the Revolution is not the conflict of proletariat and bourgeoisie, but of East, represented by the
peasantry, and West, represented by urban Russia. And
what of the Bolsheviks? The peasants cannot even pronounce the word "revolution" correctly; but they understand that it bears no resemblance to what the Bolsheviks
claim to be doing. "Beat the Communists," they shout.
"We're for the re-lo-voo-shun (*revolyukhu*)!"[3] For the
Bolsheviks, as the servants of a "scientific" ideology, are
merely defending, under another name, that whole structure of civilization which true revolution has risen up to top-
ple. Some of Pil'nyak's choicest sarcasm is reserved for
them:

> In the Ordynin house, in the Executive Committee
> (there were no geraniums gracing these windows), peo-
> ple in leather jackets, Bolsheviks, would assemble up-
> stairs. Here they were, in leather jackets, every one of
> them erect, a lusty leather lad, every one of them sturdy,
> curls spilling down the back of his neck from under his
> cap, skin pulled taut over cheekbones, folds at the cor-
> ners of the mouth, sharp-creased movements. The pick
> of Russia's soft-boned and misshapen folk. In leather
> jackets—there's no getting at them. Here's what we know,
> here's what we want, here's where we're put—and that's
> that.[4]

[3] *Materialy k romanu*, KN, No. 2 (1924), p. 77.
[4] *Golyi god* (Petersburg-Berlin, 1922), p. 132.

They are actually counter-revolutionaries. But their prideful intellects must pay: Asia triumphs, sweeping everything away, even the peasantry; and the final vision opens up an austere and eternal Paradise, which is undefiled by man's presumptuous sin of mind:

> The forest stands austere, pillar-like, and against it the snowstorm hurls itself in fury. Night. Was it not about the forest, not about the snowstorm that the *bylina* was made on how the epic heroes died? New, ever new snow-furies hurl themselves against the forest pillars, wailing, screeching, shouting, howling a female howl of frenzied rage, falling dead, and behind them more, ever more furies rush on, never relenting, ever increasing, like the head of a snake—two for every one cut off—but the forest stands like Il'ya Muromets.[5]

Pil'nyak's universe was constructed from ready-made materials. To see the Revolution as a spontaneous upwelling of the peasantry was to express a commonplace of the time. As Blok said: "Bolshevism and the Revolution exist neither in Moscow nor in Petersburg. Bolshevism—the real, Russian, devout kind—is somewhere in the depths of Russia, perhaps in the village. Yes, most likely there. . . ."[6] "Asia" called up a thousand years of history, first recorded as the chroniclers turned their eyes eastward on the hostile

[5] *Ibid.*, pp. 153-54.

[6] Quoted by Evgenii Zamyatin, "Aleksandr Blok," in *Litsa* (New York, 1955), p. 25. Many of the peasant poets—notably Esenin, Klyuev, and Klychkov—adopted a profoundly anti-intellectual stance and hailed Lenin and the Bolsheviks as a direct expression of the popular will because they had destroyed civilization. Cf. Georgii Ivanov, *Peterburgskie zimy* (New York, 1952), pp. 228-30. The attitudes of the intellectual toward the peasantry and the "soil" in this century offer possibilities for a fascinating study, which has not yet been undertaken; nor has the peasantry as a literary theme—myth would be the better term—in the writing of the last seventy or eighty years been investigated.

nomads of the far-reaching steppe; then battened into myth by the ingress of the Mongols; constantly renewed by the eastward-running expansion of Russian trade and military power; ornamented by the discovery, toward the end of the nineteenth century, of the philosophies of China and India and the literatures of Persia and Turkey; animated more recently by new religious enthusiasms that sprang from the rediscovery of Orthodoxy, the fascination with anthroposophy, and the authority of Vladimir Solov'yov. One of its offshoots, the two-Russias theme—"Asia" or "Europe," village or city, soil or salon—had absorbed intellectuals for a century or more. Pil'nyak's version owed most to the so-called Eurasians: in its contempt for the Russian intelligentsia as products of Western civilization; the rejection of Europe not so much for itself as for its irrelevance to Russian problems; the denial that capitalism (a European invention) could contribute to Russia's development; the interpretation of the Revolution as a cleansing, renewing event; and the assertion that Russians are neither Europeans nor Asians, but a mixture of both, or Eurasians.[7]

Pil'nyak pulled these familiar ideas together into a single view of the world and set them in a new literary context. He rooted the themes of Easternism and primitivism specifically in the peasantry and recast the two-Russias theme in terms of the social conflicts of his time. The result was a version of the revolutionary experience that struck an immediate response in the twenties and has haunted Russian writers ever since. It has taken on the firm flesh of myth.

[7] For a good survey of Eurasianism, cf. S. I. Gessen, review of *Evraziiskii vremennik*, IV (Berlin, 1925), in *Sovremennyya zapiski*, XXV (Paris, 1925), 494-508. Gessen traces the changes in the movement in the direction of greater moderation. Gleb Struve has a useful account of it, with an extensive bibliography, in *Russkaya literatura v izgnanii* (New York, 1956), pp. 40-49. For a literary version by a member of the Pil'nyak "school," cf. Nikolai Ognyov, *Evraziya, KN*, No. 1 (1923).

Against it pulls the Bolshevik version, the official myth which casts the proletariat as hero. But this myth has failed to penetrate the literary mind; one cannot think of a single distinguished work of Russian fiction that is built upon it. It has been imposed from above, and during periods of relative relaxation, it is all but ignored by the writers. The literature of the recent "thaw," for example, has revived all the old questions of the relationship of the intellectual to the world of the senses, the realm of nature, the soil, and the peasantry. The presence of these two competing myths, and the vain attempts that have been made to mate them, ensure that Soviet culture is in no danger of becoming monolithic within the foreseeable future.

PIL'NYAK's views of the Revolution marked him as an extreme "right-wing" fellow traveler, who teetered on the edge of counter-revolution. (As far as many proletarians were concerned, he had fallen in.) Yet he could not be dismissed or ignored, for his popularity ran high among readers and among many of the young writers as well. He held out a special challenge to the Party's policy toward fellow travelers which Voronskii was shaping: for here was a writer, if ever there was one, who required "adjustment" to the realities of the times as Bolsheviks saw them. It is significant that the first substantial critical article on a prose writer in RVS dealt not with Ivanov, as we might expect, but with Pil'nyak. And Voronskii himself did the honors.[8]

Voronskii began like a skilled boxer by softening up his opponent. He praised Pil'nyak's stories and novels as brilliantly accurate portraits of the Russian provinces during the Civil War. He was even willing to grant that in certain isolated cases the Revolution might indeed represent a peasant revolt against the city and against the Communists.

[8] "Literaturnye siluety. Bor. Pil'nyak," *KN*, No. 4 (1922), pp. 252-69.

But—and here the "but" meant everything—he could not accept this representation as a valid commentary on the Revolution as a whole. Pil'nyak's regurgitated Slavophilism had bespattered his natural talent. Even more distressing to Voronskii was Pil'nyak's primitivism, his suggestion that the Revolution merely reenacted the sex drive on a grand scale. Voronskii worked up a righteous indignation over the one sentence that was to dog Pil'nyak forever after: "I feel," says one of the characters in the story, "Heart's-ease" (Ivan-da-Mar'ya), which was not published in *RVS*, "that the entire Revolution—the entire Revolution—smells of sexual organs." "To whom and for what purpose," huffed Voronskii, "is all this pathology necessary? The result is something like the Rozanovish mysticism of sex, or the conversion of the world into a brothel."[9] Pil'nyak must jettison this rotting cargo, make his convictions worthy of his impressive gifts of observation, turn his outward acceptance of the Revolution into a true commitment. Only then could he begin to develop into a Soviet writer. "We have entered a period," Voronskii intoned, "of a real and genuine reworking and inner rethinking of everything we have experienced over the past five years. The artist who fails to understand that will quickly find himself behind the 'spirit of the time.' "[10]

So far Voronskii was saying no more than one might expect from a man who, willy-nilly, defended the proletarian myth: the castigation of Pil'nyak repeated the terms that dozens of other Bolshevik critics used at the time. But Voronskii made one important qualification: he assumed that Pil'nyak meant well, was a sincere artist, and could change. That being the case, the young writer's lapses into execrable taste and political obtuseness were obviously the result of ignorance. Once he had become aware of the reactionary

[9] *Ibid.*, p. 255. The reference is to the writer Vasilii Rozanov (1856-1919).
[10] *Ibid.*, p. 267.

nature of his ideas, he would recoil in horror and mend his ways. That was where the critic came in: he worked as a kind of ideological witch doctor who, by exposing the roots of evil, helped the writer to exorcise it. Pil'nyak's primitivism was a symptom of the age, Voronskii insisted, not some unique and exotic illness. It even had its good side, for it represented a salubrious reaction against "decadent" prewar literature in the name of reality and fresh air, and documented the deep disappointment that young writers felt in the "values of contemporary bourgeois culture." Yet basically it was unhealthy; as writers like Zamyatin had shown, it suggested "tiredness after the stormy days of Revolution," and had the power to titillate latent impulses toward escapism into a world of the exotic and fantastic.[11] Now that Pil'nyak understood that, he was bound to reform.

Voronskii adopted the tone of a dispassionate doctor perhaps in order to make it easier for Pil'nyak to work this transformation and save face: a sick man, after all, need blame only the virus, not himself. In the final analysis, however, Pil'nyak was expected to give clear indication that he had taken his medicine and restored his talent to health. The alternative was worsening illness: "sorrow, mysticism, despondency, slush, spineless romanticism" would lead to artistic death and burial among third-rate decadents like Artsybashev.[12] As if to reinforce his point, Voronskii never published in *RVS* any of Pil'nyak's blatantly "Slavophile" works, such as "Sankt-Piter-Burkh," and he excerpted *Bare Year* to exclude all the ruminations on history, the Revolution, and sex.

Voronskii's statement had special importance because it reached beyond Pil'nyak to all the young writers of the time, not just to those who had succumbed to "primitivism." It gave notice that an unfortunate class origin did

---

[11] *Ibid.*, pp. 255-56.   [12] *Ibid.*, p. 255.

not necessarily exclude a writer from a career in the field of Soviet letters. Past sins could be forgiven; and sincere evidence of a desire to change would bring sympathetic understanding and public support. Voronskii bent over backward with Pil'nyak—and, by implication, with all the new writers—to avoid seeing any evidence of malice. He even chose to ignore the obvious sarcasm of Pil'nyak's portrayal of Bolshevik activists in *Bare Year*, taking them instead as models of the new man. (It is possible that as a very literal reader in this stage of his development, Voronskii may have missed the sarcasm completely, though it is difficult to see how.) The writer, then, was being given the benefit of the doubt; if he consciously strove to reorient his "attitudes" he could expect sympathetic understanding and help. Voronskii assumed, at least for the purposes of polemic, that these young writers were sincere; and the article on Pil'nyak, in turn, stood as concrete evidence of his own good faith.

"MUCH has been given to Pil'nyak," Voronskii observed, "and the demands on him ought to be increased."[13] They were. Voronskii seems to have expected that Pil'nyak would examine his heart, sharpen his quill at a new angle, and start producing works that answered to this careful documentation of strengths and weaknesses. And it may well be that Pil'nyak tried to do just that, or at least tried to create the impression that he was doing so. *Materials for a Novel* (*Materialy k romanu*), written in 1923 and published in two installments in *RVS* in 1924, looks like a deliberate attempt to court Voronskii's favor.[14]

[13] *Ibid.*, p. 266.
[14] B. Pil'nyak, *Materialy k romanu*, *KN*, No. 1 (1924), pp. 3-27; No. 2 (1924), pp. 63-96. Quotes from the work will be identified in parentheses in the text by part (I or II) and page number. The "novel" that eventually emerged from these "materials" was *Machines and Wolves* (*Mashiny i volki*) (Moscow, 1924).

Materials for a Novel tells of the rise of industry in Russia. Like many other twentieth-century works with industrial themes—Gor'kii's *The Artamonov Business*, for instance, or Leonov's *Road to Ocean*—it covers a large expanse of time, beginning with the first tentative efforts to tame nature and ending with a glimpse of a future ruled by the machine. Somewhat in the manner of Upton Sinclair, Pil'nyak treats his setting (Kolomna and environs) with such care and detail as to create a sense of documentary reality. He focuses on two periods of violent social upheaval in Russia—1905 and 1921—and, as usual, explores their impact on a variety of people and institutions. As in *Bare Year*, we are taken to the decaying country manor, the petit-bourgeois house, and the primitive socialist collective. But this time the fulcrum is different. Pil'nyak moves his story mainly on the inner life of a factory, which is spread out over a period of some sixty years. This much certainly seems to represent an advance toward recognizing modern times. Pil'nyak goes even further, by making a distinction between the oppressive machine civilization of capitalism, and the liberating machine civilization of Comunism which he wraps in a luxuriant lyricism reminiscent of the Smithy poets. The distinction is one that the Communists themselves make, of course. As Voronskii had reminded Pil'nyak:

> The progressive movement of the human spirit is measured by man's power over nature, and if this movement has at present been brought to a halt by "complete mechanization," the reason is to be found in social inequality, in the decay and disintegration of the [social] order based on man's sway over man, and not in the fact that technology as such has destroyed everything spiritual.[15]

[15] A. Voronskii, "Literaturnye siluety. Bor. Pil'nyak," p. 258.

This very argument turns up in *Materials*, where it is put into the mouth of the Bolshevik hero, Andrei Kozhukhov. The sweeping condemnation of all technology in favor of a life of pristine simplicity is assigned to a most unattractive specimen of the old intelligentsia, the engineer Erliksov. Although pre-Petrine Russia remains the ideal, scarcely a trace remains of the "historiosophy" and "Asiaticism" that Voronskii had found so offensive in *Bare Year*. There is a new attitude toward the Bolsheviks as well. The portrait of Kozhukhov panders to the Bolshevik self-image, without the slightest tinge of irony: Pil'nyak makes him the only character to appear in both parts, fits him out with an Old Revolutionary past that was shopworn even in 1924, and endows him with the storybook qualities of resoluteness, vision, and humanity. Finally, Pil'nyak seems to play up those quirks of his style that Voronskii had singled out for special praise: the lyricism is lusher, the treatment of the various regional human "types" fuller and more detailed, the landscapes more colorful and precise. And he makes several authorial intrusions to assure the reader that the fragmentary nature of his work, which so many critics had complained about, is deliberate.

It is tempting to interpret these changes as calculated responses to the remarks that Voronskii had made in his silhouette. We cannot be sure whether they were or not; but the fact that *Materials for a Novel* was the first substantial piece of prose fiction by Pil'nyak that *RVS* ever published suggests at least the possibility that Voronskii saw them that way. If so, he was badly mistaken. Pil'nyak made no break with his earlier work but merely redeployed its components. The basic myth remained intact; only now we see it in the process of enaction: its unfolding defines history and creates the rhythm and movement of the story. Everything begins with "some men who yearned to walk along the swamp paths, who took it into their heads to raise Rus' up on her hind legs, traverse the swamps, lay out roads with a ruler, fetter themselves with granite, iron and steel, cursing tranced Rus' of the wooden huts—and they set out . . ." [I, 4]. And so the towns, cities, factories grew, subduing raw nature. But what seems like progress is really a prideful flexing of the intellect and the will which in turn teach man to fear and then to abandon the very thing that makes him whole. It is the Eden myth. In fact, Pil'nyak locates it in a kind of garden:

If you turn off the main road, drive through the field, ford Black Creek, make your way first through a dark aspen wood, then through a red pine wood, skirt some ravines, cut through a village, drag up and down dry valleys, jolt through another forest over the snags, then cross the Oka in a ferry, just as people did three hundred years ago, pass through meadows and willow groves, then where the path is lost, effaced, obliterated in the tall green grass—you will come to Kadanok, to the Kadanok swamps. Here there are no roads. Here the wild ducks cry. Here it smells of ooze, peat, swamp gas. Here live the thirteen Sisters Ague and Fever. Here on sandy islets the pines grow rank, the alder thickets stand close together, by the bogs the heather has carpeted the earth—and at night, when the thirteen Sisters Ague and Fever roam, in the swamps over the water skim green swampfires, noiseless and cold, fearsome fires, and then the air smells of sulphur, and the frenzied ducks cry in terror. Here there are neither paths nor roads—here roam wolves, hunters and tramps. Here you can sink into a bog. . . . [I, 8]

It is a self-contained universe, perfectly harmonious (the language that evokes it is invariably rhetorical); yet because it holds the mystery of life and death, it is also sinister and terrifying. It asserts itself, again and again, through "rebellion, the rising of the masses" aimed at "shattering the iron horses and the roads"; it "smashes against the concrete and iron, against the steel of the cities" and once more "vanishes in the byways" (I, 4). This savage dialectic ends just as the Marxists have predicted, with the triumph of technology. Man has won; happiness ensues.

But there is a catch. Just as the Utopias envisaged by Kirillov, in Dostoevskii's *Possessed,* or by Pozdnyshev, in Tolstoi's *Kreutzer Sonata,* depend upon the extinction of the human race—in the first case through mass suicide, in the second through sexual continence—so the Utopia envisaged by the Bolshevik hero of *Materials for a Novel* depends upon the sacrifice of man to the machine which he has created for the purpose of freeing himself from all dependence. The final scene of the story foreshadows the paradox:

> Behind the glass the turbines and the steam dynamo ran noiselessly in the glaring light. No people were to be seen. They peered in, they saw: leaning against the railing below the turbine, his head resting on his chest, slept a fitter, with a rag in his hand. A greaser entered, carrying a tea pot and a piece of bread, went over to the stairway leading to the boiler room, and walked down it.
>
> "Look," Forst said to Kozhukhov. "It's night. There's a long time to go yet before the change of shift. . . . The machine is consolidated human genius. The fitter is asleep, the greaser has gone to drink tea with the girls who haul the coal. . . . The machine is running by itself, without man. . . . Look closely, see how it's running . . . it's running all by itself, without man! . . . Remarkable. . . ." [II, 96]

Man has outsmarted himself. In the end he must face the annihilation he has tried to escape. History has come full circle. The Eden he builds is a mocking copy of the Eden he has tried to flee: smokestacks for trees, lamps for stars, generators for suns, railroad tracks for rustic paths, machine oil for primeval muck. And he settles for it with a sigh of relief, though it is infinitely more terrible than what he has pulled against. But, debrained, he can no longer appreciate the irony. He is the issue of that tradition of anti-industrial fiction that Kuprin's *Moloch*, Upton Sinclair's *The Jungle*, and Gor'kii's *Mother* had helped create for Russian literature.

ALL PIL'NYAK's works are allegories, none more obviously so than *Materials for a Novel*. The events, settings, characters, even the imagery are structured on opposing parallels that recapitulate the root myth: country/city; field/factory; soul/mind; past/present; peasant/worker, and so on, with the second element representing a corruption or parody of the first. The characters serve as vehicles of the allegory. One polarity is represented by the peasant girl Dasha, the original Eve: "from all her being wafted all the stupefying odors of her forest habitation . . . and all of her seemed to be hewn out of a cobblestone—a huge bosom, a huge stomach, a huge behind, huge hands" [I, 18]. The other is represented by the Bolshevik Andrei Kozhukhov, the pragmatic dreamer, who is dedicated to making the peaceful mindless existence of the Dashas purposeful and useful by harnessing it to the factory. Dasha is so far unspoiled; but her announcement that she plans to go to work in the factory as a cleaning woman indicates that the process of decay has already set in. What awaits her is painted in the typically lurid colors of anti-industrial fiction:

> the machine would consume her simple morality and ethics, consume her healthy flush, force her to push coal carts up to the furnaces, to inhale soot and the wisecracks of the foreman. Then the foreman would have her come to his apartment or, on a holiday, to the Lurov woods on the other side of the Oka, and there she would make the rounds, just as all factory girls do; and in those lice-infested barracks, where people live stacked one on top of the other, where there is no joy and can be none, where

the human rabble has gathered, she would consider it happiness that a foreman had taken her, because *that* and a bottle of vodka would be happiness. . . . [I, 22]

Between Dasha and Andrei moves Erliksov. He is an engineer who designs and builds machines, yet understands their terrible power, a man who yearns after the untrammelled state of the natural man, yet distrusts and fears its anonymity. He is the human version of the caged wolf he has seen at a bazaar. Through a love affair with Dasha and through friendship with Andrei, he hopes to resolve the conflict of reason and intuition and emerge a whole man. But no resolution is possible; and finally he is literally torn apart when, in expiation of the sin of intellect, he throws himself into a huge flywheel on one of those machines which he has helped to create. The god that has been brought into existence to serve man ends by subduing him.

The Russian reader, who for generations had treated the personages of fiction as flesh-and-blood individuals, found himself balked and frustrated by Pil'nyak's people. They have no individuality. They never change or develop; they lack depth, mind, motivation; they scarcely even possess a physical existence, so meager an allotment does the author give them of his not inconsiderable powers of description. As Viktor Gofman has aptly observed, they do their acting behind the scenes, and present us with the results in the form of letters, diaries, and speeches.[16] As mere emblems, mere vehicles of moods and ideas, they can, at most, open windows on events. Pil'nyak is essentially a writer of situations and settings. He is at his best in mass portraits: the proletariat, the peasantry, families, villages, towns, periods in history.

History, for Pil'nyak, is neither a story nor a random succession of incidents, but a myth that is central to all of life.

---

[16] "Mesto Pil'nyaka," in *Boris Pil'nyak. Stat'i i materialy* (Leningrad, 1928), p. 20.

Assuming different forms but remaining essentially the same, it is immune to time and to man's efforts to direct it. What looks like historical change is only an intensification of forces that have been present all along. Thus *Materials for a Novel* really ends the moment it begins back in what is conventionally called the sixteenth century, with the act of self-enslavement performed in the name of self-liberation. This concept of history is also a concept of time. The attempt to blur the reader's sense of past and present through sudden leaps in narration suggests the workings of a "subjective" time such as we expect in literature. But at bottom, a strict law operates even here. The order in which events unfold is really always the same, regardless of what men think or how the author may rearrange their components; the outcome is foreordained. Time, like history, is a constant state of being, a unity which makes all events and experiences simultaneous. We can neither allot it with our calendars and clocks, nor manipulate it with our fancies.

Pil'nyak virtually defines that change in the concept of time which went along with the decline of the novel toward the end of the nineteenth century. It is intimated in Chekhov's sense of the repetitiousness of life and in his predilection for circular structures (as in "The Cart"); it is occasionally seen in Bunin (*Brethren* is one of the best examples); but it is peculiarly a theme of the Symbolists, whence Pil'nyak took it. In the service of this concept, the usual strategies of narrative prose are sacrificed. Pil'nyak works, as he described it, through "associations of parallels and antitheses" [II, 64], not through an unfolding of a story line in time and space. We must therefore read him as we read so much modern poetry—vertically, as it were, piecing together a picture from scattered clues. He deliberately destroys scenes or episodes that threaten to develop even a rudimentary story interest. Thus he breaks off the pursuit of Andrei Kozhukhov by the police just at the point where most writers would begin to develop it. In this respect, he stands apart from the writers of the Serapion Brotherhood, like Kaverin, Grin, and Ivanov, who considered "plotlessness" one of the more unfortunate characteristics of older Russian fiction and tried to remedy it in their own writing. We are reminded instead of Belyi's technique of evoking chaos through sudden shifts of setting and perspective. But Belyi, at least in *Petersburg* and *The Silver Dove,* uses a gridwork of traditional plot to sustain his work. Pil'nyak does nothing of the kind in *Materials.* Nor does he pay the slightest respect to the conventions of genre; in fact it is in this work that the breakdown of those conventions, which had begun in the late nineteenth century, reaches its extreme. "Materials" is an apt description of the process: although "for a novel," the work is an assemblage of pages from a diary, letters, historical tracts, ethnographical sketches, anecdotes, dramatic monologues, political slogans, high rhetoric and obscene expletive, exquisitely crafted "literature" and unstructured babble. We have before us a compendium of virtually all the styles of prose language, whether literary or nonliterary, that were being produced at the time. They are juxtaposed in seemingly random fashion to support Pil'nyak's notion that all of human experience —not just what we traditionally reserve to the province of literature—serves a great timeless myth. It is his way of suggesting universality.

It was this appearance of unstructured artlessness verging on chaos that enhanced Pil'nyak's reputation at the time as a "realist," an observant chronicler of his age. Actually, art lurked beneath every utterance. *Materials for a Novel,* like all Pil'nyak's work, has a unity which is created not merely by the pervasive central myth, but also by a carefully crafted repertoire of formal devices.

Perhaps the most common of them is repetition. Here we find virtually a catalogue of the rhetorician's art: anaphora

("Gody shli: / Devyat'sot devat'nadtsatyi. / Devyat'sot dvadtsatyi. / Devyat'sot dvadtsat' pervyi. . . ." [II, 77]); paramoion ("*prishol, poshol po shasham.* . . ." [I, 4]); parachesis ("*davno narodam vosslavlennyi.* . . ." [I, 4]); paragmenon ("Muzhiku nashemu kak dikar'—sla-vya-ni-nu,—reshat'sya, reshit'sya, reshat'." [I, 6]); homoioptoton ("zhili vmes*te*, v tesno*te*, smra*de*, p'yans*tve*, verili bo*gu*, chort*u*, nachal'stv*u*, sglaz*u*. . . ." [I, 10]); and many others.

Even more strikingly, Pil'nyak has at his command a basic fund of incidents, themes, and images which travel from one work to another, not as leitmotifs (for their meaning varies from context to context) but simply as bricks and mortar. Much of *Bare Year*, for instance, was assembled from an earlier collection of stories entitled *Bygones (Byl'yo)*. Within a single work, whole phrases, lines, paragraphs, and even scenes may be repeated at various points. Sometimes the repetition is subtle, as, for instance, where the basic structure of a scene is retained, but the contents strung upon it are varied—a kind of exergasia. Usually, however, we have to do with word-for-word recurrences, so much so that *Materials* looks like a pastiche of self-plagiarisms. This technique serves several purposes. For one thing, the repetitions act as stimuli, which condition the reader to react, in predictable ways, with pity, boredom, or anger: we soon learn what is expected of us, even if we refuse to satisfy the expectation. For another thing, they provide loci (in a kind of tautotes) around which individual scenes can be structured—as, for example, the word "stove-couch" (*lezhanka*) which organizes the otherwise chaotic interior of a certain house: "in the house there is a stove-couch—by the stove-couch . . . on the stove-couch . . . by the stove-couch . . . beside the stove-couch," and, at the end, "in front of the stove-coach" [II, 63-64].

Finally, the repetitions reinforce Pil'nyak's theme that all life is fundamentally the same because it exists in a timeless present and merely recapitulates, in different contexts, all that has ever happened. In effect, Pil'nyak was writing one great work throughout his career. It was never completed, but we see parts of it in the novels and stories he did produce.

Andrei Belyi uses repetitions as well; like Pil'nyak, he has a repertoire of images that travel from work to work. But there is an important difference: Belyi is a symbolist; Pil'nyak is not. Each work of Belyi's represents an organic structure in which each symbol has a plurality of meaning that depends upon its position in the work as a whole and its interrelationships with other symbols, a meaning that reveals itself gradually, as the work unfolds, in a series of epiphanies. But Pil'nyak's use of the image is nonsymbolic. His images carry no hidden meanings; they function as signs which refer directly to concepts, and their function never changes within one work, very often not from work to work either. They are a perfect illustration of a point that one of the characters in *Petersburg* makes: "Don't confuse allegory with the symbol: allegory is a symbol that has become common currency. . . ."[17] Wolf, peasant, wind, snowstorm, factory, Revolution are the emblems, the tags of Pil'nyak's world—a static world, in which appearance and reality are one, and things are shown after they have happened, not while they are in process. By naming something he fixes it forever. The "idea" of a Pil'nyak work becomes obvious fairly early, sometimes on the very first page, as in *Materials*; what follows merely elaborates or embroiders.

Closely related to repetition is the literary echo, which Pil'nyak, like Belyi, Remizov, and Bunin, uses lavishly. One of the most striking illustrations can be found in the description of the factory in *Materials*. Here Pil'nyak cannibalizes a stock nineteenth-century Russian literary landscape. "These places," we are told, "had everything in order not to be that poetry which for centuries was considered

17 Andrei Belyi, *Peterburg*, Part 2 (Berlin, 1922), p. 87.

genuine." The landscape, in other words, does not lack anything; it contains all that the faithful reader of Turgenev
or Goncharov might expect. But it is different. Surveying the
environs, like the sensitive narrator of Karamzin's "Poor
Liza," the author observes the "ancient Moscow river," now
"choked with piles of wood, boxes of peat, barges on the
water, a whistling steamer, and the water can't be seen. . . ."
The verdant hills along the river bank? Now "hills of slag."
The winding rutted rural road? Now "two tracks of iron
rails for carts." The endearing diminutives for nature be-
loved of Karamzin and Turgenev are here too—only now
we find not "dear little birds" (*ptichki*) or "pretty little
bushes" (*kustochki*), but a "dear little locomotive" (*paro-
vichek*) and "pretty little carts" (*vagonchiki*). The rustle
of leaves has become the hiss of the factory, which is
"very boring"; the inevitable monastery on the distant hill
is "unnecessary"; the sky is something one now "does not
wish to look at"; the old estate set in the linden trees or
acacias has undergone a transformation too: "before you,
three chance linden trees, a poplar—and beyond the poplar,
in the acacias, a 'guest house,' a 'house for bachelors,' cement houses with tile roofs in the style of Swedish cottages,
houses for engineers—peaceful and solid." And the placid
rural village, complete with idyllic mother and child, has
turned into "little huts like bird houses, with front gardens
rank with poppies and burdocks, with little boys covered
in dust and with a woman by the gate and with a suckling
pig in a mud puddle. . . ." [II, 65] The literary echo, besides serving the theme of corruption and decay, adds the
dimension of memory and pathos to the story. And as an
ironic statement, it hurls an accusation as well—an accusation that the writers of the nineteenth century were either
too heavy-handed to pick out the thread of reality, or else
deliberately lied about what they saw, using "fiction" to
distort or conceal the truth. In this respect too, Pil'nyak

carried on yet another theme of the literary generation before him.

Many of these devices, to be sure, are purely ornamental.
That is to say, they do not serve the basic myth and fulfill
no essential thematic or structural role: they can be moved
from place to place, expanded or shortened, even done
away with entirely. Such, for example, are the imitations of
peasant sayings that stud *Materials for a Novel*: "Two
poods of bread is a horse, half a village of houses is a pood"
[I, 6]. At one point, Pil'nyak weaves a whole long passage
of such sayings, real and invented [I, 8-9]. Or he may employ literary references in the same way:

> A thief, a plain fool and an Ivanushka the fool, a boor, a
> toady, a Smerdyakov, a Gogolian, Shchedrinian or Os-
> trovskiian—and with them the fools in Christ's name, the
> Alyosha Karamazovs, the Juliana Lazarevas, the Serafim
> Sarovskiis lived together. . . . [I, 10]

Yet such devices—often mere catalogues—do make an essential contribution to the work as a whole; for they help
create and sustain that rhetorical, highly artificial tone
which permeates every part and confers a unity. Even the
most careless and seemingly artless effects may be elaborate rhetorical constructs. Pil'nyak's sentence structure,
for instance, which creates an impression of extraordinary
randomness, is actually built upon the principle of para-
taxis, with the word "i" serving (much as in Old Russian
literature) both to link the paratactical units and to set
them off, as relative pronouns do. The same point may be
made of many of Pil'nyak's "realistic," even "naturalistic"
descriptions. Consider the factory in *Materials*:

> smoke, soot, fire—noise, clang, shriek and iron's squeak
> —semi-darkness, electricity instead of sun—tolerances,
> gauges, cupola furnaces, open-hearth furnaces, smiths,
> hydraulic presses and presses weighing tons. . . . [II, 66]

Certainly, this is an effective piece of impressionism; but it is also highly artificial, with the rhythmic grouping (smoke, soot, fire—noise, clang, shriek), the careful contrasts of visual, audial, and light-dark effects, and the paratactical syntax. Even the machines are not so much functional pieces of equipment as brand names chosen for their exotic sounds.

This atmosphere of artificiality is deliberate. It asserts a principle of literariness which openly and defiantly manipulates the "material." Its motivation, in *Materials*, is provided by an author-persona who introduces and ends the story, makes the links between scenes and events, fades into the background when other narrators or "eyes" step forward, affects a helpless attitude in the face of experiences he pretends merely to be recording, and participates in the story himself, with his own distinctive manner of speaking. In these respects, he resembles the typical narrator of the *skaz*. But he is not that; he is too sophisticated, too conscious, too calculating a literary intelligence. Every move he makes is carefully planned. Even those passages that resemble free association are highly organized interior monologues. The author-narrator leaves us in no doubt about his function in the work, for he frequently resorts to what the Formalists call "baring the device." "I came out of Belyi and Bunin," we are told, "many people do many things better than I, and I consider myself entitled to appropriate this 'better' or whatever I can do better (Oh Peregudov and Dal', I conceal from nobody what I have taken from you for this story!)" [I, 3]. The fourth "fragment" is introduced in the following way: "from the chapter entitled 'Rubbish,' which does not fit into the plan of the tale, but which nevertheless is essential before proceeding to the development of the spectacle" [I, 15].

It is this willful, often playful self-assertiveness that gives warrant to the great variety of styles and genres in the work. No attempt is made to conceal art. On the contrary, art is thrust in the reader's face, with all its underpinnings exposed. Through arbitrariness, through artificiality, through the exploitation of a range of material seemingly seized at random, the literary mind proclaims its right to do as it pleases. In many ways, the capricious literariness of this and other works by Pil'nyak calls to mind the verbal prestidigitation of the Old Russian writer, like Daniel the Exile and Ilarion, who worked in a period when literary talent was measured by the number of sources one could bring to hand and weave together into new tapestries. From the more recent past, it carried into the twenties that cult of artificiality which the Symbolists, in particular, had practiced ("Oh, books are more beautiful than roses!"[18]), in their belief that the created world is superior to the world of nature, the inanimate higher than the animate.

PIL'NYAK exerted a powerful influence on the young writers of the time. His view of life, his stylistic mannerisms, his imagery were all widely imitated by fellow travelers like Nikolai Ognyov and proletarians like Artyom Vesyolyi. People spoke of the "Pil'nyak school" in literature, or, disparagingly, of "Pil'nyakovitis" (*pil'nyakovshchina*). Through him the new writers encountered Bunin—in the keen, almost painful sense of a lyrical nature that stands apart from man; Remizov—in the rhetoric, the love of source-snatching, the cult of ancient Russia's songs and sayings, the highly "literary" view of the world; and especially Belyi—in the word play and the sense of irony that verges on the grotesque. But none of these beginners approached their elders in quality or in range. Though both generations shared a similar view of the world, the indebtedness of youth to age was to a large extent mechanical. They took the tricks, devices, and mannerisms but ignored

---

[18] V. Bryusov, "Lyublyu ya linii vernost' . . . ," (1899), *Polnoe sobranie sochinenii i perevodov*, II, *Tertia Vigilia* (St. Petersburg, 1914), 71.

the literary systems on which they were based. Pil'nyak scooped up the husks of Belyi's symbols for the purposes of his own allegories. Belyi was well aware that people regarded Pil'nyak as his pupil, and it plainly annoyed him. He complained, according to Viktor Shklovskii, that "Pil'-nyak's things produce on him the impression of a picture that one doesn't know from what distance to look at"—in other words, that Pil'nyak merely borrowed materials and assembled them mechanically, without regard for the context from which they came.[19] But Pil'nyak showed one way in which it could be done; and it was a lesson that his followers, in turn, learned well.

AFTER *Materials for a Novel,* Voronskii never again published a large-scale work by Pil'nyak, nor a critical study of him comparable in scope and seriousness to the silhouette of 1922. The consensus among the critics in *RVS,* from the mid-twenties on, was that Pil'nyak had failed to grow, was repeating himself, and would occupy only a modest place in the history of Russian literature as a writer of period pieces.[20]

One motive for this change of heart may have been political. In the fifth issue of *New World* for 1926, Pil'nyak had published *A Tale of the Unextinguished Moon (Povest' nepogashennoi luny).* Despite his denials, everyone interpreted this story of the politically motivated murder of a prominent Communist on the operating table as a commentary on the recent death of Frunze in similar circumstances. It raised a storm. The proletarian critics seemed actually pleased, because the story was dedicated to Vo-

[19] "O Pil'nyake," *LEF,* No. 3 (1925), pp. 126-36; quotation from Belyi on p. 128. Shklovskii dislikes Pil'nyak's sensationalism, but his main objection is that Pil'nyak "has canonized the chance manner of his first piece, *Bare Year,* creating things from manifestly crumbling pieces" (p. 127).

[20] Cf., e.g., A. Voronskii, "Pisatel', kniga, chitatel'," *KN,* No. 1 (1927), pp. 226-39.

ronskii and stood, in their eyes, as eloquent testimony to the consequences of his policy of "coddling" fellow travelers. Voronskii reacted immediately with a letter to *New World*. It read in part:

> Such a portrayal of a profoundly sad and tragic event is not only the crudest distortion and extremely insulting to the memory of Comrade Frunze, but is also a malicious slander on our Communist Party.
>
> The tale is dedicated to me. In view of the fact that such a dedication is in the highest degree offensive to me as a Communist, and might cast a shadow on my Party name, I declare that I reject this dedication with disgust.[21]

There is some evidence that this letter was insincere: that Voronskii had not only approved of the story when Pil'nyak read it to him, but that he also believed the insinuation it contained was true. "I am being accused of inspiring Pil'nyak," he wrote in a letter to Gor'kii. "To be sure, he did find out something from me, but I am not to blame for the main thing."[22] The "something" is suggestively cryptic. Whatever it may mean, the incident embroiled Voronskii in deep trouble with "highly-placed people"[23] at a time when

[21] *Novyi mir*, No. 6 (1926), p. 184. The editors expressed agreement with Voronskii, considered it a "manifest and gross error" to have published the work and, in No. 1 (1927), printed Pil'nyak's apology ("Pis'mo v redaktsiyu," p. 256).

[22] Letter to Gor'kii, beginning of June 1926, in *M. Gor'kii i sovetskaya pechat'. Arkhiv A. M. Gor'kogo*, x, Book 2 (1965), 38. Gladkov asserted that Pil'nyak had read the story to Voronskii, who gave his approval. He also said that the editors of *New World* had not bothered to look at it because it was by an established writer and because Voronskii had given it his blessing (letter to Gor'kii, May 5, 1926, in *Gor'kii i sovetskie pisateli. Literaturnoe nasledstvo*, lxx [Moscow, 1963], 79).

[23] Voronskii to Gor'kii, *Arkhiv*, p. 38. Gor'kii reacted with the remark that he could not "understand your incident with Pil'nyak" (quoted from an unpublished letter dated July 24, 1926, in the Gor'-

his own position in *RVS*, for a number of reasons we shall consider in the next chapter, was becoming very shaky indeed. If we are to believe Fyodor Gladkov, Voronskii saved himself only on condition that he make a public disclaimer of just the kind he did.[24]

But the political situation could have been only a secondary motive. Voronskii, after all, never made a final break with Pil'nyak—which he surely would have done if it had been merely a question of discarding a political liability. Right up to the end of his tenure as editor, he even published an occasional story or sketch by Pil'nyak, and, in his surveys of literature, consistently treated him with respect, if not enthusiasm. More to the point, perhaps, was that Pil'-nyak's influence on the other writers of his generation had begun to decline sharply around 1925. At work here, without doubt, was a shift in literary fashion. Simplicity, straightforwardness, psychological analysis, strong characters, coherent structure—the very antitheses of the things for which Pil'nyak had been admired—defined the terms of this shift. As we shall see, *RVS* had a great deal to do with bringing it about. Pil'nyak was simply left behind—an anachronism at the age of thirty-one. Also left behind was the kind of criticism that had made Pil'nyak acceptable in the first place to *RVS* and probably to most Marxist readers. If—as is quite possible—Voronskii had published *Materials* because he thought the work represented a fundamental change in direction by Pil'nyak, then he did so while operating according to a canon that made works of fiction literal transcriptions of "life" and therefore easily mistook ripples on the

kii archive in an editorial note to Gladkov's letter to Gor'kii, *ibid.*, p. 80).

[24] Gladkov, *ibid.* The writer Chapygin remarked indignantly to Gor'kii that he considered the whole story about Frunze's death a "lie," and he excoriated Pil'nyak for adding fuel to it (letter to Gor'kii, July 8, 1926, in *Gor'kii i sovetskie pisateli*, p. 645).

surface for great upheavals in the depths, a canon that *wished* to discover such changes because it set up the critic as arbiter and assumed that the writer hung gratefully on his every word. But the new esthetic brought with it new ways of reading that exposed underlying patterns of the kind that Voronskii probably had missed; and experience undoubtedly brought an awareness that the critic and the writer are natural enemies.

But Pil'nyak had begun to change too. After 1925, he all but abandoned the "ornamental" style, the Eurasian themes, and the allegories, in favor of a kind of lyrical reportage. The irony was that neither Voronskii nor most of the reading public noticed, or cared to appreciate, the change, which this time *was* fundamental. More is the pity, because some of Pil'nyak's best work followed. The lyrical reportage stands up well even today. The novel *Mahogany* (*Krasnoe derevo*), perhaps his finest piece of longer prose fiction, was published in 1929 but never reached the Soviet reader, for it was printed in Berlin and immediatcly banned in Russia as a political obscenity. Until the end of his career, some ten years later, Pil'nyak remained an experimenter. But so decisively had his earlier writing imprinted itself on the public mind that he could not escape it; and it was his fate to be judged by lesser works (*Bare Year* excepted) at a time when something resembling a genuine literary judgment, relatively untainted by politics, could have been made.

· I I ·

Pil'nyak's closest rival for popularity in the early twenties was Vsevolod Ivanov. *The Guerrillas* announced the appearance of a new writer who had to be reckoned with; *Armored Train 14-69* (*Bronepoezd 14-69*) and *Azure Sands* (*Golubye peski*), which followed in quick succession in *RVS*, established him as practically a classic in his own time. Both writers were the first to attempt to make literature out of the experience of the Civil War. Comparison was therefore inevitable. In practically every important way, they were set poles apart, with Ivanov much the worthier specimen of what people expected of a "new" writer.

There was, first of all, the matter of style. No one could deny that Ivanov's work showed some streaks from the same brush of "ornamentalism" that had bedaubed Pil'nyak: the variety of language-levels within a single work, with special affection for dialect and regionalisms; an ear for word play and the devices of rhetoric; a tendency to lyricize nature at the expense of character. But these traits worked toward different ends in Ivanov's stories; for he focused on plot, as we would expect in a member of the Serapion Brothers. We find no great displacements in time and space; rather, we are carried along by an onflowing narrative where events seem to follow one another chronologically. Because Ivanov rarely interprets for the reader (one of Pil'nyak's worst habits), he forces us to engage the narrative directly. Working without a visible "philosophy," let alone an elaborate cosmology like Pil'nyak's, he creates the impression that he is merely interested in spinning a tale. By comparison with Pil'nyak, his colors are bland; he understates, applies the ornamentalist effects sparingly, and does not caress himself publicly.

The Siberian setting of nearly all Ivanov's early works helped make his reputation. Not that it was anything new —Pushkin had used it in *The Captain's Daughter*, Dostoevskii in *Notes from the House of the Dead*, Leskov and Shishkov in their ethnographical sketches, Mel'nikov-Pecherskii in his novels, Chekhov in the account of his trip to Sakhalin Island, Goncharov in *The Frigate Pallas*, Andrei Belyi in *Petersburg*. But the edge had not been dulled either for readers or writers: Siberia had never engaged the literary imagination to the extent that, say, the Caucasus had. And in the 1920's that area took on a far greater importance

than ever before: there brother had fought brother in some
of the bloodiest encounters of the Civil War; there foreigners
had staked out their claims and long continued to defend
them. It seemed that in those vast expanses the very fate
of the new Russia was being decided. Ivanov, himself a
Siberian (not a European Russian on a holiday, like most of
his predecessors), wrote about this land in a way that
seemed photographically accurate at the time, and therefore quite foreign to the vague, metaphysical "East" of Pil'-
nyak's work.

Like Pil'nyak, Ivanov attempts, in the personages of his
fiction, to create a sociology of literary types. But again,
his focus is different. Pil'nyak, as we have seen, is interested
in the two extremes of the social scale: the nobility and the
intelligentsia on the one hand, and the unspoiled peasantry
on the other. Ivanov has his noblemen, his intellectuals,
and his peasants too; but they are mere backdrops. Instead,
his vision angles toward the lower strata of society and
comes to rest upon those people who have only the vaguest
class ties (like artisans), or who have become *déclassés* altogether (like sailors, circus entertainers, or wanderers).
Such people have the greatest mobility; and it is mobility
that interests Ivanov. He introduced a new type into Soviet
literature: the man who is pulled out of the faceless masses
by war, steps over the shards of the old society, and har-
nesses his energies to the surge of events—a man like Seleznev (*The Guerrillas*), the rich peasant become guerrilla
leader; or Zapus, the sailor turned revolutionary (*Azure
Sands*); or Vershinin, the fisherman converted into Red
commander (*Armored Train 14-69*). These were the first
heroes of the new literature, the earliest figures in that
mythology of Revolution which Soviet writers, in the absence of living models, have been called upon to create.

But it was a certain mood, a certain atmosphere in
Ivanov's work that impressed readers more than anything
else. Voronskii seems to have been the first to devise a tag

for this mood, in an article he wrote on Ivanov in 1922. He called it "joyfulness" (*radostnost'*), by which he meant the evocation of a world "where everything is suffused with powerful, primitive vitality, with beauty, with virginal immaculacy and purity, where people, like the nature surrounding them, are pristinely whole and healthy."[25] This view of the world, Voronskii thought, rooted in Ivanov's background. His father epitomized the upward struggle of the proletariat: from mine worker to schoolteacher through relentless self-education. Ivanov himself, much like the young Gor'kii, had tramped about Russia in a variety of odd jobs. Talent, ambition, and circumstances had snatched him from anonymity: his career impressed Voronskii as a "graphic argument for the Revolution," a "graphic index of what a great step forward [the new intelligentsia of humble background] has taken, of how much fresh, creative energy it carries within itself."[26]

More than anything else, this "joyfulness" measured Ivanov's distance not only from Pil'nyak—a celebrant of disharmony, decay, gloom, and despair—but from the pre-war generation that had cultivated "egocentrism, psychologism, Andreevism, Dostoevskianism and . . . inner desolation"— in other words, the writers from whom Pil'nyak derived.[27] Readers could find in Ivanov none of those tortured examinations of conscience that some of the older writers, like Blok, had been conducting in public; none of the self-pity that characterized the protagonists of Zamyatin's stories of urban life during the Civil War; none of the tragic sense of history that drenched the recently published first volume of Aleksei Tolstoi's *Road to Calvary*; none of the cool detachment from current events that Akhmatova, Pasternak, and Bunin exemplified; none of the pathology of sex and in-

---

[25] "Literaturnye siluety. Vsev. Ivanov," *KN*, No. 5 (1922), p. 258.
[26] *Ibid.*, p. 255.
[27] "Literaturnye siluety, Bor. Pil'nyak," *KN*, No. 4 (1922), pp. 255-56.

sanity that had made Sologub's reputation. Ivanov seemed to break clean from all that, in order to write in an honest, straightforward, and unambiguous manner about the simple, yet fundamental things that touched all Russians in those times: violence, death, heroism, honor, shame, victory, defeat. He made much the same impression on readers as had the young Gor'kii with his first stories, which were regarded as reaffirmations of life against a prevailing climate of despondency in literature. (And was it not perhaps significant that Gor'kii, thirty years later, had held out his hand to Ivanov and arranged his debut in *RVS*?) But the younger writer was considered healthier than his mentor; for he seemed innocent of that sense of frustration that dogs so many of Gor'kii's characters. Intervening events had made all the difference. A rule-of-thumb formula could well have been: Gor'kii plus Revolution equals Ivanov.

THESE qualities of joyfulness, health, energy, freshness, and newness defined the image that Voronskii wished to create for his journal as well—the title, *Red Virgin Soil*, implied as much. The inauguration of the literature section of the first issue with *The Guerrillas* had a deep symbolic importance for Voronskii: he said that the work "marked out the artistic physiognomy of the journal . . . ,"[28] and put it forward as an illustration of what he meant when he talked about "new" writing. It is therefore not surprising that Ivanov became virtually the official belletrist of *RVS*, at least until mid-decade. Voronskii published more by him than by any other prose writer: thirteen short stories, three long tales (*The Guerrillas, Armored Train*, and *Khabu*), one novel (*Azure Sands*), and excerpts from another (*Severostal'*).

But, like almost all the other critics of the time, Voronskii misconstrued Ivanov. The things they found in him are

28 "Iz proshlogo," *Prozhektor*, No. 6 (1927), p. 20.

there, to be sure; and the contrast with Pil'nyak and the previous literary generation is valid up to a point. But what everyone failed to see was Ivanov's fundamentally cynical, nihilistic, and despairing view of the world.

Ivanov was proclaimed a master of character drawing. As Voronskii put it: "standing above everything is the 'joyful and intoxicating earth,' and its master—man."[29] True enough, "man," when taken by himself in these stories, *is* life-affirming, healthful, and positive. But he cannot be lifted from his surroundings, a strong temptation, especially for Russian critics with their rage for "types" and "heroes." This is generally unsound critical practice; in the case of Ivanov, it is disastrous. The fact is that Ivanov builds his work not on character, but on plot and situation. The three early long tales—*The Guerrillas, Armored Train,* and *Azure Sands*—are not vehicles for heroes, but adventure fictions, constructed of individual scenes strung upon a rudimentary plot line and arranged according to the classic adventure formula: goal—frustration—resolution.

Consider *The Guerrillas*, which tells of four happy-go-lucky carpenters who commit a crime against the established authority, take to the hills, are pursued by the law, turn into guerrillas, die heroic deaths, and become Red heroes. The tale is built on a series of scenes which are set pieces. There is a campfire scene, a barn-building scene, a hunting scene, a peasant-holiday scene, and so on. Each of these scenes carries with it a number of characters who have no function beyond its limits; they disappear with the next scene and its new set of characters. A few, like the carpenters, do turn up in a number of scenes, but they are the typical "wandering" characters of the adventure story who function merely to link one scene to another. They have no fixed or consistent personalities, but instead take on the coloration of whatever situation they participate in. Note

[29] "Literaturnye siluety. Vsev. Ivanov," p. 258.

what happens to the detachment of Polish Uhlans that sets out from the town in pursuit of the guerrillas:

> But the further they moved away from the town and into the depths of the fields and forests, the more their character changed. . . . The Uhlans, and with them Ensign Visnevskii, felt the way a tired sweating man feels on a hot day as he undresses and slips into the water. Back there, by the little squat houses of the district town, remained that which the town had imprinted on them for almost half their lifetimes—respect, restraint, and a great deal else that keeps the heart always on guard. All that was at once rubbed into dust and scattered to the winds by the endless ancient fields, the forests, the narrow ruts of the roads, overgrown with grass, and by the possibility of disposing of human life at will.[30]

The schoolteacher Kobelev-Malishevskii—Ivanov's contribution to that stock fictional character of the early twenties, the neurotic intellectual—plays informer to the Uhlans, betraying the whereabouts of the guerrillas. But when we next see him, he has himself joined the guerrilla band, with nobody apparently the wiser about his earlier treachery. We are spared any hint of how this change might have come about, how his character, weak and pathetic at the outset, turns strong and resolute. Here again it is situation that rules. An informer is necessary to motivate the pursuit of the carpenters, in order that they may become guerrillas. The teacher is the likeliest candidate, presumably because he is the only intellectual in the story, and intellectuals are not to be trusted, at least not in Ivanov's world. Later, the situation requires someone who can make posters and draft proclamations for the guerrillas; and the teacher, as the only person in sight who possesses the necessary skills, is again trotted out. There is not the slightest

[30] *Partizany, KN*, No. 1 (1921), p. 26.

suggestion that he is merely an opportunist. Actually, he is not a character at all, but a servant of the situation.

What of the carpenters, who turn up in practically every scene and appear to be the real "heroes"? They do change from dim-witted artisans to class-conscious partisans; but we are shown only the results of change, in successive stages, not the process. Furthermore, their experience is not cumulative; they themselves have no awareness of their transformation, for it depends not on inner growth, but entirely on situation. Ivanov carefully establishes them from the outset as moral, intellectual, and emotional neutrals who would not even be carpenters if physical necessity did not require it. They happen to wander into a village to celebrate a holiday. The homebrew is flowing; the law swoops down to seize the still and make arrests. In the ensuing excitement one of the carpenters kills a policeman and all four take to the hills to escape retribution. With them goes the owner of the still, the rich peasant Seleznev. A punitive expedition sets out from town, forcing the pursued to turn from flight to resistance in order to survive. Beyond some vague talk about fomenting an uprising in the town and establishing a peasant government independent of the Reds (something the Reds themselves seem to forget when they decide to canonize these men), they have no ideas, no plans, no visions. Even their martyrdom is a result of stupidity: they stumble into a trap and are killed.

Armored Train 14-69 offers a more conventional-looking hero in Vershinin, the commander of a band of Red guerrillas whose mission, deep in the wastes of Siberia, is to blockade a White armored train. The task rests heavy on him, for he can see no way of stopping tons of onrushing steel with small weapons and bare hands. The fact that he has a decision to make gives him a certain depth. Ivanov even decks him out with something resembling a revolutionary consciousness: he senses a "disorder" in the world which he wishes to put right. "My heart's squealing," he

says, "like a cat that's been tossed out into the cold. . . ."[31]
But all this is mere window-dressing. Vershinin does not
suffer from any sense of failure to measure up to his ideals,
for he has no ideals. His entire career has merely followed
the swath of the fitful wind of circumstance. A fisherman
in an obscure Siberian village, he has been conscripted to
fight the Japanese and the atamans. Later he finds himself
chairman of a revolutionary staff (revshtab) because the
job is open and he is handy. Finally, he becomes a guerrilla
commander precisely because he lacks resoluteness, will,
and mind. He is a servant of the collective will of his men,
whose ideology is superior: the private-property instinct,
we are told, still simmers within him, but his men have
moved on to an "international" or "proletarian" outlook on
life. The solution to the problem of stopping the train lies
in nothing he devises, but is the result of the intuitive needs
of his subordinates. Because this tale shows a unity of time
and situation, we are easily persuaded to take Vershinin as
a personality in his own right. Actually, he is a perfect example of the de-heroized hero, the slave of circumstance,
who graced many a work of fiction in the early twenties.

Significantly, Ivanov fails in his one conscious attempt,
during this early period, to create a major character who
stands independent of his milieu: Vas'ka Zapus, the hero
of *Azure Sands*, a novel about the fortunes of war in a remote Siberian town which is forever changing hands.
Zapus is supposed to represent a kind of universal man who
combines vision, common sense, and activism, owes allegiance to no person and no geography, and moves from
situation to situation with the ease of the folk hero, redress-
ing wrongs and scattering inspiration. Though a demi-god
(legend has already worked his name over), he possesses
those earthy qualities—a crude sense of humor and a passion for women—deemed essential for a leader of men. Yet

[31] *Bronepoezd 14-69*, KN, No. 1 (1922), p. 89.

Ivanov fails to bring him to life. He merely recapitulates the current clichés about Red military heroes. The real hero of *Azure Sands* is the chaos of war in Siberia; Zapus is merely its servant, and ultimately its victim.[32]

EACH of Ivanov's three major early works, then, is an adventure tale that experiments with a different kind of hero: *The Guerrillas* with a mass hero, *Armored Train* with an individual hero who tries to match instinct to situation, *Azure Sands* with a hero who seeks to dominate circumstance. In each case, however, situation rules. And in each of these tales the story resolves itself and ends when the heroes have fulfilled the function that situation demands of them: when the carpenters finally are martyred, when Vershinin finally heeds the collective will and sees the train stopped, when Zapus has accumulated enough deeds to ensure his status as a folk hero. Even the details that attach to them serve the requirements of structure and pace. At the beginning of *The Guerrillas*, for example, we see Ivanov hovering over the trivial daily round of four carpenters who are extraordinarily ordinary. His purpose, however, is not to establish their "characters," but to delay the unfolding of the action. Gradually he shaves the detail, quickens the pace, moves from specific to general statements, from individuals to masses, abandons the hour-by-hour time scale for a concept of time where whole months are covered in a single sentence.

Ivanov's treatment of character reminds us somewhat of early Kievan literature, where personality attaches not to individuals but to the situations or institutions that individuals represent—to princedom, not to princes; to monkhood, not to monks. Each situation carries with it a new set of requirements and attributes; and from an accumulation of situations, the reader may piece together something like

---

[32] *Golubye peski*, KN, Nos. 3 (1922)—3 (1923).

a picture of a person. Erich Auerbach has called this a paratactical technique of characterization.[33] In Ivanov's work,
however, such pictures rarely take shape, because he uses
the paratactical technique not to create personality, but
rather to destroy any possibility of personality. For him,
men are hopelessly fragmented creatures, lacking memory, incapable of learning from experiences, and unable
to exercise any control over events; they therefore act illog-
ically, irrationally, and inconsistently. If sheer accident appears to play a decisive role in their lives, that is because each
new situation presents them with a totally unexpected set of
requirements, to which they must hastily adjust or perish.
War makes the point brutally clear; perhaps that is why it
is Ivanov's most effective setting. Men's only sense of reality, even of existence, hangs on their fidelity to circumstances
moment by moment. They are at the beck of necessity.

It is a cruel necessity at that, because it is senseless and
arbitrary. Ivanov's landscapes serve it well. They are flat,
colorless, devoid of warmth, contour, or proportion; they
form an endless, trackless present through which his men
wander without purpose or goal. Ivanov's refusal to inter-
vene with commentary (as Pil'nyak could not have resisted
doing) makes this world even more remote, more awesome,
more terrifying. The marvel is that he was read as a region-
alist in those days.

It is a world in which death is the only certainty. Yet
even death is not a very important happening for Ivanov's
shadowy men; it is merely the sudden termination of a
pointless existence that they have never understood. Still, it
is the key to Ivanov's ironic vision of life. Consider the
short story "How Burial Mounds Are Made" (Kak
sozdayutsya kurgany) which was published in the fourth
issue of RVS for 1924. Here the setting is one of those dots
on the vast map of Siberia, where the fruits of battle—some

[33] *Mimesis: The Representation of Reality in Western Literature*
(Garden City, New York, 1957), pp. 86 ff.

8,000 corpses—lie stacked awaiting burial. To get them underground is both a problem in engineering and a race against time: the ground is frozen solid, making excavation impossible; the corpses are frozen too, yet spring is approaching and, with it, the prospect of rapid decomposition and plague. Finally, a grave is carved from the earth, the corpses are dumped in, and the dirt heaped up in the shape of a Scythian burial mound.

These corpses are not reminders of guilt that must hastily be shoveled out of sight; they are simply objects that, at worst, take up space and endanger health, and at best, provide temporary employment for the natives. They are regarded with the casual boredom of the observer who has seen too much of death. Though the atrocities of more recent wars have somewhat jaded our sensibilities, the tone is still effective, and we readily recognize its kinship with the shock effects that Garshin, Andreev, and Babel' cultivated so skillfully in their treatment of war. Ivanov wishes not merely to shock, but to insist on the parallel, and thereby the irony, with the Scythian burial mounds that dot the area in which he sets his story. These belong to a heroic past which comes over in a highly lyrical style that jars against the predominant laconicism:

> The burial mound we had climbed still held the smells of the last autumn, over which someone is sure to shed tears, and the earth lay in joyous spring emptiness.
>
> My companion began to speak, much more slowly than he had that morning, about the Scythians who had inhabited these parts, about the heavy bronze bits and stirrups of their saddles, about the primitive art of the burial mounds; and he went on to recall how in the sea at Kerch on a clear day you could see the columns of a Greek city that had been swallowed up, and how the sea still casts up amphoras filled with rotted black grain.[34]

[34] "Kak sozdayutsya kurgany," *KN*, No. 4 (1924), p. 3.

Ivanov's point here is man's tendency to romanticize the ordinary, and to gloss the horrible. But the Scythian burial mounds stand after all as a testimonial to death; and death lacks any romance or heroism, as Ivanov shows in his account of how modern burial mounds are made. Indeed, death, being commonplace in wars, is banal. Yet the deception will go on: "And a thousand winters from now some young archaeologist and poet will dig open the [twentieth-century] burial mound and—will understand nothing."[35]

The famous climax scene in *Armored Train 14-69* develops the irony of death much further. The White train is approaching; the line must be blocked. But how? The guerrillas have no artillery; the terrain provides no material for a physical barrier; and time has run out anyway, as the rumble of the onrushing engine grows louder and louder. Suddenly it is clear: only a body across the tracks can do the job. None of the Russian peasants in the band can bring himself to make the sacrifice; but the Chinese, Sin-Bin-U, lies on the rails, is duly mangled, and brings the train to a stop. This scene has lodged in Soviet folklore as a tribute to proletarian self-sacrifice on an international scale, and Sin-Bin-U has taken his place in the exclusive club of non-Russian martyrs to the cause of the working class. But something is strange about it. Why should one body suffice to stop a whole train? Why should none of the Russians in the group be willing to offer his own body? Obviously the presence of a single body cannot arrest the forward motion of a train. What does, then? It is the very banality of the gesture. Gunfire, explosions, and barricades are all part of the accepted genre of death, and give meaning to the heroics of resistance and counter-resistance. But a body on the tracks belongs to pulp-fiction and melodrama. The Russian peasants cannot be persuaded to lend themselves to such an enterprise, not because they fear death, but because

[35] *Ibid.*, p. 8.

they fear ridicule from the touch of something so patently absurd. Possibly this kind of death, because it is histrionic, impresses the Whites (who are comic-opera types) not as the mangling of an enemy, but as the sacrifice of one of their own. More likely, however, the very banality of the act creates such an absurdity that further resistance is unthinkable. Another minute and all are likely to burst into laughter.

This notion of death and sacrifice casts a pall upon the traditional modes of heroism. Ivanov tends to ridicule conscious heroics; yet his sense of the ridiculous is too refined to do no more than destroy them. Heroism constitutes an unsettling element in any community, particularly in the military. In acting itself out, as a kind of blood sacrifice, it helps restore a balance. But at the same time, it seems to reaffirm all the values of the ordinary, unheroic life that have been threatened.

Let us consider the little story "The God Matvei" (Bog Matvei). Matvei is a peasant who turns up in Denisyuk's front-line regiment, which has been pinned down for three weeks by the Whites. Asserting that he is God, he orders an end to the fighting. To strengthen his claim to divinity, he performs a miracle, prancing around in full view of the Whites whose bullets have no effect on him whatever. Denisyuk's peasant soldiers are appropriately awed. Then Denisyuk himself puts Matvei's divinity to the test by sending him—on a white horse, of course—in front of his soldiers' bullets. It is a joke, for the ammunition is blank; yet the soldiers do not quite believe that the bullets are not live. Then Denisyuk loads a rifle with real ammunition, fires at Matvei, brings him and his horse down, and administers the *coup de grâce*. And his soldiers, "inaudibly, and what is more, unaware of it themselves, laughed."[36] Matvei is buried, the regiment then sweeps on to overrun the

[36] "Bog Matvei," *KN*, No. 3 (1927), p. 124.

White positions, and Denisyuk himself dies the hero's death he has always wanted. Matvei has played the role of sacrificial, propitiatory victim. The peasant soldiers know perfectly well that death is natural, ordinary, and unheroic. Matvei threatens their natural world with miracles. But men do not want miracles, because they *are* out of the ordinary; they prefer assurances that their own world is real. Matvei, like all heroes, defies and in that sense ridicules the real world; his death serves to punish his presumption and to reaffirm that man, for all his frailty, still reigns supreme and still may kill his gods if he so desires.

Because heroism in *The Guerrillas* and in *Azure Sands* is set on a grander scale and deflated even more abruptly than in "The God Matvei," the irony turns savage. The action of *Azure Sands* is built upon the attempts by various combatants to capture Ust'-Mongol'sk, a sleepy and remote town which has acquired momentary importance as a military objective, although nobody knows why. At the end, all the heroes die—White, Red, and Green alike—and the town again sinks into obscurity, symbolized in the figure of the contractor Kachanov who, like the town itself, emerges unchanged by the struggle for possession. Another contractor, Ermolin, forms the frame for *The Guerrillas*. It is he who starts the four carpenters out on the adventures that eventually make them Red heroes. And it is he who has the last word: as the guerrillas are being solemnly interred, to the strains of the "International," Ermolin, who has been untouched by any of the events he has set in motion (or contracted, in the literal sense), stands over the grave and observes, with irreverent levity: "Say, they was re-e-eal good lads."[37] So much for sacrifice!

ALTHOUGH death and heroism go along naturally with the military setting that Ivanov employs in these early works,

---

[37] *Partizany*, p. 40.

they do not stand as purely martial themes. Military fiction in Russia has long provided an effective means of commenting upon human ideals and social values. The reason, perhaps, lies in the special position that the military life has occupied in Russian society as a whole. Young men from all classes of society were expected to perform service as a duty; but for the well-born it was more than a duty—it was an essential part of personal polishing and social education. In this respect, Russia differed markedly from the United States and even England, where soldiers have always been isolated from the mainstream of social life. It was, furthermore, an active kind of life right up to the last quarter of the nineteenth century, owing to continual unrest in the borderlands and an occasional foreign war. Military experience, then, provided a test of virility and ideals, not just of the soldier, but also—because of the close linkage of civilian and military life—of society as a whole. That is perhaps why Russia's defeats on the battlefield in the nineteenth century, which were relatively insignificant as purely military events, had such a devastating effect on society. The Crimean War, the conflict with Turkey in 1877-1878, the clash with Japan in 1904—all these events generated profound social crises; for the military virtues of honor, valor, and sacrifice had been the highest values of society itself. The failure of those values in a military context could not help but reflect directly upon society as a whole.

It did not take the writers long to discover and probe these connections. Turgenev's *Rudin*, for example, which was written toward the end of the Crimean War, is set in civilian society. And it is a society that asks, as does the novel, whether or not vital ideals any longer exist, and if so, where they can now be tested: are not idealists truly "superfluous" men, like the hero himself? Rudin finally puts his ideals (which are the ideals of the intelligentsia of his time) to the test in a quasi-military situation—on the barricades of Paris during the events of 1848—and perishes.

Tolstoi, however, was the master at exploring the implications of military life as a testing ground for social ideals, in works like "The Raid," *Sevastopol Tales*, and especially (even in the title) *War and Peace*, which began as an attempt to explain the Crimean defeat. The military fiction of the last quarter of the century—Garshin's "Four Days" 1877), Andreev's *The Red Laugh* (1904), Kuprin's *The Duel* (1905)—is an eloquent chronicle of the disintegration of society that culminated in the Revolution of 1917. That event created a new set of values, although they did not for many years begin to rule society as a whole; and the Civil War was their testing place. The final military victory of the Bolsheviks in 1921 was taken as implicit proof of the vitality and essential rightness of those ideals, as victory in total war usually is.

The military experience, then, had as profoundly important a symbolic value in 1921 as it had throughout much of the nineteenth century. That fact, when set within the tradition of military fiction, made the works of Ivanov far more than mere adventure tales. Most of his heroes are associated in one way or another with the Bolsheviks, and thus partake, if only indirectly, of the repertoire of Bolshevik slogans and ideals. But it is all for nothing. Ideals do not help Vas'ka Zapus shape events. They neither save the guerrillas from their doom, nor dignify their death: the old world, in the person of the contractor Ermolin, has the last word over their grave. The most "ideological" of these early works, *Armored Train*, is full of high-flown proletarian sentiments; yet they are powerless to effect a solution to the problem at hand. The ideologues talk grandly about taking over the earth, but are incapable of taking over a mere train; they are simply sanctimonious sloganeers. The theme of brotherhood fares no better. The guerrillas prepare to kill the American they capture, but instead release him when he responds enthusiastically to those international phonemes of working-class speech—"Lenin" and "proletariat." Yet another "brother," Sin-Bin-U, is sacrificed without hesitation by a collective proletarian will which cannot move by itself.

Ivanov, however, is only remaining faithful to his central vision of the world. If necessity rules all, then the values of mind and spirit cease to matter. Man's business becomes sheer survival, and even that depends not on him, but on a capricious and unpredictable fate. As Seleznev, in *The Guerrillas*, observes: "A man—what is he—you can always make a new one. A man is dust."[38] He does not scorn biological man (for that is all that counts), but rather humanistic sentimentalism—the disease of ideologues and intellectuals for Ivanov as well as Pil'nyak. Such men invariably perish. And there is no grandeur in their defeat. But Ivanov's vision is far gloomier than Pil'nyak's, for he proposes no idyll, no harmonious and balanced center: his universe is fragmented, meaningless, and without pity. Man can only bow to it.

THIS VISION brings Ivanov far closer to the writers of the previous generation than anyone suspected at the time. The wonder is that the critics, almost without exception, misinterpreted it. One could reasonably have expected that the Marxists, in particular, would have been sensitive to situation and setting, wherein lay the center of Ivanov's world. As it was, they did not seem even mildly disturbed by the inconsistencies and downright absurdities in his characters, though these are at times so obvious that one cannot help wondering whether Ivanov may not be waving them as red flags. Wish projection undoubtedly encouraged much misreading. Good writers sympathetic to Communism were needed; and Ivanov, to all outward appearances, filled the bill—with heroes from the lower classes, a style that seemed relatively accessible, an absence of phi-

[38] *Ibid.*, p. 31.

losophizing about the "accursed questions." In short, he ex-
hibited a relative freedom from those mannerisms that people associated with the old "bourgeois" literature and found
typified in Pil'nyak. With their tendency to read works of
fiction as sociological "documents," the critics did not
scratch the surface until the middle of the decade.

By then Ivanov had begun to simplify his plots and his
situations, move away from military settings, and make an
attempt at character drawing. His theme remained the
same; but now, in starker surroundings, it began to show
itself to even the hardiest misreaders. The critics grew suspicious; enthusiasm gave way to wary uneasiness; even
Voronskii's ardor cooled.[39] But Ivanov had a keener sense
of the conditions for literary survival than did Pil'nyak; he
made the appropriate adjustments. The beginnings of yet
a new style came in 1927, with the stage version of *Armored
Train*. Here Ivanov removed the sting of irony, cast out
ambiguity, and produced an unmistakably "proletarian"
work, in which Vershinin appears not as the passive and
ideologically defective agent of the collective mind, but as
a resolute, positive hero with unimpeachable credentials.

By then, Ivanov's major work was over. Nothing he did
in the last four decades of his life matched, in quality or in
influence, what he had written in those six years. Through
his early writings, Soviet literature made contact with two
of the vital themes of the previous generation: the themes
of necessity and death.[40] Ivanov's contribution was to re-
clothe them in the images of the time and, in so doing, to
show how the right trappings could make an unacceptable

[39] See, e.g., G. Gorbachov, *Sovremennaya russkaya literatura* (3d
ed.; Moscow-Leningrad, 1931), pp. 229-46. Voronskii's reappraisal is
seen in "O knige Vsevoloda Ivanova 'Tainoe tainykh,'" *Mister Britling
p'yot chashu do dna* (Moscow, 1927), esp. p. 160. Voronskii here
remarks Ivanov's chronic pessimism and his inability to reconcile the
concept of blind fate and vital, spontaneous creation.

[40] Cf., e.g., Aleksandr Fadeev's novel *The Rout* (*Razgrom*), published in 1927.

view of life acceptable. Possibly he did not think of his work in those terms; but the technique was convincing and has, no doubt, been consciously exploited by many a Soviet writer since then who has struggled with the problem of making sudden adjustments to new political situations. Voronskii's contribution was to set, in his article of 1922, the terms for the misinterpretation which made Ivanov's eminence and influence possible, and to provide, in *RVS*, a prestigious forum for his work.

CHAPTER V

Dissensions and Decisions

Sometime in 1923, a sudden change of mood occurred among the men of letters in Russia. Only two years earlier, it had been a commonplace to talk about the death of literature and the improbability of resurrection.[1] Only a year earlier, the stirrings of a new life were still feeble enough to hearten pessimism, however well-meaning, and make optimism, however tentative, look like serendipity. But now, anyone reading the reviews and articles would suppose that literary opulence was the most natural thing in the new Soviet world, an assurance of the future if not quite a reality of the present. And it was no wonder. Somehow a new literature was growing up on a scale that nobody had dreamed possible.

The trickle of manuscripts was swelling to a flood. New journals were being opened: *Young Guard* in 1922, *October* and *The Star* in 1924, *New World* a year later. New publishing houses, private and official, were being started: by 1925, three times as many were operating as in 1923.[2] New books were coming out at such a rate that the statisticians in 1927 could count three times the number of titles and

---

[1] Cf., e.g., P. Guber, "Est' li budushchee u russkoi literatury?" *Vestnik literatury*, No. 1 (1921), pp. 2-4.

[2] A. I. Nazarov, *Ocherki istorii sovetskogo knigoizdatel'stva* (Moscow, 1952), p. 115. He gives the following figures:

Date	Total Publ. Houses	No. Private	Per cent Private
June 1, 1923	678	233	30
Jan. 1, 1924	1127	442	39
Jan. 1, 1925	2055	431	20

The number of private enterprises engaged in publishing was actually somewhat higher, if one considers that many of the so-called "cooperative" publishers, like Alkonost' and Helikon, were actually private.

five times the number of copies as in 1922.[3] The newspapers and journals were airing the pros and cons of urgent
literary issues: *Pravda* ran a series of clamorous articles on
contemporary writing; *Press and Revolution* opened its
pages to a full-scale debate between Marxists and Formalists; *RVS* organized a symposium on the writer and the
Revolution that attracted nearly all the literati in Moscow.[4]
New groups, schools, movements, and factions were taking form—most destined to pass swiftly away without
trace, but some, like the Smiths, the Futurists, and the Octobrists, well armed with platforms, disciples, and journals
of their own. Young poets flocked to cafés to declaim the
verses they could not get printed. Established writers
gathered for readings and discussions in clubs, salons, and
private houses like Dr. Grekov's in Petrograd.[5] Voronskii
himself ran informal literary evenings, where writers, bureaucrats, and politicians could rub shoulders. "We would
often gather," one of them reported, "at Voronskii's, in his
double room at the Hotel National, which at that time was
called either the First or the Second House of Soviets. Having all chipped in for a bottle of red wine, we would sit
over that bottle the whole evening long, talking about literature expansively and avidly. Here Esenin read his

[3] I.e., from over 10,500 titles to over 30,000, and from 50 million
copies to about 300 million (Nazarov, *ibid.*, pp. 120-23).

[4] For the *Pravda* series, cf., among others, A. Voronskii, "Iz sovremennykh literaturnykh nastroenii," June 28, 1921, p. 2 (this article
really began the series); I. Osinskii, "Pobegi travy," April 30, 1922,
pp. 4-5, May 28, 1922, p. 2, and July 4, 1922, pp. 2-3; and L.
Trotskii, "Proletarskaya literatura i proletarskoe iskusstvo," September
14, 1923, pp. 2-3, and September 15, 1923, pp. 2-3. For the Formal-
ist-Marxist debate, cf. *Pechat' i revolyutsiya*, No. 5 (1924). For a
report of the *RVS* symposium, cf. "Sovremennye pisateli i revolyu-
tsionnyi narod," *Pravda*, August 23, 1922, p. 5.

[5] For a lively account of Dr. Grekov's house (it would have been
called a salon in the old days), cf. Konstantin Fedin, *Gor'kii sredi
nas*, Part 2 (1921-1928) (Moscow, 1944), pp. 33-56. Not only
writers, but musicians, actors, and scholars attended.

poems. Pil'nyak read *Bare Year*, Babel'—*Red Cavalry*, Leonov—*The Badgers*, Fedin—"The Orchard," Zoshchenko and Nikitin their stories. Old Bolsheviks and army commanders—friends of Voronskii's—would turn up too— Frunze, Ordzhonikidze, Eideman, Gryaznov."[6] Something like a literary life, in the lusty, disputatious Russian tradition, was taking shape. For the politicians, there were, of course, dangers—the dangers that diversity holds for any self-appointed guardians of the Truth. But the Party had worked out no norms, practical or theoretical, for a good many things, among them literature, and tolerated a relatively free discussion almost until the end of the twenties.

This policy of tolerance, within a burgeoning literary life, worked against the special position that *RVS* had held ever since the end of the Civil War. For the first time, Voronskii faced real competition from new publications and new literary groups. The most important of these, for him, were *LEF* and *On Guard*. Each asserted its intention of displacing *RVS* as the organizing center of Soviet literature. Being obscure, they required publicity; and an assault against a respectable, successful, established literary journal served the purpose admirably. So much of *LEF*'s campaign was conducted in a spirit of naughty iconoclasm that it is hard to know how seriously they took their professed ambitions. But for the On-Guardists—utterly devoid of any sense of fun—the stakes were too high for foolery: it was a fight to the death.

Freshened with a transfusion of new proletarian blood, the Futurists began to publish, in March 1923, a journal of literature and criticism which they called *LEF*, an abbreviation for *Levyi Front Iskusstv*, The Left Front of the Arts.[7]

[6] Vsev. Ivanov, "Istoriya moikh knig," *Sobranie sochinenii*, i (Moscow, 1958), 62-64.

[7] Both the group and the journal went by the name of LEF. To avoid confusion, reference will be made only to the journal, although, for all practical purposes, they were identical.

At their peak they could boast no more than twenty-five members; but they were lively, noisy, interesting, and influential out of all proportion to their size. They claimed direct succession from the pre-war Moscow Cubo-Futurists, though only Mayakovskii, Kamenskii, and Kruchonykh could actually legitimize the claim. By Soviet standards, their history was venerable. They never lost an opportunity to remind people that they had been the first literary group to recognize the Bolsheviks, and they were not shy about claiming grateful recompense as their right. Lunacharskii, eager for converts and compelled to satisfy them all—whether Proletkul'tists, Symbolists, fellow travelers, repentant noblemen, or seekers after solitude—had put some Futurists in charge of the Graphic Arts Section of the Commissariat of Education in 1918. Osip Brik, N. Punin, and Natan Al'tman, the chief staffers of the Section, subjected none of the museums under their jurisdiction to the havoc that Futurism was always threatening to visit upon the fossilized monuments of the past. Instead, they brought out one issue of a journal in 1919, called *Graphic Arts* (*Izobrazitel'nye iskusstva*), and, two years later, an interesting miscellany entitled *Art in Production* (*Iskusstvo v proizvodstve*).

The real voice of Futurism, however, echoed from the pages of *Art of the Commune* (*Iskusstvo kommuny*), a newspaper in pamphlet format which appeared more or less regularly from December 1918 to April 1919. In addition to the usual swath of disapproving commentary about the art of the past, it tried to offer a constructive program of its own. Art was defined as "action" and therefore appropriate "only to the present; behind, we have the *results of action*; ahead—*plans for action*."[8] All talk of "genius," "inspiration," and "free creativity" was branded irrelevant twaddle: any man could make art, for art had to do with

[8] Cited by N. Chuzhak, "Pod znakom zhiznestroeniya," *LEF*, No. 1 (1923), p. 24.

the "direct material creation of things." Far from "representing" or "standing for" reality, as all art heretofore had done, it was reality itself.[9] This anti-esthetic sentiment, which ran throughout Futurism, was well put by Osip Brik:

> The bourgeoisie thought that art's only task was to distort life. The proletariat thinks otherwise. Not distort, but create. And not a haze of ideas but a *material thing.* —"We gave the idea of things."—"*We don't need your ideas!* . . . If you are artists, if you can create and make— then make us our human nature, our human *things.*"[10]

In practice, the "thinginess" of art, at this point, meant service to the slogans of politics and the needs of society. "To the streets—Futurists/Drummers and Poets!" Mayakovskii cried.[11] Cubo-Futurism's insistence on the power of the self-sufficient word thus passed into Revolutionary Futurism. But so did its iconoclasm, nihilism, and primitivism. The negative part of the Futurist program attracted, as it always had, far greater attention for the colorful crudities it heaped upon all outmoded—that is, all non-Futurist—art. "Is it not better," one of them wrote, "to drop decrepit mellifluousness into the city sewage system, and set up as mighty a rumbling as we can, more in keeping with the way our ears are attuned?"[12]

With *LEF*, in 1923, the call to arms against the heathen rang as vibrantly as ever: the Revolution would find a worthy helpmeet in a new art won with the weapons of "example, agitation, propaganda."[13] But *LEF* considered itself more sophisticated than *Art of the Commune*. It looked condescendingly back at the "nihilism" of 1918, insisting that the calmer conditions of the NEP required constructive ideas. N. Chuzhak, one of the leading theorists, disap-

[9] *Ibid.*   [10] *Ibid.*
[11] "Prikaz po armii iskusstva," *Polnoe sobranie sochinenii,* II (Moscow, 1956), 15.
[12] "Pod znakom zhiznestroeniya," p. 24.
[13] "V kogo vgryzaetsya LEF?" *LEF,* No. 1 (1923), p. 9.

provingly listed the extremes to which Futurism was susceptible: a tendency to make art mere agitation-propaganda or mere formalism; an emphasis on the applied arts to the exclusion of all others (*prikladnichestvo*); the merger of art and the products of industry (*proizvodnichestvo*).[14] The trouble was that these views of art, and many others as well, had already been put forth as definitions by various people who spoke as Futurists. Nobody could agree on what art really was or precisely what role it should play in the new society. The real purpose of *LEF*, as Chuzhak saw it, was to find a common ground on which all the "left-wing" views of art could stand. That is probably why the *LEF* formulations were so hazy and the connections between those formulations and the model specimens of "new" literature so tenuous. Art's purpose, according to *LEF*, was the "building of life" (*zhiznestroenie*)[15] on a "dialectical model" of the future, in order to exert an "emotionally organizing action on the psyche in connection with the task of the class struggle."[16] As a result, a "new man" would appear. When he did, art would have served its purpose and would then merge with labor. What forms would this new art take? That was left in some doubt. For the time being, artists of the "left" were encouraged to use the old forms but to bore from within, so that ultimately these forms would disintegrate, and new ones, appropriate to the future, would emerge:

> Until art has been cast down from its self-subsistent pedestal, Futurism must make use of it, on its own ground, setting the workings of agitation-propaganda against manners-and-mores painting; a vigorous cultivation of language against the lyric; the imaginative adventure tale against psychological fiction; the newspaper

[14] "Pod znakom zhiznestroeniya," pp. 25-27.
[15] *Ibid.*
[16] S. Tret'yakov, "Otkuda i kuda? (Perspektivy futurizma)," *LEF*, No. 1 (1923), p. 199.

feuilleton and the propaganda piece against pure art; the orator's platform against declamation; tragedy and farce against petty-bourgeois drama; the movements of productive labor against inner experiences.[17]

Like so many radical programs of the past, this one was designed not to get rid of art, but to make art directly relevant to daily life. If artists would keep in mind that their business was not "form" or "content," but "purpose," all would be well.[18] Although *LEF* was interested almost exclusively in literature, it was the nonliterary arts, particularly architecture, which made the most creative use of these theories; the literature itself was disappointing. At its best, *LEF* was an anthology of the more experimental writing of the time, represented by such stalwarts as Babel', Vesyolyi, Mayakovskii, Aseev, and Pasternak. At its worst, and unfortunately most characteristic, it ran to pulpy love stories and adventure tales which were supposed to illustrate the superiority of plot to "psychology" and to create an impression of unmediated reality by various suspense devices, enabling the reader to concentrate strictly on the unfolding of the action, scene by scene, and thereby to overcome the "esthetic distance" which the old stratagems of fiction supposedly created by "interpreting" life.

These formulations by no means represented the consensus of all the contributors to *LEF* or even many of the important ones—certainly not Eikhenbaum and Shklovskii (both Formalists), nor Osip Brik (an advocate of the "production" art that Chuzhak deplored), nor Boris Pasternak (a lyricist). They were the work of the "proletarian" wing, made up of Chuzhak, B. Kushner, and S. Tret'yakov. These men had been the guiding spirits of the "Creative Work" (Tvorchestvo) group in Vladivostok, and had arrived independently at many of the ideas put forward by *Art of the Commune*. It was their presence that enabled this latest

[17] *Ibid.*, p. 202.   [18] *Ibid.*, p. 199.

version of Futurism to call itself revolutionary in the social and political sense that mattered at the time.

That claim leaned upon the argument that "futurism" was not a school but a view of the world which, like that of the proletariat, was revolutionary and militant. The fact that both Futurism and the proletariat shared a similar history of "oppression" which reached its height at about the same time (1912) suggested the syllogism. The Revolution completed it: the events of 1917 "saved" Futurism from becoming merely an abstract formalistic movement divorced from real life, giving it "individualism," "palpable form," and a new social and collective cast. Futurism, in turn, "is battling for that dynamic organization of the personality without which progress toward the commune is impossible." In short, the interests, the goals, and the destinies of Futurism and the proletariat were identical.[19]

In many particulars the theories of *LEF* and the proletarian critics showed substantial agreement: a progressive idea as the working model for art; the need to "organize" the "psyche" of the masses by means of art; focus on an ever-changing and future reality, instead of on static pictures of life; the idea that the artist is not a unique genius, but an expression of the collective will; a scorn for the art of the past—and most contemporary art as well—as "passive," "contemplative," and irrelevant to the tasks of the times. In fact, such coincidences facilitated a tactical alliance between *LEF* and the Proletkul't in 1923.[20]

But basically incompatible mentalities undid everything. To people as grimly intent as most proletarians (particularly the Octobrists) on easy communication with the masses, *LEF*'s lively sense that art should experiment, innovate, even

[19] *Ibid.*, pp. 195-203.
[20] Cf. Ch. vi, p. 237. The Proletkul't aspired to form a united front with other literary groups, but succeeded in doing so only with *LEF*, which took part in the Moscow organization and published in Proletkul't journals. For the Octobrists, however, any collaboration with *LEF* was unthinkable.

shock, seemed arcane, precious, and, at bottom, immoral. *LEF*, in turn, scarcely troubled to conceal its scorn for most contemporary proletarian writing as merely a flaccid imitation of bourgeois art.[21] Toward *RVS* the critics in *LEF* maintained a relentless hostility from the outset; in their eyes Voronskii and his writers were the sterile offspring of an utterly outmoded idea of art.[22] In turn, Voronskii, as we shall see, regarded the theories of *LEF* as basically un-Marxist. Two of the theorists of Futurism, Boris Arvatov and E. Bik (pseudonym of Sergei Bobrov), had published poems in *RVS*; but that was before *LEF* had been formed and before Voronskii himself had decided to adopt a strong line. After 1923, there were no further contributions to his journal from theorists or critics of the "left." Their writers, however— Mayakovskii, Aseev, and others claimed by *LEF*—found the door at *RVS* open to them, probably because they had contributed little or nothing to theory and could therefore be taken on their own merits as artists, without the need for embarrassing compromises.

LEF lacked the size, the unity, and the intelligibility to form the center of a new Soviet literature. Decline soon set in. Longer and longer intervals elapsed between each of the seven issues of the journal; finally, in 1925, it expired. Two years later, *New LEF* (*Novyi LEF*) signaled an attempt at revival, but that lasted only a year. And REF—the Revolutionary Front of Art—the following year was even shorter-lived.

LESS INTERESTING, but larger, more aggressive, better organized, and, ultimately, more influential was the proletarian literature movement. The groups that composed it

[21] Cf., e.g., V. Sillov, "Raseya ili R.S.F.S.R. (Zametki o proletarskoi poezii)," *LEF*, No. 2 (1923), pp. 119-29. Here Sillov shows, with devastating effect, that the proletarian poetry of the time was drenched with the imagery of sentimental bourgeois lyricism and could not therefore have any serious claim to being "revolutionary."
[22] "Za chto boretsya LEF?" *LEF*, No. 1 (1923), p. 6.

had a common parentage in the Proletarian Cultural and Educational Organizations (Proletkul't), a mass organization set up in September 1917, to give substance to the dreams that had glimmered for nearly a decade among a small group of Russian Marxists. One of those men, A. V. Lunacharskii, became Commissar of Education—the key position for rendering official aid to cultural organizations. Another, Aleksandr Bogdanov, had worked out a basic theory which was taken over by the Proletkul't.[23] In its new and simplified form, it ran as follows: any class needs culture, not merely as a reflection of its ideals and aspirations, but actually as the primary means of organizing its experience toward desired ends; the proletariat has no culture of its own, for economic and political struggles have consumed all its energies; bourgeois culture is clearly unsuited to the task of organizing the psychology of the proletariat; therefore, the proletariat must and can develop its own culture. It was assumed that given a few lessons in basic craftsmanship, anyone could become a proletarian artist. And so, in an unprecedented experiment, the Proletkul't established a system of "studios" throughout Russia—as much of it as the Bolsheviks could claim at the time—in order to impart the rudiments. Some of the results may be seen in the fifteen Proletkul't periodicals that appeared at one time or another during the Civil War. In 1920, at the Second Congress of the Third International, a bureau of the International Proletkul't was set up; to it were accredited representatives from most of the European countries and from the United States. At that point, the Russian Proletkul't claimed 400,000 members, of whom 80,000 were supposedly enrolled in studio work.

The Proletkul't was too large to remain intact for long. And it never was a monolith. Within it played a variety of

[23] Cf. esp. A. Bogdanov, *Kul'turnye zadachi nashego vremeni* (Moscow, 1911); *Iskusstvo i rabochii klass* (Moscow, 1918); and *O proletarskoi kul'ture* (Moscow-Leningrad, 1924).

opinions, not so much on the substance of Bogdanov's theses as on their practical applications: whether to accept the Russian cultural heritage, and if so, to what extent; how to reconcile the needs of individual talent with the impersonality of a mass organization; how to determine precisely what were the features of a uniquely proletarian art; how far Party discipline applied in cultural matters. Fissures soon developed and factions broke away. The first important defection occurred in 1919, when a large group of young writers, most of them poets, decided that the Proletkul't's enthusiasm for organizing the masses worked against the creative talent of individuals. They formed the Smithy (Kuznitsa), where they hoped to hammer out their verses in peace. A year later they took a fling at mass work themselves by forming the All-Russian Association of Proletarian Writers (VAPP). But they possessed neither the skill nor, when it came down to cases, the will to run a large organization. After the onset of the NEP, many of the older Smithy writers—like Gerasimov, Kirillov, and Kazin —convinced that the Revolution had been surrendered to the bourgeosie, dusted off the original idea of forming a small, elite group of writers; proposed that the badly limping VAPP be hobbled and left to die; and insisted that the Smithy be withdrawn altogether from literary politics, with its ranks closed to all but mature writers. The Proletkul't meanwhile had its wings clipped after insisting on the right to operate independent of the Party and the government. But it had passed its peak anyway, with the general revival of literature.[24]

[24] Cf. Ya. Yakovlev, "O proletarskoi kul'ture i Proletkul'te," *Pravda*, October 23, 1922, p. 2. For the text of the Central Committee's letter on the Proletkul't, cf. "O proletkul'takh (Pis'mo TsK RKP)," in *O partiinoi i sovetskoi pechati* (Moscow, 1954), pp. 220-22.

For a detailed account of early proletarian literature movements after the Revolution, cf. Herman Ermolaev, *Soviet Literary Theories, 1918-1934: The Genesis of Socialist Realism* (Berkeley and Los Angeles, 1963), pp. 9-26.

By 1922, then, a dying Proletkul't and a half-hearted Smithy group were about the only sizable remnants of a once vigorous movement. But the idea of proletarian culture still burned among the younger Smithy writers who had been dismissed by their elders as "immature." In December 1922, a group of them banded together with members of the "Young Guard" and "Workers' Spring" organizations to form "October." Naturally, they issued a manifesto, which accused the older Smiths of retarding the development of proletarian culture by ignoring organizational work and by writing "romantic" and "cosmic" poetry. They gained control of the languishing VAPP and set out to hammer it into a firm, disciplined organization modeled on the Communist Party itself. Like all proletarian literary organizations, the Octobrists accepted Bogdanov's basic ideas, but they avoided the disastrous mistake of the Proletkul't by declaring themselves firmly bound by Party discipline. Although the Smiths seemed to revive, founding *The Workers' Journal* (*Rabochii zhurnal*) in 1924, the canny Octobrists dominated proletarian literature from then on, and fixed themselves in the public mind, quite inaccurately, as the spokesmen for the movement as a whole.

With the inauguration of *On Guard* (*Na postu*), a journal of theory and criticism, in 1923, the Octobrists began to push for a position of predominance in literature analogous to the position the Communist Party held in politics. Though small in number, they had loud voices, a single-mindedness indistinguishable from fanaticism, and a highly developed sense of invective. Under the leadership of L. Averbakh, B. Volin, G. Lelevich, I. Vardin, and S. Rodov, they promptly declared war on all other literary groups of any consequence. *LEF* seemed to offer no serious competition; the Proletkul't lived on in name only; and the Smiths were badly organized. The only obstacle to their ambitions was *RVS*, and they resolved to remove it. A massive attack was quickly mounted. The first two issues of *On Guard* talked of little else besides *RVS*. Voronskii, at first taken aback, soon rallied his defenses and launched a spirited counter-offensive. And so began a battle that raged for four years, largely on the pages of these two journals.[25] It reduced all the other disputes of the time to mere skirmishes. Its outcome had great consequence for *RVS*, for Voronskii personally, and for the future of Soviet Russian literature.

ON THE SURFACE, the issue at stake was the fellow travelers. Like many proletarians, the Octobrists had long nursed a grudge against the Party's literary policy, which in their eyes showed favoritism to writers who seemed to them, at best, politically apathetic, at worst, agents of the bourgeoisie. Surely this was a mockery of the Revolution itself, which had been made to ensure proletarian predominance in all things. Worse still, virtually nothing was being done, according to the Octobrists, to help the struggling young proletarian writers: they were paid at a lower rate than the fellow travelers, discriminated against by editors, and openly despised by critics who lavished superlatives on other writers. The Octobrists did not dare to attack the Party directly. But Voronskii was fair game. Blithely ignoring the fact that he was the instrument of Party policy in literature, they fingered him as the source of all the misfortunes that had fallen on proletarian literature.

The Octobrists elaborated a theory of literature whose corners were pinned firmly to the old Proletkul't ideas, but whose fabric was tailored to the realities of the power struggle. (1) Literature serves one particular class at one particular time. Its purpose is to organize the psyche and consciousness of that class. (2) The predominant literature

[25] *On Guard* was the official publication of the Octobrists. Strictly speaking, the term "On-Guardist" should be limited to contributors to the journal. In practice, everyone interchanged the two terms, and even extended them to outsiders who followed the line of the group or the journal. I shall do the same.

of the time is bourgeois and, therefore, of no use to the proletariat, which requires its own literature in order to organize a class consciousness and achieve predominance in every respect. Since literature is a class weapon, any talk about peaceful coexistence between two literary systems is a "reactionary utopia." As Vardin put it, "if literature is not won by the proletariat, then it will serve the bourgeoisie."[26] (3) The proletariat must build its own literature. Yet it finds itself in the anomalous position of being slighted in favor of the petty-bourgeois fellow travelers, who do not sympathize with the Revolution, but are of a mind with the emigrés, and wage silent counter-revolution in their writings. Thus, Leonov's work is drenched with "reactionary mysticism," Babel's with "petty-bourgeois anarchic psychology" and "pathological excesses," and Pil'nyak's with sex, eroticism, and pseudo-philosophy—a "melange of populism, Slavophilism and obscurantism."[27] (4) The fellow travelers can therefore have no positive value for the working class. At best, they can be used as "auxiliary" forces to dull the hostility of the enemies of the Revolution, but only if they are organized around a core of proletarian writers and restricted according to a rigid "percentage-quota"—in other words, only if proletarian literature itself enjoys the hegemony to which it is entitled. (5) These arrangements are best made by a literary organization which would be a "communist cell" in literature, enjoy the full support of the

[26] "Voronshchinu neobkhodimo likvidirovat'," *Na postu*, No. 1 (1924), p. 22.

[27] The opinion on Leonov is G. Lelevich's, "Po zhurnal'nym okopam," *Molodaya gvardiya*, No. 7-8 (1924), p. 266. Regarding Babel', the first quote is from V. Veshnev, "Poeziya banditizma," *Molodaya gvardiya*, No. 7-8 (1924), p. 280; the second from Lelevich, "Po zhurnal'nym okopam," *ibid.*, p. 267. The first opinion of Pil'nyak is V. Veshnev's, "Tovarishch Sosnovskii i grazhdanin Pil'nyak," *Molodaya gvardiya*, No. 9 (1924), p. 177; the quote is from P. Poluyanov, review of B. Pil'nyak, *Mashiny i volki*, *Molodaya gvardiya*, No. 8 (1926), p. 205. Cf. also Derevenskii, "Derevnya v russkoi literature," *Na postu*, No. 1 (1923), pp. 153-58.

Party, and establish contact with Party organizations at a corresponding level.[28]

The Octobrists allowed that Voronskii's policy of patiently tolerating the fellow travelers might have been justified in 1921 as a kind of experiment, but they insisted that it had long since demonstrated its basic unsoundness: the fellow travelers were actually moving further away from Communism all the time and taking much of the new literature with them. Meanwhile, proletarian literature could buttress its claims with new works by Bezymenskii, Libedinskii, Tarasov-Rodionov, and a host of young beginners. But Voronskii apparently would not acknowledge these facts. A detailed bill of indictment was drawn up to show that he was unfit to serve as the spokesman for Soviet literature, and had, in fact, "become a weapon in the cause of reinforcing the position of the bourgeoisie."[29] He was shown in a variety of shabby guises—sometimes as a fuzzy-headed, nineteenth-century Russian liberal whose quaint ideas, harmless enough in themselves, proved "utterly hopeless in the resolution of the active political tasks of the proletariat in the field of literature";[30] sometimes as an ideological troglodyte whose unwillingness to face the real world of class struggle had made him an unwitting ally of the bourgeoisie. "Today's literature," the Octobrists reminded their readers, "is before everything else a field of fierce class battle. Writers are the conscious or unconscious warriors of various classes on the ideological front. The

[28] See the following sources: S. Rodov, *V literaturnykh boyakh* (Moscow, 1926), *passim*, esp. pp. 5-176; G. Lelevich, "Nam nuzhna partiinaya liniya," *Na postu*, No. 1 (1923), pp. 102-08; I. Vardin, "Voronshchinu neobkhodimo likvidirovat'," *Na postu*, No. 1 (1924), pp. 9-36; speeches of Vardin and Averbakh at Meeting of Press Section of Central Committee, May 9-10, 1924, in *K voprosu o politike RKP (b) v khudozhestvennoi literature* (Moscow, 1924), pp. 14-24, 40-42, 94-99; I. Maiskii, "O kul'ture, literature i kommunisticheskoi partii," *Zvezda*, No. 3 (1924), pp. 258-79.

[29] I. Vardin, "Voronshchinu neobkhodimo likvidirovat'," p. 22.

[30] *Ibid.*, p. 9.

'thick' journals are the fortresses and the beachheads of the class armies of literature."[31] As the polemic grew more bitter, he found himself being depicted as an out-and-out counter-revolutionary—the mastermind of a sinister plot against proletarian literature, an active agent of the bourgeoisie who was trying to drive a wedge between the proletarian writers and the proletarian critics, an ideological lecher who lured young writers into his journal and there corrupted them.[32]

Nor were Voronskii's colleagues spared. V. Pravdukhin, for instance, once the leading critic of *Red Grainfield* (*Krasnaya niva*) and later a prominent contributor to *RVS*, sided publicly with Voronskii, and was branded "an ex-S. R. [Socialist Revolutionary] and in fact an actual S. R."—a charge not to be taken lightly in those days—who enjoyed the protection of "such unprincipled and spineless politicians as Voronskii. . . ."[33] Vladimir Ermilov, a master of the tarbrush, painted Fyodor Zhits as a man "alien to Marxism and Communism," who "on the pages of *RVS* appears as the troubadour of a philistinism that has become insolent and obese."[34] The technique of guilt by association was employed to ferret out a number of confederates in this rap-

[31] G. Lelevich, "Po zhurnal'nym okopam," p. 261.

[32] Cf. S. Rodov, "Nazad . . . nazad . . . na (Pod obstrelom)," *V literaturnykh boyakh*, pp. 30-43; Yu. Libedinskii, "Klassovoe i gruppovoe," *Na postu*, No. 4 (1923), p. 58. They had in mind a number of their better young writers—among them Artyom Vesyolyi, Mikhail Golodnyi, A. Yasnyi, and Mikhail Svetlov—who, chafing under the rigid discipline and hysterical exclusiveness of the Octobrists, had broken away and gone over to *RVS*.

[33] The first quote is from I. Vardin, speech at Meeting of Press Section, in *K voprosu o politike* . . . , p. 20. The second is from I. Vardin, "Revolyutsiya i literatura (Dve glavy iz knigi)," *Na postu*, No. 1 (June 1925), pp. 72-73.

[34] "Pochemu my ne lyubim zhitsei," *Protiv meshchanstva i upadochnichestva* (Moscow-Leningrad, 1927), pp. 22-24. Zhits became hysterical over attacks of this kind, and threatened to give up writing altogether (cf. A. Voronskii, "V obshchem i tselom," *KN*, No. 8 [1926], p. 220).

idly growing conspiracy. Surely it was significant that I. Lezhnev, the editor of *Russia* (*Rossiya*), a journal published by a private (bourgeois) publishing house, should have declared that *RVS* was Russia's "only thick literary journal."[35] Surely it was not mere coincidence that the Russian emigré press had been following the controversy attentively and more or less siding with *RVS*. Mark Slonim, the editor of *The Will of Russia* (*Volya Rossii*), a newspaper published in Prague, was even supposed to be a "popularizer" of Voronskii.[36] Agents of "Voronskiism," as the plot came to be called, were discovered in the government publishing houses as well. Vardin reported that "New Moscow" (Novaya Moskva) had wanted to drop *On Guard*, and that other houses had refused to take the journal. That seemed proof enough that "the Party political leadership of our publishing houses is worthless."[37] The conspiracy was traced even into the highest Party circles, where Trotskii supposedly was its chief agent, though the Octobrists did not attack him openly until 1925, when his own position within the Party had weakened.

This was not the first time that Voronskii had felt the lash of dissatisfaction and jealousy. In 1922, for instance, he had been accused of cutting off the rations of twenty-seven writers—most of them Communists—associated with the "Circle" Publishing House, in order to increase the allotments for writers of the petty-bourgeoisie.[38] But never had

[35] I. Lezhnev, "Gde zhe novaya literatura?" *Rossiya*, No. 1 (1924), p. 181. I. Lezhnev is not to be confused with A. Lezhnev, the critic for *RVS*. It is one of the many ironies of Soviet life that the "bourgeois" I. Lezhnev survived all the purges and long remained active, whereas A. Lezhnev, a good Communist, was purged and disappeared from literature.

[36] I. Vardin, "Voronshchinu neobkhodimo likvidirovat'," pp. 27, 33. The reference apparently is to Slonim's article entitled "Literaturnaya cheka," in *Volya Rossii*, No. 20 (1923).

[37] "Voronshchinu neobkhodimo likvidirovat'," p. 27.

[38] G. Ustinov, "Ne s togo kontsa," *Izvestiya*, September 6, 1922, p. 5. Voronskii's reply, terming the charge a "complete fabrication," was printed in *Pravda*, "Pis'mo v redaktsiyu," September 7, 1922, p. 6.

there been anything as sustained and violent as this campaign. His first impulse had been to brush the charges off as absurd. But he soon realized that even though they might be absurd, they could not be ignored; and during the next four years, he devoted many pages of *RVS* to rebuttal. Naturally he denied the existence of any plot against proletarians, insisting that the rates of payment were the same for all, pointing to the large number of new proletarian works that publishing houses were bringing out, reaffirming his journal's policy of giving a hearing to any promising writer, whatever his background, and—what must have been supremely satisfying—reminding the Octobrists that one of the "classics" of proletarian literature—Yurii Libedinskii's novel *A Week* (*Nedelya*)—owed its final version to a virtual rewrite by none other than Voronskii himself.[39] He could not very well deny that *RVS* published a far greater number of fellow traveler writers than proletarians. But he defended the practice, on the grounds that the fellow travelers were more numerous, better educated, superior craftsmen, and perhaps even more effective ideologically insofar as they tried to reflect reality instead of bending it to fit ideology, as the proletarian writers were wont to do.[40]

Voronskii's defense of the fellow travelers—which will be considered in detail later—proceeded from what he assumed to be a position of strength. He accused the Octobrists of attacking him personally because they "lacked the courage to name the 'super-educated connivers,' lacked the courage to acknowledge that the highest organs of the Party are supervising the line that is being pursued by Voronskii."[41] He expressed confidence that the Party would

[39] Speech at Meeting of Press Section, May 9-10, 1924, in *K voprosu o politike* . . . , p. 102.

[40] "Iskusstvo, kak poznanie zhizni, i sovremennost' (K voprosu o nashikh literaturnykh raznoglasiyakh)," *KN*, No. 5 (1923), esp. pp. 372-73.

[41] *Ibid.*, p. 377.

pay no heed to "the Rodovs and the Leleviches." No doubt he felt there was little danger of that. But he had raised a vital point: granting that he *was* the Party line in literature, why then should there be any question among Marxists about the propriety of the course he was following?

Most of the high Party officials who had anything to say at all on the matter arrayed themselves publicly with *RVS*. Though they entertained important differences of opinion on the questions that had been raised about proletarian literature, they were unanimous in supporting the established policy toward the fellow travelers and in condemning the crude tactics of the Octobrists. Bukharin spoke for them all when he complained of the "endless platforms" that were consuming energies better spent in writing novels and poetry.[42] But these men were voicing their opinions as private citizens, so to speak. The Party itself made no official statement of any kind; in the first year or so of the quarrel, it would say only that no "group," "school," or "faction" had the right to speak in its name. This seemed designed as a reply to the Octobrists' complaint that the Party lacked a policy toward literature, to their demand that the Party take sides in the quarrel, and, of course, to their hope that their own theories would ultimately constitute official writ. Voronskii, too, claimed to be speaking in the name of the Party. And the Party's failure to protest implied that it considered the old policy toward fellow travelers still operative. Yet here was the Party's spokesman being subjected to charges that were serious in any event, and positively grave when flung at a Bolshevik carrying out a delicate Party assignment. Not only his authority, but his loyalty was being challenged. Why then did the Party not spring to his defense?

We can only speculate. By 1924, when the polemic was coming to a climax, the volume of writing had so increased

[42] Speech at Meeting of Press Section, in *K voprosu o politike* . . . , p. 37.

that no one could now make "literature" and *RVS* virtually synonymous; the journal accounted for only a part of the new literature—the most impressive and representative, to be sure, but a part nonetheless. At the same time, it was rapidly moving away from indiscriminate encyclopedism and developing a clear-cut theory and program for literature. Under the circumstances, the Party may well have begun to look on *RVS* as itself a "faction" or "school"—certainly not one so narrowly based as the Octobrists, but one nevertheless which now tended to make finer distinctions among the various writers than the broadly based Party policy was willing to sanction. At this point, to have reaffirmed Voronskii's position as virtually the incarnation of Party policy would certainly have alienated the Octobrists, large areas of proletarian literature, and the writers of the "left"—all people who, while often annoying, presumably gave loyalty to the regime and were therefore worth cultivating. Furthermore, the Party had no official literary tradition of its own to fall back on: classical Marxism provided very little in the way of guidance; Lenin had been concerned with the written word only as it applied to Party business. To have adopted, ready-made, the theory of any one group of the mid-twenties, even of *RVS*, would have meant freezing into dogma something experimental, tentative, and in that sense flawed. By letting a number of different theories and viewpoints clash, expose their weaknesses, and work out their imprecisions, the Party in effect was encouraging the development of a solid body of Marxist esthetics; and when the time came, there would be something substantial from which to pick and choose in order to construct an official theory.

The economic situation being what it was in 1923, literature probably did not occupy a very high place on the Party's list of priorities anyway. The Party might well have been content to let the quarrel run its course. But the debate on fellow travelers and proletarians quickly spread beyond the confines of *RVS* and *On Guard*. Practically anyone who was commenting on contemporary literature at the time registered his vote for one side or the other. The leading Party officials lined up with *RVS*. The Octobrists let it be assumed that they held the sympathies of all proletarian writers. That was certainly true as far as the big names went: Bezymenskii, their showpiece poet, and Libedinskii, their model fiction writer, gladly lent their polemical talents to the cause. But the Smithy—a proletarian group containing many more genuine literary talents than October—allied itself with *RVS*; so did a number of promising young poets who had defected from October; and "The Pass" (Pereval), a group composed largely of worker and peasant writers, actually operated out of the editorial offices of *RVS*. Even those writers who kept silent in the dispute, as did most of the fellow travelers, found themselves identified with one side or the other. Perhaps never before in Russian literature had an issue been so extensively and passionately debated—not romanticism and classicism, nor Slavophilism and Westernism, not even "utilitarian" and "pure" art in the 1860's. As Vyacheslav Polonskii described it: "Friends fell out over . . . bourgeois and proletarian literature. The accusations they flung at one another did not lead to law suits only because in a literary battle—or so it was thought—'anything went.' Party comrades treated each other as if they were class enemies."[43]

Before a year had passed, both sides were urging the Party to speak out. According to Radek, the Octobrists "have broken so much glass that the broad circles of the Party, who up to the present time have not given sufficient attention to questions of literature, have now been com-

[43] *Ocherki literaturnogo dvizheniya revolyutsionnoi epokhi* (2nd ed.; Moscow-Leningrad, 1930), p. 175.

pelled to turn their attention to literature to some extent."[44] A formal debate was scheduled by the Press Section of the Central Committee for December 5, 1923. When the time came, each side had written statements prepared, but for some reason the session was put off five months.[45] In May 1924, it finally convened and lasted for two days, the 9th and 10th. Voronskii, the main speaker for his side, marshaled impressive support in Bukharin, Radek, Trotskii, and Lunacharskii. His chief opponent, Vardin, found no allies of remotely comparable stature.[46] All the familiar issues that had unfolded in print were rehashed from the platform. But one new thing did result: a statement of Party policy toward literature—guarded and cautious, to be sure, but a statement nonetheless. Abandoned now was the old hands-off policy; legitimized was the principle of Party intervention in literary matters.

The statement defined Party policy toward literature for the next two years: it was embodied in a resolution of the Thirteenth Congress later that same month, and restated at

[44] Speech at Meeting of Press Section, in *K voprosu o politike . . .* , p. 47.

[45] L. Kishchinskaya, "Literaturnaya diskussiya 1922-1925 godov (K istorii stanovleniya ideino-esteticheskikh printsipov sovetskoi literaturnoi kritiki)," *Voprosy literatury*, No. 4 (1966), pp. 42-43. It is not clear, from this article, whether the reports presented at the May session were identical with those prepared for the previous December; but the fact that Kishchinskaya cites the December reports from unpublished archival material, whereas the May reports were fully published at the time, suggests that they were not. Unfortunately, she does not give enough to make comparison possible. One change may have been in the question of Party leadership of literature: in December it seems to have attracted little attention, but certainly it figured very prominently in May.

[46] The lineup was as follows: on Voronskii's side were A. Vesyolyi, N. Osinskii, V. Polonskii, N. Bukharin, G. Yakubovskii, Ya. Yakovlev, K. Radek, L. Trotskii, A. Lunacharskii, N. Meshcheryakov; on Vardin's were Yu. Libedinskii, F. Raskol'nikov, G. Lelevich, L. Averbakh, V. Pletnyov, S. Rodov, A. Bezymenskii, P. Kerzhentsev, D. Ryazanov, D. Bednyi.

much greater length in the famous Central Committee Resolution of June 18, 1925, entitled "On the Policy of the Party in the Area of Belles Lettres."[47] The Octobrists were rebuked for crude tactics and presumptuous appropriation of the Party's name; yet the existence of an autonomous proletarian literature was recognized and its eventual preponderance taken for granted. Hereby Voronskii, in effect, received a reprimand for his off-handed and often contemptuous attitude toward the young worker-writers. Because the statement struck a compromise, both sides interpreted it as a victory for their policies.[48] Actually, the Octobrists gained a good deal at Voronskii's expense: heretofore Voronskii had functioned as the instrument of Party policy in literature; now a large measure of his authority passed to his enemies, with the recognition that an important part of their policy also constituted Party policy.

That was not all. Voronskii soon found a check placed on his virtually absolute rule within RVS. With the June issue of 1924—one month after the debate—his two figurehead colleagues on the editorial board, Bubnov and Smirnov, were replaced by Fyodor Raskol'nikov, an editor of the journal Young Guard, and Vladimir Sorin, the assistant chief of the Press Section of the Central Committee. Since both openly supported the Octobrist line, they could not possibly have met with Voronskii's approval. Obviously their appointment was intended as a physical demonstration of the new policy of compromise; but in addition, it aimed—as Raskol'nikov bluntly admitted—at effecting "a change in the previous line of the journal."[49]

[47] For the text of the Party Congress resolution, see O partiinoi i sovetskoi pechati (Moscow, 1954), pp. 310-11; for the Central Committee resolution, see "O politike partii v oblasti khudozhestvennoi literatury," Pravda, July 1, 1925, p. 6.

[48] Cf., e.g., A. Voronskii, "Literatura i politika," Prozhektor, No. 15 (1924), pp. 26-29; I. Maiskii, "O kul'ture, literature, i kommunisticheskoi partii," Zvezda, No. 3 (1924), pp. 276-79.

[49] As cited in M. Gor'kii i sovetskaya pechat'. Arkhiv A. M. Gor'-

Voronskii's attitude toward this turn of events was the subject of a progress report that his new colleague, Sorin, made to the directing board of the Moscow Association of Proletarian Writers (MAPP) that September:

I talked with Voronskii before coming here. I talked about the need for us, in the name of the editorial board, to make an official overture to MAPP [to submit proletarian literature for publication]. He refused. He said that it would look as if he were crawling, as if he had been defeated in something and was guilty in somebody's eyes. He said that he had always kept the doors of his journal open to you, and that it was you who didn't come, you who didn't want to, but as for him, he had invited you. . . .[50]

The audience reacted with indignation. Sorin, however, was in no position to force the issue. As he admitted: "I take no part in the work of the editorial board, and I have no time to. . . ." Raskol'nikov, who suffered from tuberculosis, had gone to Italy to take the sun cure. But Sorin promised his listeners that "as soon as he gets here, he will plunge into this work, he'll take his seat on the editorial board and, together with Voronskii, will start doing business."[51]

Raskol'nikov returned late in 1924 and took up his duties in RVS. But in the January 1925 issue, Voronskii's name was nowhere to be seen; it had been replaced by an anonymous "editorial board." Articles and reviews by Vardin, Lelevich, Rodov, and Zonin—all On-Guardists—were prominently featured. In a letter to Gor'kii at the end of that month, Voronskii observed: "I've had to leave RVS. The

kogo, x, Book 2 (Moscow, 1965), p. 15, n. 1. Hereafter referred to as Arkhiv.

[50] As reported by Dmitrii Furmanov, Dnevniki, entry for September 20, 1924, in Sobranie sochinenii, IV (Moscow, 1961), 337-38.

[51] Both quotes ibid., p. 337.

journal has gone over to the On-Guardists. You know about them, and there's no need for me to enlarge on them. . . . Raskol'nikov is running things in *RVS*."[52] He went on to talk about his plans for a new literary venture—a series of miscellanies which would come out every two months or so —and he seemed to anticipate no dearth of contributors. Still, he took care to ask for Gor'kii's continued support, not merely for the good of literature, but, unabashedly, as a personal favor: "Your name would lend weight and would help me get a firm hold in a new position."[53] There was no further explanation. Although it is uncertain, one suspects that Voronskii's departure from *RVS* was voluntary. His new colleagues apparently had every expectation of working with a man whose talents, though perhaps hateful, had proven very effective, whereas the tone of Voronskii's remarks to Sorin suggests that he had no intention of associating himself with them.

Voronskii's plans for retirement, however, proved to be premature. One month later Raskol'nikov was replaced by Emel'yan Yaroslavskii—not an On-Guardist—and Voronskii was back as chief editor. Again we can only speculate on what happened. Voronskii's letters to Gor'kii tell us nothing except that the new editorial board (which continued to carry the presumably still inactive Sorin) "does not hamper my work."[54] There are several possible explanations. One is that Gor'kii's indignant reaction to the news of Voronskii's departure may have had deep reverberations. In mid-January he had received a letter from Raskol'nikov which solicited his continuing support of *RVS*, but made no mention of Voronskii. Suspecting that something was "not quite right,"[55] Gor'kii returned a tart refusal: ". . . my views

[52] Letter to Gor'kii, January 29, 1925, *Arkhiv*, p. 15.
[53] *Ibid.* Perhaps Voronskii had in mind the miscellany entitled *Red Virgin Soil* (*Krasnaya nov'*), of which two volumes appeared in 1925.
[54] Letter to Gor'kii, March 6, 1925, *Arkhiv*, pp. 17-18.
[55] Letter to Voronskii, February 12, 1925, *Arkhiv*, p. 16.

on the art of the word do not correspond with yours, as you expressed them in your speech at the session of the 'Meeting' called by the Press Section of the Central Committee on May 9, 1924. Therefore I cannot contribute to a journal in which you evidently will play the leading role."[56] In describing the incident to Voronskii (with the letter to Raskol'nikov quoted in full), Gor'kii used far stronger language. He described the On-Guardist position as "anti-revolutionary and anti-cultural," dismissed Raskol'nikov as an "ignorant and ungifted kid," expressed his regret that Voronskii had left *RVS* and his conviction that the On-Guardists would "destroy" the journal, and rounded off with a generous tribute:

> Your work in *RVS* has had great significance for Russian literature, and it goes without saying that honest men of letters, in all likelihood, are just as perturbed by your removal from a project created by you, just as perturbed about this as am I, who have a sincere regard for you. I know what *RVS* cost you.[57]

We must not forget either that Voronskii still had friends among influential members of the Party. Babel', in fact, stated that "it's clear to anyone that the man is holding on just by his personal connections . . . just by the people he knows . . . anyone else in his place would have had his nose rubbed in the dirt a dozen times. . . ."[58] Existing documents do not make it at all clear whether this is true; but the impression of someone like Babel', who stood more or less apart from literary politics, is valuable. And Voronskii himself certainly encouraged such an interpretation when he told Gor'kii, in March of 1925, that "the 'On-Guardists' are

---

[56] Letter to Raskol'nikov, January 26, 1925, *Arkhiv*, p. 82. Raskol'-nikov's letter to Gor'kii is dated January 17, 1925, and is in *Arkhiv*, pp. 80-81.
[57] Letter to Voronskii, February 12, 1925, *Arkhiv*, p. 16.
[58] According to Dmitrii Furmanov, *Dnevniki*, p. 367.

suffering defeat in the higher echelons," and that Bukharin was "helping matters along."[59] But we cannot overlook the machinery set in motion at about this season by the Literature Commission of the Central Committee, which laid the groundwork for the Resolution that would appear on June 18. At the March 3 session, Frunze (an old prison comrade of Voronskii's) measured out some harsh words about the On-Guardists. While granting that Voronskii had paid insufficient attention to proletarian writers, he insisted nonetheless that: "Comrade Vardin is wrong when he says that the activities of *RVS* have encouraged On-Guardists to defect from the proletarian camp. . . . I know that the fellow travelers are being frightened away from us not by *RVS*, but rather by those tactics and methods that the journal *On Guard* is propagating."[60] This suggests that reinforcements were being rushed to prop up the principle of compromise which had most assuredly been weakened by the recent happenings in *RVS*.

In any event, a partial cease-fire descended over the trenches. The On-Guardists suddenly seemed to lose much of their enthusiasm for attacking Voronskii. The issues of *RVS* for 1925 and the first part of 1926 contain scarcely a word about the enemy, good or bad. Considering the comradely spirit that the June 18 Resolution was supposed to create, it would have made sense for the Central Committee to restrain both parties, though we do not know whether that actually happened. Possibly the On-Guardists were simply too preoccupied with their own problems to give Voronskii much mind. They had begun to split up over the question of how the Resolution should be interpreted: a "left" wing, led by Vardin and Rodov, clung to the old policies and tactics; a "right" wing, headed by Averbakh, disavowed the past, pledged allegiance to the spirit of the resolution, and began to work out a new program for lit-

---

[59] Letter to Gor'kii, March 6, 1925, *Arkhiv*, p. 18.
[60] As cited in *Arkhiv*, p. 18n.

erature.[61] Voronskii, on his side, certainly had no reason to rekindle the quarrel which had already damaged him so much. He may have declared a détente in order to assess the meaning of these new tactics, and to allow the break-up of the opposition to proceed without any interference that might weld it together again.

WHATEVER the reasons for the lull may have been, one thing is clear: Voronskii no longer held his old position of supremacy. Though restored to his job, he was convinced that the campaign against him had not abated, but had merely moved underground. "They're not abusing me now," he told Gor'kii, "but they are composing denunciations and writing utterly loathsome articles of a personal nature. It's disgusting to read them—but shameful to answer them."[62] The quarrel once more broke into the open in the spring of 1926. Again Averbakh started it, this time with the inaugural issue of his new journal, *On Literary Guard* (*Na literaturnom postu*) which featured an article entitled "Once More About Voronskii." Voronskii shot back a rejoinder in a sarcastic pseudoclassical style in the May issue of *RVS*.[63] The specifics of thrust and parry differed little from those of 1923 and 1924. But the tone was different. If the writers of the old *On Guard* had often laced their invective with treacly protestations of martyrdom, those for the new *On Literary Guard* cut a swagger. And well they might. For by now, the Party had all but dropped the policy of encouraging peaceful competition and had begun to move toward open support of Averbakh. Voronskii's position was being undercut; and in his rebuttal to Averbakh,

[61] For a detailed discussion, cf. Edward J. Brown, *The Proletarian Episode in Russian Literature* (New York, 1953), pp. 40-57.

[62] Letter to Gor'kii, after June 18, 1925, *Arkhiv*, p. 22. Voronskii does not elaborate on the "denunciations."

[63] L. Averbakh, "Opyat' o Voronskom," *Na literaturnom postu*, No. 1 (1926); A. Voronskii, "Mister Britling p'yot chashu do dna," *KN*, No. 5 (1926), pp. 195-203.

he gave the first public indication that he understood what
was happening. Turning to Lunacharskii, he wrote:

> Anatolii Vasil'evich! You have entered into the On-
> Guardist abode, and, it would seem, you are quite at
> home there. I ask one thing: sinful am I, sins lie upon
> me (not long ago I was deeply moved even by *Uncle
> Vanya*). I love life and it is hard for my soul to part with
> my body. But if it is fated that I must accept the end,
> then let it not be from the hand of Averbakh. . . . To per-
> ish on the field of battle in frontal attacks is painful, but
> it is honorable, and—"there is intoxication in battle"—but
> to suffocate from Averbakh's "literary gases"—let this
> bitter cup pass me by.
>
> I am a quiet man. Let Averbakh flourish, but I do not
> want a shameful end. . . . But though I am quiet, I am
> also hot-tempered, and I can begin breaking glass. The
> atmosphere is stifling from these gases; I want to live;
> let me break out the window panes. Of course I shall
> frighten nobody, but why drive people to indecency?[64]

The bantering manner concealed a deep discouragement
and hurt which Voronskii poured out in his private letters to
Gor'kii.[65] His energy began to ebb and his health, never very
strong, broke down. (Toward the end of the summer of
1926, he put himself under treatment at Kislovodsk for enlargement of the heart.[66]) Yet he plunged even deeper into
his work: in addition to a full schedule of editing, he un-

---

[64] *Ibid.*, pp. 202-03. The quotation is from Pushkin's *Feast in Time
of Plague* (*Pir vo vremya chumy*). The whole stanza, which is relevant to Voronskii's sentiments, is as follows: "There is intoxication
in battle,/ And on the brink of the gloomy abyss,/ And on the
raging ocean,/ Amidst the menacing waves and the stormy dark,/
And in the Araby hurricane,/ And in the waft of Plague" (*"Est'
upoenie v boyu,/ I bezdny mrachnoi na krayu,/ I v raz' 'yarennom
okeane,/ Sred' groznykh voln i burnoi t'my,/ I v araviiskom uragane,/
I v dunovenii Chumy"*).

[65] Cf., e.g., letter to Gor'kii, June 16, 1926, *Arkhiv*, p. 35.

[66] Letter to Gor'kii, October 12, 1926, *Arkhiv*, p. 41.

dertook a course of lectures on literature at various schools in Moscow. Only his "chronic good cheer," he said, carried him through.[67] He needed all the cheer he could summon up for what lay ahead.

February 1927 marked the sixth anniversary of the founding of *RVS*. A group of Voronskii's colleagues and friends decided to celebrate the event with a gala evening at the Herzen House. Under the circumstances, this was immediately interpreted as a demonstration of support for Voronskii, the more so, perhaps, because the journal's fifth anniversary, a more logical time for festivity, had apparently passed unobserved. Arranged around a glum-looking guest of honor, for the benefit of the photographer, were Fyodor Gladkov, V. V. Veresaev, Boris Pil'nyak, Ivan Evdokimov, of the "Pereval" group, Vyacheslav Polonskii, editor of the journal *New World*, the poet Mikhail Gerasimov, Isaak Babel', and, from the Party hierarchy, Karl Radek.[68] Perhaps others attended and were not photographed; more were certainly invited, for, as Gladkov told Gor'kii, "a certain part of the public pointedly stayed away."[69] The committee which organized the affair composed a message of welcome to Voronskii, expressing confidence that he would remain at the head of *RVS*, "despite the fact that certain literary organizations have raised the question of removing you from the editorship of the journal you have created. . . ."[70] Gor'kii sent a warm testimonial praising Voronskii's "service to Russian literature" in his "splendid journal," and wishing him continued success, despite the obstacles he faced.[71]

[67] Letter to Gor'kii, June 16, 1926, *Arkhiv*, p. 35.

[68] The photograph is printed in *Prozhektor*, No. 6 (1927), p. 20.

[69] Letter to Gor'kii, March 10, 1927, *Gor'kii i sovetskie pisateli. Literaturnoe nasledstvo*, LXX (Moscow, 1963), 79. Hereafter referred to as *Nasledstvo*.

[70] Quoted from an enclosure in an unpublished letter of Ivan Evdokimov to Gor'kii, January 1, 1927, in *Nasledstvo*, p. 91, n. 4.

[71] Text of the letter, dated "middle of February," in *Arkhiv*, p. 45.

No more than a month later, however, rumors that Voronskii's removal was imminent began to circulate. The gossipy Gladkov reported as a fact to Gor'kii that three new men had been named to the editorial board of *RVS* to replace Voronskii: P. M. Kerzhentsev, an editor of *Izvestiya* and a veteran of the old *Proletarian Culture*; Vladimir Ermilov, an editor of the journal *Young Guard*; and S. Gusev, head of the Press Section of the Central Committee.[72] Voronskii confirmed the news in reply to a worried query from Gor'kii, saying that it was a matter of "a few weeks, perhaps days."[73] As it happened, both Gladkov and Voronskii were wrong. Gor'kii learned in the first week of April that the removal "has been put off. Rather, it remains open."[74] Once again we are left in the dark, without knowing why the proceedings started, or why they ended so abruptly. (They were obviously more than rumors, since Voronskii mentioned as his successors the same men that Gladkov did.) Clearly, however, the campaign against him was reaching a climax.

On April 18, Voronskii was summoned before an expanded session of the Press Section which had been specially convened to discuss his work in *RVS*. No complete transcript of the proceedings has ever been published, but references to them in various sources leave no doubt that

---

An editorial note to this letter states that Evdokimov wrote to Gor'kii on January 11, 1927, asking him to sign the message of welcome to Voronskii, which he enclosed. Gor'kii "apparently" did not, but wrote one of his own instead. As we see, there is a ten-day discrepancy in the dates assigned to this letter in the two sources quoted. Since it is highly unlikely that there were two letters on exactly the same subject so close together, one of these dates is cited incorrectly. Unfortunately, it is impossible to say which one, since neither Evdokimov's letter(s) nor the message of welcome to Voronskii have been published.

[72] Letter to Gor'kii, March 10, 1927, *Nasledstvo*, p. 90.

[73] Letter to Gor'kii, March 30, 1927, *Arkhiv*, p. 51. Gor'kii's letter to Voronskii is dated March 23, 1927, *Arkhiv*, p. 50.

[74] Letter to Gor'kii, April 7, 1927, *Nasledstvo*, p. 93.

Voronskii faced a kangaroo court. Between eighty and a hundred people were present, none of whom, according to Voronskii, could be counted a friend of *RVS*. After giving a detailed report on the activities of his journal for 1926 and 1927, which amounted to a spirited and unapologetic defense of his policies, Voronskii read off an impressive list of the new works he had published during this period, and reaffirmed his belief that good writing must count as much as sound ideology in anything pretending to the name of literature. When it came to the principal grievance of his accusers—the disproportionately few pages allotted to proletarian writers—he turned evasive. If one counted Gor'kii, Evdokimov, Loginov-Lesnyak, Furmanov, Nikiforov, and Zuev among the "proletarians," he said, then his journal had done its duty by publishing them all. But as everyone knew, neither Gor'kii nor Evdokimov was considered "proletarian" by most of the proletarians themselves; the remaining four represented only a small percentage of what by then had grown into a large, although by no means unified movement; and, as we shall see, Voronskii did not believe that there was such a thing as "proletarian" literature anyway.[75]

A letter to Gor'kii written about three weeks earlier gives us some insight into the moods that Voronskii took with him into this crucially important meeting. "I'm worn down to the limits of my strength," he had complained; yet he was convinced that he had acted for the best, and could suggest no reason for the position in which he now found himself. "I have fought against stupidity, against the failure to understand, against the lack of culture, I've fought for literature, which I sincerely love. I have made mistakes, of course, but they have been honest mistakes." He therefore refused to assume the role of the cringing penitent that was being fashioned for him, and instead prepared him-

[75] "Iz doklada o 'Krasnoi novi,'" *Mister Britling p'yot chashu do dna* (Moscow, 1927), pp. 218-27.

self for the worst: "I am 'packing my suitcases,'" he concluded.[76] Before the public, he continued to wear a mask of
disdainful aloofness; in Gladkov's words, he was "comport-
ing himself like a sage, as if he's been reading Lucretius."[77]

Now, facing his accusers a month later, he ventured the
suspicion that "a Golgotha has been prepared for me here,"
and expressed doubt that he would hold the reins of *RVS*
much longer. Yet he refused to compromise what he considered a correct policy, asserted his intention of pursuing
it just as long as he could, and informed his listeners that
he would continue to speak out against Averbakh and his
group until something resembling a working relationship
with them had come to pass—meaning, of course, on his
own terms.[78]

The most important answering speeches were made by
Gusev, head of the Press Section, by Averbakh and Zonin,
and by the writer Georgii Nikiforov, who had once been on
friendly terms with Voronskii. If Voronskii had expected
merely a recapitulation of all the old charges, he must have
been staggered to hear Gusev remark: "Approximately
until 1926, *RVS* fulfilled all the commands of the Party."
In the same vein, Nikiforov observed that "Voronskii
[successfully] ran the whole enormous business of winning
the non-Party writers over onto the Soviet platform." Averbakh, of all people, announced: "We respect the services of
Voronskii."[79] Such amenities rang as hollow as the typical
funeral oration which they were probably meant to suggest, and were quickly followed by a very substantial "how-

[76] All quotes from letter to Gor'kii, March 30, 1927, *Arkhiv*, p. 51.

[77] Letter to Gor'kii, March 10, 1927, *Nasledstvo*, p. 90. Gor'kii was
angered by the sarcastic tone of this remark: cf. his letter to Gladkov,
March 21, 1927, *Nasledstvo*, p. 90.

[78] "Iz doklada o 'Krasnoi novi,'" p. 219.

[79] All three quoted from unpublished sources by A. G. Dement'ev,
"A. Voronskii—kritik," in *A. Voronskii. Literaturno-kriticheskie stat'i*,
compiled by G. A. Voronskaya and A. G. Dement'ev, ed. by L. A.
Shubin (Moscow, 1963), p. 9.

ever." Only the tactics had changed: the flanking movement had replaced the frontal assault. Gusev called the
maneuver: the mere mention of 1926 served to remind everyone of the Central Committee Resolution, to disavow
the vindictive tactics of the old On-Guardists, and to suggest that it was Voronskii who was refusing to live by the
new spirit of comradeship and cooperation. In case any
doubts lingered, Vladimir Narbut, an employee of the Press
Section, drafted a message to the Central Committee accusing Voronskii of impermissible tactics, and had it read
to all assembled.[80]

"The question of Voronskii's fate was put point-blank.
They tried in every way possible to get rid of him once and
for all."[81] So Gladkov, who was present, summarized the
meeting's purpose for Gor'kii. But Voronskii's time had still
not come. As he himself wrote to Gor'kii the very day of
the session: "Things are bad with *Soil* just as before. How
sick I am of all this! It's interfering with my work. Recently
I was publicly 'whipped.' It was unpleasant. Apparently
I'm still hanging on. . . . But there are a good many unexpected things ahead. We'll see, we'll see!"[82] The editors of
the volume in which this letter is printed have made an
omission at the crucial spot, indicated by the ellipsis, which
may contain some explanation of just how Voronskii was
managing to "hang on." Gladkov thought that Voronskii
had "conducted himself rather firmly, though not adroitly
enough," and implies that this saved him.[83] But Voronskii's
firmness under fire was nothing new; and from all we can
gather, nobody offered him a chance (which he would not

[80] Narbut, also head of the Soil and Factory (Zemlya i Fabrika)
Publishing House, wrote extensively on problems of the press in the
twenties. The message here is described, from archival sources, in
Nasledstvo, p. 94n.

[81] Letter to Gor'kii, beginning of May 1927, *Nasledstvo*, p. 96.

[82] Letter to Gor'kii, April 18, 1927, *Arkhiv*, p. 53. Cf. Gor'kii's
sympathetic reply, April 29, 1927, *Arkhiv*, pp. 54-55.

[83] Letter to Gor'kii, beginning of May 1927, *Nasledstvo*, p. 96.

have taken anyway) to recant his "errors" and throw in his lot with Averbakh.

Very likely some behind-the-scenes maneuvering was in progress. It seems doubtful, however, that Bukharin was involved in it this time, as he very well may have been during the 1925 crisis. Two pieces of evidence suggest in fact that he had turned away from Voronskii. One is an article that he wrote for *Pravda* in January 1927, on the peasant poets in *RVS*. Though limiting himself to Druzhinin and Esenin, he launched a sweeping attack on "Eseninism" in general. By this he meant a self-pitying nostalgia for "the most negative features of the Russian village." To his mind, this was "the most harmful aspect" of contemporary literature, because it had such a tremendous appeal to young writers and readers alike: even Communist Youths were known to keep copies of Esenin under their pillows. The times pointed forward, however, not back; such sentiments were therefore "intolerable" and had to be stamped out.[84] The article makes no mention of Voronskii; but it could only have been construed as an attack on his literary policy. Any reader of *RVS* knew that the poetry section specialized in peasant lyricists who sounded very much like Esenin; and everyone was also aware that Voronskii's position was so insecure by then that even the suggestion of disapproval, in the official Party newspaper, from a high Party functionary —particularly someone who was known to have supported him in the past—was serious indeed. The other piece of evidence comes from Voronskii himself. In his April 18 speech before the Press Section, he made a direct reply to Bukharin's article, entirely in the spirit we would expect: a polite, but unapologetic begging to take exception, on the grounds that the peasant poets were fresh and original voices and deserved encouragement, not censure.[85] Further details of this dark and interesting area of literary politics,

---

[84] "Zlye zametki," *Pravda*, January 12, 1927, p. 2.
[85] "Iz doklada o 'Krasnoi novi,' " p. 223.

however, must await the publication of new archival material.

The proceedings of this April 18 session were not made officially public, even though everyone in the literary world must have known generally what went on. But the enmities that had once again been fanned there broke out in print a month later, with a series of articles centering around the newly formed Federation of Organizations of Soviet Writers (FOSP). Voronskii led off with a blistering attack on Averbakh for establishing a VAPP dictatorship over the fledgling body. S. Gusev returned an answer, accusing Voronskii of defeatism and Trotskiism. Voronskii, in turn, charged Gusev with peddling the Averbakh line under the guise of maintaining impartiality in the dispute.[86] This proved to be his final contribution to *RVS*. In May another radical reorganization of the editorial board was carried out. Yaroslavskii and Sorin, whose only visible contribution to the journal during their tenure had been a brief editorial note of disagreement with Voronskii's last article, now found themselves relieved of what they both obviously regarded as a burdensome bore. Into their places stepped V. Vasil'evskii, V. F. Friche, and, once again, Fyodor Raskol'nikov.

Although Voronskii's name continued to appear on the masthead until the end of the year, he had in effect resigned. Apparently he was given a chance to stay on as chief editor, but decided that it "made no sense to remain."[87] As he explained to Gor'kii in August: "I'm still officially a member of *Soil*, but I haven't actually done any

---

[86] A. Voronskii, "Ob uzhasnom krokodile, o Federatsii pisatelei i fal'shivykh frazakh. (Otkrytoe pis'mo tov. Gusevu)," *KN*, No. 6 (1927), pp. 238-49. The other articles in question are A. Voronskii, "O Federatsii sovetskikh pisatelei," *KN*, No. 4 (1927), pp. 214-21, and S. Gusev, "Kakaya Federatsiya pisatelei nam nuzhna?" *Pravda*, April 30, 1927, pp. 5-6. This dispute will be treated in somewhat more detail in Chapter IX.

[87] Letter to Gor'kii, June 16, 1927, *Arkhiv*, pp. 55-56.

work for a long time. I cannot work with Raskol'nikov and Friche. There's no leave of absence in prospect so far, but I'm hoping to get one."[88]

Now that it had finally happened, he expressed great relief that "for the first time in seven years I'm having a rest from manuscripts." He now had some leisure to write articles, to run the "Circle" Publishing House (though he feared it might not be for long) and—a particular pleasure —to work on his autobiography.[89] But the events of the previous two years had taken their toll. Leonov reported in September that Voronskii had "grown dreadfully thin and haggard."[90] This was the beginning of a period of even greater disappointments and uncertainties for him: expulsion from the Party, arrests, and exiles still lay ahead.

Friche wrote Gor'kii in August: "Unfortunately, A. K. Voronskii shows no great desire to work together with the new editorial board, and will undoubtedly leave it."[91] The remark sounds too pious under the circumstances. For it is hard to escape the conviction—though it cannot be proved with the existing evidence—that the return of Raskol'nikov in June was engineered, probably by the Press Section, in order to force Voronskii's resignation. There was no reason, after all, to suppose that Voronskii would be any more willing to work with him now than he had been two years previously. As for Friche, we shall see in Chapter VI that his ideas about literature would have been offensive to Voronskii; whether anything else was involved in Voronskii's refusal to work with him, we do not know.[92] Certainly Gor'kii

[88] Letter to Gor'kii, August 11, 1927, *Arkhiv*, p. 57.

[89] *Ibid.*

[90] Letter to Gor'kii, September 15, 1927, *Nasledstvo*, p. 251.

[91] Letter to Gor'kii, August 1927, *Arkhiv*, p. 57, n. 9.

[92] Friche had, however, been writing a series of articles for *Pravda* on contemporary literature at the height of this crisis. Though he makes no mention of Voronskii, he does deal with several of the writers who were featured in *RVS* at the same time. Cf. his unfavorable account of Leonov's *The Thief*, entitled "Concerning the New

seems to have been convinced that some such maneuvering had gone on. The moment he heard what had happened, he sent a telegram demanding the immediate suspension of the publication of *Klim Samgin*, which was coming out serially in *RVS*; and in a follow-up letter he stated flatly that he would have nothing to do with the journal henceforth.[93] In any event, the burden had been shifted to Voronskii himself: nobody could be accused of firing him. Remarks by Gladkov in a letter written in September suggest that counter-maneuvering of some kind was still going on: though things "seem hopeless" for Voronskii, he said, "it won't be surprising if some sudden unexpected change takes place soon."[94] We cannot say what Gladkov had in mind. The "change" that occurred was for the worse: Voronskii's name was dropped from the journal in November; the following month he was formally relieved of duties he had already relinquished, and was replaced by Vsevolod Ivanov.

Friche assured Gor'kii that "the literary platform of *RVS*, despite the already-mentioned changes in the composition of the editorial board, remains essentially the same as it was."[95] But without Voronskii, the journal lost a vital spark: from June onward, it fell off rapidly in quality, and never

Bourgeois" (O novom burzhua), *Pravda*, May 22, 1927, p. 4. The title suggests the theme. There was nothing in these articles that Voronskii did not already know about Friche's approach; but their timing was tactless, to say the least.

[93] Gor'kii's withdrawal of manuscripts was not an uncommon happening. At least once before he had done it to *RVS*, over the GUM affair (cf. Ch. I, n. 51). In this case, Khalatov, the head of the State Publishing House, induced him to relent by promising that everything was being done to improve the quality of the journal and attract new writers. Cf. letter to Gor'kii, October 1, 1927, in *Arkhiv*, Book 1 (Moscow, 1964), p. 88. Gor'kii had been informed of Voronskii's removal in a letter from P. P. Kryuchkov, June 21, 1927; the telegram was sent on June 28; the follow-up letter on June 29 (*ibid.*, p. 89n.).

[94] Letter to Gor'kii, September 25, 1927, *Nasledstvo*, p. 101.

[95] Letter to Gor'kii, August 1927, *Arkhiv*, p. 57, n. 9. According

again reached the eminence or importance it had during its first six years.

IT IS surprising that right up to the middle of 1923 Voronskii showed complete indifference to problems of literary theory. One would not expect that from a Marxist, of all people. As we have suggested, however, he may have seen no need for such a theory: since art was concerned with "ideas," and since all Marxists agreed on what constituted good and bad ideas in those times, then presumably there was no basic disagreement on what constituted good and bad art, and no need therefore for any separate theory of art. If, in fact, that was Voronskii's assumption, then the appearance of *LEF* and *On Guard* made nonsense of it. For here were two journals, also Marxist, whose ideas about art proved that no single Marxist viewpoint existed, and that differences of opinion among Marxists were fundamental, not merely tactical. Voronskii suddenly found himself forced to spell out the ideas about literature that guided a policy his opponents considered outrageous—and un-Marxist.

His article entitled "Art as the Cognition of Life," in the fifth issue of *RVS* for 1923, was the first attempt to outline a guiding theory for *RVS*. "At the Pass," a month later, sketched out a new program for literature to complement it.[96] From that moment on *RVS* ceased to be an "encyclopedic" journal. It no longer saw its primary purpose as reflecting the age in all its variety, but rather as interpreting the world through a single powerful idea. That idea would

to Friche, Lunacharskii would become chief editor if Voronskii left. But that did not in fact happen. The date of Voronskii's formal removal from *RVS* is according to an editorial note in *Nasledstvo*, p. 91.

[96] "Iskusstvo, kak poznanie zhizni, i sovremennost' (K voprosu o nashikh literaturnykh raznoglasiyakh)," *KN*, No. 5 (1923), pp. 347-84; "Na perevale," *KN*, No. 6 (1923), pp. 312-22.

find fullest development in a new department of literary theory and criticism, would guide the selection of fiction and poetry to illustrate it, and would illuminate and pull together every part of the journal. The long articles on politics and economics that had been such a marked feature of the journal to date would now assume more modest proportions, and would be carefully set off in a department of their own. The reviews would begin to talk mainly about fiction and poetry. New writers would come in and bring with them longer and more ambitious works. A small but thoroughly competent group of critics and theorists—Lezhnev, Pravdukhin, Zhits, Dynnik, Gorbov, Aksel'rod, and a few others, all of varied interests and skills, yet likeminded—would begin to form around Voronskii. The second period in the history of *RVS* had begun: that of a true thick journal.

Despite the sudden, new importance of literary theory, we find very few examples, between 1923 and 1927, of purely theoretical articles in *RVS*. Some simply discuss new books and go on to generalize from there. The old genres of criticism remain too, although they now strive for something more, something beyond inflated book reviews or half-baked excursions into sociology. But the most important articles are written as polemical rebuttals in the literary debate. They go beyond mere retort, to statements of basic principles. For example, Lezhnev's double article, "The Proletkul't and Proletarian Art," uses a point-by-point refutation of *LEF* and On-Guardist arguments as a framework on which to hang a theory of the nature and function of art.[97] It soon became clear that under the issue of proletarians and fellow travelers, the first real Marxist debate on fundamental questions of the theory and practice of literature was taking place. It is to those questions that the next two chapters are devoted.

[97] "Proletkul't i proletarskoe iskusstvo," *KN*, No. 2 (1924), pp. 272-87, and No. 3 (1924), pp. 268-82.

CHAPTER VI

The Theory of Literature

ALL Marxists agree that art, as an element of the super-structure, is socially conditioned, performs a useful social function, and, like other social phenomena, moves in certain rhythms that can be described and, to some extent, predicted. As soon as they attempt to specify art, however, to identify its particular qualities and define its role in a program of social action, they reveal that the areas of disagreement are far wider and more decisive. On many fundamental questions no consensus has been reached. Do we really need art at all, or can its functions be performed just as well by other elements of the superstructure, such as philosophy or religion? What effects does art produce, and how can they be measured? To what extent does art deal with truths that reach through all history and transcend all classes, and to what extent is it bound to the specific problems and ideologies of its own time? What accounts for the fact that change in art seems to move at a different pace from social change? What use can the arts of very different societies have for us today? Why do they continue to appeal? How can one explain the phenomenon that the forms of art seem to endure far longer than the "contents"? Does art have conventions and laws of its own that counteract the pull of society?

Marxism has not yet worked out an esthetic that accounts for these and many other problems in a way satisfactory to all its adherents. But a beginning was made in Russia during the twenties by those men who specialized in literary criticism and theory (usually without distinguishing the two). The age being what it was, a sense of urgency inspirited their work. To a society ruled by Spartan ideals they had to demonstrate that art was no mere frill. At the same time, they found before them an opportunity that critics dream about but rarely meet. An old literature had passed away, a new one was coming into existence whose development could not as yet be foreseen. Must it not be guided—and could it not be shaped—by men who knew their Marxism, yet respected the special problems of the writer? Voronskii believed that the whole future of Russian literature depended on what such men were doing then; every act of criticism virtually turned into a moral act. Certainly those writing for *RVS* took their responsibilities seriously. Though "of another cast of mind,"[1] they did not set themselves lower than the artist; quite the contrary, in many cases. But the best of them, as always, served art, not themselves.

· I ·

WE HAVE already considered *LEF* in connection with the great literary quarrel of the twenties. Through a unique amalgam of Proletkul't and Futurist theories, this group made the first, albeit maddeningly imprecise attempt at a comprehensive Marxist theory of art in Soviet times. The basic postulates of this theory, contained in the inaugural issue of *LEF* (March 1923), must be introduced into the present context; for they were aimed chiefly at *RVS*, and provoked the journal to outline its own theory in response.

Certainly there was nothing unusual in distinguishing two orders of reality, the real and the apparent; all Marxists do that. Where the theorists of *LEF* made their own special imprint was in putting this distinction in dynamistic terms. For them, real reality, called *bytie* ("becoming"), meant continual forward movement. Apparent or pseudo-reality, called *byt* ("being"), was merely the lifeless residue of the first. Now, since art deals with reality, real art must deal with real reality; in other words, it must itself be in motion, and it cannot "mirror" or "represent" anything; for to

---

[1] A. Lezhnev, "Dialogi," *KN*, No. 1 (1926), p. 259.

represent means to arrest all motion. Such art turns *bytie* into *byt*, and is therefore only pseudo-art. Real reality will have swept on, and the artist will find himself left with the fossilized remnant of what once was. Representational art is characteristic of societies which fear reality; it is the perfect medium for recording the "ossified or decadent social forms" to which such societies cling in their effort to check the onrush of reality that brings them closer to their ultimate doom. Obviously, such pseudo-art creates an "esthetic break" between the audience and reality. "The reader lives with fictitious people moving through fictitious ways of life, commits fictitious acts and fictitious faults. . . ." He is entertained but anesthetized: as the passive observer of a dead world he is persuaded to take for real, he is robbed of mind, will, and emotion, and thus becomes a useful implement of the bourgeoisie.[2]

But genuine art, according to *LEF*, always looks to the future: in order even to keep up with the relentless forward press of reality, it must run ahead of it, providing a "dialectical model" of what will be, fashioned "under the aegis of an ever-new process of eternal self-renewal and development of matter from within."[3] What is the purpose of such art? Not to tell or show anything (i.e., not to be "cognitive"); for to tell means to record, and to record means to kill. Rather, genuine art builds life by producing "things that organize the emotions";[4] and because these "things" serve a higher and still-to-come stage of reality, they exert an "emotionally organizing influence on the psyche, in connection with the task of the class struggle."[5] The true artist is therefore a "psycho-engineer" or "psycho-builder";[6] his work serves the class that serves reality—i.e.,

[2] S. Tret'yakov, "Otkuda i kuda? (Perspektivy futurizma)," *LEF*, No. 1 (1923), pp. 198-200.

[3] N. Chuzhak, "Pod znakom zhiznestroeniya," *LEF*, No. 1 (1923), p. 35.

[4] Tret'yakov, "Otkuda i kuda?" p. 199.

[5] *Ibid.*   [6] *Ibid.*, p. 202.

the proletariat, for that class has nothing to fear from reality, and therefore requires none of the deceptions, surrogates, or camouflages provided by "representational" art.[7]

With a few changes in terminology—notably "infect" for "organize"—the Octobrist conception of art ran along basically the same lines. One of the clearest statements of it came from G. Lelevich in 1924. All true art, he said, is permeated with the values of a specific class and "infects" the consumer with those values. To be sure, it is possible to present individual pieces of reality that are devoid of such values, but this constitutes mere mechanical copying, not art; a particular work may even "tell" or "show" us something, i.e., may have cognitive value, but that is purely incidental. So strong, indeed, is the infecting power of genuine art that it persists long after every other (incidental) attraction of a work has disappeared. For example, the gargoyles of Notre Dame certainly "say" nothing to modern man; yet they do retain their power to infect with the ideology of the class they were created to serve. Obviously, then, proletarians must create their own art which will infect them with the values they cherish; any other kind can only bring harm.[8]

LEF considered the pseudo-art which they vowed to destroy virtually synonymous with all the art of the past. But they found abundant examples of it even in the new society; the chief practitioners were the fellow travelers, and the chief propagators the journal *RVS* and its editor Voronskii.

---

[7] Besides Chuzhak and Tret'yakov, see B. Arvatov, *Iskusstvo i klassy* (Moscow-Petrograd, 1923), pp. 77-79, and the rebuttal by V. Pravdukhin, "O kul'ture iskusstv," *KN*, No. 1 (1924), pp. 304-05; also the "Theses" adopted at the session of the Presidium of the Central Committee of the All-Russian Proletkul't in Moscow, May 25, 1923 ("K programme," *Gorn*, No. 8 [1923], first two pages, unnumbered), and the rebuttal by A. Lezhnev, "Proletkul't i proletarskoe iskusstvo," *KN*, No. 2 (1924), pp. 274-81.

[8] "Nashi literaturnye raznoglasiya," *Zvezda*, No. 3 (1924), pp. 280-88.

192 THEORY OF LITERATURE

VORONSKII's earliest major statement on art theory was composed in reply to that first issue of *LEF*, which it followed by a mere two months, in May 1923. Considering his position in the world of letters at the time, it is difficult to imagine that he regarded this article as a defense or an apologia. Certainly he could have felt little threat from a concept of art that most Marxists regarded as eccentric and extreme. Why, then, did he bother to answer?

Probably there were several reasons. One was that his policy toward the fellow travelers had brought grumbling from many proletarian writers, whose loyalties toward the regime were already strained by the NEP. A reassertion of the reasons for that policy would not hurt. Furthermore, eccentric though the *LEF* theories might be, they did contain a Marxist logic, looked appropriately radical and new, drew from the traditions of proletarian culture, and took on a certain weight if only by being the first to outline something resembling a program for a new art in a troubled and uncertain period. Voronskii, a practical man, may have thought it prudent to nip any possibility of serious rivalry to his program. No one who held the views of art espoused by *LEF* could, after all, believe (as did the *RVS* critics) that a novel, story, or poem must tell us about a reality that we can verify with our own ordinary senses; nor could he tolerate (much less elevate) writers who, like the fellow travelers, tried to "represent" contemporary reality and infected their readers with hostile class values. Finally, it is entirely possible that Voronskii may have been ready to make some sort of statement about art anyway. The journal had developed to the point where it was moving out of the encyclopedic stage and therefore required a guiding line; and Voronskii's own hazy ideas about art had undoubtedly begun to come into focus. Probably, then, the March 1923 issue of *LEF* came at just the right time: a rebuttal of its proposals provided a framework for outlining the theories that had implicitly guided the journal's policies during the first two years and that would explicitly do so for the next two.

The very title of his article, "Art as the Cognition of Life," took issue with the fundamental thesis of *LEF*. Art tells us something: that is the assumption on which Voronskii proceeded. When Voronskii says "art," here and elsewhere, he really means "literature"; and even though he takes for granted that the terms of his theory apply to all the arts, they nonetheless are shaped, illustrated, and conditioned by the art of the word. In this respect, he honors the bias typical of Russian esthetics ever since Belinskii. In fact, this first article is a conscious tribute to Belinskii's ideas.

Like Belinskii, Voronskii begins with a statement of what art does not do: it neither gratifies a desire for pleasure nor provides an outlet for the artist's daydreams. Its purpose, rather, is to "cognize" (*poznat'*) reality. The use of a philosophical term here is important: *poznat'* means to gain knowledge of something, and this is how Voronskii wishes us to think of art—as an activity of the mind. In this respect, the workings of art resemble the workings of the intellect (which Voronskii calls *nauka*, meaning "science" or "knowledge"): both strive to discover the truth about reality, and the discovery each makes is the same.[9]

To describe the reality appropriate to art and science Voronskii resorts to the same kind of distinction that *LEF* did: between a "real" or "objective" reality—orderly, harmonious, comprehending the laws that move all life and history—and an everyday reality—random, chaotic and apparently static. His imagery, however, turns not on movement but on vision. Ordinarily, we mortals see only the physical world before us: we "cannot catch, cannot spy out that which is being born in thunder, in flood, in change, in

[9] "Iskusstvo, kak poznanie zhizni i sovremennost' (K voprosu o nashikh literaturnykh raznoglasiyakh)," *KN*, No. 5 (1923), p. 350.

catastrophe."[10] With art, however, we can see through the workaday world into the world beyond. For the artist tears away the veils of visible reality, thereby exposing "that which we pass by, that which is not yet recorded on our senses, that which is as yet unnoticed." But he does not copy what he sees, for vision in the truly artistic sense means the creation of something new out of what has been discovered:

> From trifles, from little he synthetically creates the important, the large, he magnifies people and objects in his artistic microscope, passing by that which is known and that which has been known. Life he erects into a "pearl of creation": he gathers into one those traits and peculiarities which are scattered and thrown about, he distinguishes the characteristic.[11]

If both art and science yield knowledge or truth, are there, then, no differences between them? We remember that Belinskii saw one difference—for him the chief one— in the means each employs to reach its end: "One [science] *proves* and the other [art] *shows*, and they both *convince*, the one, however, by logical arguments, the other by pictures."[12] Voronskii follows right along:

> science analyzes, art synthesizes; science is abstract, art is concrete; science is directed to man's reason, art to his sensual nature. Science is the cognition of life with the aid of concepts, art with the aid of images, in the form of living, sensual contemplation.[13]

But having held out his right hand to Belinskii for the distinction between ends and means, Voronskii then holds out his left to Plekhanov in order to obscure the distinction

---

[10] *Ibid.*   [11] Both quotes *ibid.*

[12] "Vzglyad na russkuyu literaturu 1847 goda," *Polnoe sobranie sochinenii,* x (Moscow, 1956), 311.

[13] "Iskusstvo, kak poznanie . . . ," p. 349.

again. He goes on to say that the image has no value in itself. It is simply a picture of an idea, and its value depends not on how faithfully it represents that idea, but ultimately on how true that idea is in itself. "*A false idea, a false content cannot find a perfect form* [image] . . . and if we say that the idea is incorrect, but is realized in a superb form [image], then we must understand this in a very narrow, a very special sense."[14] There can therefore be no distinction between truth and beauty; the ugliness in any work of art is proportionate to its failure to provide knowledge.

Related to the difference in means is a difference in the faculties through which we apprehend truth: in art we use not our intellect, but our emotions, giving ourselves over to "sensual contemplation." To describe how this apprehension works, Voronskii—and after him, other critics in *RVS*—resorted to the familiar notion of "infection." They used it with obvious disrelish, because of its prominence in the Octobrist esthetic and its association with religious experience in Tolstoi's theory of art. Yet they could find no better word to describe the cause of that sudden sense of rightness, indubitability, and oneness that for them betokened the discovery of truth.[15] But once again, it was not, at this point, the quality of the emotion that interested Voronskii so much as its content. The artist must deal not with what Voronskii scornfully calls the private emotions, but rather with those emotions that exist independent of him, the "great feelings and ideals of his age," the universal passions of love, hatred, suffering, and heroism; for they

[14] *Ibid.*, p. 365. This is a paraphrase of Plekhanov, *Iskusstvo i obshchestvennaya zhizn'*, in *G. V. Plekhanov. Literatura i estetika*, 1 (Moscow, 1958), 193.

[15] F. Zhits, review of V. Shklovskii, *Teoriya prozy*, *KN*, No. 1 (1926), p. 268. Voronskii admitted that the Bible and the Koran—both examples of true art for Tolstoi—were capable of infecting, but he insisted that such infection was not artistic, inasmuch as religious "images" are abstract, whereas those of art must be concrete ("Polemicheskie zametki," *KN*, No. 5 [1924], p. 313).

manifest, in different form, the same values with which science is concerned.[16] In the writings of Voronskii and his colleagues throughout this middle period, the realms of intellect and feeling are constantly linked—in the assumption, for example, that all serious art is characterized by a "lyricism of thought," or by "big feelings *and* serious thought," or by "a deeply *felt* attitude or thought."[17] The artist must "in full measure feel, think, suffer, be deliriously happy, transforming all this into images";[18] but the important thing is that these feelings and thoughts, as well as the images that embody them, must have cognitive value.

Since art serves truth, it is in the end indistinguishable from history itself. As V. Pravdukhin put it, art "is always nourished, in its content, by the general movement toward the resolution of the problem of the ultimate happiness of mankind."[19] Probably Belinskii and Tolstoi once again served as the intermediaries through which this familiar property of romantic esthetics moved into *RVS*. Tolstoi defined art as "one of the weapons of social intercourse and thus of progress, i.e., of the forward movement of humanity toward perfection," and asserted that it must bring about an "evolution of feelings" analogous to the evolution of knowledge, by promoting those feelings necessary to the good of the people, and driving out the unnecessary ones.[20] In Belinskii's formulation of the same idea, "the very essence of *art* and *thought* [Voronskii's *nauka*] lies both in their hostile opposition [for their media are different] and

---

[16] "Na perevale," *KN*, No. 6 (1923), pp. 318-19.

[17] The first quote is from A. Lezhnev, "Proletkul't i proletarskoe iskusstvo," *KN*, No. 3 (1924), p. 269; the second from A. Voronskii, "Khudozhestvennaya literatura i rabkory," *KN*, No. 3 (1926), p. 232; the third from Voronskii, "Literaturnye siluety. Dem'yan Bednyi," *KN*, No. 6 (1924), p. 264. Italics added.

[18] A. Voronskii, "Na perevale," p. 318.

[19] "O kul'ture iskusstv," *KN*, No. 1 (1924), p. 293.

[20] *Chto takoe iskusstvo?* in *Polnoe sobranie sochinenii*, xxx (Moscow, 1951), 151-52.

their intimate consanguinity with one another [for both serve the truth]."[21] Each is "equally indispensable" in promoting the "consciousness" leading to that social well-being which is the "highest and most sacred interest of society."[22]

Voronskii argued that art of this kind cannot possibly be "passive" or "contemplative," as *LEF* charged; for the knowledge it provides works to some end beyond itself, and effects changes in the life of the individual and in mankind as a whole. Just what the specific properties of the action attendant on art might be, Voronskii did not say. Earlier, when the terms of good and bad art were much simpler, he had exhorted writers to remember that they were wielding a "class weapon" with which they could either defend or attack the Revolution. The "action" he then envisaged seemed scarcely distinguishable from the sort of action that agitators' handbooks talk about. Much later, he would speak from just the opposite assumption: that the effects of art must not be confused with the programs of social activists. At this point, however, he probably had in mind something similar to Dobrolyubov's notion that art offers us, clear and clean, the great liberating ideals that lie within us all but have been sullied by society. Our sudden awareness of the disparity between the ideal and the actual creates a desire to overcome it; we then take steps to do so, while constantly refreshing ourselves at the source, through art, in order to hearten our efforts and check our progress. Certainly it is some such feeling of discontent that nourishes the creative process as Voronskii saw it: "Whenever [he really means 'inasmuch as'] a poet or writer is dissatisfied with surrounding reality, he naturally strives to depict it not as it is, but as it should be. The reality of

21 "Ideya iskusstva," *Polnoe sobranie sochinenii*, iv (Moscow, 1954), 586.
22 "Vzglyad na russkuyu literaturu 1847 goda," p. 311.

the present day he begins to examine through the prism of an ideal tomorrow."[23] The reader recapitulates the same process, though with somewhat dimmer intensity; his discontent, however, presumably translates itself into the making not of a work of art, but of a social action. It is because of art's capacity for producing action that the writer must keep his fingers on the pulse of ordinary life; only then can he make "tomorrow" relevant to "today."

Voronskii's early theory of art seems to rest on the classic tripartite division of man's being into intellect, feeling, and action, with "science" the activity appropriate to the first, "art" to the second, and "action" as the expression of both. But in this first article, and in all the writings on theory that appeared in *RVS* for the next two years, the emphasis fell upon the similarities between science and art, not the differences: both have the same starting point—the world —and the same end—knowledge or truth; both are "empirical" (*opytno*), that is, both mirror reality yet do not merely copy it, because they are selective. No doubt the reason for stating these identities again and again was to dignify art for an age that tended to respect the intellect more. For if it was true, as Voronskii said, that "in genuine art there exists exactly the same precise, objective point (*moment*) as in philosophy and science,"[24] then how could art be denied a place of honor in the new society? Anyone who considered art useless because it is cognitive must also grant that science and philosophy are useless.[25] Here Voronskii was merely restating a venerable syllogism that had been put forth for a century or more in Russia by men who at bottom had serious doubts about the usefulness of art and tried to dispel them by identifying art with something that seemed indubitably useful. Art might purvey information for the public welfare (Dobrolyubov, Pisarev), serve

---

[23] "Iskusstvo, kak poznanie . . . ," p. 351.
[24] *Ibid.*, p. 362.   [25] *Ibid.*, p. 359.

as a means of promoting fellowship (Tolstoi), or remind us of scenes and events that would otherwise fade from our memories (Chernyshevskii).

This kind of argument proves its point as far as it goes. But it cuts another way, of course: for if the functions of art can also be realized by textbooks, photographs, blueprints, machine tools, or drugs, then why have art at all? In the terms of Voronskii's theory, if art and science are alike in all essentials, then why not dispose of one or the other? The dilemma suggested here bears especially on Marxists: since they claim to know in advance what ails society and what remedies must be administered to restore it to health, why do they need art, which simply tells them the same thing? The age being what it was, one required little imagination to predict which of the two—art or science—would go if ever a choice had to be made. Some people were in fact cheerfully advocating the abolition of art, or defining its role in such a way that made its demise inevitable. M. Levidov, for example, thought that the new age had to create a new kind of basic culture, one that rested not on art (as Russian culture always had) but on science and technology. Art might be tolerated, he thought, but only as a kind of tranquilizer at the end of an honest day's labor. Even the theorists of *LEF* and October, while assigning art an honorable function as the organizer of class experience, in effect doomed it to extinction when classes disappeared.[26]

Anyone writing for *RVS*, however, took for granted that art was then, and always would be—even in a classless society—essential to the human experience. In this way, it was clearly implied that art fulfilled a function different from science or anything else. Yet within the terms of the cogni-

[26] M. Levidov, "Organizovannoe uproshchenie kul'tury," *KN*, No. 1 (1923), pp. 306-18; for a "labor theory of beauty," cf. G. Yakubovskii, "Praktika i teoriya v tvorchestve 'Kuznitsy,'" *KN*, No. 6 (1923), pp. 343-48.

tion theory, as Voronskii presented it in 1923, this implication could not be translated into a convincing statement.

WHEN IT came to the relationship between art and reality, those terms needed the most precise definition, but got the least. Voronskii recognized, but did not really come to grips with the problem of how a moving, or dialectical reality can be fixed on paper or canvas. He granted that everything is in motion, but insisted, nonetheless, that "a given thing, in certain conditions and in a definite space and time, is a given thing, and by no means something that is already transitory." If that were not the case, we would be left with an "absolute relativism," which, by denying any permanency, would make all knowledge of reality impossible.[27] Had not Lenin himself asserted that we can find, at any one moment in history, firm and reliable reference points built on accumulated experience, knowledge, and events?[28] Voronskii did not elaborate on this idea; and its meaning, unfortunately, is not entirely clear. But he did seem to be undoing one important argument of his own that he had carefully constructed in the same article: if our ability to know reality depends, after all, on "accumulated" experience—that is, on the evidence of a reality already past—then must we not always lag behind real reality? How then can we deny that art, which embodies such experience, is "passive" and "contemplative"?

When this problem is translated into the visual imagery more characteristic of Voronskii's thinking, a further difficulty becomes apparent. The contrast between the seen and

27 "Iskusstvo, kak poznanie . . . ," p. 350.
28 Voronskii quotes from Lenin as follows: " '. . . human thinking, by its nature, is capable of giving and does give us *absolute* truth, which is built up from the sum of relative truths. Each step in the development of knowledge [*nauka*] adds new grains to this sum of absolute truth, but the limits of each scientific proposition are relative, being now expandable, now contractable by the further growth of knowledge' " ("Polemicheskie zametki," *KN*, No. 5 [1924], p. 315).

the unseen is fundamental to Voronskii's esthetic; and he describes it, in this article, by means of the metaphor wherein art tears away the veils of a lower (seen) reality in order to get at a higher one (unseen). Actually, this amounts to a restatement of the *LEF* proposition that art concerns itself not with being (*byt*) but with becoming (*bytie*). Yet Voronskii immediately backs off—it is almost as if he sees the connection—and creates another metaphor which conveys something quite different: if, for *LEF* (and the Octobrists) the true artist ignores physical reality, for Voronskii he must work *through* it, seizing the "archetypal, individual characteristics and traits of the future" as they reveal themselves "in the bowels of current reality."[29]

It is this second metaphor—a metaphor not of contrast but of oneness—that underlies much of Voronskii's subsequent speculation on problems of art, particularly in those cases where he tries to apply his theories to the works of art he actually published. He never developed it—it exists really as an assumption—but if he had, it probably would have taken the following form. The dialectic permeates all of visible reality; any piece of such reality, therefore, contains some measure, however small, of "objective" reality. To be sure, all sides of reality cannot be included in every work of art, because not all represent discoveries; but they cannot simply be rejected out of hand. Art is a living organism, which suffers and finally dies if any of its parts are amputated. Hence, no set of data is intrinsically superior to any other; art must make that value judgment; for only in the work of art can a selection and purification of visible reality be made in such a way that the underlying "idea," or real reality shines through. The notion of a reality limited only to the experience of the proletariat is therefore false to reality, for it ignores a large area wherein the dialectic plays.

[29] "Iskusstvo, kak poznanie . . . ," p. 352.

The point had a practical bearing on the hotly disputed matter of how far an artist could go in showing the corrupt and dismal sides of life in Russia during the NEP. *LEF* and *October* wished in effect to exclude these sides as "untypical" of the aspirations of the proletariat. But Voronskii insisted that they must be shown, not only because they too beat to the pulse of the dialectic, but because they comprised most of visible reality in 1923, when the peasantry and the bourgeoisie far outnumbered the proletariat.

In these terms, then, the world is not a duality but a unity, and it becomes difficult to see just what art is expected to strip away. The fact that Voronskii failed in this article to develop either one of these two basically opposing metaphors suggests that he felt their pull and could see no way of reconciling them. Something like Coleridge's distinction between a primary and secondary imagination might have helped here, but Voronskii—besides never having read Coleridge, as far as we know—did not at this point think of art in terms of how it was created, but only in terms of what it showed. And that "what," being truth itself, was indivisible: he could not yet conceive that art might possibly deal with a different kind of reality than did science or even the ordinary processes of the mind.

We see, then, within this early cognition theory three large areas of tension: a tendency to obliterate the identity of art as against the insistence that art plays a unique and essential role; a tendency to make art passive as against the assertion that it is active; and a tendency to open all of reality to art as against the conviction that only a special kind of reality is appropriate to it. Even if Voronskii had felt these tensions at the time, he might not have worried much about defining them, still less about dealing with them: how elaborate, after all, did the explanation of what he regarded as a perfectly plain and workable program for literature have to be? But whether Voronskii knew it or not, "Art as the Cognition of Life" marked not just the summing up of a period past, but the beginning of a new period during which literary theory would have to undergo considerable refinement in order to keep pace with the growth of literature and of *RVS*.

WITHOUT a doubt, the theory developed to a great extent from the tensions set up by its very deficiencies: much of the work by the contributors to *RVS* during the next two years represented—consciously or unconsciously—an effort to overcome these deficiencies while preserving Voronskii's basic propositions intact.

Another impetus to development came from the practical needs of the journal: the rapid increase in the volume and variety of fiction and poetry submitted for publication made it obvious that more flexible, subtle, and sophisticated norms would be required to guide selection; and imprecisions that might remain hidden in the realm of pure theory were more likely to show forth in the concrete language of criticism.

Finally, the theory served as the ultimate justification of what was, after all, Party policy toward literature. Here the stubborn refusal of *LEF* and the Octobrists to accept that policy, or even recognize its validity, undoubtedly began to tell. They could not be satisfied with "Art as the Cognition of Life" as theory: among other things, the "art" of which it talked was not art at all in their sense of the term. But even more than Voronskii at the time, they were mainly interested in what this theory meant in terms of literary practice; and the link between these two realms existed, for them, in the concept of class. On the face of it, their argument seemed to make impeccable Marxist sense: if all art serves a definite class, then the best art serves the best class; since the best class is the proletariat, the best art is proletarian art. Why settle for anything less? If Voronskii had followed the same logic, he would have had to close his journal, or refashion it in such a way as to betray its original purpose and thereby presumably deviate from Party policy; for his program for literature—and the theory he developed to support it—was oriented on writers who, by every test of class allegiance, could at best rank only as "sympathizers" with the Bolsheviks. The fact that Voronskii devoted nearly half of "Art as the Cognition of Life" to a discussion of the fellow travelers indicated that he was well aware of the class implications of his theory. Yet he did not really pose the problem in a clear-cut way; and he found himself under mounting pressure from *LEF* and October to explain what kind of art it was that made possible an apparently un-Marxist policy like his.

THE BEGINNINGS of change in the *RVS* theory of art were marked by a shift of emphasis. From about 1924 on, writers no longer talked much about art in terms of the attributes it shared with science. To be sure, they still insisted that it was a form of knowledge, and that its purpose was cognitive. But more and more they looked on art as something with a nature of its own, and began to seek ways of defining and specifying that nature so that it could not be identified with anything else and thereby obliterated, yet so that it could continue, at the same time, to fulfill its cognitive role.

A very sharp and explicit distinction had of course been drawn by Voronskii between the medium appropriate to art (images) and to science (concepts); and it would have been natural to look for further elaboration along this line. But that did not happen: as we shall see in the next chapter, such an approach would have raised more problems than Marxist theorists were capable of handling or even formulating. Instead, attention turned to the artist himself and the process by which he created. This matter had rated no more than a few off-hand references from Voronskii, who was interested only in the purposes and goals of art. Yet, wherever he did make such references, one thing was evident: the vocabulary he employed for the processes of mind appropriate to art was different from the vocabulary that referred to the intellective or conceptual processes. For the first, he spoke of "feeling," "imagination," "attitude" (*nastroenie*), even "intuition"; for the second, of "intellect," "reason," "logic," or "ratiocination." He recognized— though he did not articulate—the operation of two different kinds of processes; and in the two years that followed this article, it became clear that the quest for art's specific nature was moving along the lines of some such differentiation.

It took the discovery of Sigmund Freud to transform this difference into an articulate conceptual distinction. Among the contributors to *RVS*, the first to use him was A. Lezhnev, whose definition of "inspiration," in an article of 1924, virtually paraphrased the idea of the dynamic unconscious.[30] But it was Voronskii, a year later, who took him up in earnest. In Freud he found what seemed to be a clear statement of the distinction which he and his colleagues had been groping for. "There is no doubt," Voronskii wrote, "that beyond the threshold of the conscious lies the vast area of the unconscious. . . . It is naïve to suppose that our conscious mind is always in control in every respect and that it subordinates our desires to itself."[31] A map of the

[30] "Proletkul't i proletarskoe iskusstvo," *KN*, No. 3 (1924), p. 276.

[31] "Freidizm i iskusstvo," *KN*, No. 7 (1925), p. 249. For a discussion of the controversies in psychology in the 1920's, cf. Raymond Bauer, *The New Man in Soviet Psychology* (Cambridge, Mass., 1952). Within *RVS*, cf., among others, Yu. Frankfurt, "Ob odnom izvrashchenii marksizma v oblasti psikhologii," No. 4 (1925), pp. 163-86 and V. M. Borovskii, "Psikhologiya bez instinktov," No. 8 (1925), pp. 173-84.

Pavlov's work on conditioned reflexes inspired a school of "reflexology" in art theory, of which G. Yakubovskii, from the Smithy, was a prominent representative. Cf. his "Praktika i teoriya v tvorchestve 'Kuznitsy,'" *KN*, No. 6 (1923), pp. 343-48; also A. Mikhailov, review of I. Ivanov, *Iskusstvo. Opyt sotsial'no-refleksologicheskogo analiza*, *KN*, No. 9 (1927), pp. 278-81.

The only Freudian literary critic of any importance in Russia was I. D. Ermakov, whose best-known work is a fascinating and sensible

mind had been discovered; and with it, the search for art's unique nature moved rapidly ahead.

To the conscious mind were of course assigned all those processes of intellection that went under the name of science. Did art then occupy the whole of the unconscious? It sometimes seemed so; Voronskii had a tendency to use the two terms synonymously. But to the "unconscious" he also assigned all the garden-variety emotions, and he always insisted that these were not to be confused with the emotions proper to art, because they expressed not universal truths but only individual quirks. For them he might well have reserved some special term like Freud's "subconscious," instead of using it interchangeably with "unconscious," as he invariably did. At any rate, Voronskii made it amply clear that art, in his view, occupies only a very small area within the unconscious mind—a "core" (*yadro*). This core "makes a real artist out of a story-teller or a simple observer," and determines his "individuality" and "uniqueness."[32] Through it pass raw impressions from the outside world, to undergo a change in kind and then reemerge as images, in the "actively operating" form of the unconscious that is called "intuition."[33]

---

study of Gogol': *Ocherki po analizu tvorchestva N. V. Gogolya* (Moscow-Petrograd, n.d. [1923]). This was the sixteenth volume in the "Psychological and Psychoanalytical Library" which Ermakov edited. All but two of the volumes already in print, and all but two of the sixteen announced for future publication were translations of the works of foreign psychologists, including MacDougall, Jung, Jones, and, most of all, Freud. A "Series on Artistic Work" existed, but Ermakov was the only one to contribute to it—as of Volume 16, at any rate: besides his Gogol', he had already published *Studies on the Psychology of the Work of A. S. Pushkin* (*Etyudy po psikhologii tvorchestva A. S. Pushkina*), and announced for the future a study of Gogol's *Dead Souls* (*Analiz "Myortvykh dush" Gogolya*) and of painting (*Organichnost' i vyrazitel'nost' v kartine*).

[32] "Zhuravli nad Gnilopyatami (Aleksei Tolstoi)," *KN*, No. 9 (1926), p. 197.

[33] "Freidizm i iskusstvo," p. 250.

What really mattered in this concept of art was not its view of the creative process—that was derivative and banal —but the fact that the "core" of creativity was radically detached from all the other operations of the mind. It was described as "objective," "impersonal," "spontaneous," and not subject to the will or volition of the artist. Against it the intellect and the ordinary emotions wage constant warfare, each seeking to advance its own claims. But the artist must resist; for these claims are irrelevant to art, being different in kind and often lamentably inferior in quality. If he finds "meaning or logical grounds" as to why he created in some particular way, he must realize that he is speaking not as an artist, but as an interpreter; artistic knowledge "is not arrived at with the aid of logic," and he must take great care not to mistake the one for the other.[34] It is entirely possible for a first-rate artist to possess third-rate intellectual equipment; if he fails to keep the two strictly apart he must inevitably damage his art, as the later career of Gogol' showed:

> As long as the writer was only an honest artist and subordinated himself to the truth of the pen, he could not help but express clearly and truthfully the real social relations of his time. Objectively, by virtue of this, he became an advanced man of the age. But because of his lack of a broad world-view and an adequate education, when the writer tried to become a moralist, a preacher, a teacher, i.e., when he tried to give something positive, ideological, he was able to express only his basic nature as a representative of the backward and obtuse "small-landowner milieu."[35]

[34] A. Voronskii, "Zametki ob iskusstve," KN, No. 6 (1925), p. 261.
[35] D. Tal'nikov, "Novaya reviziya 'Revizora,'" KN, No. 3 (1927), p. 215. Cf. Belinskii: "[talent] must be the mouthpiece not of this or that party or sect, condemned perhaps to an ephemeral existence, doomed to disappear without a trace, but of the innermost thoughts of the whole society, of its aspirations which may well be as yet

Among contemporary writers, Leonov exemplified the same kind of split personality. Critics in *RVS*, as in other journals, had been bothered by his short stories, which drew heavily on the trappings of symbolism, and by his novelette entitled *The End of a Petty Man* (*Konets melkogo cheloveka*), which showed the strong imprint of Dostoevskii—in the drawing-room scenes, the quadrille of intellectuals, the double, the gloomy prognostications of a mechanized future, and so on. Voronskii added his voice to the chorus of disapproval; yet he went ahead and printed the novelette (in No. 3, 1924), on the ground that Leonov's *artistic* nature stood in contrast to the hopeless muddle of his thoughts:

> What comes from the artist, from his intuition, is almost always strong, real, full of life, simple, true; what comes from his mind, his thoughts, is often just stuck on, doubtful, strange, confused, not thought through, at loose ends, symbolical, made strange by dreams and devils, ambiguous, and sometimes downright reactionary. Most assuredly, Leonov is being crushed by the colossal figure of Dostoevskii, to the detriment of his gift for portraiture.[36]

The artist, then, must remain true to his vision of the world, even if that puts him hopelessly at odds with his times. Of all the writers who could have been chosen to drive this point home, Mayakovskii might seem the least promising; yet Voronskii, in one of the best critical studies he ever wrote, made this poet a tragic testimony to artistic cowardice. He argued that Mayakovskii's real gift—his

---

unclear to that society itself. In other words, the poet must express not the particular and the accidental, but the general and the necessary, which lend color and meaning to his whole epoch" ("Vzglyad na russkuyu literaturu 1847 goda," p. 306).

[36] "Literaturnye siluety. Leonid Leonov," *KN*, No. 3 (1924), p. 304.

"core"—was lyrical, not declamatory. The poems on the Revolution, which had made his reputation, betrayed that gift and were therefore false. Only the love poems respected it: "In all our native poetry you will hardly find poems with such passion, such torment, poems so emotionally bared and naked." Yet ideologically these poems were the epitome of decadence. Voronskii counted it "one of the most profound tragedies of our age" that Mayakovskii was at his artistic best when at his ideological worst; nonetheless, he would take the artistic Mayakovskii in preference to the correct one.[37]

IT IS true that Voronskii felt uneasy about dispensing with the conscious mind altogether. A Marxist, after all, cannot really deny that being determines consciousness, and that consciousness rules one's actions. How can art claim an exemption? Yet the logic of Voronskii's dichotomy required that just such an exemption be made. Whenever he found the pull of the two sides too strong, he attempted to honor both by hedging. Instead of outright hostility between the conscious and unconscious mind, he would talk about "a certain contradiction," and even this contradiction would be played down: intuition, Voronskii insisted, originates in the material world and is "nothing more than the truths which have once been discovered by preceding generations through experience and reason and have passed into the area of the subconscious [unconscious]." Such, for example, are certain "social instincts," like courage or patriotism, which have become habitual and automatic and have thereby sunk below the level of the conscious mind.[38] He would also reproach Freud for opening a chasm between

[37] "V. Mayakovskii," *KN*, No. 2 (1925). The first quote is on p. 264, the second on p. 268.
[38] "Freidizm i iskusstvo," p. 263. Voronskii used "unconscious" (*bessoznatel'nyi*) and "subconscious" (*podsoznatel'nyi*) interchangeably.

the two great areas of the mind; man, as everyone should know, was neither all reason nor all instinct, but a blend of both. And because *LEF* and the Octobrists asserted that "intuition" simply refurbished the old romantic notion of Divine Inspiration visiting the Genius-Poet, Voronskii frequently felt obliged to soft-pedal that idea as well. "Intuition," he would say at such times, favors not only geniuses, but ordinary scholars, scientists, and even politicians, who experience it as a heightened state of efficiency and productivity; eminently "sensible" and "honest" poets like Pushkin and Goethe have testified to its workings; it might even visit a doggerel-scribbling schoolboy.[39]

But none of this backtracking sounded very convincing. Voronskii could not sift certain serious flaws out of his attempt at defining a "rational" unconscious. For one thing, when he talked about the amount of time that must pass between the ingestion of intuitions through the conscious mind and their reemergence, he seemed to be thinking in terms of generations. That, to say the least, made his argument academic. Furthermore, he admitted that in addition to "socially acquired" materials, the unconscious also contains atavistic drives, which may even predominate at certain times—in wars, for instance.[40] Just how important a part, if any, they played in the creation of art, he did not say; but with them, he at least recognized in principle the existence of a region of the unconscious that is impervious to the conscious mind, just as Freud did.

Despite qualifications and evasions, the fact remained that the results of intuition, as Voronskii and others in *RVS* described them, differed radically in kind from any product of the conscious mind. They were "trustworthy and indis-

---

[39] For a sampling of such views, all in *RVS*, cf. A. Lezhnev, "Proletkul't i proletarskoe iskusstvo," No. 2 (1924), esp. p. 276; A. Voronskii, "Zametki ob iskusstve," No. 6 (1925), p. 261; G. Pospelov, "K probleme formy i soderzhaniya," No. 5 (1925), p. 252.

[40] "Freidizm i iskusstvo," p. 252.

putable. They require no logical verification and often cannot be verified in a logical way, precisely because they are formed in advance in the subconscious area of our being and subsequently emerge all at once, suddenly, unexpectedly in the conscious mind, independent, it would seem, of our 'I,' without any preliminary work on its part." This is at the same time a definition of how art works; for intuition is "the main thing" there, and the image is formed "primarily intuitively." Though intuition may also operate in science, it is at best "subordinate" to reason there, and really need not come into play at all.[41] As a graphic example, Voronskii proposed Mikhailov, the artist in Tolstoi's *Anna Karenina*. Mikhailov is attempting to make a drawing that shows a man beset by anger. He has struggled with the subject, but has had no success. Suddenly his eye happens to light on an old sketch; he has rejected that too as unsatisfactory, but in the meantime it has been smeared with stearin. This alters Mikhailov's perception of it in a crucial way: at once he sees what he must do to achieve what he wants, and he knows intuitively that he is right.[42]

The concept of the impersonal, detached, creative center is familiar to any reader of romantic esthetics. It is what Belinskii called *fantaziya*, by which he meant not "fantasy" in the modern sense of the word, but the creative imagination. However, the writers for *RVS* went much further than Belinskii in setting this imagination apart from the rest of the mind: in place of the old cognitive idea of the act of creation as a perfect harmonization of all sides of the mind, combining deep feeling with profound intellect and intuition with reason, they now put forth the idea of a mind hopelessly divided against itself—perhaps to the detriment of personality, but indubitably to the benefit of art.

From here it was but a leisurely step to the proposition that the work of art reflects only the intentions of the artist

[41] *Ibid.*, pp. 250, 263.
[42] "Zametki ob iskusstve," p. 261.

and can therefore be judged only according to how well it realizes those intentions. I. Grigor'ev, arming himself with the teachings of Freud, took that step in an article printed in the July 1925 issue of *RVS*. The artist, in his view, selects materials at the behest of his "basic drives" and reworks them in his dynamic unconscious; the result—a work of art—therefore reflects no outside "reality," but rather serves as a device for "revealing" or "transposing" the "intentions of the artist," which Grigor'ev defines as his conscious or unconscious attitude toward life. Symbols fulfill in art the same function as in dreams; and they can be interpreted and analyzed, in the one case by the psychoanalyst, in the other by the critic, who compares variant drafts and ransacks biographical data in quest of the "key" that will unlock the artist's "system of ideology."[43]

If these propositions were to be accepted, then art could of course provide no knowledge of anything except the artist himself. Grigor'ev, in fact, specifically advocated doing away with "cognition" as art's basic purpose. But here Voronskii balked. He was willing to grant that "intention" sparks the impulse to create; and in this limited sense, he allowed that reality might be a "device" for expressing that intention. (That much we might reasonably expect from a reader of Freud.) But he insisted that Grigor'ev and his mentor both missed the mark in dismissing the external world: for Voronskii, that world exists, and has an objective value independent of ourselves; we can discover it through art. The alternative is an unacceptable "agnosticism." In order to determine whether the reality reflected in a work of art is valid or not, we must, according to Voronskii, establish its relationship not to the artist's "intention" (which presumably lies in the unconscious), but to external reality. That, in turn, tells us whether the "inten-

[43] I. Grigor'ev, "Psikhoanaliz kak metod issledovaniya khudozhestvennoi literatury," *KN*, No. 7 (1925), pp. 224-40. All quotes are from p. 232.

tion" is valid, whether it "helps man cognize the world or hinders such cognition."[44]

But how could Voronskii reconcile his insistence on cognition with his new enthusiasm for intuition and the unconscious? Heretofore, when faced with similar dilemmas, he had simply let them stand. In this case, he employed a tactic that was more admirable for craftiness than for honesty. In publishing Grigor'ev's article, he was in effect letting someone else state the conclusion to which his own theory led but which he could not accept: a solipsism that was undeniably un-Marxist. Yet because the conclusion was stated by an outsider—Grigor'ev was not a regular contributor to *RVS*—Voronskii did not have to accept it or even try to reconcile it with the ideology of his journal; he could attack it in a detached fashion because it no longer belonged to him. At the same time, he further diluted the force (and the threat) of Grigor'ev's argument by removing it still one step further, transferring it back to its originator: Sigmund Freud. The unconscious, Voronskii announced, had been discovered by great writers long ago and recognized by Marx himself; Freud merely repeats truisms. In this way, Voronskii chose to ignore the fact that it was Freud who gave him the formulations which helped point his theory in a new direction.[45]

The dilemma remained nonetheless. Voronskii still

[44] "Freidizm i iskusstvo," pp. 241-62.

[45] Thus Voronskii notes that all the great writers were masters of psychological analysis, but did not get the same results as Freud. So much the worse for Freud: "Despite their colossal powers of intuition, neither Tolstoi nor Dostoevskii found that psychoanalytical emotions (Oedipus complex) are predominant in the human psyche, or that unconscious intentions, anti-social in content, cover the whole area of our consciousness and direct our actions. And they knew better than anybody what importance the dynamic unconscious has in the life of man. Furthermore, in depicting their heroes, they were far indeed from giving us monotonous results; in uncovering people's intentions, they instinctively regarded them as being in dependence on the surrounding social milieu" (*ibid.*, p. 259).

thought that art deals with reality (in the special cognitive sense of the word) while at the same time working in the unconscious; yet neither he nor any of his colleagues at this point knew how to make a convincing case for it.

Two books published in 1927 suggested one way of overcoming this vexing problem: *My Life in Art* (*Moya zhizn' v iskusstve*) by Konstantin Stanislavskii, and *My Life at Home and in Yasnaya Polyana* (*Moya zhizn' doma i v Yasnoi Polyane*), by Tolstoi's sister-in-law, T. A. Kuz'minskaya. The first gave Voronskii the theory of "reincarnation" (*perevoploshchenie*); the second furnished examples of that theory at work in Tolstoi's writing.[46] Stanislavskii's "method" is so familiar to us today that we may easily underestimate the impact it had on Voronskii forty years ago. For him, it was a revelation that the artist must dissolve himself entirely in a character or scene, *become* it, in order to render it truly. In glossing this idea, Voronskii took the next step forward in his theory of art. Now he thought he could bring together the "objective" and the "intuitive" worlds. The capacity for reincarnation, he tells us, is inborn, "completely intuitive," unmediated by reason, and resistant to all conscious calculation, all flexing of the will. Only after constant trial and error does the artist, like Mikhailov, suddenly come upon the one avenue that leads into the particular reality before him. "One must," explains Voronskii interposing phrases from Stanislavskii, "detach oneself from the feelings that belong to the ordinary round of existence and instead infect oneself with creative feeling, one must scorn the 'cares of the vain world,' throw off the 'harmonious dream,' renounce the 'pleasures of the world.' "[47] Then one is prepared to meet reality on its own

[46] The term does crop up in Voronskii's earlier writings (cf., e.g., "Literaturnye zametki," *KN*, No. 1 [1923], p. 292; "Zametki ob iskusstve," *KN*, No. 6 [1925], p. 263), but he does not elaborate on it.

[47] "Zametki o khudozhestvennom tvorchestve," *Iskusstvo videt' mir* (Moscow, 1928), p. 67. The article was originally published a year earlier, in *Novyi mir*, Nos. 8 and 9 (1927).

terms and willing to follow it wherever it may lead, even if that involves, in Stanislavskii's words, "believing the most stupid or improbable thing."[48] The image presumably forges the link between the world of the artist's unconscious and the world of objective reality.

FROM THIS point on it was clear that however the theory of art might develop in *RVS*, it must always honor the idea that art looks to a world of reality outside the artist. Nonetheless, there had occurred a slow shift away from the basic theme of the original cognition theory, that art and science deal with the same thing but in different ways. By 1926 and 1927, Voronskii and his followers were saying, in effect, that they deal with different orders of reality in different ways. Not only does the world of art detach itself from the world of science, but, more important, a certain kind of world can be known only through art. Even though the image remains the means whereby we know this special world, the point now seemed to be that only this special world lends itself to reproduction imagistically. The grounds for such a distinction between art and science lay in the original association of art with "feelings," and the reluctance to see that science cannot deal with "feelings," however "cognitive" they may be. Now this distinction became fundamental. "An interesting happening," Voronskii wrote, "a curious event, an entertaining person, become facts of artistic significance only when there is concealed in them, as the larva of a butterfly is concealed in the chrysalis, an *artistic idea*, an *emotion* which is *revealed* to the writer in a special way, in concrete images. . . ."[49]

This distinction underwent fullest development in Voronskii's later articles on art. Even though one definitely, and the others most probably, were written in 1927, none

[48] Quoted in *ibid.*, p. 64.
[49] "Khudozhestvennaya literatura i rabkory," *KN*, No. 3 (1926), p. 232.

appeared in *RVS*. Perhaps this was so because they would have required a fundamental revision of the program for literature which Voronskii, by then in deep political trouble, might have been reluctant to undertake so suddenly, the more so since the form of this revision could only increase his unpopularity. Strictly speaking, then, we cannot account these articles to the *RVS* theory of art. Nonetheless, they do represent a natural unfolding of that theory as it had been worked out in *RVS* by Lezhnev, Pravdukhin, Aksel'rod (Ortodoks), Voronskii himself, and others; and there is some evidence, as we shall see in Chapter VIII, that changes in the program were getting underway too. For these reasons, we can appropriately treat the articles here.

Characteristically, Voronskii needed the push of an opposing opinion to form his own. In this case it came from Gor'kii: " 'there is no beauty in the desert; beauty is in the soul of the Arab—nor does beauty lie in the gloomy landscape of Finland—it is the Finn who has imagined it and endowed his austere land with it.' "[50] Voronskii agreed that this idea answered adequately to what he considered Gor'kii's basic theme—the world's utter chaos, with man's mind the only ordering principle. But he could not accept it for exactly the same reason he had been unable to accept the conclusions Grigor'ev drew from Freud: "if we create beauty only by the powers of our imagination, then what is nature, how does it exist?"[51] No, nature is patterned, ordered, harmonious, and if we cannot see that, the fault is ours. Again, as in the article on Freud, Voronskii beats a retreat the moment he suspects he may have gone too far. Does beauty in nature mean absolute beauty? By no means: "There is no truth in general, no beauty in gen-

[50] Quoted by Voronskii, "O khudozhestvennoi pravde," *Iskusstvo videt' mir*, p. 6.
[51] *Ibid.*, pp. 6-7.

eral."[52] Nonetheless, he is forced to admit the existence of universal concepts of beauty—his charmingly naïve example being that both the Finn and the Arab dislike thunderstorms—and indeed, the whole thrust of his thinking, despite the disclaimers, can point nowhere else. A year later, in his last major article on art, he flings caution aside, and presents the world revealed by art as "beautiful in itself, independent of us and frequently contrary to our impressions."[53] It represents an "alien, foreign life" which is "self-existing" and "is revealed in objects, in events, in people, independent of the way the artist wishes to treat them; the world, as it were, detaches itself from man, frees itself from his 'I,' from his impressions; it surrounds us in all its *self-existent* charm. . . ."[54] Voronskii still denies that he recognizes an "absolute" beauty; but it is the term he fears, not the concept. The "fully objective" world he proposes instead amounts to the same thing:

> Why does the Venus de Milo continue to set an unattainable standard for us, despite the great diversity in taste, in way of life, in feelings between us and the Greeks? Because there exists an objective beauty in nature, and the artist reveals it to us in his works.[55]

Art's purpose now is redefined as well: it is still knowledge, but knowledge of a very special kind. Man's natural state is one of harmony with the real world, the world of beauty. But the cares and routines of his daily round have obscured that world. Only at rare moments, particularly in childhood, does he glimpse it. Art serves to reproduce the "primitive and immediate sensations and impressions" of the world we no longer know; it summons up the "most elementary states" which we fail to notice because "they are

[52] *Ibid.*, p. 9.
[53] "Iskusstvo videt' mir," *Iskusstvo videt' mir*, p. 87.
[54] *Ibid.*, p. 90.   [55] *Ibid.*, p. 88.

too common and too primary."[56] In this way it restores
the natural equilibrium between us and reality:

> Man preserves in his memory, sometimes perhaps only
> as a distant and dim dream, unspoiled, genuine images
> of the world. They break through into man despite all
> obstacles. He knows about them because of childhood
> and youth; they reveal themselves to him in special, ex-
> ceptional moments, in periods of social life. Man yearns
> after these virginally bright images, and he composes
> sagas, legends, sings songs, writes novels, tales and novel-
> las about them.[57]

It is childhood especially that interests Voronskii here,
that period of life when "the controlling force of reason has
not yet had time to put its impress on immediate perceptions."[58] The genuine artist, appropriately enough, must be
ingenuous, even "stupid," if he is to create the kind of art
which turns "a clever man into a fool, a mature man into a
child."[59] For Voronskii, no one gave a more convincing
account of those perceptions than Marcel Proust. In fact,
many of Voronskii's formulations in this last period paraphrased passages from *Remembrance of Things Past*, the
second volume of which (*Within a Budding Grove*) had
recently been published in Russian translation. And, reversing a lifelong prejudice against the works of Andrei
Belyi, Voronskii also recommended *Kotik Letaev* as a suc-

[56] "O khudozhestvennoi pravde," p. 37.

[57] "Iskusstvo videt' mir," p. 84. Cf. Belinskii: "But the enjoyment
of the beautiful should consist in the instantaneous obliteration of
the *I*, in a living sympathy with the universal life of nature . . ."
("Literaturnye mechtaniya," *Polnoe sobranie sochinenii*, I [Moscow,
1953], 34). Belinskii also uses the concept of immediate, or unmediated (*neposredstvennyi*) contemplation of truth to describe the workings of art. Cf. "Ideya iskusstva," *Polnoe sobranie sochinenii*, IV (Moscow, 1954), 585-601.

[58] "Marsel' Prust (K voprosu o psikhologii khudozhestvennogo
tvorchestva)," *Iskusstvo videt' mir*, p. 154.

[59] "Iskusstvo videt' mir," p. 95.

cessful attempt at depicting the awakening realm of pure sensation in an infant's mind. The other examples he brought in from literature were supposed to illustrate either the rendition of "fresh" impressions or laments over freshness gone stale—various Pushkin lyrics on the lost youth theme, Tolstoi's "Death of Ivan Il'ich," Esenin, Lermontov, Gogol', and—need it be said?—Marx's musings on Greek literature as a record of civilization's happy childhood.[60]

There is more than a suggestion here of atavism, of that mysterious region of the unconscious mind which Voronskii recognized but never defined or assigned specifically to art. Only it is not, of course, the wild terrifying world that Freud saw, but a bright, pure world. Because it resides in each man, it is common to mankind; through it, and therefore through art, man is healed, mankind unified, the world made whole. Time and history, in effect, are undone. Herein, for Voronskii, lies the true meaning of collectivism:

> There's a lot of talking and writing these days about a new collective consciousness, but this consciousness, in contrast to the former individualism, should begin with the distinct feeling that beyond the threshold of our sensations and impressions there is a stable world, solidly given. A link with life, with people, the awareness that we are part of a great whole—this is given to us primarily because of this basic feeling.[61]

Tolstoi would not have put it much differently.

How THEN does the artist, and after him his audience, know when this perception of the world has been achieved? Is there a special kind or quality of "emotion" that attaches solely to the creation and the consumption of art? Among

[60] For Proust, cf. "Marsel' Prust . . . ," pp. 151-61; for Belyi, "Mramornyi grom (Andrei Belyi)," *Iskusstvo videt' mir*, pp. 115-30; for the others, "Iskusstvo videt' mir," pp. 81-83.

[61] "Iskusstvo videt' mir," p. 107.

the writers for *RVS*, I. Eiges at least recognized that the poetic merit of a poem is not necessarily proportionate to the intensity of the feeling it expresses or arouses; other activities may play more skillfully upon the emotions than art. But further than that he did not go.[62] The question was taken up anew by Lyubov' Aksel'rod (Ortodoks), an Old Bolshevik who had been a disciple of Plekhanov. Her reputation as a major Marxist philosopher no doubt prompted Voronskii to invite her to contribute three articles on art in 1926. Next to his own, they are the most extensive statements by a single writer that we find in *RVS*. In the main, they offer a routine, though useful, rehash of Plekhanov's views. But they go much further than their model in focusing on the question of art's specificity and in trying to define it in terms of "feeling."[63]

Art, though a social phenomenon, has its own order of existence; it "strives to produce artistic values above all . . . following its own nature [I, 153]." That nature, according to Miss Aksel'rod, is to be found not in art's ability to create images, but rather in its "esthetic" side, that is, in its capacity to satisfy man's esthetic need. The existence of such a need can be proven by considering how art began. From the earliest times (and here she follows Plekhanov entirely) man attempted to imitate, in gesture and song, the processes of labor and nature. The moment these imitative gestures lost direct connection with their models and took on the slightest elaboration, they became candidates for art. They began to undergo their own development, to have an "independent significance" [III, 165], to become "valuable in themselves" [III, 163] with no purpose beyond that of

[62] "Dialog o muzyke," *KN*, No. 10 (1925), pp. 248-49.
[63] "Voprosy iskusstva," *KN*, No. 6 (1926), pp. 146-61; "Metodologicheskie voprosy iskusstva," *KN*, No. 7 (1926), pp. 175-88; "Metodologicheskie problemy iskusstva," *KN*, No. 12 (1926), pp. 148-68. These articles are referred to in the text by Roman numeral (for first, second, and third article) and page number.

satisfying an esthetic need of the person making the gesture. How do we know that the pleasure evoked by the gratification of an esthetic need belongs truly to art and not to something else? Here Miss Aksel'rod picks up Kant's idea of the "judgment of taste" (which is also touched on, briefly and enigmatically, at the end of Plekhanov's article on eighteenth-century French drama and painting), and defines esthetic enjoyment as a "disinterested, immediate relationship" to the work of art [I, 155], something intuitive, contemplative, and utterly free of utilitarian motives.[64]

It is obvious that Miss Aksel'rod proposes some basic revisions in the assumptions made by the cognition theory. She insists that images and "infection" characterize other activities besides art and cannot therefore specify it; and the only "action" she envisages arising from art is a goalless response. Most important, according to her concept of disinterestedness, art can be only incidentally, not primarily, a kind of knowledge; and in this incidental cognitive function it takes its place beside many other human activities, and must therefore sacrifice any claim to uniqueness, if judged by this criterion alone.

Miss Aksel'rod suggested, charitably, that Voronskii proposed "cognition" not as a definition of art, but only as an attestation of his belief in a realistic art, as opposed to a romantic one. She read his motives wrong. He always insisted that imagery is art's proper medium and cognition art's proper end. Yet he not only made no attempt to rebut these articles, but even took over their main ideas—disinterestedness and immediacy—and made them an indication of the kind of knowledge that art is supposed to provide: in other words, what can we know through art in a

[64] G. V. Plekhanov, "Frantsuzskaya dramaticheskaya literatura i frantsuzskaya zhivopis' XVIII veka s tochki zreniya sotsiologii," *G. V. Plekhanov. Literatura i estetika*, ɪ (Moscow, 1958), 99-100. A useful treatment of Kant's esthetic and its setting in the history of literary theory can be found in René Wellek, *A History of Modern Criticism, 1750-1950*, ɪ (New Haven, 1955), 227-32.

disinterested, immediate way? The signs which point to the presence of disinterestedness for him are a sense of intensity, economy, universality, detachment from any individual or concrete object, and, above all, indubitability, "that which must be, that which cannot help but be." He complained that in reading most writers he saw the world "sometimes through the eyes of Andrew, sometimes through the eyes of Nataliya, sometimes through the eyes of Peter," whereas he wished to see it "the way it is in itself," and to be "convinced of its unshakable and incontestable significance."[65]

In these last articles, Voronskii differentiates three kinds of art and seems to assign each to a particular sphere or activity of the mind. The first is the art of the "simple empiricists," which merely copies visible reality, and presents not "the thing in itself" but "the thing for us"—that is to say, a picture of objects that we can verify with our ordinary senses. The second represents the feelings and thoughts of the artist himself. "People, trees, flowers are depicted not as they exist in and of themselves, but according to the whim and fancy of the artist. In the foreground stands not the world, but the artist." The art of the pre-Soviet decadents is like this; so too is art that aims at propaganda: it "wants more than it sees," and Voronskii considers it one inevitable product of the infection theory as expounded by LEF and the Octobrists. The third kind of art is the real one. Here "the artist does not invent the beautiful, but finds it in reality by means of his special sense."[66]

Even real art, however, must take account of the visible and temporal world. The artist is admonished to "plunge into life" and put himself "on the level of the political,

[65] The first quote is from "O khudozhestvennoi pravde," p. 37; the second from "Iskusstvo videt' mir," p. 107.

[66] For descriptions of the various kinds of art, cf., in the order in which the quotations are given in the text, "Iskusstvo videt' mir," pp. 107-08, 98-100, 88.

moral and scientific ideas of his age." But why, if he is concerned with truths beyond the visible world? "The eternal ought to display itself in the temporal," Voronskii explains, "but for that to happen one must know and understand the temporal."[67] Here he returns to the problem he had raised in "Art as the Cognition of Life": that of the relationship between two orders of reality. His answer now is just as banal and perfunctory as it had been then. But there is a difference: in the earlier article, as we saw, he had made an earnest and unsuccessful attempt to contrast and reconcile the two realities at the same time. Since then, however, he had wrenched them apart and identified the higher as the one that really counted for art, with the other, apparently, a regrettably necessary means of making art's message "relevant" to earthly mortals. The problem still remained, but in 1928 it did not interest Voronskii enough even to worry him. Only one new side of the problem appeared. Voronskii now suggested that conscious activity may perform a special service for art. By broadening his points of contact with the visible world, the artist presumably increases his chances of finding entrées into the invisible. He must not work by mere imagination: "People write novels and stories about counts, princes and senators whom they have never once seen and whose milieu they have never observed . . .";[68] the result is mere invention. Since the artist moves by trial and error, the more he takes in, the greater the likelihood for successful discovery. Perhaps a similar line of thinking extended to craftsmanship too, which in the main is not a matter of intuition, but of learned and consciously applied skills. Poor technique obscures cognition; truths are useless unless they can be revealed and communicated; the artist must therefore make himself a well-appointed receptacle through constant study and practice. Yet, how conscious is craftsmanship at that

[67] Both quotes *ibid.*, p. 97.
[68] "Zametki o khudozhestvennom tvorchestve," p. 30.

crucial moment of discovery if, as Voronskii says, we cannot seek the image or the color that best reveal a truth, but
must let them come to us, even though we know immediately whether they are the right ones or not? This problem
was never explored.

BENEATH these views of art the early cognition theory still
shimmers, but the contours have been washed with new
streams and have taken on new configurations. "Knowledge" is still art's main business; but now it is a very different kind of knowledge from that which Voronskii talked
about in 1923. Art now reveals not the flux of the dialectic
nor a truth that may also be ascertained through science,
but a kind of Nirvana, a Paradise that man has lost and can
regain through art. A form of "infection" still operates, but
it no longer suggests violent seizure; rather, it resembles
the glacial calm of revelation which, being disinterested
and unmediated by mind, expects no answering action.
"Class" and "ideology" at best fashion dispositions that may
favor the creation of art, but they do not bear directly on
it, or on the value of the experience that art provides. We
note that Voronskii even uses a different verb for this immediate kind of knowledge: his last collection is entitled
"The Art of *Seeing* the World" (Iskusstvo *videt'* mir), not
"cognizing." And with this, he finally succeeds in specifying art in relation to science, which would of course have
nothing to do with this kind of knowledge. Yet in doing so,
he all but despecifies it in another direction: art's function,
as he conceives it in these last articles, is virtually identical
with religion. He admits as much, but understandably contents himself with only grazing reference to it.

· I I ·

In the light of these theories of the creative process, we
can now return to the problem which stands at the fore-

front of all Marxist discussions of the nature of art: the problem of class. Let it be said from the outset that the writers for *RVS* shared certain premises with all other Marxists. Every artist, they believed, creates at the behest of a particular class. The "psychological class prism" through which he views reality may be clear or hazy, depending on the relationship of the class in question to the movement of history. As a general rule, every class wishes the artist to provide it with a "precise, empirical (*opytnoe*) cognition of life." But if the "objective truth" of life "is for some reason or other unprofitable to a given class"—as, for example, when the class has begun to decline—then the artist is "commanded" to distort life; and in doing so, he creates "pseudo-art." The ear of a rising class is more finely attuned to the great "ideas" of history than that of a declining one; and if the artist himself belongs to the rising class, he is more likely to cognize a fuller measure of truth and can therefore produce better art.[69] As Lezhnev put it:

> Talented writers and therefore talented works can appear from a declining class, but the circumstance that the class is declining and deteriorating deprives the artist who belongs to it of a broad and objective view of things, an understanding and sympathy for the great ideas of his time—in a word, it narrows his horizon and impoverishes his content. Therefore in this sense the chances of a major work's appearing are greatly reduced.[70]

Now, with this much granted, surely it is logical to proceed a step further, as did the On-Guardists, and ask: if all art is class art, then how can it have any value apart from its service to the class whose ideals it represents? If (to adopt the Proletkul't-*LEF* terminology) art organizes the reader's psyche according to the goals of the class it serves,

[69] A. Voronskii, "Iskusstvo, kak poznanie . . . ," pp. 352, 362-63.
[70] "Plekhanov i sovremennaya kritika," *KN*, No. 5 (1925), p. 264.

then must not all art serving alien ideologies be ruthlessly
stamped out, lest it taint?

For Voronskii and his fellow critics, the conclusion did
not follow from the premises. As far as they were concerned, even art created in the service of an alien ideology
might have as much value for the proletariat as proletarian
art itself, sometimes more. True enough, all art is class art;
but, they argued, appending a crucial condition, it is not
only that.

In the homeliest sense, purely external circumstances
might favor art in certain ages and work against it in
others: thus, peace is better than war, wealth better than
poverty, stability better than chaos. The artist must have
the leisure to "see" and not be tempted to "will and act,"
both of which involve faculties alien to art.[71] More important is the intellectual and spiritual texture of a given age:
for all the writers in it are subject to the "same conditions
of life," draw on the "same scientific and artistic culture of
times past," and therefore share "common merits and defects."[72] People generally assumed that certain proletarian
themes existed—industry, reconstruction, guerrilla commanders, workers of the world—and certain proletarian
images as well—steel, slag, sweat, smoke, soot—and that a
preponderance of these in any piece of writing would make
it proletarian. Voronskii admitted that there were indeed
certain moods and subjects, such as the inner life of the
Communist Party, which no fellow traveler could handle
with any degree of skill or convincingness. But he flatly denied that anything like a qualitatively distinct proletarian
literature existed. The Smiths, for instance, showed the
same obsession with peasant themes and the same sympathies with urban culture that most "bourgeois" writers
did. The stylistic experiments which the proletarian writers

[71] A. Voronskii, "O khudozhestvennoi pravde," p. 14.
[72] A. Voronskii, "O proletarskom iskusstve," *KN*, No. 7 (1923), p.
263.

passed off as radical innovations could all be found in fellow travelers as well. And even if the proletarian writers had produced some work of real value, that did not alter the fact that "all these undeniable successes are successes of that same old art which so many proletarian writers shun."[73] Voronskii challenged his readers to distinguish one writer of the twenties from another by style, theme, imagery, or even point of view:

> Pil'nyak [a fellow traveler] and Artyom Vesyolyi [a proletarian], despite all the differences in their manner of writing, have much in common: their view of the Revolution as an elemental force, their language, their mixing of planes, etc. Mayakovskii [a Futurist] and Bezymenskii [an Octobrist] have things in common. The Communist Anna Karavaeva in her "Shores" treats exactly the same theme, and in much the same way as does Aleksei Tolstoi ["old intelligentsia"] in his "Azure Cities." Aseev's [Futurist] poems about the yellow time are finding an echo in Komsomol and even Party circles; Esenin's [fellow traveler or peasant] poetry strikes a sympathetic chord in the worker and the peasant and the intellectual, and Marx was "infected" with ancient Greek art which flourished in a society based on slave labor.[74]

Another factor which counted here was the social value of art in the light of the theories that had been developing in RVS. The concept of disinterestedness virtually isolated

[73] "O proletarskom iskusstve," p. 263.

[74] "Mister Britling p'yot chashu do dna," KN, No. 5 (1926), p. 200. Gabriela Porębina notes an important distinction between Trotskii's and Voronskii's views of the fellow travelers which is relevant here: Trotskii thought that the peasant orientation of the fellow travelers put them in opposition to the workers; Voronskii, on the other hand, insisted that they were allies of the workers, despite their peasant orientation—a perfect illustration, as it were, of that comradely cooperation of two classes which was so much on everyone's mind at the time (Aleksander Woronski. Poglądy estetyczne i krytycznoliterackie [1921-1928] [Wrocław-Warsaw-Cracow, 1964], p. 23).

the individual work; for what, to a Marxist, could be less disinterested than society? Not that art lacked social value; but most of the theorists after 1925 assumed that such value was appended *after* the work had been created (much as the critic might pronounce a "logical" judgment on it, subject, of course, to all the errors of the intellect), and had no relevance to the real nature or intrinsic value of the work itself. Miss Aksel'rod was the first to develop this important qualification:

> Let us imagine that a state puts up a statue to a great man. The state's immediate purpose is certainly not to give esthetic pleasure to those who look at the monument. The erection of the monument has a great many utilitarian aims: the monument represents gratitude to a great man for his work; the monument ought to tell future generations of the glory and might of the state in question; the monument ought to serve as propaganda for those ideas which the great man expounded; the monument ought to inspire young talents and be a stimulus for their development; the monument ought to be a connecting link between the present generation and generations of other times, etc., etc. As you see, all of these are great utilitarian aims, and if the monument does not have within it, in fact, all the potentialities for the realization of the explicit and implicit utilitarian aims, then it is not doing what it was intended to do. But in order that the achievement of all the utilitarian aims should be possible, the monument ought to have an outstanding artistic form, i.e., first and foremost give those who look at it immediate esthetic pleasure—in other words, it ought to be a *work of art* before anything else. All the explicit aims can be realized by other means: by preaching, by history, by biography, etc. But all this utilitarian content, once embodied in artistic form, gives birth to another aim—the aim of satisfying esthetic need. This new aim

is what is the specificum of art, and its artist-creator ought to have it in mind above all. For, all the utilitarian aims of a work of art are realized only when the artistic task is fulfilled.[75]

Voronskii made much the same point in his later writings. We recall that in 1923 he adopted Plekhanov's two-pronged definition of the tasks of criticism: first, the sociological equivalent; then, esthetic evaluation. In 1927 he still distinguished the two actions, but he reversed their order. The "esthetic" feeling of disinterestedness, he tells us, is a "measure with whose help we evaluate to what extent this or that work of art corresponds to the truth." But this "measure," in turn, is "subject to testing, because of man's practical activity which, in a class society, has a practical nature." Such activity underlies the sociological values that we subsequently impute to a work of art. In other words, "sociological evaluation is the last, the final evaluation of the trueness or falseness of a work of art."[76]

But the main fault of the On-Guardist version of the "class" argument, in the eyes of Voronskii and his followers, was its equation of "ideology" with the "idea" underlying the work of art. For ideology belonged to those activities of the mind they called "scientific": it was logical, discursive, abstract, conceptual—all the things art must not be; it stood opposed to the "result of work on the object," that is to say, to the finished work of art itself. Ideology could not be objective, in the special sense they assigned to the word; for it concerned itself with "the transmission of the subjective attitudes, thoughts and feelings of the artist,"[77] which should have nothing to do with art. It was one thing to grant that a writer's class outlook unavoidably influences his artistry to some extent—encroaches on it would really be

[75] "Metodologicheskie problemy iskusstva," KN, No. 12 (1926), p. 167.
[76] "O khudozhestvennoi pravde," all quotes from p. 16.
[77] A. Voronskii, "Iskusstvo, kak poznanie . . . ," p. 352.

the better term—but quite another to assume, as did the On-Guardists, that he must deliberately inject a class outlook into his work. Regardless of whether that outlook be good or bad, he thereby betrays his art, for he contemplates not the world, but his own mind. His work becomes "tendentious," "discursive," "symbolic." As Pravdukhin expressed it:

> The writer ought to know how to dissolve his ideological orientation artistically in the material. The class struggle in art is carried out not by the hatred or enmity of the artist toward man, not by his praising his hero or cleansing him completely of sins, but by the artistic sympathetic understanding of his living, typical essence. The passion of the artist ought to be, in its own way, restrained, objective and cold. . . . The artist needs to worry about his results only in terms of the proper distribution of his material and the attempt to give it inner spirit. Otherwise we would never have had Chichikov or Shylock or Oblomov, or Harpagon or Tolstoi's Ivan Il'ich.[78]

The essence of the creative process, then, and of the work of art as well, is untouched by class, ideology, or even history, and may retain an "objective" value regardless of the circumstances in which it is produced. Ideology is merely another way of expressing the "progressive" idea of history; but it is not that idea itself. Genuine art, in Voronskii's phrase, "always contradicts ideology."[79] It is the critic's job to distinguish the objective content from those subjective elements which the artist inevitably introduces.

THESE opinions about society, class, and art bore directly on the rivalry of fellow travelers and proletarians, which

[78] "Molodoe vino (O romane A. Fadeeva 'Razgrom')," *KN*, No. 5 (1927), p. 242.
[79] "Iskusstvo, kak poznanie . . . ," p. 362.

the On-Guardists had put at the center of their campaign against *RVS* and had succeeded in making the *cause célèbre* of the twenties. One must admit that, given their premises about class, they had no alternative but to impose on the fellow travelers the "percentage-quota" they talked about. Voronskii, quite naturally, looked at things differently. But he did not underestimate his opponents, and developed a set of counter-arguments in defense of that policy which he considered essential to the vitality of Russian literature.

The simplest of them appealed to patriotism: the fellow travelers made a "graphic argument for the Revolution," and gave the lie to charges that the Soviet regime was spiritually bankrupt. If the new literature were to be limited to the meager and second-rate efforts of the On-Guardists and their favored writers, then Paris and Berlin would indeed have cause to cackle.[80] Or if Soviet prestige mattered so little—and proletarian pride tended to cock a snook at the opinions of the unwashed world outside—then perhaps cold statistics might speak. Turning the theory of the percentage-quota back on its inventors, Voronskii argued that since 95 per cent of political Russia consisted of fellow travelers, then literary Russia should by all rights reflect something of the same proportion, if only in deference to the "typicalness" the On-Guardists were always braying about. Plain common sense must have its say too:

we are astonishingly poor, indigent, miserable, ignorant. We are faced with a shattered economy, the savagery and backwardness of the forests and villages, the "melancholy of the fields," a hard, sometimes nightmarish way of life [*byt*]. Our cultural layer is incredibly thin. People have to be Narcissuses madly in love with themselves, or unwilling to see or hear reality, to insist that we must rid ourselves once and for all of the old art,

80 *Ibid.*, p. 371.

declare that the Ivanovs are useless to the Party and the workers, push them into the "NEP" and yet resolve to remain loyal to the Revolution.[81]

To deny the fellow travelers full participation in literary life, then, would lead to the "annihilation and suffocation of Soviet literature, both proletarian and nonproletarian."[82]

Voronskii's main argument, however, grew out of the special view of art and class that was developing in his journal. He was willing to go along with the assumption that a "progressive" writer who was in harmony with a rising class and thereby exposed to larger vistas of reality had a better chance of creating good art than did the servant of a dying class. He also granted that proletarian writers had certain built-in advantages, such as a first-hand experience of certain sides of life, and a mood of optimism which made them "emotionally stronger and firmer" than the fellow travelers and less subject to attacks of decadence. The Communist Youth poets, for instance, brimmed with an energy and enthusiasm that few fellow travelers could match. The Smithy poets had been the first to show the constructive sides of the Revolution in their emphasis on proletarian tactics, discipline, and organization. Libedinskii, Tarasov-Rodionov, and Arosev had treated truly Communist themes from a Communist point of view.[83] As we might expect, it was in his earlier writings that Voronskii emphasized these features of outlook and ideology; practically all his favorable assessments of proletarian writers date from before 1925. As ideology ceased to matter, however, the proletarian writers lost their natural advantages

[81] *Ibid.*, p. 379.   [82] *Ibid.*, p. 368.

[83] For the Communist Youth poets, cf. "Pisatel', kniga, chitatel'," *KN*, No. 1 (1927), p. 238, and "O gruppe pisatelei 'Oktyabr' ' i 'Molodaya gvardiya,'" *KN*, No. 2 (1924), p. 306; for the Smithy writers, "Literaturnye otkliki. O gruppe pisatelei 'Kuznitsa,'" *KN*, No. 3 (1923), p. 314; for the three individual writers, "Literaturnye zametki," *KN*, No. 1 (1923), pp. 290-305.

in his eyes. Under the new concepts of art, he decided that they had very little to recommend them: instead of seeking to discover reality by relaxing and letting their unconscious take over, they chattered incessantly about a reality of their own inventing and preened their ideological egos in front of their writing tables. "Class," in their hands, proved ruinous to art. The new concepts of art could only favor the fellow travelers; and their stock rose higher as that of the proletarians plunged. Voronskii no longer found it necessary to bother with statistical proofs of their loyalty, as he had in 1923. Though still shaky ideologically, the fellow travelers, he insisted, were nonetheless sympathetic toward proletarian ideals and therefore attuned to history's realest realities. More important, because they were indifferent to politics, they had no ax to grind and could therefore better resist incursions from their conscious or "subjective" selves, wherein "ideology" lodged. Because they did not fear intuition (as Voronskii thought the proletarians did) but trusted to it, they depicted a broader expanse of objective reality and gave "pieces of real life" written out of "artistically honest motives."[84] For that reason they served the cause of history better than their proletarian contemporaries:

> By depicting and reflecting the life of the present, by helping to cognize it, they . . . are capable as well of organizing the psyche of the reader in a direction necessary for communism, for we need not only political education, but also that which helps us to enrich ourselves with artistic and other knowledge.[85]

Herein lay the paradox that so baffled and enraged the On-Guardists: artistic superiority was bought at the price of ideological probity, yet in the long run served Communism better. This was what Lezhnev meant by "sincerity"

[84] "Iskusstvo, kak poznanie . . . ," p. 369.
[85] *Ibid.*, p. 373.

—a word which later hardened into dogma among Voronskii's young followers, the Perevalists, and which has
cropped up again in the controversies of the past fifteen
years.[86] Lelevich had argued that no matter how "sincere"
or artistically perfect a piece of writing might be, it was
worth nothing if it contained material harmful to the cause
of the proletariat. Lezhnev, on the other hand, insisted that
if a choice must be made, he would willingly accept the possibility of ideological deviation, for an insincere work is in-
artistic in that it reflects no reality at all and therefore can
teach us nothing. "A good article," he said, "is better than
a bad novel."[87]

One of the serious charges brought against Voronskii in
the twenties (and by practically all commentators since
then) was that he had lost sight of the primary purpose of
his journal, which was to make Communists out of fellow
travelers. The accusation contains much justice. All the reviews and articles which appeared in *RVS* between 1921
and 1923 took for granted that a writer must and could
change—we have only to recall Voronskii's approach toward Pil'nyak. But now, with the new developments in
theory, how much sense did change make? The appraisals
made of various writers from the mid-twenties on still
attempted to determine a basic "outlook" or "attitude"; but
now this attitude was located in the "core" that lay
deep in the writer's unconscious and resisted all change. A
writer therefore had to be accepted as he was—warts and
all—and not expected to violate himself in the name of
some irrelevant "ideology." Voronskii, for example, strongly
disapproved of the idea he found at the core of all Aleksei

[86] Cf., e.g., V. Pomerantsev, "Ob iskrennosti v literature," *Novyi
mir*, No. 12 (1953), pp. 218-45. Cf. Ch. IX for a discussion of the
Perevalist theory of art.

[87] The quote is from his review of L. Gumilevskii's *Sobachii
pereulok, KN*, No. 1 (1927), p. 256. The rest of the argument comes
from "Literaturnye zametki," *KN*, No. 7 (1925), p. 268. Lelevich's
argument is here summarized from Lezhnev's paraphrase.

Tolstoi's work—that life represents a hopeless conflict between dream and harsh reality—but he insisted that the idea, like it or not, must be respected as an artistic reality.[88]

Thus, it made no sense to a critic in *RVS* to group writers under class labels; they had to be treated apart from the factions that claimed them. In the long dispute that raged over whether proletarian culture could exist in the sense of "a developed and internally harmonious system of knowledge and skill in all areas of material and spiritual creativity," it is not surprising to find *RVS* supporting the position that such a culture is impossible. But the reasons were literary, not political; and this fact in itself constituted the journal's chief contribution to the baggage of theory that piled up around the dispute.[89]

[88] A. Voronskii, "Zhuravli nad Gnilopyatami," *KN*, No. 9 (1926), pp. 194-208. Writing in 1923, Voronskii linked this "core" to a class experience: "The writer, particularly in our tempestuous and fast-moving times, usually experiences several fundamental social changes, turning-points, periods, but only one of these puts its basic mark, its primary coloration on the writer's artistic self" ("Literaturnye otkliki. O gruppe pisatelei 'Kuznitsa,'" *KN*, No. 3 [1923], p. 298). Voronskii never developed this interesting theory. It reminds us of Pereverzev's idea that a writer can never change class, but is indelibly stamped by his origins.

[89] The most prominent spokesman against an autonomous proletarian culture was L. Trotskii; the quotation is from his *Literatura i revolyutsiya* (2nd ed.; Moscow, 1924), p. 146. For a position between the two extreme views that enjoyed some popularity, cf. N. Bukharin, "Proletariat i voprosy khudozhestvennoi politiki," *KN*, No. 4 (1925), pp. 264-65. Though *RVS* published this article, it more or less identified itself with Trotskii's views. This dispute has been too much written about to bear repeating here. A short but serviceable account can be found in Edward J. Brown, *The Proletarian Episode in Russian Literature* (New York, 1953), pp. 35-40.

One thing that has been neglected, however, and deserves thorough study, is the terminology of the dispute. Everyone, for example, more or less agreed on the meaning of "proletarian revolution"; but what about "proletarian" art, music, painting, literature? As a political label, the adjective could mean "Party member," but not all people who called themselves proletarians were. As a class designator, it usually called up pictures of workers toiling sweatily in factories, but not all "proletarians" did that. It could also mean "pro-Soviet,"

To be sure, Voronskii and his colleagues continued to use the terms "fellow traveler" and "proletarian." But they did so with increasing reluctance—Voronskii in particular—and for the most part only in polemic. A steady reader of the journal might notice a tendency to equate "proletarian" with "bad," in matters of literature, and "fellow traveler" with "good." Prejudice certainly had its say, and Voronskii showed it more than the others, particularly as his opponents' attacks became more personal. But it was not a systematic prejudice, as his ecstatic reviews of Bednyi and Fadeev prove. In his critical articles he tried to pick out separate strands within the proletarian literature movement—Smithy, MAPP, Perevalist, Octobrists, Young Guard, and so on—and even threads within the strands—the Smiths who showed defeatist tendencies in the NEP as against those who remained steadfast, or those October poets who followed Futurism as against those who echoed more "classical" strains. And, having found them, he adopted a different attitude toward each. He much preferred, however, to discuss writers as individuals, and he always seemed more generous toward anyone who was not closely involved with a group, such as Dem'yan Bednyi among the proletarians, and practically any of the fellow travelers.[90]

"Marxist," "non-Party Communist," or just plain "good" when people talked about political loyalties; but "fellow traveler" could mean all those things too. Racially, so to speak, it could describe working-class provenience, but that obviously excluded most of the high Bolshevik leaders. Nobody could even agree whether a proletarian had to be born or whether he could be made by giving him a "proletarian" viewpoint, whatever this was. Cf., e.g., V. Polyanskii, "Kto zhe yavlyaetsya proletarskim pisatelem (Zametki publitsista)?" *KN*, No. 3 (1929), pp. 198-205; B. Ol'khovyi, "O poputnichestve i poputchikakh," *Pechat' i revolyutsiya*, No. 5 (1929), pp. 3-18 and No. 6 (1929), pp. 3-22; A. Lezhnev and D. Gorbov, *Literatura revolyutsionnogo desyatiletiya* (Moscow, 1929), pp. 53-86.

[90] Cf., e.g., "O gruppe pisatelei 'Oktyabr' ' i 'Molodaya gvardiya,'" *KN*, No. 2 (1924), p. 298. We remember that he also tried to distinguish two basic groups of fellow travelers. In his disregard of class

He thought that each writer was unique and must be taken on his own merits. This idea, which seems so self-evident to us, was revolutionary among Marxists in the twenties; and not the least of *RVS*'s accomplishments was to show that it made sense.

IN MAKING class virtually irrelevant to art, *RVS* stepped squarely into the other great controversy of the twenties: the question of what was to be done with the Russian art of the past. Was it to be junked, locked up in a museum, or handed over to the masses?

The lines here ran much straighter than on the battlefield of proletarian culture. Speaking for the nays were the radical wing of the Proletkul't and *LEF*, whose tactical alliance lasted long enough to produce, in 1923, a set of "theses" concerning the art of the past, or, as they put it, the "art of bourgeois capitalist society." Their argument held no surprises for anyone who was familiar with their views of art and reality. The incarnation of that "cognitive" art they so despised was all the Russian literature up to 1917 and all the new literature that in any way resembled it— literature, that is to say, which reflected "ossified or decadent social forms," threw a veil of fantasy over real life, lulled readers into a bovine contemplation of the world while infecting them with insidious ideologies, celebrated art for art's sake, and fetishized the creative process with talk about such "unscientific" things as "inspiration" and "intuition."[91] The real issue was whether art of this kind

---

designators, Voronskii anticipated the time, nearly a decade in the future, when such labels for writers would be declared outmoded and a single designation—"Soviet writer"—applied to all. But his reasons were, of course, quite different. For the review of Bednyi, cf. "Literaturnye siluety. Dem'yan Bednyi," *KN*, No. 6 (1924), pp. 303-28; for Fadeev, "Staroe i novoe," *Prozhektor*, No. 7 (1927), pp. 20-21.

[91] These theses were adopted at the session of the Presidium of the Central Committee of the All-Russian Proletkul't in Moscow on May 25, 1923, and were published in the journal *Gorn* ("K programme," No. 8 [1923], first two pages unnumbered).

could ever have any conceivable value for Soviet man. Chuzhak insisted that it could not, because history had moved on and left it behind; yet by arguing that all great literature had always been "futuristic" because it stood ahead of its own times, he had been compelled to admit that the art of the past must at least be accepted on its own terms and be allowed an "auxiliary" function insofar as it provided a documentary picture of what the past had been like.[92] Lelevich, speaking for the stricter Octobrists, was unwilling to grant even that much. If art retained its power to infect people with the values of the class it served even after its content had grown obsolete, then clearly any art that did not reflect proletarian values—meaning all the art of the past—must be quarantined in museums and libraries, if not destroyed outright. It was admittedly a little difficult to imagine a calloused Russian working man being contaminated by the medieval ideology wafting from the gargoyles of Notre Dame; but Lelevich's argument applied to familiar works of Russian literature as well. For instance, he labeled Pushkin's novel *The Captain's Daughter* unfit for proletarian consumption because the author, being a nobleman, could not present an objectively true picture of the Pugachov rebellion: he had muffled class contradictions and distorted the significance of that great mass uprising. Consequently:

> individual elements are systematized in such a way that the reader is "infected" with emotions that correspond fully to the "social command" of the nobility: the greatest sympathy for Catherine II, for Grinyov [the hero], for Ivan Kuz'mich and other "noble" representatives of the ruling class, respect for Savel'ich's attachment to serfdom [Savel'ich is Grinyov's servant] and hostility toward the masses who have risen in revolt.[93]

[92] "Pod znakom zhiznestroeniya," *LEF*, No. 1 (1923), pp. 21–22, 35.

[93] "Nashi literaturnye raznoglasiya," *Zvezda*, No. 3 (1924), pp.

These, however, were minority opinions. Most Marxists at the time believed that a place could be found for nearly all the Russian classics in the Soviet scheme of things. And to this issue the high Party officials brought a consensus such as they had failed to achieve in the dispute over proletarian culture. Almost without exception, they registered strong disapproval of the viewpoint of *LEF* and the proletarians. To be sure, the government had really foreclosed the matter by "nationalizing" the classics in 1918, along with art galleries, museums, and other repositories of the national heritage; and reprints had accounted for a healthy proportion of the titles published in Russia since then. General guidelines were supposed to follow automatically from a policy known as "selective absorption," which in effect set up a scale of ideological values, from acceptable to unacceptable, and ranged the old writers along it. Preference went to the political martyrs, like Radishchev and Ryleev, to some of the satirists, like Saltykov-Shchedrin, perhaps to those "naturalists" who painted particularly lurid portraits of tsarist society, like Gor'kii or Dal', and to a few chronic malcontents like Lermontov. At the other end stood the religious enthusiasts, like Dostoevskii, the secret police agents, like Bulgarin, and the defenders of the status quo, like Leskov in his "anti-nihilist" novels. Actually, "selective absorption" remained only a vaguely articulated ideal. For no systematic literary criticism had as yet been created to determine who was "reactionary" and who was not—Marxists did not even agree on what the term meant—or which writers could be wholly accepted, which must be wholly rejected, which might be partly accepted and partly rejected, and so on. In practice, the publishing houses continued turning out mass editions of certain works by Tol-

---

282-84. See also S. Rodov, speech at Meeting of Press Section of Central Committee, May 9-10, 1924, in *K voprosu o politike RKP (b) v khudozhestvennoi literature* (Moscow, 1924), p. 71.

stoi, Dostoevskii, Pushkin, and Gogol' which, by purely ideological standards, would certainly seem to qualify as "reactionary." The fundamental question raised in the *LEF*-Proletkul't theses of 1923 went unanswered: why accept any of this? Once a person granted that some writers of the past were unacceptable—and even their most passionate admirers had to admit as much—then was it not conceivable that all might be tainted? And if one had to omit writers who had espoused causes of which Marxists disapproved, like Tolstoi with his quietism and Dostoevskii with his primitive Christianity, or who resisted ready paraphrase in political or sociological terms, like most of the lyric poets, then what sort of a classical heritage could one really construct?

No one seriously questioned the need for continuity in science and learning; could not the same unspoken sense of need apply to art as well? Vyacheslav Polonskii, for one, thought that it could. Culture, he argued, is a collective concept embracing "all the possible achievements of science, art, and technology." Thus, if we accept the "material" culture of the past (tools, machines, and so on), as we must if we are not to revert to the caves, then we must also accept the "spiritual culture," which of course includes art. The two cannot be separated, and neither is superior to the other. The Russian revolutionary intelligentsia, in his opinion, never fought against what was best in the old culture, nor did the masses rise up against it; their aim was to "shatter not culture itself, but only the privilege of the few to its possession."[94]

Arguments of this kind, which were common in those days, not only begged the question, but, in terms of the

[94] "Zametki o kul'ture i nekul'turnosti," *KN*, No. 3 (1923), pp. 272-74. This rebuts M. Levidov's article, "Organizovannoe uproshchenie kul'tury," *KN*, No. 1 (1923), pp. 306-18. Levidov in turn answered Polonskii: cf. "Ot 10-i do 4-kh i ot 4-kh do 10-ti," *LEF*, No. 3 (1923), pp. 148-53.

RVS theory, actually worked against art by identifying it with science. They also smacked of sentimentalism—the sentimentalism of sensitive men who had been imprinted with the classics-oriented gymnasia education. Such men talked a great deal about "prestige," about the "guardianship of a glorious heritage," about the need to "educate" the masses in a "great" and "humanistic" tradition. But the fact of the matter was that most of the defenders of the past could advance no compelling Marxist arguments for their position which were any match for the ruthlessly consistent viewpoint of the Octobrists and *LEF*. Voronskii was as sentimental as any man when it came to times gone by.[95]

[95] Voronskii was sent to Prague as a delegate to the Sixth Conference of the Social Democrats early in 1912. Of his stay there he wrote many years later:

I developed a deep attachment to the Czech capital. It was steeped in centuries of antiquity. The first European university had been opened in Prague. Here lived, raged and suffered Jan Huss; I saw his church. . . . On the heights beyond the bridge medieval castles were falling into decay. The austere inspired Gothic of churches, palaces and palazzos, with soaring lines that seemed about to pull away from earth, with lancet windows and light lacy moulding, plunged one into the age of crusaders, tournaments, beautiful ladies, religious orders, monasteries, guilds, ballads, hunts, feasts and troubadours. . . . In the National Museum were preserved armor, chain mail, visors, shields, rusty swords . . . lances, crossbows, bows, the first cannon and guns, iron trunks with such complicated lock mechanisms inside the covers that one could not help thinking of the assiduous, painstaking labor, the wonderful handiwork of the old masters. With the decayed, stagnant odor in my nostrils . . . I recalled my early youth, my passion for historical novels, tales, stories of the Middle Ages. To my surprise I began to have a strong and deep feeling that [all these things] were incomparably closer to me than our own kremlins, our Russianized Byzantine style, our tower-chambers and popular assemblies, our Suzdals and monasteries, our bogatyrs and Robber Nightingales, as if I really had once lived here, in Prague, in the Middle Ages, and the days and years of that life had left an ineradicable poetic imprint on my soul. It was as if this was my real motherland, my cradle . . . [here] generations of people once had lived, loved, suffered, worked, rested, their life, their daily round had gone their

But together with his collaborators in *RVS*, he went on to put solid ground under his sentiment, developing a philosophy of the past that made "acceptance" not only possible, but essential. This philosophy became common currency among defenders of the past, and it has provided the chief justification for the program of absorption which the Soviets have followed ever since. Very possibly the major contribution by *RVS* to Russian literature lay in the ability to show persuasively how the past could be made a respectable and usable part of the new culture.

IN THE long discussions within *RVS* concerning art and class, there was another argument which never really took on substance, but lurked not far beneath the surface. We can best approach it by referring to the more familiar terms of Tolstoi's *What Is Art?* For Tolstoi, all good art is animated by a religious impulse, which means a desire to serve a higher ideal. This ideal takes various forms at various times—the State, the Emperor, God—but it is the presence of some ideal, rather than its specific form, that matters. History does show a general upward movement toward higher and higher ideals, with Christianity at the summit. Christian art is therefore the best; yet in essence it represents merely an intensified and refined version of the same ideal that informs even the crudest art.[96]

---

normal way, and now none of this existed, would never exist, and no one had time or sympathy for it.

I was living a double life: I was reading foreign underground literature, with its variety of doctrines and currents, having friendly arguments with my friends, waiting and preparing for the Conference, discussing plans for traveling around Russia after our session—and at the same time surrendering myself to my new country, to the dreamy past, the sad and sweet reminiscences of that which I had never known, but which was stronger, brighter and more cherished than anything I had experienced in real life itself.

(*Za zhivoi i myortvoi vodoi*, Book 2 [Moscow, 1929], pp. 195-97.)
[96] *Chto takoe iskusstvo?* in *Polnoe sobranie sochinenii*, xxx (Moscow, 1951), esp. 151-58.

Now, if for the word "religion" we substitute "humanistic ideals" (justice, truth, freedom, etc.), and for "Christianity," "Communism," we are restating an important but unspoken assumption about art in *RVS*. In the terms of this assumption, it is impossible to hold, as *LEF* and the Octobrists seemed to do, that the ideals of Communism are qualitatively different and therefore unquestionably superior to all other imaginable ideals. Rather, it is necessary to say that they represent merely an intensification of those ideals which are the subject of all good art in all periods of history. Good art therefore cannot be limited to Soviet Russia; it exists wherever those ideals predominate, whether in the fifth century BC or the nineteenth century AD. For *RVS*, as for Tolstoi, such art appeals to all men, because it is always relevant to their highest aspirations.

This assumption supported the argument for objective value that had been worked out in *RVS*. Both denied the relevance of time for art, and in that sense, the relevance of class as well—at least, class as a definition of history; for both held that the values appropriate to art may reside in a writer from any class and from any period of history. "Good" and "bad" art were still distinguished, but the distinction could not be made synonymous with "present" and "past"; it was necessary to think first of an ever-present, ever-vital society of writers.

It is not surprising, then, to find *RVS* insisting that virtually all the major writers of the nineteenth century, however invidious their "ideologies," must be incorporated into the cultural heritage. The "reactionary" sides of Leskov, or the later Gogol' and Tolstoi occasioned only slight discomfort. Readers were invited to consider that Leskov's position as a "petty-bourgeois" (*meshchanin*) gave him a feel for social democracy and alienated him from the nobility and the landowners sufficiently for him to observe their negative features.[97] Pushkin, despite his compromises with the Tsar, turned out to be an unconscious revolutionary, much of whose work after the Decembrist affair was a sublimation of his "progressive" ideas.[98] Even Dostoevskii briefly enjoyed a reputation as a progressive writer, whose vision of a great and noble Russia supposedly forecast the Revolution; his work could "teach us to . . . find enjoyment in its very torments," and to follow its "thundering torrent with eyes full of horror and rapture. . . ." True enough, he was a celebrant of Christianity, but it was a Christianity of the masses (Jesus and Mary, we are solemnly reminded, were really members of the proletariat), and an anti-establishmentarian Christianity at that.[99] Indeed, virtually any writer of the past with a solid reputation, from the Greeks onward, qualified for admission to the fraternity of artists, although Shakespeare and Goethe stood highest among the Europeans (yet another of the many judgments that Romanticism passed on to Marxism) and Tolstoi and Pushkin among the Russians.

It was the literature and culture of the recent past—from the turn of the century onward—that raised real problems. In their bill of particulars, Voronskii and his colleagues echoed the opinions of virtually all Marxists in the twen-

[97] Ark. Glagolev, review of selected stories of Leskov, *KN*, No. 8 (1926), p. 237.

[98] L. Voitolovskii, "Pushkin i ego sovremennost'," *KN*, No. 6 (1925), pp. 228-59.

[99] A. Lunacharskii, "Dostoevskii, kak khudozhnik i myslitel'," *KN*, No. 4 (1921), esp. pp. 206-08. The example is perhaps unfair. Lunacharskii was speaking on the centenary of Dostoevskii's birth, and obviously had to say something nice about him. But if there were any hesitations about Dostoevskii's acceptability, the publication of the long-suppressed chapter of *The Possessed*, entitled "Stavrogin's Confession," laid them to rest as far as many Marxists were concerned. S. Bobrov, who only a few issues earlier had been defending Dostoevskii as a healthy realist ("Koni o Nekrasove i Dostoevskom," *KN*, No. 4 [1921], pp. 246-49), now decided that he was "sick" and had no place in Soviet Russia ("Ya, Nikolai Stavrogin . . . ," *KN*, No. 2 [1922], pp. 332-36).

ties, whether radical Proletkul'tists or tolerant Old Bolsheviks. The Symbolists stood for "narcissism," "mysticism," "pornography," "melancholia"; the Acmeists for an Olympian detachment from the great issues of the time; the Futurists for neurotic individualism and compulsive craftsmanship—all of them symptomatic responses to the "commands" of a class which had reached the final stages of decay. Could even the hardest digging uncover any "objective value" beneath these deposits of "subjectivism"? Not at first. But slowly hostility eroded: the critics in *RVS* began to prepare a place in the literary heritage even for these writers. A number of factors converged to make this change possible. During the encyclopedic phase, the conviction that the journal must be "representative" no doubt was responsible for the publication of a few poems by Mandel'shtam (an Acmeist) and by Khodasevich and Voloshin (near-Symbolists). As time went on, the preoccupation with craftsmanship undoubtedly had its say: for who could deny that most of the "decadents" wrote more skillfully than any young aspirant of the twenties and might therefore serve as teachers, provided of course every precaution was taken against infection with their unhealthy ideologies?[100] In the development of literary theory, the separation of a creative "core" from the rest of the mind had brought with it a distinction between artist and ideologue; and this distinction made it possible to welcome the contributions of the Futurists Mayakovskii and Aseev, and to reevaluate the "decadent" Pasternak as a major poet.[101] But the one argument that made all the others palatable turned on the conviction that a national literature is a unity which cannot be broken. The "decadents" had carried the line of Russian literature from the nineteenth century into the twentieth; and the Soviet writers, whether they liked it

[100] Cf., e.g., A. Voronskii, "Literaturnye siluety. Dem'yan Bednyi," *KN*, No. 6 (1924), p. 321.
[101] Cf. A. Lezhnev, "Boris Pasternak," *KN*, No. 8 (1926), p. 218.

or not, were their immediate heirs. The consequences, however unpleasant, had to be faced:

> we cannot simply wave away the sharpness of perception, the dynamic quality, the refinement of artistic devices, the rich susceptibility to impressions, the new forms, style, power of striking the reader which were introduced into our literature by the impressionists and, in general, by the individualistic schools just before the Revolution. . . . The problem art faces today is how to achieve the most objective representation of the world with the help of the extremely acute, subjective devices developed earlier. . . .[102]

WOULD such extenuations apply even to those writers who had committed the gravest sin of all: left their native land? The official attitude toward them was ambivalent. Good riddance vied with political expediency. On the one hand, the government put few obstacles in the way of those who wished to leave, and even expelled a good many itself. On the other hand, returnees had obvious propaganda value, and the door was left cautiously but visibly ajar. *RVS* adopted this same attitude. The critics produced a few survey articles on emigré literature, but made no attempt to give a systematic or detailed accounting of it: in six years, only three works out of what was, after all, an extraordinarily rich crop of writing received individual reviews.[103] Yet *RVS* was constantly, almost morbidly preoccupied with making a good impression on the Russians abroad who read and reviewed the journal. Fascination alternated with repulsion: repulsion because the emigrés were, after all,

[102] A. Voronskii, "Iskusstvo videt' mir," *Iskusstvo videt' mir* (Moscow, 1928), p. 114.

[103] S. Monosov, review of M. Aldanov, *Devyatoe Termidora, KN,* No. 2 (1925), pp. 279-81; D. Gorbov, review of A. Drozdov, *Chelovek shagaet, KN,* No. 9 (1926), pp. 226-27; V. Yakerin, review of Teffi, "Nichego podobnogo" and "Vchera," *KN,* No. 4 (1927), pp. 231-32.

traitors who now wallowed in capitalist luxuries, hatched plots against their motherland, and betrayed their talents by turning out spiteful examples of the worst kind of decadent scribbling; fascination because many of them might well be brought to reason with a somewhat more vigorous application of the same techniques that had worked so well for the fellow travelers.

The groundwork was laid early. In articles in the third issue of *RVS* for 1921, Nikolai Meshcheryakov, head of the State Publishing House, and Pyotr Kogan, the eminent critic, made a case for admitting the emigrés to the new society—a case intended as much to appease those at home who considered forgiveness treason as to show those abroad how they might undo their unfortunate error. Meshcheryakov built his argument around a familiar Marxist syllogism: the intelligentsia, itself not a social class, always allies itself with the class which best serves its interests; now that the bourgeoisie was in decline, the intelligentsia obviously should turn to the proletariat as the only class which "is in a position to build a new society, in a position to raise the falling productive forces and again to broaden the area where the labor of the intelligentsia can be applied." The "national Bolshevism" espoused by the so-called "Changing Landmarks" (Smena vekh) movement he interpreted as a sign that this shift of loyalties had already got under way within the emigration; and he recommended it as a useful transition stage for those who wished to return but feared to take the plunge all at once.[104]

---

[104] "Novye vekhi," *KN*, No. 3 (1921), p. 269. "Changing Landmarks" was a movement among a relatively small segment of the emigrant intelligentsia which accepted the Revolution as a fact, but not Marxism or Bolshevism. Cf. also "Russkie smenovekhovtsy," *KN*, No. 2 (1922), pp. 337-42, where Meshcheryakov sees the example of the "Changing Landmarks" group being followed in Russia by the group editing the journal *New Russia* (*Novaya Rossiya*) in Petrograd. Cf. also V. Polonskii, "Zametki ob intelligentsii," *KN*, No. 1 (1924), pp. 189-208.

Kogan's case was more original and more sophisticated. Essentially it embroidered one of the hardiest items in that familiar national merchandise, the Russian soul: the notion that writers, if cut off from their native soil, become sterile. He was convinced that many of these writers would soon get their fill of European "democracy" and return home. In an argument strikingly though unwittingly predictive of the "sincerity" doctrine, he appealed to the pride of the prodigals:

> The Tolstois and Bunins, contrary to their poetic will, are forced to set the supposedly ideal structure of life of European "democracy" against the new Russia. Because of one of those great misunderstandings that so often occur in periods of historic cataclysms, the emigré writers were forced to declare themselves ideologists of emotions and aspirations alien to them and take a hostile stand toward that outbreak [the Revolution] which sooner or later must find a natural response in their souls.[105]

Kogan postulated that Russian literature is traditionally "in opposition"; that Communism itself is an opposition movement directed against "the swamp of petty-bourgeois narrowness so hated by the Russian writer"; and that the emigrés therefore could return and remain in the best dissident traditions of Russian literature. The clincher was supposed to be his bland assertion that many non-Communists and even anti-Communists were writing and publishing freely

[105] P. Kogan, "Russkaya literatura v gody Oktyabr'skoi revolyutsii," *KN*, No. 3 (1921), p. 242. Kogan's contributions to *RVS* are confined to the journal's encyclopedic period, for he later became its bitter ideological enemy. The "sterility" theme is, of course, not a Marxist invention; it seems to be part of the Russian literary mythology, despite the fertility of writers like Turgenev and Dostoevskii while abroad. Cf. V. Khodasevich, "Literatura v izgnanii," *Literaturnye stat'i i vospominaniya* (New York, 1954), pp. 257-71; M. Osorgin, "Rossiiskie zhurnaly," *Sovremennyya zapiski*, xxii (Paris, 1924), 429.

within Soviet Russia—which was true enough, but hardly a fact that *RVS*, with its insistence on "contemporariness," liked to advertise.[106]

The case of Aleksei Tolstoi indicated what a writer who heeded the call and actually returned might expect. As one of the most prominent writers in emigration, blame lay heavy upon him. Kogan's view of him as a once-talented writer who had lost his gift was rather more charitable than most appreciations. Nikolai Aseev, for instance, dismissed his story "N. N. Burov and His Sentiments" as "so flabby, boring and pitifully crude that one might think it had been written to dictation."[107] The novel *Road to Calvary* (*Khozhdenie po mukam*)—as much of it, at least, as had come out serially in *Contemporary Notes* by late 1921—was treated to one of the harshest appraisals *RVS* ever made of a major work of fiction. Tolstoi's unflattering portraits of the Bolsheviks upset the reviewer—Voronskii—more than anything else: they constituted a "tendentious lie," a "slander"; they were full of "improbable banalities," and gave proof of the author's "countish hatred, his lordly disdain, his spite, bitterness, fury."[108] Voronskii bracketed the novel with General Krasnov's *From the Two-Headed Eagle to the Red Banner* which in those days was synonymous, for Bolsheviks, with utter ideological depravity. Even so, Voronskii left the door open a crack, by pausing in his bitter invective to observe that Tolstoi had once moved in progressive and radical circles and had taken a satirical attitude toward the nobility and toward the decadent intelligentsia of his time.[109] With Tolstoi's decision to return from abroad, announced early in 1922, the door was pushed wide open. *RVS* began to publish the novel *Aelita*, and critical opinions

[106] "Russkaya literatura v gody Oktyabr'skoi revolyutsii," pp. 239-41.

[107] "Po moryu bumazhnomu," *KN*, No. 4 (1922), p. 239.

[108] A. Voronskii, "O dvukh romanakh," *KN*, No. 2 (1921), p. 223.

[109] *Ibid.*, p. 221.

toward Tolstoi underwent sudden revision. Tolstoi was now divorced from the turn-of-the-century decadence, linked to the best traditions of nineteenth-century realism, elevated to the ranks of such senior fellow travelers as Gor'kii and Prishvin, and pronounced worthy of study by apprentice writers. Even *Road to Calvary*, which had once towered as a monument to White Guardist spleen, now gained qualified readmittance to Russian literature as the best work that had been produced abroad.[110]

Tolstoi, then, stood as the model of a writer who "because of his sensitivity, honesty, and desire to create has long since broken with the underwater kingdom of the dead."[111] But what about the writers who did not return? Here *RVS*, in keeping with its concept of literature as a continual present, went much further than the official line. As the twenties wore on, fewer and fewer were the critics in the journal who automatically wrote off the entire literature of the emigration. By 1926 one of them, Dmitrii Gorbov, was even willing to concede that much of that literature was "not inferior to the best which several of the writers mentioned [Bunin, Remizov, Zaitsev, Shmelyov, Merezhkovskii, Gippius] produced in their prime and in conditions more favorable to creativity than those in which they are writing now."[112] From then on a tacit distinction was made between writers whose political and social opinions were merely "reactionary," and those who used their art for outright anti-Bolshevik propaganda. The first—Remizov, Zaitsev, and Shmelyov being primary examples—were accorded some respect as craftsmen. The second—Aldanov, Merezhkovskii, and Gippius most prominently—called down wrath-

110 V. Dynnik, "Tretii Aleksei Tolstoi," *KN*, No. 2 (1926), pp. 215-23; cf. also A. Voronskii, "Zhuravli nad Gnilopyatami," *KN*, No. 9 (1926), pp. 194-208.

111 Cf. N. Smirnov, "Solntse myortvykh," *KN*, No. 3 (1924), p. 253.

112 "Novaya krasota i zhivuchee bezobrazie," *KN*, No. 7 (1926), p. 240.

ful invective, for they had forfeited any claim to art by ad-
mixing ideology.

Under these new rules, one of the best contemporary
writers, Ivan Bunin, found himself restored to the Pan-
theon, even though he stubbornly remained abroad. Earlier
appraisals had depicted him as a pathological liar whose
major literary efforts, in emigration, created propaganda of
the kind that debated whether or not soup made of human
fingers was on the menu in Russia.[113] But in 1926, Gorbov,
scarcely mentioning politics, made him the only emigré
artist whose work embodied "the principle of genuine art,
free from extra-artistic biases, petty spite, and personal interests."[114] There was no question of his being "contemporary." Gorbov found the value of his work, rather, in its
artistry, in the "clean, precise, aristocratically dry lines" of
the prose, and in the pictures of a dying class, which had a
depth "hardly accessible to artists of a class in the ascend-
ancy, who are compelled to depict their antagonist only
from the outside."[115] Like Aleksei Tolstoi, Bunin became
"a legitimate heir of our classical literature," the "best representative of Russian classicism in its last stage."[116]

THE SPECIAL view of class, history, and reality that developed in RVS made it possible, then, to accept potentially
the work of any writer, past or present. At the same time,
the insistence that all sides of reality are potential candidates for representation in art, inasmuch as all embody, to
greater or lesser extent, "eternal" ideas, meant that no subject was unfit, a priori, and that no writer could be dismissed out of hand for addressing himself to themes that
were unpleasant or ideologies that were hateful—the more
so since each writer had a distinct point of view that was

[113] A. Voronskii, "Ob otshel'nikhakh, bezumtsakh i buntaryakh,"
KN, No. 1 (1921), p. 293.
[114] "Novaya krasota i zhivuchee bezobrazie," p. 238.
[115] Ibid.
[116] N. Smirnov, "Solntse myortvykh," p. 253.

probably valid in its own right. In this way, the essential oneness of Russian literature was affirmed. As a literary event, 1917 no longer had much importance. Time had been erased: all writers became contemporaries.

· I I I ·

The cognition theory, in its early and late phases, was heavily derivative. From Tolstoi came the idea of infection. The concept of art as the servant of a constantly progressive ideal echoed one of the key ideas in *What Is Art?* but might not have been a direct borrowing, any more than many other resonances of Tolstoi, such as immediacy and the almost religious function of art. The parallels probably sprang from common assumptions about art, particularly from a common emphasis on universals. We see a heavy positivist strain in the notion that nature operates according to laws which art must imitate, but not copy; that race, moment, and milieu, so to speak, are not art's real business, but only incidental factors; and that art must concern itself, as Taine said, not with "simple physical appearances" or the "palpable exterior of beings and events," but rather with "the totality of their relationships, that is, with their logic."[117]

Stanislavskii and Freud contributed some terminology and therewith neater formulations of ideas that for the most part had already been hazily conceived. "Immediate impressions" and the opposition of unhealthy rationalism to salubrious instinct remind us of Bergson, who was very much in vogue when the theorists for *RVS* were youths. There is no evidence that Voronskii ever read him; if he had, he would probably have said so, for he loved to show off his library and was always charitable about acknowledging sources. But others may have, Miss Aksel'rod in particular, who seems to have used the term "immediate

[117] Hippolyte Taine, *Philosophie de l'art*, I (Paris, 1921), 27-29.

impressions" before anyone else in *RVS*. Still, vitalistic philosophies suffused the air around the turn of the century (Artsybashev's fiction is a virtual catalogue of them), and may have been taken in unconsciously, just as many people take in Marx and Freud without ever reading them. They are also implicit in the Marxist vision, which is probably why Lunacharskii turned so readily to them in his early writings.

As for the possible influence of other Marxist theories in the twenties, we do notice some striking parallels with the school of V. F. Pereverzev. Both he and *RVS* define art as a mimesis of the harmony that pervades the world, in order to provide knowledge; find the specific property of art in the image, which is a "dialectical unity of subject and object";[118] insist on the primacy of the text in any act of criticism; see the critic's task not in defining what a work of literature is about, but rather in determining how it reveals reality; make "harmony" the criterion of artistic excellence; and believe that the writer, once formed, cannot change. We certainly see much open admiration for Pereverzev in the journal: A. Glagolev wrote an ecstatic review of his book on Dostoevskii; G. Pospelov, a disciple, contributed a fair amount to the journal's theory of criticism between 1925 and 1927; and Voronskii printed an article by him on Pisarev.[119] But all this is actually no more than a coincidence of viewpoint and of premises that derive from a common Marxist heritage. The areas of disagreement are fundamental: for example, *RVS* could not have accepted

[118] V. F. Pereverzev, "Neobkhodimye predposylki marksistskogo literaturovedeniya," *Literaturovedenie. Sbornik statei* (Moscow, 1928), p. 14.
[119] Glagolev's review is in *KN*, No. 6 (1925), pp. 298-99. Pospelov's articles are: "K probleme formy i soderzhaniya," No. 5 (1925), pp. 245-62; "O metodakh literaturnoi nauki," No. 9 (1925), pp. 250-58; and "K postanovke problemy zhizni i smerti poeticheskikh faktov," No. 1 (1926), pp. 237-49. Pereverzev's article is "Nigilizm Pisareva v sotsiologicheskom osveshchenii," No. 6 (1926), pp. 162-76.

Pereverzev's idea that "social psychology" is the solvent of the work of art, nor his insistence that a writer's system of imagery is grounded in the class to which he belongs. Voronskii always showed a fierce determination to keep his journal detached from any other contemporary "school" of theory or criticism: it was the independent stance, the skill in blending and resolving various points of view, that had brought him success.

Strong and implicit was the imprint of German idealist esthetics: the contrast between base reality and the reality of "real" ideas with which art must deal; the idea that art is not a copy of nature but a representation of the spirit in matter; the assumption that art and science both advance mankind by introducing an ennobling principle into the world; the definition of the supreme esthetic experience as harmony, with art mediating between the receptor and the objective world—all this, and much more, passed into Russian romanticism, and into Marxism. The striking parallels between the ideas of RVS and certain key tenets of Symbolism—the contrast between the "abstract" language of science and the "concrete" language of art (Vyacheslav Ivanov's Logos versus Mythos); the concept of the cold, impersonal, creative self as opposed to the empirical, non-artistic self; the notion that any piece of visible reality is permeated with an "idea"—these probably derived in both cases from the Romantic tradition: Voronskii and his colleagues despised Symbolism too much to borrow from it consciously, and probably knew too little about it to borrow unconsciously.

Although many Russians were far more systematic disciples of Romanticism than Belinskii, it was he who provided the richest lode of Romantic ideas for RVS. His presence weighed more heavily in the journal than that of any Marxist, even Plekhanov. Because he and the Marxists proceeded from a common tradition in so many fundamental problems of esthetics, they could live together amicably.

But perhaps Belinskii held a special appeal for Voronskii for other reasons too: both combined the talents of theorist, critic, and practical journalist; and both worked in periods which had uncannily much in common. In any case, it was largely through Voronskii's efforts that Belinskii entered Soviet esthetics, where he has been a powerful force ever since.

The great quarrel over the nature of reality had its counterpart in virtually every other discipline in Soviet Russia during the 1920's. "Passive" versus "active," "cognitive" versus "constructivist," "mechanistic" versus "dialectical"— these were some of the terms then current. In the sciences, for instance, the "mechanists" advocated a strict empiricism, which tended to disparage not only dialectics, but all philosophy as a violation of reality through the aprioristic imposition of abstract schemes on it. In the social sciences, "mechanism" shaped Bukharin's view of society as a system in balance with nature, where movement occurs only as the balance is disturbed and then reestablished on a new basis. In art theory, "dialecticism"—represented by *LEF*, the Octobrists, and later, socialist realism—held that the historical process would unfold, but that the artist could foresee its course, race ahead of it, and in that way speed it up. The "mechanists," like V. F. Friche, insisted that art can mirror only what is placed before it and must therefore always trail history. *RVS* tried to accommodate both extremes in the notion that becoming is seen through being, future through present, intangible through tangible; but by making art an imitation of reality (and, in the later phase, an unchanging reality at that), it approached the "mechanistic" position. It is tempting to see this quarrel—concerning art, at any rate—as a recapitulation of the famous polemic between the conservatives and the radicals in the 1860's. Indeed, there are many parallels.[120] But they must not be

[120] Some of the points, for instance, that A. V. Druzhinin made against "didactic" art would not have been out of place in *RVS*

256   THEORY OF LITERATURE

pressed too far: for one thing, the proletarians, unlike the
radicals, emphasized the infecting and organizing role of
art at the expense of any knowledge or information it might
contain. Yet we may safely characterize the polemic of the
twenties as one more reflex of the long and deep-running
dialogue in Russian letters between the partisans of a utili-
tarianism and the defenders of self-sufficient values.

The critics in *RVS* refrained scrupulously from using
their sources as weapons in the polemic. Such weapons
would have made little dent anyway. No nineteenth-century thinker could yet be invested with the garb of authority; that was the business of the thirties. In fact, there was
no tradition on which all Marxists could agree. It may also
be that the critics in *RVS* did not wish to tie themselves
too tightly to "authorities." (Even Marx is scarcely mentioned!) That would not have answered to their purposes.
They probably took for granted that because they were
Marxists, and therefore servants of progress, they had a
license to update, correct, and revise their predecessors,
Marxist and non-Marxist both. And they were right in the
sense that they had to create a theory for their own purposes, a theory that could shape practical criticism and
speak to the literature of their own time.

Much of the writing on art in *RVS* is refreshingly un-
Marxist in its lack of dogmatism. To some extent this reflects a genuine humility, a feeling that any claims must be
balanced against the realities of the literature that actually
was being written and against the requirements of a jour-
nalistic enterprise. But there is also much that is half-baked,
fudging, poorly expressed, imperfectly grasped—the fruits
of hasty composition, great gaps in reading, and unsureness
of touch. Because Voronskii was the most prolific of the
theorists, his faults glare brightest. What are we to say, for

sixty years later. Cf. "Kritika gogolevskogo perioda russkoi literatury
i nashi k nei otnosheniya," 1856, *Sobranie sochinenii*, vii (St. Petersburg, 1865), 189-242.

example, of his stubborn insistence that the artist is "active," when the logic of his own argumentation indicates just the opposite? Creation, he tells us again and again, starts with an act of the will whereby the artist seeks to bring his "subjective feelings, words and thoughts" into correspondence with "the nature of the object being studied."[121] But one almost feels that Voronskii is playing with the grammatical ambiguity of the Russian word for "cognition" (*poznanie*, literally "cognizing"), a gerund that combines process and result. The fact remains that the artist must know what to will, and that is an intuitive process. Undoubtedly Voronskii here was over-protesting against the jeers of *LEF* and the On-Guardists that the "cognitive" artist was merely a "copyist": Voronskii would not grant this, remembering perhaps that Chernyshevskii had unabashedly made the same point, and thereby reduced art to an *aide-mémoire*. He did not see until much later that his way out depended on showing that the artist represents a certain *kind* of reality which bears no resemblance to the reality the On-Guardists had in mind; and when he finally groped his way to it, he shrank at the specter of "absolute truth" that rose up before him. The relationship of the conscious to the unconscious was yet another part of his theory that he could never express to his satisfaction. Actually, he had defined the relationship, but he would not accept the terms imposed by the definition: as a Marxist, he had to account for the role of the conscious mind in art, yet to be true to his theory, he could not regard that mind as anything more than a window. In short, we should not overlook an unwillingness to accept consequences as one of the reasons why so much discussion of art by Marxists is so unsatisfactory.

WERE THESE later views of Voronskii and his followers "un-Marxist," as their opponents at the time charged, and as commentators on *RVS* have repeated ever since? Did the

[121] "Iskusstvo, kak poznanie . . . ," p. 353.

journal swerve from Marxism in its special concept of class, in the ideas of intuition, the unconscious, immediate impressions, disinterestedness, reincarnation?[122] It is difficult to say, largely because Marxism, as applied to the theory and practice of literature, had never before been followed out so far. What began, in the heat of polemic, as an attempt to justify a specific policy, grew into an esthetic, which claimed relevance to every aspect of the art of writing at the time. Perhaps it would be better to say that we see in *RVS*, in Voronskii's last articles, and in the writings of those who followed him, the logical consequence of the premises that Marxism holds about art. Not that all equally honest attempts to let ideas develop of their own momentum would have reached the same end; the starting points were often too different. But we cannot deny that *RVS* shows an inner consistency: the later theory developed organically out of the earlier, even though it proved to be radically different in kind.

We must also keep in mind that the theorists in *RVS* could not afford the luxury of sheer theorizing. Unlike many of their opponents, they bore a fairly immediate responsibility for what they said: as makers of a journal and (they believed) of an important new literature, their ideas had to translate readily into working norms and prove flexible enough to respond to the pressures set up by a practical venture. We need look no further for an illustration than to those ideas we have just mentioned—disinterestedness, sincerity, objective value. They could make any writer acceptable, but obviously, if taken literally, they would also make criticism impossible. If, furthermore, reality cannot be known except through the individual writer, if each writer is unique, and if he is deemed competent provided he remains true to his uniqueness—then the critic apparently could produce nothing but plot summaries and apprecia-

[122] Cf., e.g., I. Grossman-Roshchin, "Iskusstvo izmenyat' mir," *Na literaturnom postu*, No. 4-5 (1929), pp. 28-34.

tive mewlings; for who is to gainsay talent? Perhaps such exercises would be preferable to the grim prescriptiveness of the criticism in the early twenties, but they would ultimately destroy a literary journal: no selection could be made; no "line" could ever develop; the encyclopedic phase would be prolonged until finally the sheer weight of material would cause complete collapse. Journals have perished from over-tolerance as well as from rigidity. But any journal that claims to print the "best" or the "most representative" must of course operate with some fairly clear set of expectations and models, particularly as the inflow of manuscripts increases. Standards must be devised— standards that depend not on the whims of critics or writers, not on shifting fashions, but on norms which can serve for all literature. Yet, like literature, they must have a specificness of their own which distinguishes them from the methodologies of other disciplines and makes them concrete enough to serve as practical tools of analysis and assessment.

The standards set up by *RVS* represented the first serious attempt, within the context of Marxism, to devise a specific program for literature. Because that program unfolded in a literary journal, it had teeth, for it not only determined who would appear there and who would not, but could also call on a body of distinguished literature for constant illustration.

CHAPTER VII

The Program for Literature

THE rudimentary cognition theory raised the question of art's form by defining the image as the medium through which art exists and achieves its ends. Further accounts of imagery in *RVS* pawed clumsily around this statement without opening any new doors; the reader in 1927 found himself much where he had been in 1923. Still, these accounts should be examined carefully, not only because they document a characteristic weakness of Marxist theory, but also because they lead into the larger question of literature's mode of existence, which underlay the journal's practical program.

· I ·

In the common usage of *RVS*, an image presumably resulted from the meeting of the objective world and the artist's mind, whereupon it was transferred to paper or canvas. It was something generalized, disinterested, universal, detached from any particular object.[1] At the same time, however, it was in itself concrete and specific—a kind of picture. In this respect it differed from what Voronskii called a "symbol," by which he meant something abstract and conceptual—a product of the realm of "science." In this ideal balance of universals and particulars, the image was thought to reflect, in miniature, the qualities of the work of art as a whole. Now, it was not fortuitous that Voronskii took a painter, Tolstoi's Mikhailov, to illustrate how the creative process works, for he thought of the image as something that could be seen, if not with the eye, then with the mind's eye. Of course, the eradication of boundaries

---

[1] A. Voronskii, "O khudozhestvennoi pravde," *Iskusstvo videt' mir* (Moscow, 1928), pp. 10-11.

among the arts, particularly the verbal and the visual, had been a common enough practice in European esthetics during the preceding seventy-five years. Among Voronskii's immediate predecessors, Plekhanov regularly linked the two (one of his most famous essays bears the title "French Dramatic Literature and French Painting of the Eighteenth Century from the Viewpoint of Sociology"). This particular linkage appears to be characteristic of cognition theories, which posit an Idea, or a world of ideas, made visible by brush or pen. Sight, for them, is the highest sense through which knowledge is gained. An artist is a man who "sees" ideas. That is why the word "art," as used by *RVS* and in fact by most Marxist estheticians, is both broad and restricted: restricted in that it draws almost exclusively from literature for illustration; broad in that the insights provided by literature are presumed applicable to all the other arts as well. It is not surprising, then, that the relatively few articles on the nonliterary arts which began to appear in *RVS* after 1924 employed the same approaches and the same terminology as did the articles on literature. This notion of the image as a picture—typical of theories, like the cognitive, which regard art as a mirror of reality— derived essentially from Belinskii. Many theorists in the twenties—most persuasively, the Formalists—considered it hopelessly old fashioned. Only V. F. Pereverzev and his disciples suggested some ways of developing it that promised to yield fruitful results in practical criticism; but their work ended before it got very far off the ground.[2]

The work of literature, then, was regarded as an assemblage of word-pictures, each of which possessed the characteristics of a pre-Impressionist painting: concreteness, dimension, depth, color, line, vividness, and a "subject" or "plot." The rule-of-thumb test for a successful image

[2] V. F. Pereverzev, ed., *Literaturovedenie. Sbornik statei* (Moscow, 1928). For a Formalist attack on the image, cf. V. Shklovskii, "Iskusstvo, kak priyom," *O teorii prozy* (Moscow, 1929), pp. 7-23.

tended to be crudely literal; it seemed to hinge on whether or not the reader could construct a corresponding mental image that made sense to his own experience of the visible world. When Esenin likened Kalmyk carts to wooden turtles (in the poem "Pugachov"), the "image," in Voronskii's opinion, was felicitous because it "corresponds to their slow pace, to their covered-up external appearance." But when Esenin wrote of the dawn as "hitching up its tail like a cow," Voronskii grumbled that the picture was "outrageous and imageless" (*bezobrázen i bezóbrazen*). Similarly, Pravdukhin thought that Andrei Belyi's penchant for synecdochic personifications was misguided: "The cook's cap peeked through the open door" (from *Petersburg*) was not, after all, how things really happened.[3]

One difficulty was that imagery, being visible and palpable, inevitably called to mind "form"; and the mention of "form" induces queasiness in most Marxists. The endless disputes about "form" and "content" in Marxist writings could be dismissed, for the most part, as puerile or silly, did they not have such grave practical consequences for art. The range of attitudes seems to run from amazement at the discovery that art does, after all, have form, to fear that form must, like a dead fish in the sun, bloat into something loathsome, namely "formalism." The word *forma* to a Russian Marxist may suggest at least three entirely different things: the identity (usually in terms of genre) of a work of art as a whole; the technical apparatus employed by the artist to convey his ideas with the greatest possible precision and economy; and the perverse flaunting of this apparatus in order to distract the audience from ideas that are false, or to conceal the fact that the work contains no ideas whatsoever.

The lack of an adequate vocabulary made a discussion

[3] A. Voronskii, "Literaturnye siluety. Sergei Esenin," *KN*, No. 1 (1924), p. 288; V. Pravdukhin, "Literaturnaya kor'," *KN*, No. 7 (1923), p. 285.

of "form" all but impossible. Is art nothing but images? Is the image lodged in an individual word? If so, what kind of a word? What, after all, is a word? What is the difference between the image and the figure of speech? Obvious questions of this sort remained not only unanswered but unasked. The men writing for *RVS* seemed to assume that the meanings of "image," "style," "genre," "form," "language," and so on, were self-evident. Yet they could not establish order even within their own workrooms. "Style," for instance, was sometimes made synonymous with "form," sometimes with "language" or with "genre" or with "imagery" or with "tropes"; and all might be interchangeable.[4] The only real attempt at a distinction that we find in *RVS* is Voronskii's opposition of image to symbol; but he never chose to illustrate it with a text.

One must admit that the premises of the cognition theory largely eliminated the need for such a basic vocabulary. If the work of art is merely an idea recast and made visible, then no disparity exists between ends and means, between what is represented and the way it is represented. Plekhanov put it well in his famous dictum that only a "true" idea can produce a "good" form and a superior work of art. From here flow the pious and heartfelt statements, familiar to all readers of Marxist esthetics, about the "inviolability" and "indivisibility" of form and content—something we all take for granted, but not necessarily for the same reasons Plekhanov did. Even as late as his last major article on theory, Voronskii could only elaborate on this truism. In reply to a rhetorical question—what new forms will art take in the years ahead?—he wrote:

it is perfectly plain that, appropriate to revolutionary proletarian art will be any form that brings us closer to

[4] Cf., e.g., I. Kasatkin, "Literaturnye ukhaby," *KN*, No. 7 (1923), pp. 252-53; V. Pravdukhin, "O kul'ture iskusstv," *KN*, No. 1 (1924), p. 296; S. Klychkov, "Lysaya gora," *KN*, No. 5 (1923), pp. 385-94; A. Lunacharskii, "Marksizm i literatura," *KN*, No. 7 (1923), p. 237.

life and gets us away from the subjectivism of the artist, any style, plot, device, or manner that help us perceive the world in a special way, independent of what we contribute to it. One must begin with the material.[5]

If the importance of form lies in its ability to make the idea visible, then the best form is obviously the simplest, that which gives easiest access to the idea. Communication between the audience and objective reality may be short-circuited if the form is too difficult to be penetrated at once; what the artist needs to find is an efficient and unambiguous signaling system.

To ALL purposes, "form" in *RVS* meant a concern with the surface texture of the work of art, with "language" in its most obvious sense. Given the assumptions that we have discussed, one could set the norms for such language virtually without reading any of the critical articles in the journal. Like the image itself, language should represent a judicious balance between the general and the particular: it must be particular enough to engage the attention of the modern reader (Homer's imagery, to take Voronskii's example, was appropriate to "the primitive and concrete thinking" of ancient times, but not to an "adherent of Einstein's theory of relativity");[6] yet not so particular as to become capricious and self-seeking—the sin of "ornamentalism"; general enough to open a route to the world beyond; yet not so general as to become abstract and "symbolic"— the sin of much proletarian writing. Just how this delicate balance was to be struck and maintained, no one in *RVS* ventured to suggest. Presumably some tingling of the sensibilities would inform reader and writer that the proper combination had been found. P. Zhurov, for instance,

---

[5] "Iskusstvo videt' mir," *Iskusstvo videt' mir* (Moscow, 1928), p. 112.

[6] "Literaturnye siluety. Sergei Esenin," p. 287.

talked about a "melodic I" that hums within every man and apparently sets the wave length.[7] In any event the writer could not go wrong if he remembered that "beautiful simplicity" was the norm, a new *dolce ed utile* which would contain nothing to violate the "economy of the reader's attention," but would strive instead for symmetry, right proportion, and, ultimately, pleasure.[8] In effect, conversational standard Russian would provide the vehicle, and the writer's sense that nothing was amiss, the rudder. The important thing we must note here is that the uses of language in literature hang not upon the requirements of the individual work, but rather upon a standard made common to all works of literature. In reading the criticism in *RVS* we would be hard-pressed to know, were we not told, whether a commentator is speaking about fiction, poetry, essays, or drama. Yurii Sobolev, for example, in reviewing a collection of Aleksandr Neverov's plays, made no distinction between dramatic dialogue and short-story dialogue.[9] It was taken for granted that a fund of "devices," "images," "tropes," and styles existed that could be drawn on at will, for any purpose. Pushkin's poetry could therefore be recommended to proletarian prose writers as a model of style—provided, presumably, that specific references were updated.

Perhaps this is norm enough, if one is going to practice the kind of negative criticism that countenances any "style" provided the eye does not notice it. Much of the criticism in *RVS* does read that way: it fences off instead of fencing in. But negatives mirror positives; admonitions carry prescriptions; and when it became necessary, as ultimately it did, to teach the writer what he ought to seek as well as avoid in order to write well, the lack of a theory of language began to tell. Slowly it dawned on the reviewers and critics that the right ideas, however lofty in themselves,

---

[7] "Smysl slova," *KN*, No. 7 (1923), p. 278.
[8] The quote is from V. Pravdukhin, "Literaturnaya kor'," p. 285.
[9] Review of A. Neverov, *P'esy*, *KN*, No. 1 (1924), pp. 313-16.

must be communicated; that communication depends on knowing what to do with language once it is in hand; and that in the torrent of new stories and novels one could find very few that showed enough sense of language to qualify as competent even by the loosest standards. The young pro-letarians, eager to crash into print before they had acquired the rudiments of a literary education and spurred on by the flattering solicitude of their sponsors among the critics, had to carry the heaviest burden of responsibility for the propagation of shabbiness, ignorance, pretentiousness, and illiteracy that the reviewers for *RVS* found increasingly evident in the literature from 1926 on. But other writers, in growing number, also stood accused: many of the old favor-ites, even among the fellow travelers, lost their luster. Indeed, the taint was traced in all but a handful: discover a disease and the sick-list mounts. "Craftsmanship," by 1927, had become virtually an obsession in *RVS*; what profits it a man, they asked, to write about the right things if he bury them under an avalanche of ineptitude? By the time they began to conclude that "form" might have some very practical applications, it was too late: the journal had begun to decline.

No way was ever found of marrying "idea" and "form" to create a useful tool of criticism. Critics found it difficult to shed their prejudices and impossible to talk a language they did not know. Here, for example, is how a usually sensible and sensitive man like Fyodor Zhits reacted to the suggestion that the Russian classical writers might have cared about "form":

> it was not in search of some pretty little rhyme that Nekrasov paced the floor of his room in a delirium for days on end while he was creating; it was not because of "formal" birth-pangs that Leonid Andreev was on the verge of insanity when he was writing his moving "Tale

of the Seven Who Were Hanged"! These artists were filled to overflowing with an agitation of the emotions.[10]

One wonders whether *RVS*, and Russian Marxists in general, might not have made more progress in matters of form (there has been virtually none in the forty years since these opinions were uttered) if the Formalists had not been writing so prolifically at the time. For the first three or four years, *RVS* manifested all the typical Marxist prejudices toward the Formalists. They were "naïve realists," mere collectors of "devices," skillful at taking things apart but utterly lost when they tried to account for the "infecting wholeness"[11] of a piece of writing. Because they lacked a theory of literature, they could not explain, but only describe literary phenomena; yet their concept of literature— as a sum of "devices," as making things "strange"—was so warped that no theory could be coaxed from it. Petrovskii's famous article "The Composition of the Novella in Maupassant" was dismissed scornfully as a "pupil's 'composition' on a set theme, full of minute observations of a general nature which tell us nothing about the novella, or about Maupassant as the 'composer.' "[12] Lezhnev, in a crude but colorful metaphor, summed the movement up as "a belated belch of idealism."[13] It was a pity that these men, who were tolerant of so many things, should have accorded so little respect to the only minds grappling seriously with the problems of language in literature. As their own sense of the importance of craftsmanship sharpened, they began to show some sympathy for the kind of close text analysis in

[10] Review of V. Shklovskii, *Sentimental'noe puteshestvie, KN,* No. 2 (1925), p. 268.

[11] The term belongs to F. Zhits, *ibid.*

[12] S. Bobrov, review of *Nachala,* No. 1, in *KN,* No. 1 (1922), p. 318.

[13] "Sredi zhurnalov," *KN,* No. 4 (1924), p. 312. Cf. also N. Bukharin, "O formal'nom metode v iskusstve," *KN,* No. 3 (1925), pp. 248-57.

which the Formalists excelled, although they did not attempt anything comparable. They borrowed a few terms *ad hoc*, and hostility mellowed to tolerance. But further than that they would not go.

THE FACT that these critics defined "form" almost wholly in terms of "language" had one important consequence: those other aspects of literature which usually were assigned to the category of "form," now being excluded from it, escaped the paralyzing strictures that "form" laid upon language. And it was in such aspects—theme, structure, character, and genre especially—that the new program for literature developed; for the cognition theory clearly implied, when it did not actually state, that certain kinds of writing and certain qualities of artistry were appropriate.

Almost from the moment that Voronskii made his first venture into theory, he and his colleagues decided that the sort of literature which had been produced between 1921 and 1923 would no longer do. In retrospect, that period now looked like one of "primitive accumulation": reality had consisted of random impingements of strange and new experiences upon the senses, and writers had patiently recorded them "drop by drop," often in such stark detail that they might furnish primary source material for sociologists, historians, and ethnographers. A "rich and necessary" material had been gathered; now the time had come to show what it meant. In Voronskii's words:

> There have been a great many themes—but there has been no *one theme*. There have been very many heroes— but there has been no *one hero*. People have written about very many astonishing, amusing and sad events— but there has been nothing about *one event*; just as in a cinema, thousands of types, of human faces have flashed before us—but there has been no *one type*. Our writers have presented thousands of small details, they have crawled around in all the most remote, tiny corners, they

have told us about astonishing and unheard-of things
and they have constantly left out, forgotten something
important.[14]

That "something important" was the reality which the
cognition theory had made art's business. Writers who
could not penetrate to it through the shimmer of events
must flounder in "ethnographism," "naturalism," "wingless"
and "naïve" realism, "foam-skimming." As so often happened, the work of the young proletarians yielded the most
nutrient examples. Dmitrii Gorbov regarded their pictures
of the NEP period—gloomy enough in its own right—as too
detailed to be truly realistic. Such "naturalism," he thought,
was merely another form of bourgeois estheticism, in that
both stared at the trees and could not discern the forest. "A
bourgeois dress coat," he concluded, "does not become a
worker's smock simply because it is put on inside out and
smudged with dirt."[15] But a good many of the fellow travelers were not proving flexible enough to suit the critics
either. Particularly suspect were those who had won celeb-
rity as local colorists and could be identified with specific
regions—Pil'nyak with Kolomna, for instance, or Vsevolod
Ivanov and Lidiya Seifullina with Siberia, or Aleksandr
Yakovlev with the Volga. What had made their reputations between 1921 and 1923 now threatened to unmake
them.

To describe such a decisive turn in literature no one,
strange to say, came up with a more imaginative term than
"neo-realism." Voronskii invented it, but he employed it
rarely and always seemed embarrassed about it. His stabs
at a definition missed the mark: he talked about "a distinctive blending of romanticism and symbolism with realism,"
or a movement in which "the symbol is endowed with a

[14] "Na perevale," *KN*, No. 6 (1923), p. 315. The quotes in the
preceding paragraph belong also to Voronskii, "Literaturnye otkliki.
O gruppe pisatelei 'Kuznitsa,'" *KN*, No. 4 (1923), p. 321.
[15] "V poiskakh temy," *KN*, No. 12 (1926), pp. 238-39.

realistic nature, and realism becomes symbolic and romantic."[16] It was not so much that his usual amplitude of mind failed to extend to definitions; rather, his practical sense was suspicious of them. He thought it sufficient to envisage a literature that innovated within tradition (and that is what these phrases mean), and to leave the results to a continuing dialogue between critic and creative writer.

COMMON to all aspects of the new realism was bigness, or monumentalness. This applied, first of all, to subject matter. The critics worried a great deal about the limited range of themes in contemporary literature. Writers seemed reluctant to move off the familiar territory of the Revolution and Civil War. One of the reviewers observed:

> When I see a Chinese on the first page, I already know that on the second there will be an armored train, and on the third a general with the inevitable *tabes dorsalis*, and on the fourth a snowstorm will be raging and shrieking. And conversely, when on the first page there is an armored train, I already can sense that on the second there will be a general with a gray handlebar mustache, on the third a snowstorm, and on the fourth again a Chinese.[17]

Writers were urged to turn their eyes to all society. Reviewers complained especially about a dearth of literature on the "new" countryside, the life of the Communist Party, the pre-Revolution underground movements, the mind of the fellow traveler, and, most seriously, the workers. But what would guarantee that contemporary reality, base and coarse as it often was, would be shown in such a way that the reader might not fall into sadness or confusion, but find himself uplifted and made whole? Presumably, the presence of a true "idea," which would put the material, how-

[16] The first quote is from "Literaturnye otkliki . . . ," p. 320, the second from "Na perevale," p. 317.

[17] Andrei Sobol', as quoted by A. Lezhnev, review of *Pisateli ob iskusstve i o sebe*, KN, No. 3 (1924), pp. 322-23.

ever lowly, into proper perspective: since the idea lodges even in the grossest matter, the artist need only record what is there. In this way, many of the controversial literary themes of the time would gain some respectability, at least in the eyes of *RVS*. Barbarism in the villages, bribe taking, rampant bureaucracy, flagrant thievery—all must be depicted in art because they existed in life; but, if presented properly, they would contrast with real reality, and thereby reveal themselves as only temporary phenomena.

The writers of the early twenties had all but dispensed with the hero as an organizing principle of fiction. But bigness, when applied to character, required that he should be at the center of the literary universe. It was therefore not surprising that the chief defect which *RVS* found in new writing from 1924 on was the failure to depict "the hero of our day, with complete fidelity to life and with artistic plausibility."[18] Most Marxists at the time—no doubt because of a common patrimony—considered a strong hero indispensable to good literature.[19] Here *RVS* and the Octobrists found themselves in agreement. But it was an agreement in principle only. For the Octobrists, the hero not only offered a convenient way of personifying and thereby "humanizing" the lesson that every work of literature should contain, but also stood as a model of enlightened social activism, a perfect amalgam of thought and deed, word and gesture. We meet him in countless specimens of proletarian literature in the twenties and later, of course, in the productions of socialist realism. Now, when Averbakh and his followers in the journal *On Literary Guard* disavowed this concept of the hero as too crude, and insisted instead on a "living man,"[20] they were really appropriating, virtually

[18] A. Voronskii, "Na perevale," p. 315.

[19] The "positive" hero as an intellectual and literary idea has been brilliantly treated by Rufus W. Mathewson, Jr., in *The Positive Hero in Russian Literature* (New York, 1958).

[20] Cf. Edward J. Brown, *The Proletarian Episode in Russian Literature* (New York, 1953), pp. 77-82.

intact, the idea of the hero that had already been worked out in *RVS*.

What in the cognition theory justified the reappearance of the hero, even made him essential? We must work by extrapolation, for no theory of the hero was elaborated there. Art, as the critics never tired of reminding their readers, is by definition a human activity. Man is the only creature capable of creating it; great human emotions form its very substance; and a human mind is the only means through which it can communicate. The cognition theory itself is built on an analogy to man's nature as mind, emotion, and action: both art and man are unique in their capacity to synthesize all three. Thus art ought to deal with human beings, who are best able to imitate its processes. Furthermore, from the assumption that each work of art holds a hard core of truth at its center, it is only a step to the assumption that a single character, a hero, most economically and effectively embodies that core, or, in other words, imitates the idea of the work of art in miniature. Then, history itself, an organic process, takes on flesh in the highest living organism, man, whose rich and contradictory nature alone can reflect the dialectic. Just as at any particular time in history one idea predominates, so in any work one personage predominates, for there are no conflicting truths, only conflicts of priority. Finally, if it is true, as Voronskii said, that "there is no genuine art without an intuitive probing into the unconscious sphere of human intentions and motives,"[21] then art must deal with the individual, human, psyche, the more complex the better.

The earliest characterizations of this new hero belong to the primitive phase of the cognition theory and therefore take no account of the "unconscious." Voronskii described him as "a fighter for social justice, a healthy, strong, disci-

[21] "Zametki o khudozhestvennom tvorchestve," *Iskusstvo videt' mir* (Moscow, 1928), p. 74. Original italics omitted.

plined man who is struggling for a new social structure,"[22] a sort of Russian American who performs prodigies of economic and social reconstruction, solves the riddles of the cosmos with science, and displaces the superfluous heroes of traditional Russian literature. In fact, his prototype is the Russian revolutionary here:

In this stormy time, we need, as never before, a special warrior, a special soldier of the age. He is always a warrior, always on watch. He is never demobilized, he never rests long or easily. He is always in the masses, with the masses. He is with them in the trenches, in the dugouts. He must develop in himself a scorn for death. His intimate, personal life should be so merged with the social that it is no hindrance at all in the camp life he must lead. He must carry only the minimum of personal belongings, but full military equipment . . . in the old society he ought to feel as if he were in an enemy camp, like a scout. He ought to be able to hate the old world as his personal enemy, he is always ready. He has no "home." . . .[23]

This leaf from the penny catechism of Marxism answered splendidly to the expectations of the ideologues who masqueraded as critics in *RVS* in the early twenties. It could well have aroused the envy of the staunchest On-Guardist too. But how much sense did it make to an accounting of the human—and literary—character that ran as follows?

Human character is made up of remote back roads; it is an impenetrable thicket, often murky and dark. In the human being lodge not one but many personalities, and they wage unrelenting war among themselves. One's age,

[22] "Polemicheskie zametki," *KN*, No. 3 (1924), p. 320.
[23] "Literaturnye siluety. Dem'yan Bednyi," *KN*, No. 6 (1924), p. 313.

a new situation in life, a new social milieu shatter our old mortal "I" at its roots, and it re-forms itself in an entirely new way. There is nothing finished, nothing static, the human psyche is unsteady, subject to all manner of vicissitudes.[24]

This was written in 1928 by the same man—Voronskii—and effectively summarized the views that had been current in the journal for the past three years. So much for the "naïvely rationalistic view of man's mind" that he himself had once propagated. He regretted that most of the young proletarian writers still honored it. Obviously they had not yet learned that "there is no need to paint the hero in one color, in order to show the social value of his attitudes and views." Actions, class position, job, ideology do not, Voronskii reminded them, sum up a man: he may be a Communist yet a scoundrel, a bourgeois yet an honorable individual.[25] Man is neither all mind nor all instinct, but combinations of both; it is literature's business to explore the combinations. The result, Voronskii thought, would almost certainly be a portrait of a deeply flawed, inconsistent, self-contradictory, bewildered personality, for the claims of the various selves compete. Writers who could not grasp this point were urged to study Tolstoi's method of constructing a world of "hidden, secret, unconscious intentions that man usually does not even suspect" beneath the world of "external actions and utterances."[26] Lezhnev suggested that the contemporary writer might explore such conflict by showing "how the proletarian world view, the new structure of feelings and practices [all lodged, presumably, in

[24] A. Voronskii, "Marsel' Prust. (K voprosu o psikhologii khudozhestvennogo tvorchestva)," *Iskusstvo videt' mir* (Moscow, 1928), pp. 156-57.
[25] "Staroe i novoe," *Prozhektor*, No. 7 (1927), pp. 20-21. The quote is from p. 21.
[26] *Ibid.*, p. 20.

the conscious mind] struggles inside man with the Ancient Adam of traditional habits, attitudes, tastes, with the deposits of centuries past that have clung to the proletariat, with the imprint left in his heart by the ruling classes. . . ."[27] Voronskii found the conflict most dramatically represented in what he considered the characteristic hero of the fellow travelers: the "superfluous man," who had found fulfillment in the irresponsibly adventuresome life of the Civil War, but could not adjust to the pedestrian realities of the NEP.[28] Every class, every social group, however, should contribute specimens of this new hero: although their origins would be different, the spiritual qualities of conflict and quest would be identical. Aleksandr Fadeev's novel *The Rout* (*Razgrom*) provided a virtually unique model, Voronskii thought, for what could be done in proletarian literature: the heroes were "intuitive" and "nonrationalistic"; their "intellect and conduct" were "subordinate to the subconscious principle in man"—so much so that in an ostensibly political work they cared nothing about politics, and did not even disclose their attitude toward the Bolsheviks.[29]

Lezhnev and Voronskii admitted that the writer working with "psychological realism" could, in his preoccupation with the mysterious sides of the mind, fall prey to morbidity or even perversity. He would do well to remember that conflict is "not absolute but relative," and, like the dialectic itself, must move forward and upward: the new man

[27] "O gruppe proletarskikh pisatelei 'Pereval,'" *KN*, No. 3 (1925), p. 262.

[28] "Puti i pereput'ya. (Po povodu poslednikh veshchei L. Seifullinoi)," *Prozhektor*, No. 22 (1927), pp. 20-21. Among the works that Voronskii mentions by way of example are Leonov's *The Thief* (*Vor*) and *The Badgers* (*Barsuki*), Aleksei Tolstoi's "Azure Cities" (*Golubye goroda*), and Loginov-Lesnyak's *Herds of the Steppe* (*Stepnye tabuny*), all of which appeared in *RVS*.

[29] "Staroe i novoe," pp. 20-21.

should be seen "forging ahead step by step, scraping off the deposits of the past, obliterating its traces."[30] That is why Voronskii, while admiring both Proust and Dostoevskii as masters of the inner mind, gave preference to the former as a writer who did not "torment the reader" by aimless wallowing in "psychology," but carried his heroes toward an insight, a resolution.[31] And when Voronskii warned that the "superfluous men" had run their course, he seemed to expect that their successors would be better adjusted: the ideal, after all, remained a harmony of all the selves. But he did not essay a description of these successors; and the time of happy harmony lay somewhere in the misty future of Communism. Writers meanwhile were obliged to show man as he was, "with all his almost agonizing disharmonies and contradictions, doubts and dislocations."[32] It was admittedly simpler and safer to create heroes who did and said all the right things; but they were neither convincing, nor realistic, nor heroic. "Psychological realism" was considered worth all the risks involved.

NOT THE least important meaning of "bigness" or "monumentalness" was the literal: physical dimension and moral grandeur. Herein lay much of the infecting power of art. The greater the size, the greater the intensity; the greater the intensity, the greater the infection; the greater the infection, the better the work. We are reminded of the neoclassical doctrine of the "simplicity of grandeur that fills the imagination," as Dr. Johnson described it, and the related idea of the sublime. Fyodor Zhits, in a metaphor very much like Longinus', pronounced *War and Peace* superior simply because it was bigger than any other piece of prose

[30] The first quote is from A. Voronskii, *ibid.*; the second from A. Lezhnev, "O gruppe proletarskikh pisatelei 'Pereval,'" p. 262.
[31] "Marsel' Prust . . . ," p. 157.
[32] A. Voronskii, "Pisatel', kniga, chitatel'," *KN*, No. 1 (1927), p. 231.

fiction. "From the point of view of formal mastery," he explained, "any ten-line miniature can be just as good as *War and Peace*; but in significance, in artistic and ideological (*ideinyi*) influence, there is as much difference between them as between a small stream with clear water and a mighty navigable river."[33] In the same spirit, D. Aranovich insisted that architecture was the only art capable of capturing and reproducing the spirit of the Revolution, because it was the most massive. Painting must be reckoned passé, because it could not "reproduce the epic structure of the revolutionary age of exceptionally large scales within the restricted 'golden' frame of the extremely conventional and flat surface of a two-dimensional canvas."[34]

A "monumental" view of literature tends to reorder genre in a radical way. In effect, it creates only two genres—the monumental, and the nonmonumental—to which the traditional genres are assigned according to size. No real distinctions are made among an epic poem, a novel, and a drama: all are deemed capable of expressing reality in a monumental manner. The quantitative difference between large and small implies, of course, a qualitative difference as well, which may be expressed in terms like "high" and "low." (*RVS* did not translate the value judgment into terminology, but it is there nonetheless.) The various components of the "big" or "high" genre come to be judged as

[33] Review of V. Shklovskii, *Teoriya prozy*, KN, No. 1 (1926), p. 268. Cf. Longinus, *On the Sublime*, trans. and ed. by W. Rhys Roberts (Cambridge, 1899), p. 134: "Wherefore not even the entire universe suffices for the thought and contemplation within the reach of the human mind, but our imaginations often pass beyond the bounds of space, and if we survey our life on every side and see how much more it everywhere abounds in what is striking, and great, and beautiful, we shall soon discern the purpose of our birth. This is why, by a sort of natural impulse, we admire not the small streams, useful and pellucid though they be, but the Nile, the Danube or the Rhine, and still more the Ocean."

[34] "Na put'yakh k sovremennoi skul'pture," KN, No. 7 (1927), p. 240.

virtually identical in structure, function, and purpose, and
are accorded the privileges of peerage. This seems to be
what K. Loks meant when he said that the epic poem and
the novel are both party to the "heroics of history," in
that we can "philosophize, quarrel, and reason" about
them, whereas for the lyric we must "listen, feel and keep
quiet."[35] "Smaller" or "lower" forms naturally occupy a far
more modest position in a system that is structured on size.
Aranovich, in an argument strikingly reminiscent of Pisarev's,
proposed that they should be junked entirely, or, at the
very least, altered radically. Painting, for example, would
be relegated to museums; sculpture would be limited to
bas-reliefs, which would add an "epic" sense to architecture, the "big" genre.[36] For literature, we can only speculate; nobody in *RVS* actually worked out a genre system
such as the one we have proposed, but it is clearly implied.
The smaller genres would presumably continue to fulfill
certain useful and practical functions that "big" literature
could not, and indeed must not, at the risk of enmeshing itself in particulars and falling into the pit of naturalism.
Ethnographical sketches, for example, might furnish documentary material on which novels and epic poems would
draw. The feuilleton and other light forms might help prepare the masses for more serious encounters with art. The
lyric poem might offset the inevitable aridities of awesome-
ness and sublimity.

Prose fiction was the preferred narrative medium, perhaps
because it best suggested the flow of life and appealed to the
largest audience, and also because it had been the glory of
nineteenth-century literature. Voronskii, in fact, regarded
an over-emphasis on poetry at the expense of prose as one
of the major weaknesses of proletarian literature. And of all

[35] Review of I. Sel'vinskii, *Ulyalaevshchina*, *KN*, No. 3 (1927),
p. 234.
[36] "Na put'yakh k sovremennoi skul'pture," p. 247. Cf. D. Pisarev,
"Razrushenie estetiki."

the genres of prose, the novel was taken as the one most worthy of a monumental literature. For one thing, it was, or could be, the bulkiest and most commodious, as *War and Peace* showed. The appearance of Konstantin Fedin's *Cities and Years* in 1924 evoked an audible sigh of relief from those critics who had gloomily remarked the reign of short forms and fretted about the lack of novels: there could be no doubt now that literature would revive, for bigness betokened an art's maturity and an age's magnificence. By 1926, Voronskii was noting with satisfaction that long works, in both prose and poetry, were the rule rather than the exception.[37]

More than sheer bulk was at issue, however, in the preference shown the novel. Lezhnev called for "an art which will be able to reproduce life in its uninterrupted development, in its becoming, an art which in the reality of today will be able to show the sprouts of what will be tomorrow, the kernels of what is to come, an art which will be capable of reproducing life in the constant renewing of its forms."[38] At the same time, this dialectical art was supposed to serve the purposes of "representativeness" (*izobrazhatel'nost'*), to create the feel of palpable reality that could be verified by one's ordinary senses and experiences. Surely the novel could best answer to this double view of experience, in its preoccupation with process and with what a recent critic has termed "coherent moral structure," unfolded through a leisurely yet purposeful time and space that are made convincingly concrete by a tissue of details.[39] Again, it was Tolstoi who pointed the way:

[37] "Pisatel', kniga, chitatel'," p. 227. For a review of Fedin's *Cities and Years* (*Goroda i gody*), cf. N. Belen'skii, *KN*, No. 5 (1925), p. 271.

[38] "Proletkul't i proletarskoe iskusstvo," *KN*, No. 3 (1924), p. 273.

[39] The recent critic is Ian Watt, *The Rise of the Novel* (Berkeley and Los Angeles, 1959), p. 117. Belinskii's views on the novel—a new genre whose importance he was the first to recognize, breaking

In a purely artistic [fictional] work of Tolstoi, everything is accomplished in time and space; there everything lives and everything dies. . . . Birth and death, good and evil, beauty and ugliness, joys and sorrows, all these and similar contradictory values appear not as *absolute, eternal forms* in the creations of our master of genius. They are not irreconcilable metaphysical entities, but, on the contrary, chains in a single, common, living, unbroken chain, where the qualitative value of each individual link is determined by quantitative relationships. . . . This, precisely, is the dialectical view of things, and at the same time, the most human view. . . . In other words, Tolstoi's work rests on experience, just like sci-

---

with the Hegelian view of drama as the supreme genre—bear a striking resemblance to those of *RVS*:

The novel and the tale have now taken the lead over all other genres of poetry [i.e., imaginative literature]. All of belles lettres is contained in them, so that beside them, any other work seems like an exception or an accident. The reasons for this lie in the very essence of the novel and the tale as genres of poetry. In them—in better and more convenient fashion than in any other genre of poetry—fiction mingles with reality, and artistic invention merges with simple albeit faithful copying from nature. The novel and the tale, even when they depict the most ordinary and hackneyed prose of the daily round, can be representative of the extreme limits of art, of the highest creative act; on the other hand, even when reflecting only the choice and lofty moments of life, they can be lacking any poetry at all, any art. . . . This is the broadest, most comprehensive genre of poetry; in it, talent feels itself limitlessly free. All the other genres of poetry come together in it—the lyrical, in the form of an outpouring of the author's feelings on the occasion of an event he is describing, the dramatic, as a sharper and more salient way of making the characters in question express themselves. Digressions, disquisitions, and moralizing, which are intolerable in other genres of poetry, can have a legitimate place in the novel and the tale. The novel and the tale give full scope to the writer as concerns the predominant traits of his talent, character, taste, turn of mind, etc. That is why there have been so many novelists and writers of tales in recent years.

("Vzglyad na russkuyu literaturu 1847 goda," *Polnoe sobranie sochinenii*, x [Moscow, 1956], 315-16.)

entific investigation. Following this strictly scientific method, Tolstoi was a realist in the genuine sense of the term.[40]

Such properties of the novel made it the perfect arena for the new hero; it simply did not occur to the critics to imagine one without the other. Boris Guber, for example, thought nothing of denying the name of "novel" to a new work because "there is no *hero* in the book, which is particularly noticeable in the abundance of characters that perform the same function as far as story goes."[41] The ideal novel they envisaged was what another age might have called a well-made work. The artist was expected to create "a single powerful, integral, harmonious picture" of life, symmetrical in all its parts.[42] The plot line must be strong enough to motivate the dialectical process that was being imitated. This was not plot in the sense that the Serapions and *LEF* and the Formalists understood it: superior because it could yield a clean, spare, almost pure form of art that focused ruthlessly on event and thereby excluded authorial incursions and "psychologizing." The literature *RVS* had in mind possessed precisely those qualities which others deprecated: a leisurely, even rambling narrative style; a sturdy sense of chronological time; involved plots with strong character portraiture; and an explicit moral orientation. The critics strongly disapproved of the unresolved endings which were favored by many contemporary writers and admired by the Serapions and the Formalists as imitations of "real," unstructured, and unestheticized life. That was one reason why Voronskii disparaged the work of Zamyatin: it made the "moment"

[40] L. I. Aksel'rod (Ortodoks), quoted by A. Voronskii, "Iskusstvo, kak poznanie zhizni, i sovremennost' (K voprosu o nashikh literaturnykh raznoglasiyakh)," *KN*, No. 5 (1923), p. 356.

[41] Review of M. Marich, *Severnoe siyanie, KN*, No. 11 (1926), p. 243.

[42] A. Voronskii, "Na perevale," *KN*, No. 6 (1923), p. 315.

(*mig*) of individual rebellion the central point of the typical story, but ended by reaffirming the inhuman and impersonal life against which this rebellion had been directed.[43] The same stricture applied to unresolved characterizations. Lezhnev criticized Boris Guber for breaking off his story "Sharashkin's Office" (Sharashkina kontora) at the structural climax, instead of following through to a "psychological culmination":

> Such endings were all right in Chekhov's time, when life developed on an even plane: the unexpectedness of an ending which was suddenly broken off was then only a purely external unexpectedness, an external effect of structure. We can take any slice of the life of a Chekhov hero and determine without any difficulty what its future course will be. This is not the case in our time, when the plane is broken up by lines of sudden change. To break the ending off *now* at a point of sudden change means in fact to present a fragment, something lacking an inner center, a culmination, an unfinished artistic organism.[44]

This insistence on denouement probably reflected a tendency to view the individual work of art as a living organism with its own life-cycle of growth, maturity, and death; it would be as false to art as to life to suggest that there is more. The reader must be carried through to the end of the life-cycle, and not left to grope for himself in an infinite or circular world; his innate sense of harmony demands a sounding of the tonic chord, in art as in life itself.

FOR RVS, then, the value of a work of art depended on two things: the intrinsic importance of the idea that was being imitated, and the fullness with which the work of art revealed this idea. Ideas either were or were not appropriate

---

[43] "Literaturnye siluety. Evg. Zamyatin," *KN*, No. 6 (1922), pp. 304-22.
[44] "Literaturnye zametki," *KN*, No. 7 (1925), p. 264.

to art: no degrees of appropriateness seemed to exist. That being the case, the burden fell upon the work itself; excellence was measured by the amount of reality that it accurately revealed. All sides of reality did not give equal scope to the ideas appropriate to art, but they had to be accounted for. All genres of art could reveal the idea with equal fullness, but the "monumental" ones offered the best likelihood of success.

This new idea of realism did away with the inclination to treat contemporary literature half-apologetically as a kind of Baedecker. At one time, political reports, sociological studies, economic surveys, ethnographical sketches, poems, short stories, and sketches had all been accepted as more or less equally valid sources of "information" about Soviet Russia. But now the line between belles lettres and other kinds of writing was again etched in and sharpened by changes in the structure of *RVS*. Articles on nonliterary topics and reviews of nonfiction dropped off and finally all but disappeared. The ethnographical and reportorial sketch, which had once cohabited comfortably with fiction, were now banished to the "Soil and Towns" department. An effort was made to restore the old literary genres —the novel and short story in particular—and to stock the first third of the journal with them. Criticism no longer aped the political tract, but now tried to identify and discuss the problems peculiar to literature.

· I I ·

By 1924, the critics knew pretty well what contemporary authors should be writing and what a journal like *RVS* should be printing. A program for literature had developed hand in hand with the cognition theory. Needed now was a criticism which would give that program authority; any journal that claims to be prescriptive—and a thick journal by nature makes that claim—must respond to such a need. But the cognition theory, especially as it developed the concept of "disinterestedness," put up some formidable obstacles. One was a tendency to move away from the work of art itself toward philosophy on the one hand and toward psychology on the other. Another was the "sincerity" doctrine which in effect sanctified any intention the writer might have and made criticism irrelevant. Still another was the inability, for reasons we have suggested, to give "form," "imagery," and "language" any rein at all. Nevertheless, the critics in *RVS* continued to insist that any discussion of the nature of literature must focus on the work of literature itself; otherwise no accounting could be made of that side of human experience—the "emotional"—which is knowable only through art. This being the case, the next question obviously had to be: *What* in the work of literature actually evokes the proper emotion, and how can it be shown to the writer so that he may employ it to achieve similar effects?

"Disinterestedness" at least specified the emotion particular to art. But in itself, it could not serve as a working rule for practical criticism. Esthetic needs, after all, are broader than art, and may satisfy themselves with a variety of objects that have nothing to do with art: X may derive as much pleasure from contemplating a gyroscope as Y does from contemplating a painting. Lezhnev suggested that all esthetic needs could be served by things that are also practical and useful, and he tried to define art as something made with a deliberately esthetic end. (One wonders what he would have said of Marcel Duchamp, who created "The Fountain" merely by appropriating a porcelain *pissoir*.) We quickly come face to face with the unshakable proposition *de gustibus*; but who is to say that tastes are not corrupt or perverted? "Disinterested" enjoyment can indicate that a work may have value as art, but it apparently cannot tell us what that value is or where it lies. To Kant, the recognition of this problem was the first step toward a solution of it in the trans-sense sphere. Neither Plekhanov nor Miss Aksel'rod could follow Kant, even though consistency de-

manded it, because they insisted that historical and social
factors must somehow figure into any accounting of the
experience of art. Predictably, Miss Aksel'rod criticized
Kant for making an "absolute essence" out of the capacity
of the esthetic object to evoke pleasure, and (in an argument reminiscent of Voronskii's against Freud), of turning
"individual, specific psychology into a metaphysical system
of transcendent value, devoid in essence of historical and
social roots."[45] Plekhanov tried to sociologize Kant, when
he wrote that disinterestedness is a matter of personal, not
social perception, and cannot therefore apply to social man;
yet *because* one has in mind social man, there is room for
Kant—that is to say, one may talk about the disinterested
contemplation of art. Perhaps this is Plekhanov's way of
trying to have his cake and eat it too; for the argument
could easily be pressed to mean either that criticism is
valueless, inasmuch as each act of appreciation is wholly
individual and therefore not measurable, or that criticism,
because it must take account of the "surrounding conditions" which supposedly shape art, cannot really be concerned with art as art. Plekhanov, however, would insist
on changing the "either-or" to "both-and": the experience of art is socially conditioned *and* disinterestedly appreciated.[46] Voronskii, as we saw, made the same distinction.

There is a strong suggestion here of a kind of criticism by
consensus. What is "good" at any time is what men judge to
be good. If that is so, then criticism becomes a study not so
much of individual works of art as of what people think
about them, and how they react to them. The sum of disinterested appreciations, so to speak, eventually establishes
a pattern. But one does not need to poll the reader, or even

<hr>

[45] "Voprosy iskusstva," *KN*, No. 6 (1926), p. 160.
[46] "Frantsuzskaya dramaticheskaya literatura i frantsuzskaya zhivopis' XVIII veka s tochki zreniya sotsiologii," *G. V. Plekhanov. Literatura i estetika*, I (Moscow, 1958), 100.

a mass of readers, to discover whether or not disinterested reactions are taking place and whether the works in question are therefore artistic. One needs only to look at the sum of disinterested appreciations, so to speak, as expressed in a judgment of taste at any given time. A book's popularity by itself, then, can give some indication that it is "artistic."

Clearly this is not a very satisfactory standard for contemporary works, where motives for enjoyment (expressed, perhaps, in the act of purchasing a book) may be anything but disinterested. But with works of proven appeal and durability, the case is easier. What has endured may be presumed to be infectious—that is, to bear within it that which is capable of producing disinterested reactions. What has endured the longest may be assumed to have the most universal appeal, to contain, in the parlance of the cognition theory, eternal emotions and artistic ideas. A standard of beauty, and of criticism, can thus be constructed from what man thinks is beautiful; and this standard, the sum of these works of literature, can be studied to find what it is that is likely to have caused infection. Voronskii's redefinition of art as a recapturing of immediate impressions does not go quite so far as to say that the older anything is the better it must be; but it does tell us that what we seek to make us whole lies in the past: for it is there that those impressions shine brightest, and we can bring them back through the art which is closest to them. The interest of the critic, then, falls not on the process of enjoying the work of literature, or even on the disinterested emotion itself, but rather on what is contained in the work of literature that should cause it to be enjoyed. Since enduringness counts most, it is the classics—works which, by definition, have endured—that must be studied to determine what in them continues, generation after generation, to depict and communicate the kind of emotion peculiar to art. On them are built standards of criticism and guides to writing.

· I I I ·

We come to the final link in that chain of logic forged by
the cognition theory in order to bind the Russian classical
writers to modern literature. The divorce of art from class
had made these writers acceptable, the concept of art as an
unrendible fabric had made them essential, and now the
needs of a practical criticism would make them supreme.

The classics always stood on the level of their age, and
many of them were clairvoyants and diviners of the future. They were deeply imbued with ideas (*ideinye*);
they were sympathetic to the best human ideals of their
time . . . the souls of the great artists "ached" not with a
spineless, boring, inert melancholy, but with that which
transforms life. . . . And therefore he [the writer] did not
create innocuous little fairy tales, did not let his thoughts
go gushing all over the paper, did not get hopelessly
mired in his material, did not dissipate himself in attention to petty details, did not narrate instructive and interesting events and anecdotes, but rather created monumental things, made gigantic generalizations, opened up
the broadest perspectives and horizons, made himself a
teacher of life, a preacher and a prophet; similarly he did
not bog down in sterile pigeonholing, in declarations or
proclamations, in sheer invention or in premeditated,
pompous tendentiousness. . . . The great gift of generalization, the wholeness of the creative process, the harmony of the work of art, the power of its influence on the
reader, were in direct and immediate dependence on the
degree to which the writer was permeated with the great
feelings, ideas and ideals of his age.[47]

One could hardly ask for a better summary of what Voronskii thought was wrong with the literature of his own
time, and how it should be put right. A writer had only to

[47] A. Voronskii, "Na perevale," *KN*, No. 6 (1923), pp. 318-19.

turn to the classics for models of the manner deemed appropriate to the new literature: Pushkin for the clarity, directness, and sweet simplicity that defined the new style; Tolstoi, as the novelist of novelists, for the dynamic of reality that throbbed beneath daily events, and for a ruthless honesty that stripped away the veils of artifice and falsehood. Making the necessary concessions to the modern reader in language, specific detail, and so on, the writer of the twenties was urged actually to "imitate" the classics, to strive for the monumental effect and the large vision, to cultivate the whole range of themes, genres, and forms that his illustrious predecessors had at their disposal, with special emphasis on the novel.[48]

Marxists take for granted the fundamental unity of a work of art: the "idea" that is present, if it is "true," exercises the almost magical power of pulling everything together. It would seem logical then to assume that if "content" determines "form," any changes in the first must bring changes in the second. And among Marxists, it was V. F. Friche who gave amplest illustration to just such an assumption. In his view, the history of a country unfolds as a succession of "styles" that shape economic relations, government, the arts. In seventeenth-century France, for instance:

> Political economy, an absolutist state, Cartesian philosophy, and classical poetry—these are merely the manifestations in various areas of seventeenth-century culture of a single style—the style of mercantilism, of a certain stage in the development of commercial capitalism, whose vehicles were the gentry that was engaged in commerce, the owners of large factories, the bourgeoisie of noble and merchant origin. The classical literary style, therefore, is merely one particular manifestation of

[48] The only major genre in which RVS took no interest was the drama, perhaps because it does not qualify as "literature" in the same sense as genres that are merely written.

those rationalistic forces which operated at the same time in philosophy and scientific thought, in the economic and political structure.[49]

It then becomes the task of the critic to determine the relationship of the various "poetic" styles to the various "economic" styles. Change occurs, Friche says, either in an evolutionary or revolutionary way—that is, either gradually or by leaps. Again, it is the "style" of the time that determines which tempo prevails:

The development of poetic forms proceeds by leaps in cases when radical displacements occur in production, or when one class replaces another, or, finally, when fundamental and radical changes occur in the psycho-ideology of a class as a result of external forces. The development of poetic forms proceeds, on the other hand, by means of partial changes "in an evolutionary way," when comparative stability prevails in the economic base, in the class structure, and in the psycho-ideology of the class, and when there is no place for really fundamental changes and dislocations.[50]

Friche's propositions—hauntingly reminiscent of Auguste Comte[51]—do allow for some complications and subtleties. For instance, they recognize that styles may be borrowed which do not conform to the underlying economic condi-

49 "Problema sotsiologii literaturnykh stilei," *Problemy literaturovedeniya* (2d ed.; Moscow-Leningrad, 1931), p. 112.
50 *Ibid.*, p. 120.
51 Within each stage of human development (theological, metaphysical, and scientific or positivistic) Comte posited the existence of a basic trend of thought from which the political and, in turn, the cultural regimes took their form. For instance, the theological stage broke down into: Scholastic Theology (reaching its height in Aquinas); Theocracy (of the Middle Ages); and, culturally, Feudalism, with the appropriate forms of social and economic life, and Christian art and architecture. (According to the summary in Edmund H. Ziegelmeyer, "August Comte and Positivism," *The Modern Schoolman*, xx, No. 1 [November 1942], 11-12.)

tions,[52] and that writers of different class psychologies may be at work in a single stylistic period of history. But the one question that Friche does not touch upon arises naturally in the mind of any historian of literature: how can we explain the fact that certain forms, such as the sonnet, the short story, the tragedy, seem to defy the succession of styles and continue to cast their spell on writers and readers over a span of many generations? Or, put another way, can a Marxist assume—as Voronskii did—that the literature of one age can simply clothe itself in the forms of another, quite different age? The point seems not to have bothered Friche at all; but it has bothered some Marxists. Georg Lukács, for one, thinks that each genre has an idea peculiar to it, though all of them are reflexes presumably of the dominant idea of the time. The tragedy and the epic, for example, depend respectively on a sense of fate and a sense of

[52] Cf. Plekhanov's observation that the culture of a country may, through importation, run well ahead of the economic and social situation, as in Russia of the early nineteenth century:

In Russia capitalism has not yet completely gained the upper hand over the old order. But Russian literature, ever since the time of Peter the Great, has been under the very strong influence of Western European literatures. Therefore it has frequently been penetrated by influences which, though fully corresponding to Western European social relationships, correspond much less to the comparatively backward social relationships in Russia. There was a time when certain of our aristocrats were infatuated with the teaching of the Encyclopedists, which corresponded to one of the final phases of the third estate's struggle with the aristocracy in France. Now a time has come when many of our "intellectuals" are infatuated with social, philosophical and esthetic teachings that correspond to the period of the decay of the Western European bourgeoisie. This infatuation anticipates the course of our own social development in just the same way as did the infatuation of the people of the eighteenth century with the theory of the Encyclopedists.

(*Iskusstvo i obshchestvennaya zhizn'*, in *G. V. Plekhanov. Literatura i estetika*, I [Moscow, 1958], 175-76, translated as *Art and Social Life* [Moscow, 1957].) Unfortunately, Plekhanov carries this interesting observation no further.

harmony with nature in a closed universe. But those ideas, Lukács argues, are no longer viable, and the tragedy and the epic, like all the traditional genres, are therefore outmoded and must be discarded.[53] Among Soviet Marxists, it remained for the Octobrists and *LEF* to carry this line of thinking out to its ruthlessly obvious conclusion:

> all existing literary forms have arisen as a way of communicating a content which should answer to the ideology of a given class in a given period. All of them have social roots which are profoundly different from the social roots of the poetry of the working class. For that reason, not one of them is a form that is suitable for proletarian literature.[54]

They therefore argued that Soviet literature could no more adopt the forms than the ideas of classical literature. All old forms, the novel in particular, must be discarded, and forms worthy of the new ideas that animate the proletarian cause somehow found. Just how this would be done, they did not suggest. Nor did they seem embarrassed by the fact that some of the better proletarian writers had started turning out short stories that bore the stamp of tradition.

Most Russian Marxists have been too bedazzled by the nineteenth century to follow logic this far. Yet they have not succeeded in devising an alternative theory that would account for the apparent disparity between changing ideas and virtually unchanging forms. The problem remains unsolved. In *RVS*, however, we can discern the dim outlines of a concept of literary change that straddles this disparity while allowing all the traditional genres to be kept. This concept always remained an unspoken assumption; but

[53] *Die Theorie des Romans. Ein geschichtsphilosophischer Versuch über die Formen der Grossen Epik* (2d ed.; Berlin-Spandau, 1963).

[54] G. Lelevich, "Otkazyvaemsya li my ot nasledstva?" *Na postu*, No. 2-3 (1923), p. 55.

there are enough clues to allow us to suggest what it might
have looked like had it been articulated.

We can take as our point of departure an exchange between Viktor Blyumenfel'd and A. Lezhnev concerning the
nature of the lyric poem. Blyumenfel'd, writing in the proletarian journal *The Furnace* (*Gorn*), insisted that all the
traditional verse forms must be abolished, particularly the
lyric, which arises from individualism and religiosity, expresses the illogical, instinctive sides of man, and can therefore offer nothing of value to a new culture built on
collectivism, optimism, and reason.[55] Lezhnev objected.
"Every form," he wrote, "is *relative*, and the lyric poetry of
the Greeks is just as real as decadent lyric poetry. And
from the proletariat's point of view, the lyric poetry of the
Greeks will perhaps prove more real than the 'decadent.' "[56]
Lezhnev's meaning is unclear, probably because he is using
—or so it seems—the word "form" in two different senses
simultaneously. One refers to the specifics of language,
style, and imagery that depend on time, place, and national
culture, and therefore differ from work to work, country to
country, generation to generation: they are "relative." The
other refers to that aspect of form which makes the novel
a novel, the epic an epic, the lyric a lyric. It is what is
usually called "genre"; for Lezhnev it presumably depends
on a point of view or idea that is not subject to the erosions
of time or the quirks of topicality, and can therefore transcend the barriers of language and social structure, speaking
as plainly to the Russian proletarian as to the ancient Greek
slave-holder: it is not "relative." The seeming paradox of
unchanging change is explained by the operation of these
two orders of form within the same work; and these two
orders, in turn, correspond to the two orders of reality distinguished by the cognition theory: the palpably, physically

[55] "K iskusstvu slova. Obshcheizvestnoe v primenenii k stikhotvornoi
forme," *Gorn*, No. 9 (1923), pp. 89-106.
[56] "Proletkul't i proletarskoe iskusstvo," *KN*, No. 3 (1924), p. 271.

real, which does change according to time and place, and the really real, which does not change. Presumably it was the first kind of form that Voronskii had in mind when he insisted that the writer must "update" the imagery of his work without altering the essential characteristics of the genre; after all, the "world" we see before us changes constantly without working essential changes on the real world beyond it.

Genres do, however, go in and out of style. Certain ones predominate at certain times, like the epic in early Greece, or the novel in eighteenth-century England. The Marxist, like Lukács, who assigns a specific idea to each genre encounters no great problem in explaining this: a change in idea automatically brings about a change in the genre that reflects it. But *RVS*, as far as one can determine from scattered and scanty evidence, made no such assumption. Rather, it took for granted that each work of art imitates, more or less adequately, the same eternal world of ideas. That being so, what matters is how much of that world any given genre takes in. Certain ideas and techniques are considered "false," not so much for themselves as because they block access to the reality with which art ought to be concerned. The question: "How good is a work of art?" depends on the answer to the question: "How commodious is it?"

With size the criterion of excellence, preference automatically goes to the larger genres, such as the novel. But even smaller genres are accorded a certain respect. Presumably this is so because no single genre can reveal all of reality: we need the smaller ones as supplements, to provide us with pictures of things for which the larger ones, in their grandeur, have no space. If we have correctly stated the tacit line of argument that runs through *RVS*, then we see suggested here a kind of great chain of genres, with the novel standing at the top, and the brief nonfictional fragment, let us say, at the bottom. Each move up the chain opens a larger vista of reality; and the chain, in its entirety, gives us as nearly complete a view of reality as possible. If art is an imitation of reality, then it should, in the totality composed of all the individual works of art ever created, imitate nearly all of reality. Such an assumption encourages the proliferation of genres and also operates to preserve those already in currency: the more representations of reality we have, the better.

RVS took for granted that the predominance of larger forms at any particular period in history betokens the existence of a mature literature. Such was the nineteenth century, despite political and social backwardness. Surely Soviet literature ought to display at least as much maturity, particularly since it was developing in an enlightened political atmosphere. As of the mid-twenties, however, small forms were still the rule. Voronskii could therefore assert that "for our age . . . Gogol', Tolstoi, Pushkin, Chekhov, Maupassant, Anatole France, Balzac, and others, will suffice"; and he could go on to argue that his summons to "return" to the classics was not reactionary, as the Octobrists charged, but "progressive"—a call "forward to the classics, to Gogol', to Tolstoi, to Shchedrin,"[57] to the vital stream of Russian literature.

Russian classical literature, then, commended itself to young writers, not merely because its endurance proved its infecting power, but because its mastery of the novel proved maturity. Surely Soviet literature could aim no lower. It became a commonplace of criticism in *RVS* to measure a contemporary writer by appropriate predecessors: the closer the kinship, the better the writer. Thus, Voronskii made Tolstoi directly responsible for the "physiological" strain in Soviet prose—the celebration of flesh, blood, love, death, sex; presented Seifullina as a continuation of the "village" tradition of the Populist writers, of

[57] "Na perevale," p. 316.

Bunin, Turgenev and others; tied Babel' with Maupassant, Chekhov, and Gor'kii (standing for skepticism, sadness, and romanticism, respectively); and compared *Red Cavalry* at some length to *War and Peace*.[58] He spilled much ink over a pedigree for Dem'yan Bednyi, in an effort to prove that he was a serious poet, something people had doubts about even then. "Aesop, Pushkin, Nekrasov, Krylov," Voronskii declared, "to them Dem'yan is related to the same degree as he is to popular collectivism, to the anonymous creator of *chastushki*, songs and tales." Bednyi's diction touched the springs of the "Pushkinian folk simplicity" that had been subverted in the age of decadence but again "freed" by the Revolution. Voronskii also discovered in Bednyi's favorite characters a dependence on the classics; though their "skin" be new, their "heart" is the same: "We meet them in Nekrasov, in Uspenskii, in Shchedrin, in Korolenko, and elsewhere. They are our old friends in Russian literature." The populist streak in Bednyi's work carried on the best traditions of classical literature, as did his "civic-mindedness." By the time Voronskii had finished, the reader had reviewed Russian literature, and had grasped the point.[59]

The Soviet writer, when confronting the classics, supposedly had many things in his favor—among them a superior ideological foundation and a society that was sympathetic to his efforts. He was expected to press these advantages in order to rise above his predecessors and to discover new artistic truths. V. Pravdukhin thought that Fadeev had "overcome" Tolstoi by tying the inner world of his characters in *The Rout* to their class backgrounds.[60]

[58] "Literaturnye siluety. I. I. Babel'. II. L. Seifullina," *KN*, No. 5 (1924), pp. 284ff.

[59] "Literaturnye siluety. Dem'yan Bednyi," *KN*, No. 6 (1924). All quotes are from p. 326. *Chastushki* are rhymed quatrains, humorous and ironic.

[60] "Molodoe vino," *KN*, No. 5 (1927), p. 239.

Seifullina's writings on village life were deemed richer and more realistic than anything in the long history of the village genre.[61] Bednyi, when set against the tradition of Russian civic poetry, stood out as the most civic-minded, and, when considered as a writer of fables, outshone the master fabulist himself:

> The fables of Krylov lack great social content; they are of a narrow, everyday character. The fables of Dem'yan are a sharp stiletto with which he inflicts blow after blow on the vicious class enemy. It is a thoroughly social fable.[62]

By 1924, critics detected signs that literature was turning more "classical," more "monumental." The poets—particularly Esenin, Kazin, and some of the Octobrists—seemed to be refurbishing their styles in a manner that looked very Pushkinian, with a new emphasis on simple, straightforward diction. "Ornamentalism" now looked like the last refuge of a few die-hard eccentrics: the hated "Belyi" influence had begun to fade. Larger works were making an appearance; the novel was reviving; ethical and moral problems were reentering literature.

But who could say that anyone was writing as well as Pushkin? Or that any satirist could match Shchedrin? Or that any novelist could rival Tolstoi? Fadeev might have "overcome" Tolstoi in one aspect of characterization, but, as Pravdukhin was forced to admit, his failure to create full-blooded characters, characters that really seemed to breathe and move, gave ample evidence that he had not approached the most rudimentary "imitation" of Tolstoi's technique.[63] It became increasingly apparent to the reviewers for *RVS* that in everything that really mattered

---

[61] A. Voronskii, "Literaturnye siluety. I. I. Babel'. II. L. Seifullina," pp. 295-96.

[62] A. Voronskii, "Literaturnye siluety. Dem'yan Bednyi," p. 320.

[63] "Molodoe vino," p. 241.

in a work of literature Soviet writers lagged far behind their predecessors.

Part of the reason for the normally optimistic Voronskii's growing disillusionment with contemporary literature was precisely a quickening sense of its failure to measure up to the classics. He had expected progress to be at least palpable, if not dramatic, but he was now swinging to the conclusion that he had underestimated the obstacles that the new literature must overcome. The most serious of them, he thought, was the graphomania of raw proletarian youths —particularly the so-called "worker-correspondents" (*rabkory*).[64] He sharply revised his opinion of the established proletarian writers too: scarcely seven months passed between his enthusiastic endorsement of the work of Libedinskii, Bezymenskii, and Tarasov-Rodionov, and his flat pronouncement that they all lacked talent.[65] His disillusionment eventually touched even the fellow travelers. Though competent—certainly of classical stature beside the proletarians—they began to bore him. By 1927, he felt that he could virtually predict what they would say next. It seemed clear to him that no writer of the present generation could do much "overcoming." Patient resignation ensued.

And how much sense did it make, after all, to expect "overcoming" in the light of those attitudes toward the past that *RVS* had worked out? The Soviet writer was constantly reminded that innovation "is legitimate only to the degree that the artist masters what has been done before him."[66] Yet the universals which inspired the nineteenth-century writer still had vitality: "those things in the art of the past which seem to be a stage already overcome, actually

---

[64] "Khudozhestvennaya literatura i rabkory," *KN*, No. 3 (1926), pp. 229-35.

[65] "O proletarskom iskusstve i o khudozhestvennoi politike nashei partii," *KN*, No. 7 (1923), pp. 257-76; "O gruppe pisatelei 'Oktyabr'' i 'Molodaya gvardiya,'" *KN*, No. 2 (1924), p. 293.

[66] "O proletarskom iskusstve . . . ," p. 262.

exist and are perceived as new truths, as discoveries," because they are viewed in new conditions. Therefore, the characters of Gogol's *Dead Souls*—Chichikov, Nozdryov, Sobakevich, Plyushkin—"to this very day . . . have a universal significance, not a narrowly historical or a limited ethnographical one."[67] The point was proved by the continued appeal—the infectiousness—of Gogol' and of the other classical writers. Since no Soviet writer could claim as much, he must humbly try to pry out their secrets. The concepts of "objective value" and "organicism" had all but erased the lines between past and present anyway, and made the classical writers and the Soviets contemporaries. A judgment, even an opinion, passed upon a classical writer turned almost automatically into an admonition for his twentieth-century colleague.

Even the circuits of communication with the masses—an unwaivable proposition for all Marxists, whatever their other differences may be—were routed through the classics. The critics in *RVS* assumed that the ideal reader—who was, of course, the "mass reader from the lower classes"[68]—took the Russian classics as his norm of good literature, not only because they reflected his own ideals best, but because Lunacharskii had seen to it that they dominated the school curriculum and circulated in cheap editions. Voronskii constantly reminded the writers that literature from the Symbolists onward had been the concern of a tiny group of writers whom the "average" reader neither could nor would understand.[69] The *ergo* was not hard to make. Put another way, a demand to return to the classics was at the same time

---

[67] The first quote is from A. Voronskii, "Iskusstvo, kak poznanie . . . ," *KN*, No. 5 (1923), p. 382; the second is from A. Voronskii, "O proletarskom iskusstve . . . ," p. 261.

[68] A. Voronskii, "Literaturnye siluety. Vsev. Ivanov," *KN*, No. 5 (1922), p. 274.

[69] A. Voronskii, "Literaturnye siluety. I. I. Babel'. II. L. Seifullina," pp. 276-77.

a demand that literature must respond to the command of the masses. Thus contact between literature and the reader could once again be established, and the points of contact would presumably be broadened by further educating the masses—and the writers—in classical literature. Literature would thus become accessible and communicative, and the reader could function as a true co-creator, inasmuch as he and the writer would be thinking in the same tradition.

There is a very revealing passage in Voronskii's last collection of articles which shows how far the identification of criticism and literary scholarship had gone to make the new writer dependent on his predecessors.

The attitude of both Tolstoi and Dostoevskii toward the unconscious requires, from our point of view, very substantial corrections. For Tolstoi, only the unconscious is a creative force; he does not trust reason. . . . For Dostoevskii, on the contrary, the unconscious is a diabolical, destructive, ruinous principle. . . . In conformity with the attitude and outlook of a new, ascending class, in conformity with the most recent discoveries in the field of psychology, our artists—whether they are depicting social life and events or analyzing the soul-states of indivual man—are obliged, each in his own way, to throw light on the problem of the interrelationships of the conscious and the unconscious. Once they have thoroughly grasped and assimilated the artistic discoveries of Tolstoi, Dostoevskii and other masters of the word, they must be able to show the ways in which the contradictions between the conscious and unconscious are relative and conditional, to *limit Dostoevskii's pessimism with Tolstoi and to adjust Tolstoi's optimism with Dostoevskii*. Only then shall we be able to "overcome" the old classics and move on ahead.[70]

[70] "O khudozhestvennoi pravde," *Iskusstvo videt' mir* (Moscow, 1928), pp. 27-28. (Italics supplied.)

The classics, that is to say, will be overcome by—the classics. What Dr. Johnson saw as the writer's misfortune—being born too late[71]—Voronskii's followers came to see as his advantage.

Such an attitude poses great dangers to the vitality of a literature. Lezhnev's testy observation that just because Bal'mont wrote decadent poetry one could not conclude that Pushkin's lyrics were also decadent may or may not be true; what matters is his shock and outrage that anyone should presume to speak of the two poets in the same breath.[72] With the standards of criticism oriented on the past, there was an inclination in RVS to assume that the classics were better just because they were classics. Innovation, except in matters of detail, tended to excite suspicion: who was the Soviet writer, unproven by the test of infectiousness, to claim superiority in essentials to his nineteenth-century predecessors? The talk about the "new" novel and the "new" lyric seemed increasingly to point to the "classical" novel and the "traditional" lyric, with the details brought up to date. Under socialist realism, this respect for the past has turned into totemism. What the classics were originally invoked to elevate—standards of criticism and writing—they have helped to crush; for who can question authority? Perhaps this is the real reason why Marxist scholarship on the nineteenth-century writers, with

[71] Johnson writes, in *The Rambler*, No. 36:

I am afraid it will not be found easy to improve the pastorals of antiquity, by any great additions or diversifications. Our descriptions may indeed differ from those of Virgil, as an English from an Italian summer, and, in some respects, as modern from ancient life; but as nature is, in both countries nearly the same, and as poetry has to do rather with the passions of men, which are uniform, than their customs, which are changeable, the varieties, which time or place can furnish, will be inconsiderable. . . .

[72] "Proletkul't i proletarskoe iskusstvo," *KN*, No. 2 (1924), pp. 274-81.

very few exceptions, has been so inconclusive and vague. It was *RVS*, with every good intention, that set up the shrines and worked out the rituals of worship. What began as liberation from the tyranny of the present ended, with socialist realism, in enslavement to the past.

· I V ·

Early in the 1920's it became obvious that under the broad canopy of Marxism luxuriated a great variety of art theories and approaches to criticism. Literature might serve as the point of departure for a study of social history, as with critics like L'vov-Rogachevskii or Kogan. It might be made, as with V. F. Friche, an expression of the "mind" of a given period, whose contours are fashioned by economic relationships. "Sociography," as practiced by G. Zalkind, derived the characteristics of a writer's style from a detailed study of his ancestry, his life, his times, and his immediate physical milieu.[73] B. Arvatov assumed that the work of literature was shaped by the writer's economic relations with society, such as the amount of money he could earn from his pen.[74] M. Levidov proceeded from the

[73] Cf. G. Zalkind, *G. P. Kamenev (1772-1803) (Opyt imushchestvennoi kharakteristiki pervogo russkogo romantika)* (Kazan', 1926). He scrutinizes the portraits of the poet's ancestors for evidence of the genesis of his "dreamy" nature, and makes detailed lists of the objects in Kamenev's household, finding there objects typical of the milieu of both the merchant and the nobleman. From that he concludes that Kamenev was really more a merchant than a nobleman, and that this fact, in turn, produced emotional conflict in him and was the cause of his romantically melancholy cast of mind. The term "sociography" is applied to Zalkind's method by U. Fokht, "Problematika sovremennoi marksistskoi istorii literatury," *Pechat' i revolyutsiya*, No. 1 (1927), pp. 68-69.

[74] "Utilitarizm v literature," *Oktyabr'*, No. 12 (1925), pp. 100-06. Cf. also B. Eikhenbaum, "Literatura i pisatel'," *Zvezda*, No. 5 (1927), and T. Grits, V. Trenin, M. Nikitin, *Slovesnost' i kommertsiya (Knizhnaya lavka A. F. Smirdina)*, ed. V. B. Shklovskii and B. M. Eikhenbaum (Moscow, 1929).

"commands" that the writer receives from the public.[75] Others saw works of art as useful artifacts, neither better nor worse than rugs, steam shovels, or flatirons.[76] A concept of art as the expression of a life-force enjoyed some vogue for a time.[77] Many other theories also invested themselves with the mantle of Marxism.[78]

No doubt Voronskii was shocked to discover—as he soon did—that such variety existed, and that it could provoke violent disagreement. Yet, like virtually all Marxists, he took it for granted that somewhere there existed a grand esthetic that would absorb the warring theories and under-write a technique of practical criticism which all could use. Indeed, he had to make such an assumption. For Marxism abhors the fragment. It must explain everything in terms of a central illuminating truth—i.e., despecify phenomena—while accounting for the separate existence of the components of that truth—i.e., specify phenomena. As Bukharin defined the problem:

> You can isolate any phenomenon of social life you like, any fragment or series (*ryad*), but if in this fragment, in this phenomenon or in a complex of phenomena you do not see its life-function, that is, if you do not re-

[75] "Samoubiistvo literatury," *Proletariat i revolyutsiya* (Leningrad, 1925), pp. 160-69.

[76] B. Arvatov, *Iskusstvo i proizvodstvo* (Moscow, 1926).

[77] A. V. Lunacharskii, *Osnovy pozitivnoi estetiki* (Moscow, 1923).

[78] For a good discussion, from a Marxist (Pereverzev) point of view, of the various methodologies of literary study, cf. U. Fokht, "Problematika sovremennoi marksistskoi istorii literatury," *Pechat' i revolyutsiya*, No. 1 (1927), pp. 61-72, and the continuation in No. 2 (1927), pp. 78-92. For a brief account of the nineteenth-century background, with which Fokht deals very little, cf. P. N. Sakulin, "K problematike sovremennogo literaturovedeniya," *Pechat' i revolyutsiya*, No. 8 (1926), pp. 75-79. For an excellent annotated bibliography of the various currents in theory and criticism, cf. A. Voznesenskij, "Die Methodologie der russischen Literaturforschung in den Jahren 1910-1925," *Zeitschrift für slavische Philologie*, IV (1927), 145-62; V (1929), 175-99.

gard it as a certain organic part of a *social whole*, if you do not regard it from the point of view of this social whole, then you will never understand these phenomena.[79]

The difficulty, as nearly all serious Marxist thinkers have been forced to concede, is that areas of human experience exist which do not lend themselves to "social" explanations. Among these are the emotions that seem universal: the impulse to religion, to beauty, and so on. One solution has been to write these off as "inborn" and therefore outside the purview of Marxism. Like any Prime Mover argument, this begs the question; but many Marxists have used it (notably Plekhanov) and have even gone as far as to grant that the products of such impulses, among them art, lie to some extent outside the competence of Marxism. The other solution has been to limit human experience to what Marxism can handle. This we see in the On-Guardist concept of art as a class product, and later in some extreme versions of socialist realism, which admit, for example, that man does carry mysterious and murky impulses within him, but insist that, since such impulses are un-Marxist, they can find no place in art. Either solution has obvious weaknesses: the first undermines the claims of a "total" science, the second patently contradicts experience. *RVS* attempted to strike a balance, by suggesting a distinction between art as it is and art as men think it is—the first standing outside history and society, the second being a product of history and society. Perhaps this is, in fact, the only solution; but it rather inconveniently leaves the most essential part of art untouched by the most essential concerns of Marxism.

A SIMILAR problem arises with regard to criticism: it should account for the specific nature of art, while remaining sociological, that is, nonspecified. Christopher Caudwell has put the matter well:

[79] "O formal'nom metode v iskusstve," *KN*, No. 3 (1925), p. 255.

physics, anthropology, biology, philosophy, and psychology are also products of society, and therefore a sound sociology would enable the art critic to employ criteria from these fields without falling into eclecticism or confusing art with psychology or politics. There is only one sound sociology which lays bare the general active relations of the ideological products of society with each other and with concrete living—historical materialism.[80]

Marxists have located art's specific nature variously; but any serious accounting of it, for the purposes of criticism, comes back ever and again to craftsmanship, or "form." So the experience of *RVS* showed: art was defined as a special kind of emotion, yet this emotion could be known only through the forms of art. And in erecting a world of literary models that would provide standards and norms for writers and critics, *RVS* moved slowly toward overcoming a major weakness of Marxism: the inability to account for "form" in any usable way. This world of literature, however, lay almost entirely outside the purview of sociology. As in the process of creating and experiencing art, so too in the act of criticism two motions were being distinguished and set quite perceptibly apart: the descriptive (esthetic), and, following upon it, the sociological.

This meant in effect that Marxism must relinquish its claim to being *the* method of criticism, and take a more modest place as merely one of several possible methods. For instance, Piksanov's *Two Centuries of Russian Literature* (*Dva veka russkoi literatury*) advocated a number of different critical methods on the ground that literature is a complex phenomenon. Sakulin's monumental *Science of Literature: Its Results and Perspectives* (*Nauka o literature, eyo itogi i perspektivy*) proposed that Marxism would ultimately form but one part of some towering synthesis.

[80] *Illusion and Reality: A Study of the Sources of Poetry* (London, 1955), pp. 11-12.

RVS, despite what it practiced, refused to acknowledge such conclusions in principle, insisting that there could be only a single method—a "Marxist" method—and that somehow these two apparently separate motions of the critical act must be linked, if not merged.[81] The solution, for *RVS*, lay in seeing the act of criticism as a series of steps, all of which must be taken before a complete evaluation could result. As Gennadii Pospelov explained it: since the problem of criticism is basically a problem of literary scholarship, of discovering wherein lies the infecting power of great art, we must then proceed in three stages: (1) the collection, classification, and description of material; (2) the discovery and statement of the laws of the appearance and change of literary phenomena (3) the explanation and interpretation of the literary phenomena of the past and present, and a forecast of literature's future directions. Of immediate urgency, as he saw it, was collection and classification. This would involve a detailed analysis beginning with "form," in order to establish literary movements and schools according to thematics, stylistics, and devices of composition, with the aim of determining what has "worked" in the past, thereby giving the critic some basis for deciding what is "artistic" in contemporary literature.[82]

Pospelov's idea—the basically simple one of distinguishing description and interpretation in the act of criticism—had occurred to other Marxists as well. It was regarded as a promising solution to the admittedly vexing problem of how to be at once specific and sociological. It also seemed to offer a practical method of bridging the gap that separated the two major approaches to literature in the 1920's:

[81] A. Glagolev, review of N. K. Piksanov, *Dva veka russkoi literatury*, *KN*, No. 4 (1925), pp. 297-98; G. Pospelov, review of P. N. Sakulin, *Sotsiologicheskii metod v literaturovedenii*, *KN*, No. 10 (1925), pp. 288-90, and of *Sinteticheskoe postroenie istorii literatury*, *KN*, No. 3 (1926), pp. 265-66: these were two of the projected fifteen volumes.

[82] "K probleme formy i soderzhaniya," *KN*, No. 5 (1925), p. 260.

Formalism, and various reflexes of sociology. The Formalists objected to any approach, including the Marxist, which went outside literature itself for an explanation of literary phenomena, or, in the jargon, turned a question of literary evolution (the intrinsic development of literature) into a question of literary genesis (the influence of extrinsic factors like sociology and psychology).[83] The Marxists, in turn, argued that Formalism was not a method at all, but only a technique, and therefore unworthy of meeting on equal ground with a fully scientific explanation of life and art. But the way to compromise had been opened. LEF had attempted to meld Proletkul't theories with a concept of language renewal and "estrangement" that came from Futurism but had been taken up by the Formalists as well. Eikhenbaum himself observed that points of contact existed between Formalism and Marxism "inasmuch as both these systems deal with the fact of [literary] evolution."[84] And as early as 1923, A. Tseitlin laid down the lines along which the accommodation would finally be made: pointing out that the sociological implications of literary facts could not be discussed until the facts themselves had been established, he suggested that Formalism should make the necessary ordering of the facts, and Marxism the interpretation.[85] This came to be known as the "formal-sociological" method, and enjoyed a great vogue in the later twenties. Many Marxists took it up. The Formalists themselves had been moving toward a recognition of social influences on literature,[86] and now many of them became

[83] This for them was an illegitimate attempt to explain the phenomena of one "series" (literature) in terms of another (sociology, psychology, etc.). Cf. Yu. Tynyanov, "O literaturnoi evolyutsii," *Arkhaisty i novatory* (Leningrad, 1929), p. 45.

[84] "Vokrug voprosa o 'formalistakh,'" *Pechat' i revolyutsiya*, No. 5 (1924), p. 9.

[85] "Marksisty i formal'nyi metod," *LEF*, No. 3 (1923), pp. 114-31.

[86] Cf. Yu. Tynyanov and R. Yakobson, "Problemy izucheniya literatury i yazyka," *Novyi LEF*, No. 12 (1928), pp. 36-37. The authors

more "sociological" than the Marxists themselves, especially as Formalism came more and more to be identified with political heresy.[87] But the formal-sociological method did not work. For one thing, as Ul'rikh Fokht, a disciple of Pereverzev, pointed out, each "side" really constituted a distinct method in itself, not a single "organic" or "eidological" (*eidologicheskii*) method that united two different approaches.[88] In practice, people emphasized one side or the other: the result was a great variety of criticism under one banner, ranging from the virtually pure formalism of those who, like Tseitlin or Sretinskii, made "interpretation" the task of an indefinably remote future, to those who continued to study "content" and "ideas" while regarding form as a less important concern. For another thing, many more "methods" are involved here than Fokht imagined: "description" alone requires an almost limitless number. Furthermore, generations must pass before the act of description envisaged by Pospelov could approach a reasonable state of completion. Would Marxism, however, be content to withhold evaluation until all the evidence was in, and even be prepared, as a genuine science must, to alter its premises accordingly? The answer seems to be self-evident: Marxism is too aggressive a view of life for that.

---

state that the immanent laws of literary history allow us to characterize changes, but do not explain either the tempo of change or the reasons why certain evolutionary directions are chosen. Only an analysis of the differences between literature and other historical phenomena can do that.

[87] Viktor Shklovskii, for example, granted Formalism a minimal usefulness in the same terms Marxists had been using throughout the twenties: it could help with terminology and "technical" matters, but Marxism was the only acceptable "method." Cf. "Pamyatnik nauchnoi oshibki," *Literaturnaya gazeta*, No. 4, January 27, 1930, p. 1.

[88] "Problematika sovremennoi marksistskoi istorii literatury," *Pechat' i revolyutsiya*, No. 2 (1927), p. 90. This was a stock argument of the Pereverzev school.

Finally, in its own critical practice, *RVS* had demonstrated that the very act of establishing norms is in itself an act of evaluation, and that the "sociology" which is supposed to follow on it really constitutes not so much a second stage of criticism as a completely different discipline: that of measuring social attitudes toward art, not the values of art itself.

Fyodor Zhits, in assessing the multitude of critical approaches in the twenties, observed: "We shall be forced, perhaps for a long time, to put together an opinion of a writer according to the principle of the child's picture puzzle: you have a tail and a hoof and a mane and a head, and everything put together gives you a horse."[89] This is most disturbing to a Marxist: scientific truth does not admit of puzzles; the picture should be substantially complete before one begins. But it is still incomplete to this day, as far as conscientious Marxists are concerned. Perhaps it will always remain so. Can a truly "synthetic" method ever be devised that satisfies both the needs of art and the premises of Marxism? At the very least, the sort of preliminary work envisaged by *RVS* and the formal-sociologists would have to be a necessary precondition for even a tentative answer.

Perhaps only the Formalists and the disciples of Pereverzev made more than a start at a workable sociology of form.[90] But their efforts came too late. With the onset of the first Five Year Plan, free investigation and experimen-

---

[89] Review of V. Shklovskii, *Teoriya prozy*, *KN*, No. 1 (1925), p. 268.

[90] Cf., e.g., Yu. Tynyanov, "Literaturnyi fakt," *Arkhaisty i novatory* (Leningrad, 1929), pp. 5-29; V. F. Pereverzev, ed., *Literaturovedenie. Sbornik statei* (Moscow, 1928), *passim*, esp. the articles by I. Bespalov, "Stil' rannikh rasskazov Gor'kogo," pp. 273-347, and by Pereverzev himself, "K voprosu o monisticheskom ponimanii tvorchestva Goncharova," pp. 201-09. The Pereverzev school was original, interesting, and too sophisticated for its detractors in the twenties. There are signs that it is now being "rehabilitated." (Cf. the recent reprinting of a 1937 book by Pereverzev, *U istokov russkogo realisticheskogo romana* [Moscow, 1965].)

tation in art and thought became difficult; by 1934, it was all but impossible. The Formalists were branded heretical for their earlier preoccupation with what their name suggests, the Pereverzev school for the "vulgar sociologist" error of insisting that a writer's outlook and style are unalterably determined by the class from which he springs.

Generally speaking, Marxist literary theory and criticism was frozen at a stage where many of its deficiencies, imprecisions, and self-contradictions had not been defined, let alone worked out. The form-content dichotomy, for instance, still defies resolution. The problem of innovation and tradition is locked in paralysis: the pull of tradition has proved so strong as to discourage innovation, and no one has yet suggested how one can imitate without enslaving himself to the model. Critical terminology, by and large, still thrashes about in a semantic jungle that has grown up from political jargon, philosophical cant, and a few Formalistic bons mots. Scholars have done excellent work on language and stylistics, but it has not found its way into socialist realism, and is not, in any event, recognizably "Marxist"; instead we find a rehearsal of the same attitudes held by *RVS*—and, earlier, by the so-called "positivists" (Pypin, Skabichevskii, Ovsyaniko-Kulikovskii) three quarters of a century ago and more—wherein the word fulfills a kind of sign function. In short, virtually no progress in literary and critical theory has been made in Russia for four decades.

By the end of the twenties, Marxist critics were just beginning to mature into adolescence. They were asking some basic questions and becoming aware of how enormous was the distance that separated any final definition of criticism from the work that must precede it. But very much indeed remained unasked, unseen, unimagined. Even the contributors to *RVS*, who were among the most sophisticated practitioners of Marxist criticism in those years, operated within very narrow limits. We find practically no attempt to account for—let alone make use of—the rich discussions of critical theory going on outside Russia in those years, discussions which were in the main non-Marxist, to be sure, but relevant nonetheless to many of the problems Marxism needed to consider and could have considered creatively just then, before it hardened into dogma. For Russia itself, there was a heavy bias in favor of sociological methods, an uncomprehending intolerance of Formalism, and a rather mindless generosity toward a few "academic" studies of the Russian classics, presumably because they did not flaunt any "method" and might thus qualify as preliminary investigations along the way toward the grand synthesis.[91] The wonder is that *RVS* accomplished as much as it did.

But the journal's achievement in criticism, despite unpromising beginnings, must be reckoned substantial. Its contributors were the first in Soviet Russia to attempt a definition and characterization of the literary movements of their time, to show the links that attached those movements to the literature of the past, and to insist that they must be interpreted as part of a living, ongoing tradition. At a time when there were no established writers, except from an earlier generation, they picked out a number of young and virtually unknown talents, encouraged them, publicized them, and made living classics of them. At a time when practically no precedents existed, they worked out techniques and approaches for a practical Marxist criticism. Their work had many limitations and defects. It was often crude, but, as things turned out, rarely wrong in the final estimation it made of a writer's worth. It was often hasty, but it set high standards for writers and expected them to be lived up to. It was sometimes overbearing, but usually courteous and well-meaning. It neglected much interesting liter-

[91] Cf. e.g., I. Sergievskii, review of L. Grossman, *Pushkin v teatral'nykh kreslakh*, *KN*, No. 10 (1926), pp. 244-45; I. Rozanov, review of K. Chukovskii, *Nekrasov. Stat'i i materialy*, *KN*, No. 1 (1927), pp. 262-64.

ature by concentrating almost exclusively on writers who were publishing in *RVS* and in the almanac *Our Days*, but it did perceive that these writers were creating the most significant literature of the time. All in all, this criticism passed four crucial tests: it dealt with the best writers in a civilized way; it persuaded the public to accept them; it made judgments that have for the most part become commonplaces; and it still stands up: we want to read the books it talks about.

Most important of all, perhaps, was *RVS*'s insistence on obeisance to the works of literature themselves. If art is the only way of knowing an important part of the world, then that world, as nearly as one can know it, is really the sum of all the works of art that have ever been created. The critics understood that if one made external reality or personal experience a criterion of the merits of a work of art, there would be no way of verifying whether the world depicted by a writer of the past was true or not; each work would have meaning only for its own time. They insisted that one must refer neither to one's own feelings, nor to some standard set by society, but rather to the whole history of literature. They saw the world of art as a phenomenological world in itself, within which one must evaluate the individual work, and even the real world itself. In making the world of literature self-sufficient, they overcame that disparity between "genesis" and "evolution" which the Formalists had considered a weakness of Marxist theory. The act of criticism thus was closed to the ideologue and the impressionist both, and the emphasis was placed on tradition—specifically, on those works of literature that have endured. The critic—more properly, the historian of literature—was urged to look to the past for indications of what, so to speak, had worked. He would then present his findings for the instruction of the writers of his own time. A movement back to the classics became a movement toward the universal, which the artist would resist at the price of immortality.

CHAPTER VIII

The New Literature, 1923 to 1928

IF PROSE FICTION in the early twenties had been concerned with mapping out the contours of the strange and terrifying new world that man was entering, then from 1923 on it tried to interpret those ridges and depressions, and to explore the meaning of man's journey through them. For man stood squarely in the center of this new world. No longer an adjunct of history or a victim of blind fate, he now possessed a deep awareness of himself and of his surroundings. Novels and stories were no longer primarily chronicles of events, moods, and impressions, but arenas into which the issues of human existence were thrust and brought to battle. "Problem" writing, so long considered outmoded, again appeared. And man was forced to face the problems unflinchingly. He might be defeated, but he was no longer allowed to withdraw: he might find no solutions, but he was now obliged to seek them. Through him, fiction recovered an ethical dimension.

This new relationship between man and the world was examined in a far greater range of themes, settings, and forms than at any time since 1917. It was particularly the province of the young men and women who began writing after 1923. The most talented of them, with few exceptions, sent their best work to *RVS* and thereby gave body to the new program for literature. Not that the old standbys were forgotten: Pil'nyak, Ivanov, Seifullina, Ognyov, Nikitin, and Vesyolyi kept up their contributions to the journal and even tried, with varying degrees of success, to recast their writing in the new manner. But they no longer had a decisive influence on the journal. Voronskii tended to identify them with the "ornamentalism" or "ethnographism" that he had repudiated. Now he played up his new discoveries—among them Babel', Karavaeva, Leonov, Kataev, Lidin, and

Olesha—and gave them national reputations with the work he published between 1923 and 1928. He still stood by the old policy of trying to represent writers from all the major classes and groups, but he found it harder to honor as time went on, certainly where prose fiction was concerned. Prose writers from the peasantry were a scarce item in any event. Proletarians were not—their number seemed to grow geometrically by the month—but, as we have seen, Voronskii felt that he could take very little of what they had to offer. By any standards that made class provenance the measure, *RVS* was not "representative." It now belonged almost entirely to the fellow travelers. But they, after all, were saying most of the worthwhile things in the literature of the time.

Voronskii also continued, and even expanded his policy of linking past and present with offerings from the older writers. Gor'kii, though living in Italy by now, still set the mark. "*RVS*," Voronskii wrote him in 1927, "has been basically oriented on you, on your literary tradition, I would say on your school. When I used to think, when I still think about the literature of our time, I always have you in mind—Tolstoi and you. That is the honest truth. I followed you more than anyone else when I was in the revolutionary underground."[1] This last phrase is the key one: Voronskii had serious reservations about much of Gor'kii's writing and would have been hard put to find traces of its influence in the new literature he chose for publication. Actually, he was paying tribute to a personal friendship that had come to mean much for him, to a direct connection with a worthy political and literary past, and most of all, to an institution. Considering the obligations incumbent on a grand old man

---

[1] Letter to Gor'kii, November 26, 1927, *M. Gor'kii i sovetskaya pechat'. Arkhiv A. M. Gor'kogo*, x, Book 2 (Moscow, 1965), 60. It is not clear which Tolstoi Voronskii has in mind: "literature of our time" suggests Aleksei, but Lev was always his favorite writer, and that comparison would of course flatter Gor'kii more.

of literature—obligations which Gor'kii readily assumed in his voluminous correspondence and his indefatigable perusal of manuscripts—the wonder is that he managed to produce any literature at all in those years. Somehow he did, and *RVS* got a good sampling of it: some short stories and literary reminiscences, and excerpts from two big novels, *The Artamonov Business* (*Delo Artamonovykh*) and *Klim Samgin*. Aleksei Tolstoi ran a close second among the senior writers, with three short stories (including the famous "Azure Cities") and yet another novel in the science fiction vein, *The Hyperboloid of Engineer Garin* (*Giperboloid inzhenera Garina*). Beside the familiar names of Prishvin, Shishkov, Kasatkin, and Chapygin appeared some that were new to the readers of *RVS*, though well-known to the public at large: Evdokimov, Klychkov, Sokolov-Mikitov, Sergeev-Tsenskii, and the wondrously prolific Panteleimon Romanov.

THE NEW literature certainly met one of the key requirements of "monumentalness": sheer size. *RVS* between 1923 and 1928 published no fewer than ten complete novels, including Leonid Leonov's *The Thief* (*Vor*), Yurii Olesha's *Envy* (*Zavist'*), Aleksei Chapygin's *Stepan Razin* (*Razin Stepan*), Fyodor Gladkov's *Cement* (*Tsement*), and Sergei Budantsev's *Locusts* (*Sarancha*), along with nine others in excerpts. Thirty-seven novelettes (*povesti*) came out in the journal during this same period, the best being Vsevolod Ivanov's *Khabu*, Valentin Kataev's *The Embezzlers* (*Rastratchiki*), Leonid Leonov's *The Badgers* (*Barsuki*) and *End of a Petty Man* (*Konets melkogo cheloveka*), Lidiya Seifullina's *Virineya*, and Nikolai Nikitin's *The Crime of Kirik Rudenko* (*Prestuplenie Kirika Rudenko*). Other traditional genres reappeared too, notably the short story. The attractions of "ornamentalism" faded: writers now insisted on a sharp distinction between literature and nonliterature, and strove after a unified tone, simpler language, tighter plots, and a far greater economy of means. Many of the shorter works, in fact, seemed designed as exercises in pure form, unhampered by topicality: the mood story, such as A. Smirnov's "On the Shoal" (Na perekate, No. 9, 1925), which tells, in a very Gor'kiian manner, of the vague yearnings evoked in a fisher boy by passing ships and by the perfume of a beautiful lady who appears mysteriously out of the night; or the adventure tale, like Boris Zhitkov's *Elchan-Kaiya* (No. 11, 1926), with its ship made of stone, its gold, Greeks, and Turks; or the nature piece, such as Leonid Zavadovskii's "On the White Lake" (Na belom ozere, No. 9, 1925); or the numerous specimens of humorous anecdote and *skaz*.

Pil'nyak offers an especially fascinating subject for a literary autopsy. He abandoned ornamentalism, or, more accurately, let it fall apart into its separate components— allegory, anecdote, diary, sermon, *skaz*, and so on—picked each up and recast it, in relatively straightforward language, as a new genre. "Speranza" (No. 6, 1923) is one of his earliest attempts to find a different voice. Supposedly it is a mood study of man's endless and pointless quests, symbolized in his tireless tracking of the seas. But here the theme—one of his favorites—has been stripped of its ornamental splendor, and exposed as the rather tiresome allegory it is. "A Story of Springs and Clay" (Rasskaz o klyuchakh i gline, No. 1, 1926), which tells of the return of exiles to the Palestinian homeland, might well have been written by a foreign correspondent. "Roots of the Japanese Sun" (Korni yaponskogo solntsa, No. 3, 1927), an account of the author's visit to Japan in 1926, is a specimen of the artistic travel diary. Pil'nyak's scattered flings at ornamentalism in the later twenties, as in the tale *Ivan Moscow* (*Ivan Moskva*, No. 6, 1927), merely recapitulated the mannerisms of yore, and confirmed the impression that his talent displayed itself to best advantage in a kind of lyrical journalism that focused on event and situation at the expense of character and moral problems.[2]

The Civil War still cast its spell, but few writers found fresh approaches to it. Most still trod the familiar paths of romance and adventure. For instance, O. Savich's *In the Mountains* (*V gorakh*, No. 9, 1925)—a saga of love and war in Central Asia—is a veritable catalogue of themes and characters from earlier fiction in this vein. Tyudelekov, the impulsive, vodka-swilling Red Commander, and Domashnev, the sensitive but resolute and calculating political commissar come straight out of Furmanov's *Chapaev*. Yumashev embodies the theme, established by Nikolai Nikitin's *Fort Vomit* and Yurii Libedinskii's *A Week*, of impotent intellectuals unable to grasp the harsh terms of revolutionary necessity, and made absurd by ceaseless self-pity, which Yumashev voices in the sign that he will "perish." And perish he does, debased and humiliated, at the hands of Khoroshaev, a satanic White officer who is a faultily fused composite of traits snatched from Lermontov's Pechorin, Dostoevskii's Stavrogin, and innumerable villains out of Vsevolod Ivanov. That such inferior work should appear in *RVS*—and therefore presumably represent the best of its kind—might have suggested that the theme of the Civil War had by now run dry. It took writers like Babel' and Leonov, as we shall see, to show that such was not the case.

The more remote past began to yield up some themes that writers were quick to explore; Soviet historical fiction took its beginnings around 1923, with revolutionaries and

[2] The career of Nikolai Ognyov, one of Pil'nyak's most ardent disciples, shows a parallel development, from the extreme "ornamentalism" of *Eurasia* (*Evraziya*, No. 1 [1923]) to the reportage or diary style of *The Diary of Kostya Ryabtsev* (*Dnevnik Kosti Ryabtseva*, excerpts in No. 10 [1926] and No. 1 [1927]).

literary personalities the favorite subjects.[3] But it was contemporary Russia—the Russia of the NEP—that attracted most of the new writers. And *RVS*, during the middle twenties, offered an unparalleled literary physiology of it.

THAT every aspect of life must find its way into literature was one of the less sophisticated, but by no means insignificant requirements of "neo-realism." For the sake of thematic range and variety, Voronskii was willing to sacrifice a great deal—including quality. It is hard to explain in any other way the appearance in *RVS* of much writing that falls well below the journal's usual standards. We find a kind of pseudo-reportage, for example, like D. Sverchkov's "Case No. 3576" (*Delo No. 3576*, No. 2, 1927), which describes the tensions that build up in a marriage from the pull of the new emancipated sex mores against the old; or "physiologies" of supposedly representative NEP "types," like the self-employed semi-skilled artisan in N. Nikandrov's *Damned Cigarette Lighters!* (*Proklyatye zazhigalki!* No. 6-7, 1923); or the boardinghouse genre which uses various milieux of communal life as menageries of social types, like G. Alekseev's *The Apartment House* (*Zhiloi dom*, No. 9, 1926) or, for the emigrés, O. Savich's *The Von Offenberg Pension* (*Pension fon-Offenberg*, No. 8, 1926).

One might have expected more from works dealing with the inner life of the Communist Party. Voronskii insisted, again and again, that this was an important theme which

---

[3] Cf., e.g., Ol'ga Forsh, *Contemporaries* (*Sovremenniki*, excerpt in No. 6 [1925]), on Gogol' and his times; N. Ognyov, "Visions" (*Videniya*, No. 10 [1925]), on the poet Polezhaev; on revolutionaries: K. Trenyov, *The Pugachov Era: A Folk Tragedy* (*Pugachovshchina. Narodnaya tragediya*, No. 2 [1924]), A. Chapygin, *Stepan Razin* (*Razin Stepan*, Nos. 1-2 [1926]); I. Evdokimov, *The Bells* (*Kolokola*, Nos. 2-6 [1926]), on the Bolshevik underground; A. Malyshkin, *February Snow* (*Fevral'skii sneg*, excerpt in No. 3 [1927]), on the February revolution.

writers had unaccountably neglected ever since Libedinskii's and Furmanov's first novels. In this way, he as much as announced that he would take what he could get. The two samples we find in *RVS* are among the poorest pieces of fiction he ever published. Dmitrii Stonov's *Bolsheviks* (*Bol'-sheviki*, No. 6, 1924) is built on the familiar conflict between duty and sentiment in the Communist. As chairman of the Executive Committee of the local Party organization, Komlev, the hero, initiates a campaign to expropriate the property of the town's bourgeoisie, who have grown fat and sleek at the expense of the workers during the NEP. The catch is that his own wife and mother are bourgeoises to the core, scorn his politics and his work, and press him to exempt them from revolutionary justice. Komlev's dilemma virtually destroys the Party organization—herein lies the moral of the tale—but all are welded together at the end by a telegram from the Center, and move purposefully onward. Stonov, though utterly innocent of any techniques of character drawing, at least shows some knack for sheer storytelling. A. Arosev, the author of the other saga of inner-Party life published in *RVS*, lacks even that. Obryvov, the hero of "On the Earth Beneath the Sun" (Na zemle pod solntsem, No. 9, 1927), is a Cheka official who, for no apparent reason, hands himself over to his comrades as a "traitor." As it turns out, he does this to expiate a moral crime: years before, one of his best friends had been killed by an anti-Red mob which thought it was disposing of Obryvov, while the intended victim stood by and made no effort to correct the mistake. Obryvov failed to act, not out of any idea that he might be more necessary to the Revolution than his friend (which was, in fact, the case, and always constitutes a permissible motive for duplicity in Communist fiction), but simply because he wished to live. In effect, he committed the murder himself. Has he now the right to live? In earlier works, such as *Torment*, Arosev treated such conflicts as hopeless moral dilemmas that slowly tore the hero apart. But now, with a crank of the handle, he lowers a wise Bolshevik father-confessor onto the stage, who reduces the moral problem to simple over-scrupulousness, and returns Obryvov to useful service with the Cheka.

The most serious thematic lacuna in those years would seem, on the face of it, to be the least probable one: the industrial worker. But Voronskii was right when he observed in 1923: "Neither in the poetry nor in the prose of our Communist youth is there any *real* production worker. . . . There are many words about the factory, but there is no genuine factory."[4] Gor'kii's *Mother*, then nearly twenty years old, had been the last substantial piece of industrial prose fiction in Russian written with anything like sympathy for the proletarian point of view. Since then "the factory" had found a literary home mainly in verse. In 1914, there had been the famous anthology of proletarian poetry edited by Gor'kii. After 1917, the poets from Ivanovo-Voznesensk and from the Smithy had written about the new machine civilization in passionate, but not very proletarian strains: they tended to make the factory either the agency of a personal rebirth through mystical attunement to a universal life-force, or the arena of struggle between a dying village life, recently abandoned and nostalgically recalled, and an impersonal and enslaving modernity. Where were the new novels, the new stories showing the machine as an instrument of the working-class will, a liberator of man from nature? This was another of those cries which Voronskii flung repeatedly into the wind. Although he did get his prose fiction, it was neither "new" nor "Communist" in the senses he meant. It came, the best of it at any rate, mainly from the Smithy group, which began to attract some prose writers after reviving in 1922. One of them, Georgii Nikiforov, made what seems to be the first

4 "O gruppe pisatelei 'Oktyabr'' i 'Molodaya gvardiya,'" *KN*, No. 2 (1924), p. 293.

serious treatment, outside poetry, of the much-neglected industrial theme; it was published in the first issue of *RVS* for 1925.

Ivan Brynda is set sometime between 1921 and 1923 in a large, provincial textile town—probably Ivanovo-Voznesensk. At first life seems undisturbed by the Revolution. The factories hum on; a few people go off to fight and then return; and faithful old workers like Ivan Brynda, with thirty-five years of service, toil away as contentedly as ever. Then the NEP comes: one by one the factories shut down, and 12,000 men find themselves without jobs, Brynda among them. At first he makes a passable living by selling second-hand goods. But his honest proletarian conscience gags, and together with two friends he goes off to Moscow in hopes of locating good clean work in a factory. Finding conditions no better there, he and his companions are forced to hire out to a small shopkeeper. The petty-bourgeois atmosphere soon works its poison: one of Ivan's friends acquires a lust for money, the other takes to drink and crime. Ivan himself remains pure at heart, quitting before temptation speaks, and trudges back to his native town utterly discouraged. Steadfastness is rewarded, however: the factories have again begun to roll, and the reader is assured that Brynda will return to his bench.

This story is a savage commentary on the state to which the proletariat was reduced by the Revolution that had been made in its name. Tsarist times appear idyllic by contrast: then Brynda worked hard but happily, felt himself a complete man, and developed a sense of proletarian "pride" that contained not a hint of rebelliousness, but only demanded work well done. Now all he asks is a return to that old existence, so that he may again "get up at six o'clock, and walk along the familiar road he had walked for more than thirty years, at the summons of the whistle."[5]

[5] *Ivan Brynda*, No. 1 (1925), p. 145.

There are at least two things seriously wrong with this work, if it is judged by the usual standards of *RVS*. For one thing, it is mawkish, wooden, obvious, and trite. For another, it reflects that defeatist attitude toward the NEP which infected many proletarians at the time, and which Voronskii considered characteristic of the Smithy group. (Gerasimov and Kirillov, in fact, resigned from the Communist Party.) Some of the gloomiest pictures ever penned of the new society are to be found in the works of these writers. (For once, no one could blame the fellow travelers, most of whom did not touch the themes of industry or reconstruction.)[6] Voronskii faithfully echoed the Party line that the NEP represented merely a temporary tactical retrenchment. Nikiforov's story, however, did give a good sense of a very real and widespread mood of the times; and it may be that Voronskii decided to make for him the same allowance he had made for the Smithy poets: despite an ideology seriously flawed with "factory romanticism," "symbolism," and "metaphysics," their verses, he said, smelled "more of workers' sweat and machine oil" than did the bloodless abstractions of the young Communist writers.[7]

The other major piece of industrial fiction in *RVS* was Fyodor Gladkov's sprawling novel *Cement*, which ran serially in the first six issues for 1925. Here we have the testimony of a very ruffled author that Voronskii considered this work devoid of literary merit but worth publishing for its theme.[8] There was probably more to it than that: Glad-

[6] One notable exception was Vsevolod Ivanov's novella *Khabu* (No. 2 [1925]), which revolves around the building of a railroad in the trackless *taiga*. Contrary to the usual Ivanov formula, nature is defeated. The critics praised Ivanov for allowing reason to triumph over instinct, but they missed the irony: the positive hero, one Leizerov, "that black-eyed Jew from Minsk," is a comically absurd figure who dies the moment his dream is realized.

[7] "O gruppe pisatelei 'Oktyabr' ' i 'Molodaya gvardiya,' " p. 293.

[8] Letter to Gor'kii, October 22, 1926, *Gor'kii i sovetskie pisateli. Literaturnoe nasledstvo*, LXX (Moscow, 1963), 81. Cf. also letter to Gor'kii, before January 20, 1926, *ibid.*, p. 73.

kov, after all, was the first writer to project the theme on a truly "monumental" scale, with an attempt at problem-ridden protagonists, powerful conflicts, an impressive flow of language that Lezhnev characterized as "a heroic monumental style that corresponds to our age,"[9] and an ambitious double plot (rebuilding a cement factory in the face of shortages and sabotage, and reconstructing a marriage eroded by the free-love morality). The trouble is that ambition outstripped performance. *Cement* pretends to be a novel, but is really a romance. Everything passes immediately into action. The love theme comes out of pulp fiction; the reconstruction theme merely renames the clichés of military fiction: the shock troops of industry, commanded by resolute leaders, move out to storm objectives defended by wily enemies. There are no hidden thoughts, no ambiguities. Although the characters take on a semblance of complexity by moving from situation to situation, in themselves they lack depth and consistency. The profusion of subplots and situations, the welter of characters, even the injection of "accursed questions" (a man responsible for the death of his brother, the clash of idealism and careerism in Party members, and so on) all provide splendid examples of the uses of retardation in literature. In most cases they have no relevance to the main thrust of the romance, and at the end are left to dangle. *Cement*, then, is a novel only in name. Still, it does stand out as the first novel-length attempt in Soviet fiction at an industrial romanticism that challenges the clinging nostalgia for the Civil War and the gloomy portents for the future by depicting hard work as an exciting adventure and setting it against a surcharged lyrical landscape borrowed from Bunin, Gor'kii, Vsevolod Ivanov, and the Smithy poets.

[9] "Literaturnye zametki," *Literaturnye budni* (Moscow, 1929), p. 201.

WHEN IT came to the contemporary Russian village, writers needed no special encouragement: this theme was epidemic in the literature of the twenties. Proletarian and peasant writers, on the whole, took sharply defined approaches consistent with their class outlook. The first tended to see the peasants as willful, greedy, and savage obstructionists of the Revolution; the second, in the main, looked on themselves as members of a dying culture and struck appropriately nostalgic poses.[10] Far more complex were the attitudes of the fellow travelers. In ideological terms, these writers sympathized with the proletariat, yet looked to the people as the real protagonists in the drama of Russia that was being played out. In their work they emphasized the conflicts that arose from the encounter of the new ways with the old; especially popular was the "return" motif—the return of the thoroughly Bolshevized son to his patriarchal village, or the dispossessed landowner to estates now run by his former peasants.[11] The theme gained a topical urgency because it echoed one of the most serious problems the new regime had to face: the clash between the starving towns and the relatively prosperous countryside, which had become a virtual civil war by the mid-twenties. For many of the fellow travelers, this was merely the latest version of the age-old antagonism of two cultures, rural and urban, that had so long entranced the Russian intelligentsia.

RVS printed a good sampling of fellow-traveler literature on this theme. Two works, both dating from 1924, merit special attention. *Virineya*, a novella by Lidiya Sei-

[10] For an example of the proletarian approach in *RVS*, cf. A. Sytin, "Boi paukov," No. 12 (1927). There are no really good examples of this kind of peasant writing in the prose fiction published in *RVS*, but it is characteristic of the lyric poetry.

[11] Cf. M. Chistyakova, "Chetyre dnya," *KN*, No. 7 (1923); I. Sokolov-Mikitov, "Pyl'," *KN*, No. 7 (1925).

fullina, represented one of the earliest attempts to show the kind of synthesis that many Marxists at the time believed might result from the conflict of the two great classes. She assumed that despite the virtual savagery of rural life, the peasantry unconsciously pursued the same ideals as the proletariat, and that no reason therefore existed for enduring antagonism. The heroine, who gives the tale its title, demonstrates the point by beginning as a mindless rustic, ripening into a Bolshevik activist, and finally dying a martyr to the cause. Leonid Leonov's *The Badgers* (*Barsuki*) was much more ambitious and complex, but its theme was essentially the same. This first long work by a promising young writer (it was styled a tale [*povest'*], but really should have been called a novel) is an allegory of war between anarchy and self-discipline, drift and goal, instinct and reason, vegetation and activism, as represented by two brothers, Pavel and Semyon Savelich. Both spring from the black peasant earth; but great spiritual wounds isolate them from one another, and circumstances drive them in separate directions—Pavel into Bolshevism, and Semyon into a meandering existence that finally brings him into a band of peasant anarchists (the Badgers) who are resisting the Bolsheviks' attempts to rule the countryside. In the end, the two brothers come face to face, as Pavel, now a commissar, metes out revolutionary justice to the Badgers, whose leader is Semyon himself. But it is a curiously amiable and undramatic encounter: Semyon recognizes that there is really nothing to fight against, because the Saveliches, like all men, are brothers who crave decency and freedom and a sense of identity.

Both these works fail, Leonov's the more frustratingly because it is the more ambitious. And they fail for the same reason: a want of technique and of sensitivity in the handling of the heroes. Virineya is not a personality but merely the composite of those scenes in which she happens to participate. Semyon, the chief protagonist of Leonov's novella, offers interesting possibilities as a driven man in search of meaning. But Leonov refuses to confront him; he remains vague, impalpable, unmotivated, unconvincing, a character utterly unworthy of the great issues with which his creator surrounds him.

This kind of failure seemed to dog virtually all the writers who treated the peasantry and the proletariat; none of their works on these themes had the makings of important literature. Yet with other settings, the same writers showed that they could often perform impressively. Leonov's second novel, *The Thief*, is a good example. Granting that he had gained experience and assurance in the three years that elapsed since *The Badgers*, the fact remained that his hero, Mitya, was the same sort of person as Semyon, and Leonov's techniques of characterizing him were basically unchanged. Yet faults became virtues when Leonov wrote about a *déclassé* in an urban setting. Why should this be so?

One reason, perhaps, was the tendency of Soviet writers, even fellow travelers, to imprison themselves in the myths about proletarians and peasants, to see them not as individuals but as representatives of classes and inhabitants of milieux endued (by Russian history and literature, and by Bolshevik ideology) with certain characteristics that persist, as in saints' lives, from birth to death, and even from generation to generation. Of these myths, none has proved hardier than that of the simple, direct, naturally good and morally radiant man of the soil or factory. No writer of the twenties—and no writer to this day—managed to make first-rate literature out of him. The old primitivist ethos no longer enjoyed the same authority it had earlier; but significantly, when it did turn up in literature, peasants and workers were usually its carriers.

Let us mention by way of example Valentin Kataev's "Rodion Zhukov" (No. 7, 1926), the story of a sailor who deserts the mutinous battleship *Potyomkin* in Rumania and makes his way through formidable obstacles back to Russia in response to the pull of the soil; or the "a-psychological" stories that Vsevolod Ivanov wrote in the mid-twenties when he stripped off his lush style, exotic language, complex plots, and mordant ironies, and began to focus on a single character, often the terrified little man (peasant or artisan) who is driven to self-destruction by a malevolent fate he never understands ("Night," "Fecundity," "The Life of Timothy Smokotinin"), or who, conversely, is saved from doom by a mysterious surge of the vital force ("The Water Patch").[12] Leonov and Seifullina tried to throw off the myth of the mindless peasant and show that he could be complex, but they did not heave hard enough. Semyon takes on a pseudo-complexity only through association with a range of other characters and, like Virineya, through confrontations with obstacles. But he remains on one plane, innocent of thought or guile, as Leonov's refusal to grapple with him suggests. The creators of "positive" heroes in the novels of the thirties faced similar problems.

THE FINEST new writing of the time moved around intelligent heroes who are exquisitely aware of their world. Most have fought in Russia's recent wars, where they have tasted glory and savagery and have come to know the hearts of men. Certainly they are the most experienced and, in some ways, the most sophisticated heroes in Russian literature. But they grope in a shadow-shot tent of doubt, bewilderment, and constant questioning. They are passionately committed to life, yet they cannot accept life as they see it—capricious, willful, patternless, and ultimately absurd. Despite their avid, desperate search for meaning, they can find nothing that takes full account of the experiences they have undergone. War has eroded their class identities, along with the other marks by which men

[12] "Noch'," *KN*, No. 6 (1926); "Plodorodie," *KN*, No. 3 (1926); "Zhizn' Timofeya Smokotinina, syna podryadchika," *KN*, No. 3 (1926); "Polyn'ya," *KN*, No. 5 (1926).

steer. Their restless quest for a sense to life brings them closer to the intelligentsia; but in other important respects they are far removed. Ideas hold little interest for them: they talk badly, and move more by touch than by reason. Their experience has exposed the bankruptcy of the old humanistic values, and they have learned to distrust, if not to escape the mind's love of system.

In addition, they have rejected the traditional Westernizing mission of the intelligentsia. They look on Europe as the source of those values that have failed, those claims that have deceived. The literature of these years gapes with the wounds inflicted by Europe on men like Startsev, the hero of Fedin's *Cities and Years*, who lives abroad for five years or more, steeping himself in a dying culture, and then returns to Russia to discover that he is utterly irrelevant. These men are passionately Russian; but they cannot find a Russia that will accept them, or a Russia they themselves can accept. Like their predecessors in the literature of the early twenties, they associate the real Russia with the peasantry, whom they regard with mixed feelings of awe, fear, and reverence. But they can make no meaningful contact with the soil, for they are too conscious of themselves to surrender to primitivism, and too experienced not to know that they can never be accepted by the peasantry. But this entrancement with the soil, this new nationalism, alienates them from the other major class as well, the proletariat which, ironically, has assumed the traditional roles of the intelligentsia—as internationalist, Europeanizer, and spiritual activist. These new men are estranged from society and from themselves. They can find no runnels for their moral energies. Although they feel their estrangement acutely, they cannot articulate their anguish, but can only continue to seek its meaning.

A prototype of this hero stands at the center of Isaak Babel's *Red Cavalry*, the cycle of stories written largely during the NEP, but set during the Polish campaign of

1920. Much has been made of the forced association of two traditional enemies, the Jew and the Cossack.[13] Actually, a good deal more than that is at stake here. Lyutov, the narrator-protagonist, is a Russian, a Jew, an intellectual, a Bolshevik; but it is others who pin these tags on him: he belies them all. He is a Russian only in Poland; at home he is a Jew. Yet his Jewishness taunts the scornful Cossack image of the passive Semitic "four-eyes," and in turn finds itself mocked in the spectacle of the dirty, illiterate inhabitants of the Polish *shtetls*, who also style themselves Jews. He is a Bolshevik whose loyalties are eroded at every turn by scruple, sentimentalism, and a deep sense of a past both dead and vital. He is an intellectual who is incapable of defining the welling problems of conscience, morality, and ethics forced on him by experience. Lyutov, then, stands outside everything. But he is of a different breed from those outsiders who people the fiction of the early twenties, such as Surikov, the young Cheka functionary in Libedinskii's novel *A Week*, who brings a flawed sensibility to what he regards as a perfect cause, and greets death gratefully as expiation for the sin of imperfection. Lyutov longs to find an allegiance that will pull together all these conflicting and incomplete identities; yet circumstances compel him to make constant acts of allegiance that he knows fall far short of perfection. Earlier Soviet war fiction normally gave its protagonists only two choices—total commitment or total destruction; *Red Cavalry* suggests a third way—the way of qualified commitment. Lyutov neither withdraws nor immolates himself, though both recourses tempt him in moments of despair. His problem is how to act—and act in the right way for the right reasons. He must do his duty to-

[13] Cf., e.g., Lionel Trilling, "Introduction," *Isaac Babel: The Collected Stories*, ed. and trans. by Walter Morison (New York, 1960), pp. 9-37. Fourteen of the *Red Cavalry* stories (with a few variations in title) were published in *RVS* in 1924 and 1925. For the sake of convenience, all references are to the book edition (*Konarmiya* [3d ed.; Moscow-Leningrad, 1928]).

ward himself while observing his obligations toward others; and it is the pull between these two concepts of duty that creates the book's moral dimension.

It is no easier for men like Lyutov to find bearings in the society of the NEP; the demands on their allegiance and the threats to their identity are as great. But their battleground is now most often the city or the town—a savage, chaotic, urban world where the only law is a jungle law of exploiters and exploited, a world that derives partly from the literary tradition, but also reflects to some extent actual conditions. So many of these dreary provincial towns and sordid city quarters—with their mud-holed streets, bug-ridden hotels, leaden skies, and grasping officials—come straight out of an ancient Russian past untouched by the machine age. They represent everything the Revolution has fought against; and their survival betokens the Revolution's defeat. What Blok had intuited seems to have come to pass: in attempting to destroy the values of the old world, the Revolution has ended by destroying all values, and ultimately, itself. As one of the characters in Valentin Kataev's story, "Fire," puts it:

we are flying. . . . We are mounting higher and higher. . . . We are in the upper layers of the atmosphere. There's nothing more to breathe, the blood beats in the temples. Oh! . . . But higher, higher. Perhaps further on we'll find angels and God? But no they're not there either. Icy cold and the black impenetrable gloom of airless space surround us. And the huge, cold, crimson, rayless, lightless, immense disc of the sun seems to be falling headlong on us out of the terrible icy space of eternal night. But where are the angels? Where then is God? It's all just an ignorant lie of the priests. They're not here either. Cold. Ice. Silence. Fire. Death.[14]

[14] "Ogon'," Rastratchiki. Povesti i rasskazy (Moscow, 1927), p. 187.

It took the NEP to give Soviet society a tragic dimension, by betraying the idealists of the Revolution just as the Revolution itself had betrayed an earlier generation of idealists.

MANY of the protagonists of this new fiction are criminals. Lootings, rapes, murders, and arson abound. But these are not the acts of heroic criminals who create a world of self-assertive activism in defiance of conventional society.[15] The time for heroics is past; society is unworthy; idealism is dead; and there is nothing to defy, for all men have become criminals now, and all society is their territory. (Kataev's bumbling embezzlers are immediately recognized but are taken for granted and even helped along their way.[16]) Often these criminal acts are punishments visited upon society itself: the acts perhaps of a Buzheninov, the protagonist of Aleksei Tolstoi's "Azure Cities," whose dream of a gleaming Moscow (the Communist society of the future) has dissolved into the reality of the dreary little village he has always known. In destroying this village, he destroys, yet avenges the dream.[17] Such acts of violence aim at the self as well: for as makers of the Revolution, these men are both perpetrators and victims of the crime against the Revolution that they see rampant in the NEP. The extinction of all values has turned them into objects, surrogates of the dead world in which they move; but their act of destruction, whether directed outward or inward, is a final flexion of the will that makes them men again.

One of the most celebrated criminals in the fiction of the twenties is Mitya Vekshin, the hero of Leonid Leonov's novel *The Thief*. Like many returning veterans, Vekshin encounters, with sudden and unmistakable directness, a

[15] Just as Civil War literature had its golden warriors, so the literature of the NEP created some romantic criminal-heroes; Il'f and Petrov's Ostap Bender is perhaps the most famous.

[16] *Rastratchiki, KN*, Nos. 10-12 (1926).

[17] "Golubye goroda," *KN*, No. 4 (1925).

society that is indifferent to deeds and sufferings, contemptuous of men of action, and mistrustful of idealists:

> That day he was standing by a grocer's shop; San'ka Babkin was with him. It was stifling hot, and the fat was dripping from a headless sturgeon in the window, and Mit'ka was hungry. A woman—the wife or daughter of a Nepman [a speculator], young, smartly dressed, as splendrous as an Arabian morn, was about to go into the shop. Mit'ka, with well-meaning courtesy, reached out his hand to open the door for her, but she misunderstood his gesture. With her glove she struck the hand that had grasped the handle, and Mit'ka, feeling stupid and humiliated, just managed to pull his hand back to avoid being struck a second time. San'ka Babkin, who had been a witness to Mit'ka's glory and to his inglorious fall, made a move forward, ready for a fight if it came to that, but he was stopped by the vacant expression on Mit'ka's face.[18]

Mitya then turns to stealing, and practices his new profession with a skill and daring that quickly make him famous. His motives, however, turn on more than mere revenge for the humiliation he has suffered. The flick of the glove reopens an old spiritual wound inflicted during the Civil War. There was nothing at the outset of the war to indicate that Mitya's part in it would be different from that of thousands of other young men who fought with the Reds. His involvement would perhaps be more intense, for he seemed to have found in it an outlet for his restless, aimless, discontented nature. But one night at the front changes everything. Mitya's horse is shot out from under him. The White officer responsible is captured and locked up for interrogation. Mitya abducts him and executes him. Justice is done, but Mitya is never the same again. That single

[18] *Vor*, KN, No. 1 (1927), p. 40.

stroke of the saber which hacks away the life of the prisoner severs some vital part of Mitya as well. He begins to bleed to death spiritually. Twisted, crippled, lacerated, he hobbles into the city.

What has caused this disfiguration? Mitya, after all, has killed many men before. But that night had its special magic:

> That night [Firsov writes] he abducted Sulim's murderer from headquarters (where he had been taken for interrogation), and led him out behind a thin, scraggly, sorry little birch grove. He was assisted by his trusty arms-bearer, San'ka Babkin, who was petrified with sympathy for Mit'ka's sorrow. Somewhere in the dark side-scenes of the sky . . . hung the round carmine moon. Not a leaf rustled in the stillness.
>
> "Do you know who it is you have killed?" asked Commissar Vekshin in a slow relentless voice, gazing at the torn tunic of the youth (who had risen to the rank of captain in just the first few months of the Civil War). The latter mumbled something faintly, because he had killed many people that day, and he did not know who was meant. "You have killed my Sulim!" Vekshin answered for him, and his thin eyebrow twanged straight like a bow that has shot off its arrow. "All right, now salute me!"
>
> The youth submitted, because too penetrating and too disquieting were the crimson light of the moon, and the blue paleness of the night's distances, and the silence of the hushed, frozen grove, and the mysterious black depths of the commissar's eyes. As he raised his arm indecisively, Vekshin gave a swing of his saber and hacked off the captain's arm, the murdering arm. And only San'ka Babkin, the most faint-hearted of all three, gave a muffled groan, and squatted on the dewy grass. . . .[19]

[19] *Ibid.*, p. 38.

The whole episode, so carefully staged, suggests a cheap vaudeville show, with the painted props, the jester-character ("trusty arms-bearer"), the confrontation of Good and Evil, the hero's declamatory pose, mobile eyebrows, and stentorian rhetoric, and the melodramatic triumph of Justice. It is as effective a piece of anti-heroics as one could wish. The symbols and trappings of manhood are destroyed —and with them, the slogans emblazoned on the banners of the Revolution. For Mitya suddenly awakens to the fact that the justice he metes out in the name of the Revolution —the justice of law—is in fact only revenge veneered by principle, and contradicts a deeper kind of justice—that of man to man. The moment he makes this distinction, even though it is largely unconscious, he becomes an outlaw, not merely from the Revolution, but from society as a whole: for great causes, like societies, do not recognize two kinds of justice, but assume that their justice is an adequate codification of natural justice. Mitya's tragedy is that by acting in the name of one kind of justice, he has ended by cutting himself off from both. *The Thief* is the account of his attempt to resolve the contradiction.

The outlaw society into which he steps bears no resemblance to the exotic realm of romantic fiction that twits convention and feeds the secret yearnings of respectable men. Rather, it stands for the whole society of the NEP, which knows neither the rule of justice nor the rule of law— the logical issue, as Leonov strongly suggests, of the Revolution, from which the pretenses to principle have been stripped. All men are now outlaws, estranged from one another and from themselves. The glove incident makes a profound impression on Mitya, not because it precipitates a sudden decision to take up a vengeful life of crime (he has been a criminal ever since that night at the front), but because it thrusts on him the final proof of his estrangement from all men. Who, after all, is he? The bold, resourceful, romantic hero of crime that Zinka sees? The arrogant loud-mouth who proclaims: "No one must sleep when Dmitrii Vekshin is awake!"? The pale, erect youth whose mask-like face conceals a soul so desolate that snow will not melt on his overcoat? The passionate lover? The cynic? The sentimentalist? He is all these and more. His selves are the creations of the people who surround him, but he cannot be known adequately by any one of them, or even by their aggregate. Something in him, while craving definition, shrinks from it, and he can find no way of making these various selves live together harmoniously. He is another one of Leonov's collective characters; but unlike Semyon, he is convincing, for Leonov turns him loose in a setting that fits him perfectly—an opalescent world of flitting shadows.

Men like Mitya know that they have suffered a severe spiritual wrench (the term Leonov uses is *obida*, "injury," "wrong," "insult"), but they are less concerned with defining its nature than with finding some way to heal it. The traditional humanistic values offer no guide; they have proven utterly inadequate to the questions raised by the experience of war. Yet they continue to press their claims, for they make up a spiritual inheritance that can no more be erased than biological inheritance. And against the parents who have passed on these spiritual genes the sons rebel: the fiction of the twenties is full of actual and symbolic fathers whom these new men sometimes pity for their naïveté, sometimes patronize for ineffectual good intentions, but more often scorn for having detected the symptoms of fatal sickness and passing it on to their helpless children anyway.

When one stops to consider how vacuous Mitya Vekshin's mind is, one cannot help but admire Leonov's achievement in sustaining a very long piece of writing. Though far from stupid or insensitive, Mitya is barren of education and innocent of culture: he goes out into the world with little more than the rudimentary literacy the sons of humble laborers might, with luck, acquire. Probably he has never read a novel, visited an art gallery, seen a play, heard a symphony, or argued an idea. The only specimen of the Russian intelligentsia he has known at all closely is Manyukin, the drunken buffoon who sells stories and treacly musings on the meaning of life. Mitya despises him, more deeply than he has ever despised anyone. There may be a tinge of natural class revulsion here, the feeling that might well up in a working man at the appearance of an especially repulsive specimen of the bourgeois liberal. But if so, it is largely unconscious: though Mitya's social pedigree is presented in some detail, his wandering life has tended to make him a virtual *déclassé*, which, of course, lends support to the role of Everyman in which Leonov tries to cast him. No, more than class feeling is involved. Mitya's reaction runs far deeper than the amused scorn which the other characters bestow on Manyukin: it is one of violent physical loathing. For he realizes with horror that he is drawn to this man. He does not know why; but Leonov drops enough hints to make it clear that Mitya thinks of this horrid creature as his father—not, to be sure, a biological father, despite some annoying mystification about the whole matter, but a spiritual father to himself and to the generation he represents. True enough, Mitya does not know Manyukin's world—the world of the liberal intelligentsia—well enough to put its values to the test in any conscious or systematic way; but he seems to feel that his own failure is somehow linked with Manyukin, and perhaps even mocked, again and again, in the old man's buffoonish performances: the traumatic scene at the front, in its pompous bathos, would have been worthy of Manyukin's talents. But Leonov leaves us unsure of just where to seek the link; muddy motives are one of the novel's weaknesses. It is at least clear, however, that Mitya's failure reflects upon the motives of the Revolution itself: and in those motives may lie the link between Manyukin and himself, a link between an old "liberal" persuasion that clamored for revolution in the name of justice and humanity, and those who actually went out to make this revolution only to discover that justice and humanity took no account of the brutality and suffering of their own experiences. Mitya himself was never an idealist in the same sense as Manyukin; but his experience casts aspersion on idealistic causes of any kind, including the Revolution as Bolsheviks see it. That may well account for the chilly reception accorded this novel in the Soviet Union practically from the moment of its publication.

Lyutov, by contrast, is steeped in the rich tradition of humanism. He is an *intelligent*, a member of the intelligentsia, which means, among other things, that he firmly believes his values have application to the practical problems of life, if not always to bring a solution, then at least to make a definition. His experience with the Cossacks discredits this belief: he perceives that his intellectual and spiritual heritage provides no meaningful guides to a way of life with which he must somehow come to terms. The famous story "Dolgushov's Death" (Smert' Dolgushova) points up the dilemma dramatically. Dolgushov is a Cossack who has been disemboweled in battle, but still clings to consciousness. He begs Lyutov to finish him off before the advancing Poles can get to him and play their tricks. But Lyutov cannot do it. And Afon'ka, the Cossack who finally releases Dolgushov forever, spits angrily at Lyutov: "You four-eyes got about as much pity for the likes of us as a cat for a mouse."[20] Lyutov's pity—a pity born of a humanistic reverence for life—fails miserably: it is a legalistic pity that blankets all men whatever the circumstances and therefore fails to respect them as individuals; a selfish pity that shields the sensibilities of the pitier and props up a self-righteous sense of virtue by

[20] "Smert' Dolgushova," *Konarmiya* (3d ed.; Moscow-Leningrad, 1928), p. 59.

feeding on the sufferings of other men. Lyutov's plea to
fate to "grant me the simplest of abilities—the ability to kill
a man" cries out for some way of translating conviction
into effective action.[21] All around him he sees the spoor of
his dead humanism, in ruined castles, crumbling letters,
and vacant churches. Toward them he feels that nostalgia
of the romantic, the curiosity of the Russian in Europe—
but not the detachment of the tourist: for they speak to
him persuasively, seductively. They are European, these
trappings of humanism; but they acquire a hold on him
only through his Jewishness, with its peculiarly formalistic
sense of history and its worship of what is dead as something living. And it is the Polish Jews, without any of the
colorful trappings of Odessa, who really bring this fateful
aspect of his Jewishness home to Lyutov, clinging as they
do to a desolate and filthy life, yet worshipping their rags.
It is easy enough for Lyutov to despise them; but perhaps
not until his visit to the shop of Gedali, the old patriarchal
Jew, does he realize how much of himself is explained by
them:

> In this shop there were buttons and a dead butterfly, and
> its small owner was called Gedali. All had abandoned
> the market; Gedali remained. He wound in and out of
> a labyrinth of globes, skulls, and dead flowers, flicking
> a bright feather duster of cock's plumes and blowing
> dust from the dead flowers.

Gedali's dream of an International composed entirely of
"good" people is but another lifeless, dust-sprinkled object:
Lyutov knows that the International "is eaten with gun-
powder and seasoned with the best blood." Yet he feels no
scorn or hatred toward Gedali, this father figure—only pity,
and a strange, warm pull away from the chaos of his own
life.[22]

[21] "Posle boya," *ibid.*, p. 163.
[22] "Gedali," *ibid.*, pp. 37, 39.

NOWHERE do the sons more ruthlessly strip their fathers naked than in Yurii Olesha's short novel *Envy*. The hero, Kavalerov, is far more richly endowed than Mitya Vekshin with imagination, vision, dreams, aspirations, and a sense of the past, and is far more intense about them than Lyutov. He opens up a veritable encyclopedia of the values of the cultivated bourgeois, with high principles (altruism, pity, sensitivity, refinement) seeking respectable incarnation in tangible rewards (comfort, fame, money, adoring women). In the time-honored way of the stock literary *intelligent*, he is incapable of putting his dreams into action. But he really does not need to, for his fantasy has the power of clothing these dreams in flesh and sending them out as wish-fulfillments into the real world. All the characters of the novel—who are linked by a system of imagery that clusters around food, beds, and the mysteriously sexual "hollow" (*vpadina*)—spring from Kavalerov's brain.[23]

[23] There is no space here to demonstrate this contention satisfactorily, but let us cite one brief example. The observant reader will note that Andrei and Anechka, Kavalerov's landlady, have much in common physically, and in their relationship to Kavalerov as well. Both, for instance, are concerned with food, performing miracles with dead bodies, and working with entrails. Both are fat and resemble sausages themselves. Kavalerov first sees them performing their ablutions, half naked, with pieces of their hair floating in the wash basin, etc. The "hollow" (*vpadina*) describes the location of Anechka's sinister stove and is suggested by the appearance of Andrei's groin. Both take in strays—Anechka cats, Andrei people—provide Kavalerov with a bed, humiliate him, and threaten to devour (castrate) him. Ivan himself clusters many of the crucial images the first time Kavalerov sees (rather, invents) him: "He was carrying a pillow [bed]. He was holding, by the corner, a large pillow in a yellow case [sausage]. It was banging against his knee. From that, hollows [*vpadiny*] would appear and disappear (Yu. Olesha, *Zavist'*, *KN*, No. 7 [1927], p. 78). While working this out for a lecture, I discovered that my colleague, William E. Harkins, had been thinking along the same lines. He has embodied his conclusions in an interesting article: "The Theme of Sterility in Olesha's *Envy*," *Slavic Review*, xxv, No. 3 (September 1966), 443-57.

The most important of them is Ivan Babichev. As a father image, he is expected to demonstrate that the lofty ideals preached by his generation and imposed on Kavalerov's—passion, refinement, sensitivity, and so on—are superior to the menacing mindless pragmatism of the new Soviet society. Ivan fails. His grandiose inventions collapse or turn back on him; his splendid speeches come off only in sordid taverns; his spirituality proves to be a grotesque mockery of the life of Christ. He proves to be merely a buffoon—more lighthearted than Manyukin, to be sure, but just as sinister, for he possesses a fearsome immortality. No failure daunts him; he even returns unscathed from a painful and apparently final death.

Ivan's younger brother, Andrei, appears to be his opposite in practically every respect; he is a dreamer, to be sure, but also a practical man of action, who knows how to translate his vision into reality. He is the special object of Kavalerov's envy; for among the things Kavalerov envies is the ability of people to turn visions into realities. But Andrei's dream—a sausage, about which he can rhapsodize as extravagantly and lyrically as Ivan can about any of his loftier visions—is a grotesque parody of idealism. And Andrei is as sterile as Ivan himself; he is a hermaphrodite, with the furious drive of a man and the soft jiggling breasts of a woman, a sort of male mother, who takes in waifs (Kavalerov and Volodya), provides them with food and comfortable beds, but exacts a terrible price: their manhood. The sausage-maker, a fearsome devourer of flesh, is merely another version of the castration fantasy that centers in Anechka, the hag who walks around festooned with entrails, a huge knife in hand. Kavalerov stands in dread of Andrei, but views Ivan tolerantly and even affectionately—until the end, that is, when suddenly the depths of his hatred open up in that final scene, a classic of the Oedipal literature, where father and son, Ivan and Kavalerov, vie for the favors of Anechka, the wife-mother.[24] The failure of Kavalerov's projections proves the sterility of his own fantasy and of the values that underlie it: they are exposed as banal, cheap, undistinguished, a mish-mash of tawdry romances and petty-bourgeois aspirations, as his name, Cavalier-off, suggests. Such dreams, like all dreams, Olesha seems to say, prove to be onanistic and self-destructive. Even his envy is pointless, for Andrei is as sterile as Ivan. Kavalerov at the end achieves what his unconscious mind has really desired all along: extinction in the great womb-bed of Anechka.

THESE heroes reject not merely the past, however, but all ready-made values. Any ideologue quickens suspicion, yet fans temptation; for on the chaos of the world he imposes a pattern within which everything, even absurdity, takes on meaning. The novels and stories of the twenties teem with men who have succumbed to the temptation, the intellectuals turned Bolshevik. And all of them illustrate how truly heroic the way of the ideologue is, for it demands nothing less than the sacrifice of the mind. Great indeed is the faith that ennobles suicide. Levinson, the hero of Aleksandr Fadeev's novel *The Rout* (*Razgrom*), is this kind of man. Like Lyutov, he is a Jew. Indeed, one might call him Lyutov's wish-fulfillment, for he has succeeded in blocking off those incursions of memory, sentiment, wonder, doubt, and scruple that prohibit Lyutov from fulfilling the role he envisages for himself: passing unnoticed in a Cossack regiment. *The Rout* is set in a place identified only as Eastern Siberia—a world where space and time are so vast as to lose all importance, and where every action of man, be-

---

[24] We may recall that Kavalerov, in looking at the portrait of Anechka's dead husband, is reminded of his own father. And Anechka tells Kavalerov that he reminds her of her husband.

ing magnified, takes on an absolute quality, and therefore a meaning, however pointless it may seem to be.[25]

Levinson offers a perfect example of the merger of thought and action. As such, he holds out great temptation for the intellectual, who harbors deep doubts about the efficacy of his mind, and to the fragmented soul, who seeks a spiritual glue to make him whole. But Levinson carries a taint of the absurd. Neither he nor his men ever know exactly where they are, or where they will be going. They ride on and on, eternally wandering through an endless present, simply because they are where they are: necessity rules all.

Men like Mitya and Lyutov possess a keen sense of distance that gives them an eye for absurdity and makes the way of the ideologue—and the activist—unacceptable to them. They admire the heroic gesture that immolates the self to an ideal. But whenever they are tempted to try it themselves, they ape the buffoon. Mitya has his Manyukin, Kavalerov his Ivan. Even Lyutov, who should know better, falls into the trap, so desperate is he to find a way into the world of the Cossacks, that fairy-tale world of high adventure and self-assertive action that pulls at him with an almost sexual power:

> Savitskii, Commander of the Sixth Division, rose when he caught sight of me and I marvelled at the beauty of his giant's body. He rose, and the purple of his riding breeches and the crimson of his tilted cap and the decorations nailed to his chest clove the hut as a standard cleaves the sky. From him wafted a scent of remote perfumes and the sickly and cloying cool of soap. His long legs were like girls, sheathed to the shoulders in gleaming jackboots.

[25] A. Fadeev, *Razgrom* (Moscow, 1935). This was not published in *RVS*.

How can a pallid four-eyes like Lyutov ever win a place beside this magnificent specimen of bogatyr? The challenge is flung: "You go ahead and mess up a dame, and a real fine dame at that," the quartermaster tells him, "and the guys'll treat you real good."[26] Lyutov does "mess up a dame" but characteristically, it is a symbolic assault that he makes on her, in that grotesque scene in which he crushes the head of the landlady's fat, strutting goose, skewers the body with his sword, then thrusts it at her and orders her to cook it. The Cossacks do not laugh. They offer him food, allow him to read Lenin's latest speech to them, and appear to take him into their company. But the challenge turns out to have been baiting at its most fiendish. For Lyutov's action—the slaying of the goose-dragon—is an obvious parody of the heroic gesture, worthy of Gogol'. The Cossacks do not laugh at this absurdity, perhaps because it is so absurd as to constitute a far greater violence than they would ever perpetrate—a violence against the dignity of the self. Lyutov does what a clown or a jester would do; and the Cossacks in fact seem to take him as a kind of jester, a lightning rod for the absurdities with which the universe can threaten that dignity which is more precious to the Cossacks than life itself.

The ideologues and the activists mistrust and fear men like Lyutov, who have a disquieting talent for making life absurd. The intellectual, in fact, is one of the stock villains in proletarian fiction—a divided, ambiguous, and therefore untruthful man who tries to apply the Revolution as an unguent to his wounds, but discovers that it demands more of him than he is willing to give. Marxist theory insists that the ideal hero combine complexity of mind, richness of spirit, and effectiveness of action, all in perfect harmony. But no writer has ever managed to create a convincing portrait of such a superman. On a more down-to-earth scale, one scratches vainly in the literature of the twenties

[26] "Moi pervyi gus'," *Konarmiya*, pp. 40-41.

for signs of a Bolshevik intellectual, or an intellectual Bolshevik. By then the image of the monolithic revolutionary had lodged too deeply in the Bolshevik mythology to allow of the paradoxes that other writers (Dostoevskii, Sartre, perhaps Pasternak in *Dr. Zhivago*) have recognized and explored in the personality of the revolutionary: self-sacrifice and aloofness, doubt and certainty, wonderment and conviction. Heroes like Mitya, Lyutov, and even Kavalerov—all rebels in search of a cause—come closest to this type. The literary Bolsheviks, however, join hands with those literary intellectuals of a somewhat earlier vintage who illustrate the mind's terrible capacity to destroy itself in the name of salvation: in creating systems to ward off the chaos of the world, it builds its own prisons.

ANOTHER temptation to the man in quest of safeguards against experience has been art. In the fiction of the twenties it is proposed again and again, and rejected. Pil'nyak finds in the timeless rituals of Japanese life a promise for taming nature without disposing of man.[27] Kavalerov is an artist who fleshes out his fantasies and peoples the world with them. The aerial ballet created by Mitya Vekshin's sister Tanya is, like any work of art, a precarious but precise projection over the pit of life that constantly tries to pull it down. Firsov's novel attempts to give form to the amorphous material of Mitya's world. But all these artists fail. Japan's ceremonial gestures turn men into jerky puppets; Kavalerov's creative gift is a grunt that produces the scatological sausage; Tanya soars too far and pays with her life for her defiant pride; Firsov finally leaves off resisting the caprices of his subjects and abandons his work. But these failures are tinged with sadness: man is freed from delusion, but he has lost a gift.

[27] Cf., e.g., "Rasskaz o tom, kak sozdayutsya rasskazy," *Sobranie sochinenii*, VI (Moscow-Leningrad, 1929), 219-35.

A few writers extended the indictment of art to the form of their own works, in a final flash of the anti-esthetic protest that had flared up in the earlier twenties, but gradually died down during the revival of the novel and the short story. Leonov was not one of them: even though the constant deflation of Firsov's pretensions at insight may legitimately be read as a parody of the omniscient author-narrator of nineteenth-century fiction, *The Thief* owes too much to the traditional strategies of fiction. *Envy*, on the other hand, is a declaration of rebellion against "significance" and "meaning." Reality has no objective value; it is the creation of one individual. We are completely at the mercy of Kavalerov's fantasies, which work in unpredictable ways, and must therefore follow them where they will, taking them, as we do real life itself, on whatever their terms are at any particular moment. We are prisoners of a ruthless present, the world of what is actually happening. There are no accurate interpretations of events, no proper explanations or summings up, few of the trappings of conventional novels. From the viewpoint of traditional fiction, there is a shocking extravagance of means in *Envy* in the pure actions and pure gestures that are absolved from service to the underlying symbol-pattern that unifies the book. On top of this Olesha erects a scaffolding that has all the stark simplicity of a formula plot: two "old" characters (Ivan and Anechka) versus two "new" ones (Volodya, Valya), with Kavalerov and Andrei Babichev providing the bridge. But it is a trap to catch the careless reader, and most critics, hypnotized by the symmetry, have fallen into it, reading the work as a conventional novel of manners, not as the symbolist fantasy it is. Very likely Voronskii was among them and therefore found nothing in *Envy* to contradict his idea of what the well-made "monumental" work should be.

WITH the values of civilization in doubt, the primitivist ethos continued to pull on a few writers. By now, however, it had lost most of its exotic savagery and had taken on the ethical coloration of the mid-twenties, in the theme of "brotherhood." Khadzhi-Murat Muguev's "The Death of Nikola Bunchuk" (Smert' Nikoly Bunchuka, No. 11, 1927) is typical of the way the theme was handled in the conventional war setting. Bunchuk, a young Cossack in the service of the Whites, has been detailed to a firing squad that is to dispose of a group of Red prisoners. Moments before the execution, Bunchuk's best friend, Shiba, lowers his rifle, refusing to shoot. He is promptly arrested. Bunchuk is assigned to the guard escort, frees Shiba at gunpoint, and both desert to the Reds. Political conviction, however, plays no part in this action. Shiba's defiant gesture reflects an instinctual reverence for life, and awakens it in Bunchuk as well. Yet the outcome is tragic, for humanism of this kind has no place in a world split by warring ideologies that demand choice: Bunchuk, in fleeing, is caught between the Red and White lines, and is killed. We do not even know the color of the bullet.

Vsevolod Ivanov extended the "brotherhood" theme to more intelligent types. In "Duty" for instance, a Red officer saves the life of a White, and later, when the tables are turned, the White returns the favor. In "Cotton," an English secret agent and a Red commissar discover that the common struggle for survival dissipates their class hatred.[28] The so-called "Pereval" (Pass) writers made this theme their trademark. The proletarian critics dubbed it "new humanism" and traced it to A. Lezhnev's doctrine of "sincerity," which we discussed in an earlier chapter. Ivan Kataev's story "Milk" (Moloko) served as an object les-

[28] "Dolg," *KN*, No. 5 (1923); "Khlopok," *Sobranie sochinenii*, II (Moscow-Leningrad, 1928), 101-24.

son: the Communist hero, swayed by the appealing human qualities of his kulak adversary, chokes down his class revulsion and gives vent to a feeling of "sympathy" for his fellow man. The critics granted that Kataev might well have been "sincere," but insisted that by presenting the kulak in such an attractive light, he made mockery of the dispossession campaign then going on, and eroded the natural class antagonism of the reader.[29]

The brotherhood theme, in any case, had a limited appeal to writers. For the questing hero, it offered yet another easy temptation to shrug off the torments of the search and grasp a ready-to-hand solution. Mitya, Lyutov, even Kavalerov stand alone in the universe: no other man can share their special agony. And when they come to sense their solitude, as they do, and begin to understand that they can confront nothing if they do not at first confront themselves, fully and ruthlessly, they have discovered a goal for their quest. They struggle to avoid this final confrontation, while sensing that it must come and moving toward it. And when it does come, it brings a sudden but unmistakable intuition of that meaning which has eluded them, and their quest, along with their story, reaches an end. Again *Red Calvary* suggested a pattern for subsequent works. Most of the stories end in sudden clearings of an atmosphere that has thickened and charged itself to such a point that it can hold nothing more. And this sudden clearing yields a meaning—often underplayed, but always surprising.

Let us look at the opening story, "Crossing the Zbruch," as an example. It is built on constant shifts and contrasts in time (eternal nature, the century-old highroad, the year of the war, the day of the march, the night of the bivouac), in style (the laconic communiqué from the front, the bejeweled description of the march, the lyrical apotheosis of nature, the earthy speech of the Jewess), in perspective

[29] M. Serebryanskii, "Epokha i eyo 'rovesniki,'" *Na literaturnom postu*, No. 5-6 (1930), p. 23.

(the Russian empire, the dirty Jewish hut), in characters
(the splendid young Cossacks, the wretched Jews), and in
setting (the fields, streams, poppies, moon, as against the
broken crockery and human excrement that are the flora
of the *shtetl*). These are laid down, slab-like, side by side.
One interrupts the other, at first rather casually, then faster
and faster, in a frenzied rivalry that creates a tension which
threatens finally to tear the story apart unless some great
violent gesture is made to restore order. And it is made, in
the sudden cry of the daughter over her slaughtered father:
". . . I want to know where else in the whole world you will
find another father like my father?"[30] The gesture by itself
is flat. But because of Babel's scrupulous preparation, we
react with a sense of relief. The sinister intimations of violence that throb from every part of his universe—the road
laid down on peasant bones, the lopped-off head of the sun,
the disemboweled mattress—augur some great catastrophe,
the more terrible because it is utterly impersonal. The slit
throat of a miserable old man, however, makes a sacrificial
gesture that brings violence down to human proportions,
renders it acceptable, and seems to buy it off, fairly cheaply
at that, with a mere Jew rather than a sturdy Cossack. The
story ends because the tension is broken. Yet the sacrifice
has given the Jew an importance and a dignity he never
possessed in life; he has been deemed a worthy gift to the
gods. And Lyutov is suddenly made aware of that paradox
of violence that dogs him throughout the book: its degrad-
ing yet ennobling nature.

Each of the stories ends in a moment of sudden insight.
Lyutov struggles to link them into a meaningful pattern
that will finally reveal what his experiences have all been
about. But he fails, for each insight stands alone, the result
of a collaboration of circumstances that change from moment to moment, and never accumulate to form a system of

[30] "Perekhod cherez Zbruch," *Konarmiya*, p. 7.

meaning or a guide to life. The point is reinforced by the cyclical structure of *Red Cavalry*, which permits an infinite number of stories, or life-experiences, to be added. Lyutov does not wish to accept this fact, for he craves order and pattern. But it is so, nonetheless: man can never learn from his experiences, but can only accept each one as it comes, live it as fully and passionately as possible, and be content to discover its unique meaning for him.

Many of the restless literary heroes of the NEP follow a similar pattern of quest and epiphany, although circumstances and experiences may differ greatly. The version offered by *The Thief* is not only the most extensive, but has made the strongest impression on subsequent writers. One of the crucial moments in Mitya's life comes early in the book, after a journey he has made with Panama, an accomplice. On the train he has met a pretty girl; Panama steals her suitcase and turns it over to him; and in the solitude of his room he opens it "with a smile of curiosity." Here is what he finds:

> In the suitcase there were underwear, dresses, several pairs of black and light-blue tights, some unaccountable feminine knick-knacks, and a variety of inoffensive odds and ends with an unfamiliar smell. Rummaging in them, he threw the things directly onto the floor and carelessly pushed them aside with his foot. A surprise awaited him in the bottom compartment, where there was nothing except long silk cords with tight knots and nickel pulleys attached. Each of them ended in a permanent noose, and the soft silk shone from long and constant use. Mit'ka, flustered and bewildered, flung them aside almost superstitiously.
>
> This particular aspect of the profession of thief seemed repellent to him. The scattered rags, the rubbish that someone else had worn, seemed to narrow the room with their unfamiliar smells, their rustlings, and their

varied colors; they seemed to hamper living and moving. . . .

. . . he felt terrified at the invasion of unnecessary, flabby things desecrated by another person's touch, things he must burn, get rid of, give away, throw into the river, and destroy entirely. . . .[31]

These are not ordinary possessions, as Mitya's reaction to them suggests. His curiosity gets more than it bargained for. Lodged deep in the suitcase is an old photograph of two children. In them Mitya recognizes himself and the girl on the train—his sister Tanya, whom he has not seen since he left home. This sudden encounter with his childhood in an assemblage of objects throws his past open before him, that baggage of memory he has been struggling both to cast off and to ransack for clues to the meaning of his condition.

This same kind of experience recurs in many crucial moments of his life. When, for example, he leaves home and prepares to step across the threshold of manhood:

Then his stepmother took a small birch-bast box . . . and packed it full of everything she hadn't the slightest use for herself; she did this so that nobody would say that her son had been chased out hungry and naked. . . .

.   .   .   .

His first night away from home he spent on the road, but along the way he paused at all the places he had known intimately in childhood. . . . At dawn, when the dew began to steam up from the ground, Mit'ka warmed himself at a fire. Then with a resolute gesture he flung his stepmother's rubbish out of the box. With this he renounced, as it were, his paternal home. Now the only thing on him that was not his was that cross his real mother, whom he did not remember, had hung around

[31] *Vor*, No. 1 (1927), p. 43.

his neck. He lost that three years later, and he did not mourn the loss: his neck felt freer. . . .[32]

This episode compresses the whole thrust of the novel, with the pattern of search, confrontation, rejection, and final freedom. The crucial action, however, is the rejection: for in the objects confronting him, Mitya glimpses the hell that tempts the wanderer at every step in Leonov's world—the hell of certainty.

Leonov's works are full of people who assemble objects in hopes of creating a three-dimensional world, a world whose solidity withstands the relentless eroding flow of time and gives its maker a kind of immortality, a world whose symmetry shuts out the chaos of the universe and gives its maker an identity by offering him something to touch and name and arrange as he will. There is Dr. Yolkov, who gathers and labels living human specimens like index cards, in preparation for his definitive work on the nature of man (*The End of a Petty Man*); in *The Thief* there are Pukhov, with his antique shop, and Tanya, with the straps and belts and nooses of her death-defying (actually, life-defying) act.

But all have exchanged their freedom and their lives for a terrible kind of immortality: they have created museums of frustrated dreams and futile quests, forever mummified in a dead world of objects. They are Lucifers as well, anxious in their pain and despair to drag down others. Dr. Yolkov's "evenings" are gatherings of the damned; Pukhov's junk-crammed shop symbolizes the comforting but suffocating myth of Christian salvation that he urges on Mitya; even Tanya works to ensnare her brother in his own guilt-laden memories of the past. Mitya scents the traps and tries to step around them. But it is Tanya's fatal fall that turns suspicion into certainty—the flutter of a fallen angel, strangled in the noose of pride that she has fashioned in her ef-

[32] *Ibid.*, p. 56.

fort to overcome life. In fact, each of the characters in the novel holds a claim on Mitya's soul—Masha the dignity he has offended, Manyukin the world of his past and the constant memory of his failure, San'ka the boundless devotion of the lackey. Mitya learns that these claims are too insistent to be sidestepped; he must battle with each of them in order to win the right to reject it. Extending his rejection to all the people around him, he casts them off like dirty objects from a trunk. That is why, though respected, he is disliked. San'ka perceives what Mitya is up to when he calls him a thief, meaning that he takes devotion from everyone and gives nothing in return; and it is in this sense that we should understand the title of the novel. Mitya replies that the real test of love is the ability to forswear love, and let people go. Only Zinka understands that, and she resolves therefore to take Mitya for what he is, in order not to lay any claims on him. But even that constitutes a claim; for Mitya hates what he is, and is trying to break out into freedom from himself.

Leonov's point is that all human relations, like physical objects, encumber. He has a cruel view of men as tyrants who lust for domination over one another, with love perhaps the most savage and most powerful weapon they wield. The lackey-love of San'ka, like any more-than-casual meeting of two individuals, carries strings with which he tries to bind Mitya in order to shield himself from life—just as he crams his room with gewgaws, among them, significantly, a bird cage, in an effort to create a respectability and peace he has never known. Such love must be cast off, Leonov seems to be telling us, in order that we may be free. Only after man has settled all the claims that are made on his soul can he, like Mitya, attain to an undistracted, unwavering contemplation of himself: naked he stands then, ready to experience rebirth as a whole, vigorous, and unflawed man. The truly free man is the outlaw—not a "circumspect thief," as Mitya contemptuously calls the acquisitive Zavarikhin—but a man beyond all law save a mysterious urge to life that links him with the eternal world of nature, beyond man's defiling touch. *The Thief* ends: "And as he stepped into the forest, seeing this, his second homeland, with new eyes, the sun, long-maned like an untamed horse that seeks its rider in the world, was rising over the earth."[33]

At one point, Firsov observes: "In those years [of Revolution and Civil War] various people fought for the supreme welfare of people, while giving little thought to the people themselves. Their great love, distributed to all equally, had no more warmth than a stearin candle."[34] He asks in effect whether one sincere and selfish love is not better than all the abstract love in the world. Leonov thinks that it is not. He wishes us to believe, apparently, that man is too complex a creature to be measured by any one person's claim. This is a characteristic theme of Leonov's, but one which unfortunately he has neither the skill nor the insight to handle with that final touch of assurance and convincingness that makes great art. Leonov's readers are well aware that his works are complicated, none more so than *The Thief*. He peoples them with platoons of secondary characters. None of them is complex in his own right, but they need not be, for their sole function is to embody one idea or course of action that entices the protagonist, Mitya. Leonov handles them well: they argue their case convincingly, and stamp their quirks on our memories. But Mitya is unworthy of the great effort they make to sway him: he essays no real encounter with any of them, but merely listens, like a schoolmaster, while they have their say. Then he rejects them. Leonov does succeed in conveying the impression of a confused man beset by alternatives, but not a man who is genuinely tempted by them. For that reason, the renunciations appear frivolous.

[33] *Ibid.*, No. 7 (1927), p. 63.
[34] *Ibid.*, No. 1 (1927), p. 38.

The failure here is partially one of technique: Leonov is unable to solve the problem of making his hero truly involved, yet keeping him disentangled enough to pursue his quest. But it is also a failure of compassion, a deafness to the dialogue of human relations. Mitya's original sin was the sin of abstraction, of principle that translated itself into pride. At the end, he returns to abstraction, as he heaves off his entire life, dying a symbolic death in the great sickness he undergoes, and reawakening freed from the burden of memory and the curse of experience. One feels that never again will anything touch him deeply. His self-contained world, despite Leonov's intentions, is a sterile Utopia, much closer to Kavalerov's, which also rejects man and turns back into itself, than to Lyutov's, which insists on the uniqueness of the individual experience, but finds it through deep involvement with other men. Leonov is not a cynic who says that the thief will out: he represents the renunciation as something clean and good. But he makes it unconsciously callous, for it is unworthy of the magnitude of the problems that Mitya meets but never really confronts. The stakes are high—nothing less than the salvation of the soul—yet they are dismissed without a suggestion of irony. What should be high tragedy, or high comedy, verges on cheap self-seeking. Like all Leonov's heroes, Mitya is a cripple, whom we are expected to take as a whole man.

· I I ·

To all appearances, Voronskii had made a brilliant success of finding new works of literature that complemented his journal's "monumental" program—works that in the main returned an alert and often complex hero to the center of the literary stage; emphasized movement, process, development in a variety of themes, settings, and moods; and cultivated the familiar terrain of the "classical" forms, particularly the novel and novella, while striving for a simpler and starker language. But Voronskii was chronically dissatisfied. And as the twenties wore on, dissatisfaction turned to disaffection. Too many writers, he complained, were still rooting in the slough of naturalism. Others disregarded actual life altogether, and churned out windy, dull, abstract treatises that travestied novels. Literature as a whole, he thought, lacked excitement and dash; writers had turned into industrious ants patiently piling up the familiar forms. Even Babel' and Leonov seemed to prefer letting their literary capital collect interest before making any further speculative investments. In his final major survey of literature for 1927, Voronskii could not find one writer to single out for the praise and encouragement he usually bestowed so lavishly.[35]

Voronskii had always been rather fickle in his enthusiasms, as Leonov, Ivanov, Seifullina, Romanov, and many other writers could testify from having been taken up in the euphoria of discovery and then abandoned to the comfortable toleration accorded familiar and well-worn objects. But more than fickleness was at work here. His gnawing sense of literature's inadequacy reflected a growing disparity between the program for literature that *RVS* had evolved, in the doctrine of "monumentalism," and the directions in which the journal's theory of literature had begun to move after the mid-twenties.

Whether from an insufficiency of candor or of insight, Voronskii was not prepared to admit in so many words that such a disparity existed. In his opinion, literature's decline (it was never his journal's deficiency) could be traced to the atrophy of what he sometimes called "romanticism," but more often "lyricism." One set of meanings he attached to the term involved passion, fire, enthusiasm, excitement. And he now began to look back nostalgically on the orna-

[35] "Pisatel', kniga, chitatel'," *KN*, No. 1 (1927), pp. 226-39. Cf. also "O tom, chego u nas net," *KN*, No. 10 (1925), pp. 255-56.

mentalists, who had been out of fashion for what amounted to an age, as the frenzied pace of the twenties measured things. Voronskii wished not to spark a revival, but to show that, whatever their other faults, the ornamentalists certainly had not been dull. Even Pil'nyak's *Bare Year*, which critics in *RVS* around 1924 had tended to dismiss as fatuous ethnographism, now struck Voronskii as still one of the finest "lyrical" portraits of the Revolution. But the term meant more than merely a kind of adrenalin for droopy writers. The other sense in which Voronskii used it developed out of the modifications he was beginning to make in his theory of art at just about the time his disaffection with contemporary literature reached a peak. "Lyricism" described an intuition of eternity, of a world of pure feeling unsullied by petty human concerns and caught up in an "immediate impression" that eradicates time and history. In both senses of the term, all art, as Voronskii saw it, should be lyrical.

The enormous amount of lyric poetry that Voronskii published in *RVS* tempts one to speculate that he may have been trying to counterbalance the deficiencies of prose fiction as he saw them. Voronskii regarded his journal in the way we should read it: as a unity. Perhaps therefore he thought that if prose could not be intrinsically lyrical, then lyricism could be introduced through the back door, in the poetry section, and the impression produced by the literature section as a whole improved. This poetry cannot be rated "monumental" by any of the most elastic definitions of the term. For one thing, it is physically too modest: nearly all the 130-odd poets who published in *RVS* over a six-year period—representing practically every "school" in existence during the twenties—specialized in the short lyric. There were very few epics, ballads, narrative poems, and so on—those genres, in other words, that we would expect to find if "monumentalness" were really operating as a selector. For another thing, the themes and moods are all wrong. A few poems, to be sure, do beat the gongs of topicality—

war, conditions in coal mines, proletarian brotherhood, oppressed minorities, the romance of two agitation-propaganda workers—but most cannot be reckoned "contemporary" in any of the senses then current, for they lack "message," "social" content, and even recognizably modern settings. Their creators preferred the "pure" love or nature lyric (Il'ina, Utkin, Zarudin, Golodnyi); or the traditional modes of sadness and yearning for a departed past (Poletaev, Esenin); or the familiar contrast between the eternal world of nature and the time-driven world of daily life (Klychkov, Kazin); or the assaults of urban civilization upon innocence (Prishelets, Obradovich, Druzhinin). Significantly, the three principal contributors—Esenin, with 51 poems, Pyotr Oreshin, with 24, and Sergei Klychkov, with 22—were all peasant lyricists, which meant that they specialized in the moods and themes we have been describing.[36] Even the majority of those poems that by virtue of theme might conceivably qualify as "revolutionary," "proletarian," or "civic," beat to the lyrical pulse: the worker yearning for the open fields of his native province (Kazin), the eulogies to Revolution in the cosmic style of Blok and Belyi (Zharov, Yasnyi, Kirillov), the tear-drenched portraits of aged blacksmiths, starving children, and decrepit horses (Aleksandrovskii, Pozharova, Korenev).

Marxists react to poetry of this kind with a wide range of negative emotions—rage, indignation, scorn, disgust, contempt—but never with indifference. Those few who do like it are invariably apologetic or defensive about what they suspect is a deep perversion in themselves: the confessional

---

[36] The same contrast between the natural and the created world—the one permanent, the other changing and menacing—runs throughout Soviet literature, but is especially strong in the twenties and in the recent "thaw." It would be interesting to study it as a reflection of a curious dualism in the Communist mind. Olesha's joke, in *Envy*, of the machine with feelings (Ophelia) is very modern, to be sure; but the violation of human dignity by machines is one of the root myths of Marxism too, as any reader of *Capital* knows.

literature by Marxists who enjoyed reading Esenin, for instance, forms an interesting and rather pathetic minor genre in the twenties. For lyric poetry opens up areas of the mind that Marxism has only the crudest tools to deal with, and it brings to life—for Russian Marxists at any rate—all the prejudices against the "decadent" *fin-de-siècle* moods with which they tend to identify it. In fact, the fortunes of the lyric impulse in Soviet Russia mesh with the rhythm of censorship: periods of severe repression, which tolerate no ambiguity, have told upon lyric poetry; conversely, periods of relaxation, such as World War II and various phases of the "thaw," have all been characterized by a resurgence of lyric moods in poetry and prose. Any casual reader of the literature of the last five or six years has been struck by the intensity and skill of the nature writing. This pattern was set in the twenties. One of the first outward signs that *RVS* had begun to feel the growing power of the literary bureaucracy was a sharp drop, beginning early in 1927, in the number and the quality of lyric poems published there, and the appearance of those longer genres, well garnished with "contemporary" subjects, that the "monumental" esthetic had led one to expect all along.[37]

In the early twenties Voronskii felt as sheepish as other Marxists about the sort of poems he was publishing. At least, he felt obliged to defend them; and his defense took essentially the same approach that most Marxist apologists for lyricism take. The article on "Art as Cognition" digressed to make the point that good lyric poetry is really the same as a good piece of prose fiction, since both deal with reality. Only the angle is different: "the lyricist observes himself, the prose writer has to do with objects outside himself: the writer's artistic attention is just shifted."

[37] E.g., V. Bugaevskii, "The Post Office" (Pochtamt, No. 4 [1927]); L. Ivanova, "On the Death of Nicholas Sacco" (Na smert' Nikolaya Sakko, No. 9 [1927]); E. Bagritskii, "The Lay of Opanas" (Duma pro Opanasa, No. 10 [1925]), a ballad about the Civil War.

What the lyricist observes, however, is not the riot of subjective fantasies, but the cognitively valuable self: the
true lyric poem communicates feelings that have "universal or class interest."[38] After Voronskii stopped trying to
please everyone and gained more confidence in his own
ideas, he gave up apologizing for lyric poetry. In fact,
it was not long before he made "lyricism," in both the
senses we have described, the ultimate test of a poet's quality, something that could extenuate virtually any other fault.
It was the one thing, for instance, that made the Smiths
bearable to him despite their "cosmism," "pantheism," and
spleen.[39] He saw no reason why the test should not apply
to prose fiction as well.

The important thing about this enthusiasm for lyricism
was that it reflected the direction in which Voronskii's
theory of art was moving, yet at the same time pulled
against his journal's program. For "monumentalism" had
been erected on the cognition theory as it existed around
1923, wherein literature was seen as an imitation of process
mediated through a tissue of daily details: a horizontal
view of experience, if we may put it so, which seems particularly appropriate to the novel. But according to the
later version of the theory, expressed most fully in Voronskii's articles of 1928, art operates not to make us sense
process or the passage of time, but rather to overcome time
by plunging us, in a single sudden insight, into union with
the timeless universe: a vertical view of experience, which
belongs more to poetry, particularly the lyric, than to the
novel. Voronskii's disgruntled comments on the state of
literature in 1927 seem to indicate his groping toward some
combination of these two concepts of experience—the monumental and the lyrical, epiphany within process, passion

[38] "Iskusstvo, kak poznanie zhizni, i sovremennost' (K voprosu o
nashikh literaturnykh raznoglasiyakh)," *KN*, No. 5 (1923), p. 351.
[39] "Literaturnye otkliki. O gruppe pisatelei 'Kuznitsa,'" *KN*, No.
3 (1923), pp. 297-312.

within universals. One of his last essays contains a long and admiring appreciation of the scene in *War and Peace* which he regarded as the high point of Tolstoi's art and perhaps even the finest moment in all Russian literature— the wounded Prince Andrei on the battlefield at Austerlitz:

> He opened his eyes, hoping to see how the battle between the French and the artillery men had ended, wanting to know whether the red-headed artillery man had been killed or not, whether the cannons had been captured or saved. But he saw nothing. Above him there was now nothing but the sky—the lofty sky, unclear, yet immeasurably lofty, with gray clouds gliding quietly across it. "How quiet, peaceful and solemn it is, not at all the way it was when I was running," thought Prince Andrei, "when we were running, shouting and fighting. How is it that I have never before seen that lofty sky? And how happy I am that I have found it at last. Yes! Everything is empty, everything vanity except that infinite sky. There is nothing, nothing but that. But even that does not exist. There is nothing but silence and peace. And thank God! . . .[40]

What impressed Voronskii about this passage?

> Prince Andrei lies wounded on the field of battle. What a felicitous theme for the artist, it would seem, what scope for the imagination, how many sad and tragic pages could be written, and in fact, how much is heaped up and invented in our days while describing such scenes. But there is nothing of that in Tolstoi. . . . No doubt, other thoughts came into Andrei Bolkonskii's head besides his thought about the sky; while lying on the battlefield, he experienced other complex and varied sensations too, but Tolstoi did not need them: he limited

[40] *Voina i mir*, Part 3, Chapter XVI, *Polnoe sobranie sochinenii*, IX, (Moscow, 1937), 344.

himself to those feelings and states of mind that are understandable to all, obligatory for all, that are the most characteristic and the most authentic. Prince Andrei *had* to think about the sky; everything else that he saw and thought might or might not have been true, and therefore Tolstoi did not reproduce these other states of mind.[41]

Andrei, then, glimpses a universal truth, which is independent of society, class, and conscious choice:

Habits, prejudices, petty cares, sorrows, insignificant joys, back-breaking labor, conventions, illnesses, heredity, social oppression, the deaths of loved ones, the banalities of one's surroundings, current opinions and ideas, distorted hopes and aspirations, fantasies, fanaticism—all these things, from our earliest years, veil our eyes, dull the sharpness and freshness of our perception and our attention, push into the depths of our conscious mind the most powerful and joyful impressions, and make the most precious and beautiful in life and in the cosmos imperceptible. . . . Distorted social man necessarily possesses distorted perceptions, images and conceptions of the world. Reality is reflected in us in distorted forms, as in a mirror with an uneven surface. We are more like sick people than like normal people. Survivals of the past, the dominant capitalist environment, make millions of people sick and abnormal. In today's society, an equilibrium, even a very relative one, between man and his environment is a rare and happy exception.[42]

Andrei achieves such an equilibrium. His experience resembles Lyutov's, Mitya's, and even Kavalerov's, in the

[41] "O khudozhestvennoi pravde," *Iskusstvo videt' mir* (Moscow, 1928), p. 34.
[42] "Iskusstvo videt' mir," *Iskusstvo videt' mir*, pp. 83-84.

sudden and unexpected cessation of motion, the sense of harmony, rightness, wholeness, the sudden irruption of insight into the horizontal flow of narrative. Time stops; the experience thus passes from the realm of history into the realm of myth.[43] A world of pure sentience opens up; petty human concerns are left behind. It is an experience that makes a final affirmation of each man's identity as an individual; for it is unique, self-contained, and incapable of being translated back into the horizontal world as a guide to living. Andrei dies; so, symbolically, does Kavalerov; Mitya's future can only be hinted at; Lyutov continues his quest for a recipe of life that he will never find. Their epiphanous experiences seem to come closest, in literature, to what Voronskii described in his last writings on theory as the experience and effect of art.

IN THESE last writings, Voronskii expressed the belief that a new period in literature was about to open. Everything indicated to him that the forms which had so recently risen to prominence were now sinking into senescence, particularly the novel. Perhaps it had not "outlived its time"; but Voronskii was certain that "in all probability it will occupy a more modest place than it has heretofore, and will be subjected, indeed perhaps even now is being subjected to very striking changes."[44] Complexity, conflict, a keen perception of the workings of the subconscious mind—even these no longer seemed so important; Voronskii found it necessary to temper his praise of Proust's skill in those areas with a warning that they had their limitations and were better left to the older writers.[45] Just what was emerging to replace

[43] Voronskii's notion of the image as a kind of snapshot, an instantly capsuled truth, seems to hang on a vertical view of experience. If so, perhaps that helps explain his failure to develop any workable theory of imagery consistent with the early "horizontal" cognition theory.

[44] "Iskusstvo videt' mir," p. 113.

[45] "Marsel' Prust. (K voprosu o psikhologii khudozhestvennogo tvorchestva)," *Iskusstvo videt' mir* (Moscow, 1928), p. 161.

the novel Voronskii found difficult to put into words. He looked for it in the kind of piece that Mikhail Prishvin specialized in: "not tales, not the novel, not short stories," but "sketches, notes, observations";[46] in the components of Babel's *Red Cavalry*; in the reminiscences by Gor'kii (there is no mention of the super-novel *Klim Samgin*); in Belyi's *Notes of a Dreamer*—that is to say, in brief, highly lyrical forms on the margin of fiction and the documentary. Much of the writing of the Perevalists seems to be like that; perhaps that is why Voronskii rated it so highly, and why his later theories of art were so readily adopted by those young writers. He might well have taken his own output after 1927 as an illustration too. Besides his autobiography, which forms a series of semi-fictional vignettes, his writings include stories—intensely lyrical, often sentimental, and much closer to sketches than to anything resembling a typical short-story form.[47]

It is highly likely that, with these new expectations launched, Voronskii would eventually have had to abandon "monumentalism" as the program for *RVS*. Because of his purge, we have no way of knowing. But one thing is certain: he would have taken exception to the way the theme of epiphany developed in the literature of the thirties. There it followed the pattern suggested in *The Thief*. The positive hero of socialist realist fiction is an outsider too, but he has already had his vision before he puts a foot on the stage. We might suppose that he is the way Mitya Vekshin would have been if Leonov had written a sequel to his novel. He no longer wonders, but asserts; no longer seeks,

---

[46] "Iskusstvo videt' mir," p. 112.

[47] Gabriela Porębina makes the interesting observation that the character Valentin in *Waters of Life and Death* is a double of the narrator (Voronskii); and she shows how several of Voronskii's key ideas about the nature of art are carried through, in semi-fictional form, in this book (*Aleksander Woronski. Poglądy estetyczne i krytycznoliterackie [1921-1928]* [Wroclaw-Warsaw-Cracow, 1964], pp. 137-39).

but moulds reality to his vision. He has the same horror of physical reality that moves Mitya: again and again in socialist realist novels that reality is the realm of the villain, entrance into which is signaled by a sudden thickening of the style, as nouns and adjectives rise up on every side to trip the traveler. (We may recall the well-stocked kitchen of Mr. Bixby's dreams, in Valentin Kataev's *Time, Forward!*, or the cluttered office of the treacherous collective farm chairman Polyanitsa in Sholokhov's *Virgin Soil Upturned.*)[48] But unlike Mitya, he is never tempted to make a journey through hell. Even the petty cares of daily life do not exist for him; he hardly ever eats, sleeps, or makes love. When essential to the movement of the story, these functions are assigned, in socialist realist novels as in Racine plays, to secondary characters, who themselves never intrude on greatness. One of the crises in Valentin Kataev's construction novel *Time, Forward!* occurs when the shock brigade engaged in the cement-pouring competition finds itself short a pair of hands to push a wheelbarrow. Although the project teeters on the edge of disaster, it never occurs to anyone that Margulies, the hero, could pitch in and help: his role is the far loftier one of creating incentive with his full-blown vision of a contest already won. Such heroes have joined the company of the kings, queens, and warriors who people the neo-classical drama.

VORONSKII had seen enough intimations of this kind of hero in proletarian fiction of the twenties to know that it was disastrous to literature as he conceived it. In fact, he parodied it in a brief sketch he wrote in 1927. His protagonist, Comrade Mikeshin, heads a "typical" Soviet enterprise, and embodies all the virtues of the storybook Bolshevik— among them, arriving at work half an hour early in order

---

[48] Valentin Kataev, *Vremya, vperyod!* (Moscow, 1935); Mikhail Sholokhov, *Podnyataya tselina*, Book 2, *Sobranie sochinenii v vos'mi tomakh*, VII (Moscow, 1962), 191-92.

to set an "infectious" example for his employees; disposing of all harmful luxuries, such as a car; and always keeping his office door open to those who seek wise paternal counsel.[49] The literary hero, for Voronskii, was not a superman, but an ordinary person who finds heroism in the daily round. Any man can experience the kind of vision Voronskii had in mind, presumably; but through the experience he ceases to be an ordinary man. Literature, Voronskii felt, could serve this vision not by prescribing spiritual exercises, as the proletarians seemed to think, but by showing that man must seek meaning through deep involvement in the here and now, and not in the formulas of the ideologues. The proletarian, and later the socialist realist ethic made no distinction between outer and inner man. But Voronskii always insisted that real literature, like real life, works in that area of constant becoming, mediating between what is and what should be. The finest writing of the twenties did just that; and nowhere do we find it better represented than in *RVS*.

[49] "Odin oglushitel'nyi aplodisment," *Al'manakh "Krug,"* vi (1927), 176-84. The joke was not appreciated by proletarian critics. Cf. P. S. Kogan, "Literaturnye zametki," *Pravda*, August 7, 1927, p. 5.

CHAPTER IX

The Decline of the Thick Journal

AT THE CENTER of literary life in the mid-twenties stood the thick journals, now restored to sovereignty, after nearly fifty years, as arbiters of taste and showplaces of talent. No reader could consider himself cultivated, let alone *au courant*, who did not follow at least one of them regularly. No writer stood much chance of winning a reputation who did not publish in them. No critic could hope to sway the public so effectively through any other medium. *RVS* still attracted the brightest talents. But it no longer stood alone —rivals had risen. Naturally, each claimed to offer something unique; but each modeled itself on the structure, if not the program, of Voronskii's journal. Whatever else the editors—a notoriously cranky lot—might have quarreled about, they evidently agreed on the form and purpose of the thick journal.

· I ·

The first real rival of *RVS* was *Young Guard* (*Molodaya gvardiya*), which began in 1922. Though an official publication of the Central Committees of the Russian Communist Party and the Communist Youth (Komsomol), in fact it moved in orbit around the Octobrists. The membership of the editorial board changed frequently, but it always included staunch supporters of that line, among them, at various times, Averbakh, Vardin, Bezymenskii, Ermilov, Kirshon, and Libedinskii. For that reason the journal had no hope of carrying out its announced policy of representing all young writers who supported the Revolution, regardless of class provenience or group allegiance. Instead, *Young Guard* catered to the proletarians. Although the lynch-pins were writers who had already made their repu-

tations, like Malashkin, Yasnyi, Golodnyi, Nikiforov, and
Romanov, the journal concentrated on unknown talents. For
most of them, to be sure, publication posed no threat to obscurity, but at least they had a hearing. Describing its mission
as "the struggle with ignorance, with ineptness and with
the lack of culture,"[1] Young Guard aimed at a far less
sophisticated audience than did RVS. That explains several
unusual appendages to a structure that otherwise is typical
of a thick journal: profuse illustrations, both drawings and
photographs; a chess department; a series of do-it-yourself
articles on such practical matters as organizing a sports
club or learning to swim; and a strong—some even said
morbid—interest in the mores and morals of the younger
generation. The literary criticism was flabby and insignificant, but that did not matter: everyone knew perfectly
well where the journal's sympathies lay, and with On
Guard as aggressively active as it was, Young Guard
would merely have labored the obvious if it had attempted
to flesh out a criticism department of its own.

Around 1926, Young Guard decided to try for tone. The
illustrations, the practical articles, and the chess section
were dropped. A more dignified and somber look now
made this journal physically indistinguishable from RVS
or New World. But the proletarian reader evidently was
not pleased with the change: from 9,000 copies in 1922, the
average pressrun had leveled off to around 7,000 over the
next two years; in 1926, however, it dropped to somewhere
between 5,000 and 6,000 an issue. Yet no drastic counter-
measures were taken until 1929, when tone was sacrificed for liveliness. Publication was stepped up to twice a
month, the average number of pages reduced to one hundred per issue, and the format cut down to a size that could
slip into an overcoat pocket. Photographs and line drawings reappeared, each issue sported a snappy cover printed

[1] "Molodoi rabochei gvardii," Molodaya gvardiya, No. 1 (1922),
p. 3.

in three colors, and a breezier style was introduced with new contributors like Mayakovskii and Tret'yakov from the old *LEF*, and Sel'vinskii from the Constructivists. The renovations worked: circulation nearly tripled. But they converted *Young Guard* from a thick journal into a popular magazine for the proletarian family with cultural pretensions.

In June 1924, *October* (*Oktyabr'*) put out its first issue. The editors announced that any proletarian writer would be welcome, regardless of what group he might belong to. In that way, they hoped to present a solid literary front by uniting a movement that was badly split among the Octobrists, the Smithy, and the young poets who had defected to *RVS*.[2] Oddly enough, it seems to have been Voronskii who secured the official authorization for this new journal.[3] What his motives were we do not know: fair play, perhaps; more likely, some hope that such a journal would draw off the steadily mounting pressure on *RVS* to publish more young proletarians; possibly an attempt to diminish the growing power of the Octobrists by creating a strong rival. In any event, he must soon have regretted his move. *October* was an official organ of the Moscow Association of Proletarian Writers (MAPP) and later of the VAPP; and that made it, in effect, a mouthpiece of the Octobrists. If nothing else, the make-up of the editorial board for the first issue proved it: there sat Averbakh, Bezymenskii, Lelevich, Libedinskii, Tarasov-Rodionov, and, as chief editor, Rodov. Even though the journal dutifully tried to serve the collective spirit by drawing editorial staffers from literary groups in the largest factories of Moscow, Leningrad, Rostov-on-Don, Khar'kov, and various towns in Siberia, its line

<hr>

[2] "Ot redaktsii," *Oktyabr'*, No. 1 (1924), pp. 3-5.

[3] According to S. Rodov, as reported by L. Kishchinskaya, "Literaturnye diskussii 1922-1925 godov (K istorii stanovleniya ideino-esteticheskikh printsipov sovetskoi literaturnoi kritiki)," *Voprosy literatury*, No. 4 (1966), p. 43.

always echoed *On Guard* and later *On Literary Guard.* Nor could *October* pretend to any originality in its literature section, which was indistinguishable from *Young Guard's* and had the same core of established proletarian writers, surrounded by young unknowns. The price of facelessness was paid in a steadily dwindling number of readers—from something between 4,000 and 5,000 printed copies in the first two years down to 2,500 in 1928. But in 1929, sweeping changes were made in *October*, as in *Young Guard*. Dying or dead departments were restored to life; many new contributors were brought in; a virtually new editorial board was installed. A. Serafimovich remained as chief editor, but was now assisted by three of the best-known young writers in Russia—Fyodor Panfyorov, Aleksandr Fadeev, and Mikhail Sholokhov. The literary criticism faithfully echoed the views of RAPP, for *October* was an official organ of that group; but it was livelier and more contentious than ever before, perhaps because RAPP was riding high at the time. Circulation shot up to as high as 10,000 copies an issue. The crisis had passed.

The one outstanding proletarian journal that remained independent of the Octobrists was *The Workers' Journal* (*Rabochii zhurnal*), the official organ of the Smithy group. It rested on a hard core of contributors to the old *Smithy*, which had managed to put out nine issues between 1920 and 1922 before folding up forever: Aleksandrovskii, Gerasimov, Kirillov, Lyashko, and Sadof'ev. The editor was Georgii Yakubovskii, the group's leading theoretician and a frequent contributor to other journals, both proletarian and nonproletarian. *The Workers' Journal* maintained high standards of writing, criticism, and physical makeup; but it lasted only a year, and produced a mere six issues.

None of these journals, with their exclusively proletarian cast, posed a real threat to *RVS*. But others were forming which drew on essentially the same writers Voronskii used; if they did not become rivals, it was precisely because they lacked originality and aggressiveness. The most important of them was *New World* (*Novyi mir*), which put out its first issue in June 1925, and has been going ever since. A. V. Lunacharskii and Yurii Steklov were the editors then: later I. I. Stepanov-Skvortsov replaced Steklov, and in 1926, Vyacheslav Polonskii joined the board. *New World* carried the usual departments of the thick journal. Special interest attached to two: "The Tribune" which was intended as a forum of controversy about literature and the arts; and "At Home and Abroad" which consisted of review articles on new Soviet and foreign literature, and on a variety of nonliterary topics, frequently off-beat, such as the Chinese theater and a newly discovered alphabet of the monolithic age.

But these were the journal's only distinguishing features. *New World* cowered in the shadow of *RVS*. Many prominent writers contributed to the prose and poetry sections —Prishvin, Sergeev-Tsenskii, Aleksei Tolstoi, Pil'nyak, and V. Lidin most frequently—but gave them virtually no important works, except for Tolstoi's *Road to Calvary* (Part II) and *Peter the First*, and Gor'kii's *Klim Samgin*. Although fellow travelers got the most attention, *New World* also published many proletarians—more, proportionately, than *RVS*, with Gladkov, Nikandrov, and Bakhmet'ev the most prominent. Few new talents appeared, however; the editors played safe with established names. But they had to settle for second-best: these writers tended to use *New World* as a kind of dustbin for their less successful efforts.

In the literary quarrel, *New World* clearly favored *RVS*, without wishing to come right out and say so. It published an important article by Voronskii, "Remarks on Creativity in Art" (Zametki o khudozhestvennom tvorchestve, No. 8, 1927), gave his *Waters of Life and Death* a very favorable review, consistently showered praise on the new writers that *RVS* discovered, and, in 1927 and 1928 when *RVS* began to decline, took in many of those writers. Lezhnev, Pakentreiger, Glagolev, and Gorbov were the best of the critics who moved from *RVS* to *New World* at the same time. But they failed to pump life into a department that had always served up a bland middle-of-the-road Marxism, despite the superior talents of its leading contributor, Vyacheslav Polonskii. All these men had ideas and could write well; but the atmosphere of *New World* proved anesthetic. The journal shrank from controversy. It dropped "The Tribune" after two issues; took no firm stand in the literary quarrel; and made virtually no contribution to literary theory. Instead of judgments on new writers, it offered little more than content summaries of their works. Only in 1929 did it begin to stir, with a series of articles on contemporary literature written in a provocative and polemical tone. No one could, of course, foresee that thirty years later, in very different circumstances, *New World* would turn into the boldest and most exciting of all the Soviet journals. Still, its very tameness seemed to appeal: it never printed fewer than 10,000 copies an issue in the twenties, and sometimes went as high as 25,000.

All these new publications were based in Moscow. Not until 1924 did the former capital, on the verge of becoming Leningrad, have its own Marxist thick journal. The first three issues of *The Star* (*Zvezda*) might have caused readers to wonder just where Marxism was headed in the second city, for the literature department was made up largely of Aleksei Tolstoi, Blok, Belyi, and some exhumed Chernyshevskii. But soon the young writers began to respond: Lavrenyov, Lidin, Slonimskii, Nikolai Nikitin, Arosev, and Semyonov sent in stories; Konstantin Fedin gave permission to print excerpts from his new novel, *Cities and Years*. And it was from such more or less established writers that *The Star* drew nourishment sufficient for health, though not for any sustained display of literary brilliance to which the readers of *RVS* were accustomed. The two best works *The*

Star ever published were Yurii Tynyanov's novel *The Death of Vazir-Mukhtar* (*Smert' Vazira Mukhtara*), and Fedin's *Brothers* (*Brat'ya*)—both respectable, but not first-rate. Wisely, however, *The Star*, instead of attempting to compete with *RVS*, cultivated a specialty—the Leningrad writers, many of them virtually unknown, who gave the journal its own distinctive personality.

The Star set itself the task of "serving the cause of the Marxist education of the new worker-peasant intelligentsia that has been brought forth by the Revolution."[4] Although writers of virtually every ideological shade within the accepted spectrum were represented on its pages, clear preference went to the proletarians. *The Star* published more of their work than either *New World* or *RVS*, gave them consistently favorable reviews, and always included one of their spokesmen on the editorial board. This naturally drew the journal into the dispute between *RVS* and the Octobrists. The editor-in-chief, I. Maiskii, began by striking a middle position: he expressed enthusiasm for the idea of proletarian culture, and twitted Voronskii for treating it in a cavalier manner while playing up the fellow travelers; yet he also took issue with the Octobrist view that only full-blooded proletarians were capable of producing a worthy new culture.[5] Extensive rebuttals by Lelevich and Rodov followed and tipped the balance toward their side, where it remained. *The Star*, nonetheless, stood as the only example of a major journal which sympathized with the Octobrists but somehow did not become a satellite. It tolerated a variety of critical opinion, took a far keener interest in problems of literary craftsmanship than most proletarian publications, and made several valuable contributions to literary theory, among them Boris Eikhenbaum's "Literature and the Writer" (Literatura i pisatel', No. 5, 1927),

4 "Ot redaktskii," *Zvezda*, No. 1 (1924).
5 "O kul'ture, literature i kommunisticheskoi partii," *Zvezda*, No. 3 (1924), pp. 258-79.

and Grigor'ev's "The Concepts of Material and Device in the Theory of Literature" (Ponyatiya materiala i priyoma v teorii literatury, No. 2, 1926).

For a long time it looked as if *The Star* must set. Until 1926, it managed to put out a mere six issues a year, each of which, with an average of 150 pages, was about half the size of *RVS* and *New World*. Some issues carried only one piece of fiction or one critical article, and padded the rest with disquisitions on general topics or book reviews. The circulation hovered somewhere between 5,000 and 6,000, then suddenly, late in 1928, plummeted to 3,300. Subsequent transfusions of talent and money restored some color to *The Star*, and it has steadily built itself up since then into one of the leading Soviet journals.

ALL THE journals we have mentioned were published by the State Publishing House, and therefore bore an official stamp, despite the differences of opinion that frequently set one against another. But for the better part of the twenties, some journals—about thirty in all—operated beyond the reach of all officialdom except the censor. They were the enterprises of private publishers who pursued their activities under the protection of a decree issued by the Council of People's Commissars (Sovnarkom) in 1921.[6]

Let us first mention the three that had the same editor: I. G. Lezhnev. *New Russia* (*Novaya Rossiya*), which appeared in Petrograd in 1922, cultivated an appearance of political neutrality, but actually had strong sympathies for the so-called "Changing Landmarks" movement (Smena vekh).[7] When it failed, Lezhnev simply tried again, this time with *Russia*, first in Petrograd—where he printed 10,000 copies an issue in a newspaper-like format that ran to about thirty-two double-columned pages—and then in

[6] The Sovnarkom decree of December 12, 1921, was aimed at stimulating the production of specialized literature by private houses.
[7] Cf. Ch. VI, n. 104.

Moscow, where he adopted the typical "thick" format of 200 pages or so, and had to cut his pressrun in half. The "Changing Landmarks" line was now soft-pedaled, but still audible, particularly in the articles by N. V. Ustryalov and by Lezhnev himself. Most of the effort, however, went into the literature section. *Russia* served no particular school, and hoped to appeal to all writers. Several of the younger fellow travelers contributed, but *Russia* depended mostly on writers who were considered "bourgeois" and "right-wing" by the Communists: Belyi, Erenburg, Mandel'-shtam, Pasternak, Zamyatin, and Khodasevich. It closed abruptly in 1925. An attempted revival the following year, under the original title of *New Russia*, lasted a mere three issues.

Among the private journals, *The Russian Contemporary* (*Russkii sovremennik*) deserves special mention. Although it began and ended in 1924, with a total of four issues, it offered a more concentrated display of superior literary talent than any other journal at the time, including *RVS*. Published in Moscow by N. I. Margaram, and edited by A. N. Tikhonov, it was unabashedly a straight literary journal, with only three departments: belles lettres; criticism, surveys, and reviews; and "Panopticum," which made light comments on contemporary literary life. Criticism was oriented on the Futurists and the Formalists, with V. Shklovskii, B. Eikhenbaum, Yu. Tynyanov, L. Grossman, and G. Vinokur the chief contributors. In belles lettres, preference went to the more experimental writing of the fellow travelers: Pil'nyak, Babel', Pasternak, Kaverin, Fedin, and Zamyatin shaped the prose; Akhmatova, Pasternak, Esenin, Mandel'shtam, Tsvetaeva, and Khodasevich the poetry. Oddly enough, Gor'kii, that literary amphibian, turned up here too: his name stood first among those with whose "closest participation" the journal appeared, and several of his reminiscences of Russian writers were included. Each issue came to 350 pages on good, heavy paper, in a printing of 5,000 copies. There were no signs of trouble ahead. Advertisements had already been published for a fifth issue, which would feature Gor'kii's story "A Sky-Blue Life" (Golubaya zhizn'), Zamyatin's "God's Scourge" (Bich Bozhii), stories by Babel', and articles by N. Punin, K. Chukovskii, and Eikhenbaum. But that issue never appeared. *The Russian Contemporary* was dead. We do not know why it closed with no warning at the height of its success, as did *Russia*, too. But success may well have been its undoing. The Soviet press constantly attacked these two journals as organs of the petty-bourgeois "insulted" intelligentsia (insulted by the Revolution, that is), and the permissive decree of 1921 notwithstanding, the government lost no opportunity to badger private enterprises during the NEP. In all likelihood, pressure of this kind forced *The Russian Contemporary* and *Russia* to fold up.

NOT LONG after the Civil War ended, literary life in the provinces began to revive. Most of the larger towns, even in very remote areas, could boast a club or group or movement, and even a journal or newspaper—like Omsk's *Art* (*Iskusstvo*), Irkutsk's *Flame of the Revolution* (*Plamya Revolyutsii*), or *Yakutsk Heat Lightning* (*Yakutskie zarnitsy*). The proletarians were especially strong outside Moscow and Leningrad; indeed, they had made Rostov-on-the-Don practically a third literary capital. One of their best journals was *Lava*, an official publication of the North Caucasus Association of Proletarian Writers. The first issue rolled off the presses in April 1925. Most of the writers associated with it have long since vanished into oblivion; but Aleksandr Fadeev sat on its editorial board, along with another well-known proletarian writer, the playwright V. Kirshon.

But it was Novonikolaevsk (now Novosibirsk) that eclipsed all the other provincial towns with a thick journal that in influence and quality could rank with virtually any in the two major cities: *Siberian Lights* (*Sibirskie ogni*). The idealistic young men and women who put out the first issue in March 1922 felt certain that, like Vsevolod Ivanov only a year earlier, there must be many an aspiring writer looking for an outlet. They hoped to do for Siberia what *RVS*—their model—was trying to do for Russia as a whole: to form a center which would bring such writers together. Like *RVS*, *Siberian Lights* outlined a typically "encyclopedic" program, denouncing "narrow dogmas" and expressing the intention of "accepting everything that reproduces in artistic form the age of the socialist revolution and its special reflex in Siberia, everything that is 'responsive' to the age, and, finally, outstanding works of general content."[8] How well they succeeded may be judged by the fact that, of the fifty or so delegates to the First Congress of Siberian Writers in 1926, more than half had entered literature through *Siberian Lights*.[9] Editors in Moscow and Leningrad followed the journal closely and brought many of its discoveries to national prominence—among them, Anna Karavaeva, Leonid Martynov, Iosif Utkin, and, of those especially close to *RVS*, Lidiya Seifullina and V. Pravdukhin.[10]

· I I ·

As I suggested earlier, *RVS*, in recapitulating the essential stages of the development of the nineteenth-century

[8] "Ot redaktsii," *Sibirskie ogni*, No. 1 (1922).

[9] S. Kozhevnikov and N. Yanovskii, "Stareishii zhurnal," *Pisateli-sibiryaki. Literaturno-kriticheskie ocherki* (Novosibirsk, 1956), pp. 298-321. As a whole, this volume gives a useful survey of Siberian literature.

[10] Few other journals have inspired the warmth and enthusiasm in their contributors that *Siberian Lights* did. For an idea of what the journal meant to them, see the remarks of two of its most distinguished alumnae: Lidiya Seifullina, "Pamyatnoe pyatiletie," *O literature* (Moscow, 1958), pp. 271-92; Anna Karavaeva, "Iz vospominanii starogo 'Ognelyuba,'" *Po dorogam zhizni. Dnevniki, ocherki, vospominaniya* (Moscow, 1957), pp. 709-19.

thick journal (albeit in much foreshortened form), was obeying a law which guides the development of all thick journals. Still stronger evidence of such a law is provided by the other thick journals of the twenties. Most skipped the encyclopedic phase, probably because literature after 1923 had revived to an extent that made it unnecessary. But otherwise they followed the same general development as *RVS*: that of a slow but relentless conversion into purely literary journals, with the disappearance of the departments of politics, economics, and science; the decline in the quality, reach, and sharpness of criticism; and the erosion of individuality. By 1928 they were no longer thick in any but the purely physical sense. They had turned into literary almanacs, random and faceless collections of prose and poetry that happened to come out regularly. Writers no longer gave their primary loyalty to any single one, but published wherever they could.

This change provoked extensive commentary in the later twenties. Typical was Dmitrii Tal'nikov's complaint that the journals were "toothless," "lacking in authority," "inarticulately mumbling"; in one a reader might find "a chance literaryish article on a few little books, or a jubilee article necessary only to the individual whose jubilee it is; in another . . . a literary hodge-podge, light-weight pieces that are suitable for weeklies."[11] Some observers welcomed these developments as a sign of healthy literary progress. I. Vareikis, the head of the Agitation-Propaganda Department of the Central Committee, thought that the way was being cleared for a kind of publication that would serve the needs of workers and peasants better than something which had been imported from bourgeois society.[12] As far back as 1924, Viktor Shklovskii had forecast exactly what

[11] "O kritike, redaktore i 'tolstom' zhurnale," *Prozhektor*, No. 32 (1928), p. 22.

[12] "Ob udeshevlenii i rasprostranenii pechati," *Pravda*, March 3, 1925, p. 1.

now was happening: he insisted that the conditions of the 1840's no longer applied, and that any attempt at "reviving" the thick journals must therefore fail. He called for "a new journal which, in placing side by side various pieces of esthetic and extra-esthetic material, would show us—even if only by chance—how things of a new genre could be built, and from what." (*New LEF*, which began to appear two years later, seemed to fulfill the prescription very well.)[13]

Most of the observers of *genus journalicum*, however, ran up the battle flags and swore to defend the thick journals to the death. They assumed that the journals themselves had courted decline, and that drift, inaction, and flabbiness could be purged with a few strong injections of willpower. Editors must thin out belles lettres, reintroduce general articles on nonliterary topics, restore surveys of provincial life, and revive the kind of literary criticism that, in Tal'nikov's words, "causes excitement, the kind that in its time [the nineteenth century] impelled young people to hasten to cut the back pages [which contained the criticism] of the journals they were receiving—the kind that organizes reader and writer alike, organizes literature and expresses through itself the dominant idea of contemporary life."[14] Surprisingly, even the proletarians turned out in force to speak for the thick journal.[15] One might have expected them to adopt some position close to Shklovskii's or Vareikis', which at least sustained hostility toward the forms and slogans of a past they had found so objectionable. But the past by now had become respectable; and

[13] "Zhurnal, kak literaturnaya forma," *Zhurnalist*, No. 11 (1924), p. 41. He suggested that it would be instructive to check the libraries to see whether any pages in *RVS* had been cut besides those in the belles lettres section.

[14] "O kritike, redaktore i 'tolstom' zhurnale," p. 22.

[15] Cf., e.g., V. Ermilov, "Put' 'Molodoi gvardii,'" *Molodaya gvardiya* No. 5 (1927), pp. 191-95.

respectability, in the end, holds out a brighter appeal to the culturally self-conscious than does defiance.

Still, the chorus of complaints which mounted steadily throughout the twenties suggested that something had gone fundamentally wrong with the thick journals. Was Shklovskii perhaps right? Were the defenders merely sending up clouds of perfume to mask the reek of decay? The tentative answer is yes; and the clues lie in changes that were taking place in the literary and political world.

ONE WAS the growth of specialized publications in all fields. An enormous increase in brochures and pamphlets helped subvert the traditional popularizing role of the journals. And each of the intellectual disciplines by now had its own journals which tended to siphon off material that otherwise would have found its way into the departments of sociology, economics, and politics in the traditional thick journal. A growing daily press gradually took over most of the reportorial functions that had been fulfilled in the old chronicles and surveys. The various departments of the newspapers offered much the same variety as the journals, but in far more accessible form. Then too, the new popular magazines undoubtedly drew off many readers who might otherwise had been educated into taking weightier fare. Some of them successfully combined the light touch with high standards: *The Flame* (*Ogonyok*), for instance, an illustrated weekly that was founded in 1923; *Red Pepper* (*Krasnyi perets*, 1922-1926), a satirical journal that enjoyed huge popularity during its relatively brief lifetime; *The Crocodile* (*Krokodil*) which, since 1922, has been perhaps the most popular forum for exposing the vices and foibles of Soviet man; and Voronskii's own *Searchlight* (*Prozhektor*, 1923-1935) which often resembled a popularized version of *RVS*. One suspects that for many readers, these better magazines did not replace a regular diet of thick journals, but supplemented it.

The upsurge of literature also worked against the individuality of the thick journals. For one thing, with more and more novels coming out, editors were faced with the choice of excerpting or serializing. Most chose the latter. Voronskii, for instance, ran Leonov's *The Thief* for an entire year. Now, this meant that if literature were to go on occupying roughly a third of each issue, fewer and fewer new works could be printed. Some of the issues of *New World* for 1926 and 1927 carried only two or three pieces of long fiction. Rather than become increasingly less "representative" of contemporary literature, the journals simply opened up more space to it; and soon it began to occupy entire issues. Furthermore, with the appearance of more and more writers, the old distinctions between "proletarian," "peasant," and "fellow traveler" began to break down (as Voronskii had insisted they must). In particular, hostility toward the fellow travelers slowly eroded. Many of the young proletarian and peasant writers came to understand that they had much to learn in matters of craftsmanship from skilled workmen like Babel' or Ivanov or Leonov. The new literary groupings which began to form around the middle of the decade tended to play down the old virtues of exclusiveness in favor of a brotherhood of writers: the Pass (Pereval), for example, embraced workers, peasants, and some members of the intelligentsia, and took the fellow travelers for teachers. The Central Committee Resolution of June 1925 had called for a fraternity of Soviet writers; the following year, *On Literary Guard* extended the hand of official proletarian recognition to the fellow travelers for the first time. Practically all the Soviet thick journals had built their "line" upon just such distinctions as were becoming obsolete. If now they wished to offer the most representative writing of the time, they must in effect abandon these "lines," and with them, the essential condition of their "thickness." No journal that hoped to remain competitive could afford to specialize in "peasants" or "proletarians,"

any more than in novels or short stories. Thus the proletarian journals began to accept the writing of fellow travelers; this brought quality and tone to otherwise dreary
departments of literature, but of course made nonsense of
any "line" that insisted on "proletarian" purity. It is hardly
surprising, then, that one journal soon began to resemble
another.

WE MUST also consider politics. By 1926, the NEP was drawing to a close and, with it, a period when differences of
opinion had been tolerated within the Party and throughout the country. The proletarians were growing more aggressive, unpleasant, and menacing. No one knew just how
much real authority they actually had or how far they
would be permitted to impose it on others; but it was obvious that the Party had bestowed on them the blessing
they had so long considered their due. Voronskii's troubles
were evident to all, and the future of the fellow travelers
seemed doubtful. Party policy had changed sometime during 1925 and 1926, but it was anyone's guess just what it
meant or how far it would go. Amid such uncertainties,
circumspection had obvious merits. Writers might well
have considered it prudent to spread their talents in order
to avoid being associated too closely with any one school
of literature or journal that might later prove to contain the
seeds of political heresy. It was no wonder that criticism
became cautious and evasive: better to have no teeth at all
than sink them into something poisonous. The future
looked too uncertain for people to risk taking strong stands.
Naturally, the thick journals felt the effects at once.

IT MAY be, however, that the most important factor in the
decline of the thick journal was one that many Marxists,
surprisingly enough, overlooked: money. The economics of
publishing were still very chancy in the middle and late
twenties. No editor, perhaps, had to face what Voronskii

did when he started his journal. But money was not easy to come by; and purely literary ventures tended to get short shrift in the Soviet system of priorities. The number of journals of all kinds in the Soviet Union rose steadily throughout the decade. In July 1924, for instance, 810 were being published; by the new year of 1927, some 1,082 were coming out in the Russian Republic alone; just six months later, the number had risen to 1,291.[16] But this growth occurred in nonliterary journals—Party organs and specialized publications; the total number of literary journals actually declined by 30 per cent between 1923 and 1925.[17] Some 74 had been registered in the Book Chamber (Knizhnaya Palata) during 1923 and 1924; but by October 1 of the following year, a mere 53 could be counted throughout the country.[18] A similar pattern took shape in book publishing. Though titles and circulations increased, a relatively small part of the total output was devoted to belles lettres—some 13 per cent in 1923, and only 9.7 per cent in 1924.[19] Of the 2,000 or so publishing houses that were supposedly operating in 1925, no more than thirty or forty published prose and poetry; of these, roughly half were "private" firms, which in turn accounted for about half the titles published in belles lettres during that year.[20] On the Soviet side, six publishing houses accounted for about 33 per cent of all titles published in all subjects; but even though one of them —"Soil and Factory"—specialized almost exclusively in belles lettres, titles in that category still made up a relatively

[16] A. A. Maksimov, "Iz istorii pervykh 'tolstykh' sovetskikh zhurnalov (1921-1925 gg.)," *Uchonye zapiski L.G.U.* [Leningradskogo Gosudarstvennogo universiteta], No. 245, Seriya fililogicheskikh nauk, No. 43 (Leningrad, 1957), p. 71.

[17] *Ibid.*

[18] V. Narbut, "Khudozhestvennaya literatura v 1924 i 1925 gg.," *Zhurnalist*, No. 1 (1926), p. 15.

[19] V. Narbut, "Knizhno-zhurnal'noe delo," *Zhurnalist*, No. 5 (1925), p. 17.

[20] V. Narbut, "Khudozhestvennaya literatura v 1924 i 1925 gg.," p. 13.

small part of the total production of the Soviet houses.[21] The figures are even smaller for contemporary literature; many of the titles published—up to 85 per cent in the case of the State Publishing House—consisted of the Russian classics.

To be sure, the decline in the number of literary journals may not betoken financial failure in all cases. According to V. Narbut, one of the faithful chroniclers of publishing statistics for the twenties, this decline occurred largely in the provinces and reflected a decision by many newspapers to abandon their magazine supplements and print literature directly on their own pages.[22] He does not say, however, why the newspapers adopted this policy. Could not paper shortages and other expenses have been the reason? We must also bear in mind that a good many of the journals that sprang up in the twenties were, like their Civil War ancestors, the flimsy vanities of ambitious, but small groups that lacked money, talent, and a public.

Still, even the established journals rested on a rather shaky foundation. Their average monthly circulation reached slightly more than 6,000, which was small considering the size of the country and the respectability of "culture" in those days. Most of this circulation was confined to the large cities, of course. As of mid-1923, Moscow and Petrograd published only 30 per cent of all the journals in Russia, but had 90 per cent of all the circulation.[23] An extensive network of libraries and reading rooms in the provinces undoubtedly boosted readership of the major journals well above the circulation figures. But so chaotic were

[21] *Ibid.* The six houses were: Gosizdat (The State Publishing House), Lengiz (The Leningrad State Publishing House), Priboi (Surf), Molodaya Gvardiya (Young Guard), Zemlya i Fabrika (Soil and Factory), and Novaya Moskva (New Moscow).

[22] *Ibid.*, p. 15.

[23] D. Lebedev, "Zhurnaly SSSR," *Zhurnalist*, No. 7 (1923), pp. 35-36.

the procedures for distributing periodicals and books that one wonders just how effectively this network functioned: not until 1930 did the government, after much wavering, attempt to create a centralized system of distribution.[24] Standards of printing and makeup often left much to be desired, even in the best journals; but when one reads accounts of the incredible disorder that reigned in publishing houses in the twenties, one marvels that anything came out at all. At one point, for instance, the State Publishing House had fragmented into sixty separate departments, all of which were working independently.[25] Periodic attempts have been made ever since the twenties to streamline the publishing industry, always in the direction of greater centralization; but, like the distribution system, it remains a sprawling problem to this day.[26]

The so-called "press workers"—typesetters, editors, and reporters—were at least regularly salaried and more or less organized against the ravages of inefficiency and waste. As early as 1918 at their First Congress, they had tried to form something like a union. Although their attempt failed, they had vocal and influential spokesmen like Vardin, Ingulov, and Sosnovskii, and their power grew with each

[24] For an account of the distribution problem, see B. P. Stepanov, *Rasprostranenie, ekspedirovanie i dostavka gazet i zhurnalov v SSSR* (Moscow, 1955).

[25] Cf. A. I. Nazarov, *Ocherki istorii sovetskogo knigoizdatel'stva* (Moscow, 1952), pp. 87-88; G. I. Broido, "Iz itogov raboty Gosizdata za 1925 god," *Pravda*, May 7, 1926, p. 5.

[26] Cf., e.g., the Central Committee Resolution of August 15, 1931, "Ob izdatel'skoi rabote," *O partiinoi i sovetskoi pechati* (Moscow, 1954), p. 422. It noted duplication and waste in journals, and thereafter the total number of journals dropped, presumably as a result of streamlining, from 2,112 in 1932 to 1,861 in 1934. With the first Five Year Plan, the publishing system was reorganized. Many houses were merged with Gosizdat in 1928 and 1929. In 1930, OGIZ (Ob'edinenie gosudarstvennykh knizhno-zhurnal'nykh izdatel'stv RSFSR), a super-organization which included Gosizdat, was formed. Cf. Nazarov, *ibid.*, p. 158.

congress and conference.[27] The writers enjoyed no such solidarity. Despite the volume of propaganda that circulated about the need for discovering new talent, theirs was a dismally familiar story. Those with no reputation found it almost impossible to break into print. If they wanted a hearing, they had a choice of publishing at their own expense or hiring a hall for a reading. Those who had attracted some attention, perhaps for a single story or poem, more often than not discovered that fortune is fickle even in a planned society: Moscow teemed with young men and women who had thrown up routine jobs in the provinces to pluck the fruits of fame in the capital, and found themselves utterly ignored.

The professional writer at least had some name, but he lived in poverty. Up to 1921, a writer of "average" productivity probably received something between 180,000 and 240,000 roubles a month, compared to the 350,000 roubles paid the unskilled worker.[28] It was only after a vigorous protest by the State Publishing House that the pay raises for numerous occupations, announced in 1921, had been extended to "literary workers" as well. After that, if he were able to turn out three or four printer's signatures (48 to 64 printed pages) of finished work a month, as the State Publishing House estimated he should, then he might have earned a decent living, for the rates of payment per signature were based roughly on that estimate. But V. V. Veresaev, himself rather productive, thought that even a conscientious wielder of the pen could produce no more than half a signature in that amount of time.[29] Since poets were

[27] Cf. the following, all in *Zhurnalist*: "Tri s' 'ezda," No. 4 (1923), pp. 3-8; "O zadachakh sektsii rabotnikov pechati," No. 1 (1922), pp. 52-53; "Konets razbrodu," No. 1 (1922), pp. 3-4; "Partiinoe soveshchanie o pechati," No. 1 (1923), pp. 59-60.

[28] "O literaturnykh rabotnikakh," *Pravda*, September 2, 1921, p. 2. See also "Oplata literaturnogo truda," *Pechat' i revolyutsiya*, No. 2 (1921), p. 236.

[29] "K polozheniyu rabotnikov iskusstv," *Pravda*, April 28, 1925,

paid at the same rate and according to the same signature system as the prose writers, one could well imagine their plight. Veresaev estimated that they were lucky if they earned one or two *chervontsy* a month.[30] A questionnaire sent out by the Central Council of the Section of Press Workers in 1925 revealed that the average annual income of professional writers—derived from honorariums for new works and reprints, and from advances— was 1,600 roubles. One writer among those interviewed had earned 2,846 roubles the previous year; but 80 per cent of his output had been journalism.[31] Even at that, discrepancies apparently existed in the rates of remuneration, especially in the provinces. Publishing houses there sometimes tried to make up deficits by cutting back on salaries or honorariums, which were low enough as it was.[32] Not the lightest of the writer's burdens was his legal status as a member of a "free profession." That meant, in practical terms, that he had to pay a higher income tax and more rent than the white-collar worker. Of his annual earnings, 25 to 38 per cent went for rent, taxes, and various "communal services," whereas such expenses generally accounted for no more than 20 per cent of the white-collar worker's wages.[33] The assumption was, of course, that he had something on which to pay rent. Many of the younger writers took to the park benches at night. Among the professionals interviewed by the Central Council, all at least

---

p. 5. The rate of payment, after the currency reform of the mid-twenties, ran around 105 roubles per signature. For an explanation of the "signature," cf. Ch. I, n. 24.

[30] *Ibid.* The *chervonets*, introduced in 1922 and maintained until 1947, equaled ten roubles. Veresaev does not specify which kind of signature he has in mind.

[31] S. Ingulov, "Kak zhivyot i rabotaet sovetskii pisatel'," *Pravda*, September 30, 1925, p. 3.

[32] V. Topor, "Pora uporyadochit' oplatu literaturnogo truda," *Zhurnalist*, No. 11 (1925), pp. 26-27.

[33] Ingulov, "Kak zhivyot i rabotaet sovetskii pisatel'," p. 3.

had a roof over their heads, but not one had a room of his own in which to work.[34]

The younger writers tended to regard "service," however vague or undirected, as a serious social obligation, and deeply resented the bureaucrat's apparent conviction that literature was only a frill. Many considered their status as members of a "free profession" insulting—it was almost like calling them gypsies—and smarted at the requirement that they had to be licensed.[35] From the day he became editor of *RVS*, Voronskii tussled with the prejudice against literature in the minds of the men who held the purse strings. Writing in *Pravda*, three months after his journal's debut, he brought strong representations against any sacrifice of literature to the self-aggrandizement of the state bureaucracy. While shortages of paper made it almost impossible in 1921 and 1922 to get an issue of a literary journal into press, the offices that controlled the allocations of money, supplies, and publishing permits nevertheless managed to grind out a mountain of reports, resolutions, and minutes.

Considerable "extraordinary" and "extra-budgetary" sums are allocated which do not come under the control of the Rabkrin [Workers' and Peasants' Inspection], and meat, cloth, tobacco, flour, etc., are obtained "to expedite matters." Before you know it a "report" is ready in two weeks, whereas the works of often first-rate artists, scholars and thinkers lie around from one month to the next.[36]

[34] *Ibid.* Cf. also A. Voronskii, "Dela literaturnye," *Prozhektor*, No. 22 (1923), p. 21; V. Polonskii, "Zametki zhurnalista," *Pechat' i revolyutsiya*, No. 7 (1926), pp. 86-90.

[35] The "license" (*patent*), issued by the Regional Financial Section (*raifinotdel*), was required of everyone who wished to write for a living. It stated that the bearer was allowed to pursue private work within a specific time period. It had to be renewed every six months, and cost 32 roubles each time. Cf. V. V. Veresaev, "K polozheniyu rabotnikov iskusstv," p. 5.

[36] "O khudozhestvennom slove v nashi dni," *Pravda*, September 11, 1921, p. 1.

Was literature, then, less "useful" than the pen-pushing of these bureaucrats? On the contrary:

> A Party purge is now going on. Before me I have S. Pod''yachev's excellent ethnographical sketch "The Ailing Man" (*Bolyashchii*): in it there is exposed a village Communist of the type long since nicknamed—and rightly so—the "hanger-on" [*primazavshiisya*]. Why are articles about these hangers-on more necessary and preferable to stories and sketches written in the spirit of Comrade Pod''yachev's? Articles are often roundabout, they use familiar expressions, they are a cliché, whereas the image created by Pod''yachev is fresh, bright, and full of life and truth.[37]

This, of course, was more a metaphor than a formula, a tactical argument designed to shatter official lethargy by making indifference toward literature a political delinquency. Throughout the twenties, Voronskii played the gadfly. His insistence on literature as a useful social activity—and one therefore entitled to full support—was directed as much at the Party as at hostile Octobrists. Yet he never expressed what must have been on the tip of his tongue: wonderment that the Party, once having decided to woo the writers, should then in effect toss them to the whim of fate. But he kept needling, cajoling, complaining, persuading, despairing, in an effort to move officialdom to do something about the financial plight of the writers. He painted gloomy and foreboding pictures of the conditions in which young writers had to live, and warned that the consequences might be politically serious, as well as artistically disastrous:

> The absence of a book market, the financial failures and crises of various publishing houses, including—first and foremost—the state houses, have created acute unem-

[37] *Ibid.*

ployment among writers. The proletarian writers are starving, the fellow travelers are starving, there are no apartments, it is difficult to place works, today's writer is paid starvation wages. The most serious attention must be directed to this matter. To a large extent, Bohemian attitudes among writers are fed by the lack of living space and the lack of money.[38]

Voronskii's prodding helped ultimately to force a definition of the relationship between literature and state. Support came, in the thirties, but at a terrible price. Conditions were so desperate, however, that nobody in the twenties thought to question the desirability of the state's rendering the necessary assistance. Indeed, only the state could do so. There were widely differing opinions as to the form this assistance should take. Most people resisted any proposals that made writers the salaried employees of literary bureaucracies like the publishing houses, and envisaged instead an arrangement whereby the state would foot the bill and attach no strings, so that the writer could create pretty much as he liked. But people were not divided over "intervention" or "nonintervention"; and probably everyone assumed that the state, if it did act, would do so in literature's best interests, that is to say, would respect the writer's individuality. But the state remained silent, and the clamor for action grew.

The writers stood pressed to the wall. Since the Soviet system had made it impossible to live off inheritances or unearned income, the less prolific or less talented had but two choices: either to write part-time, while earning their bread in field, factory, or office; or to become professional with a vengeance, which usually meant moving into journalism, where the rates of pay were not high, but where one could turn out much more. Either choice takes a heavy

[38] "Dela literaturnye," p. 21.

toll of creative energies, as writers in every country have discovered.

Interestingly enough, it was the partisans of proletarian culture who had plumped for the benefits of part-time writing. Like Tolstoi, they abhorred the whole notion of the "professional" writer, with the white collars, ink-stained fingers, and flower-studded lapels the term called up to them. They firmly believed that the only preparation a proletarian writer needed was a rudimentary education and plenty of practical experience in the workaday world. During the day he would toil at his machine; at night he would transfer his impressions into poems and stories: there would be a perfect synthesis of art and labor, mind and body, muscle and brain. Most people, however, realized—even Bogdanov had reluctantly done so—that a mature literature must be fully professional, and that young writers need time to practice, make mistakes, and polish their craft, without worrying about the next loaf of bread. But time in the twenties was perhaps the scarcest commodity of all.

Oddly enough, the economic situation seemed to have little effect on the numbers of people seeking to enter literature, which suggests something of the prestige that the art enjoyed among writers and the public, if not among the bureaucrats. But standards did suffer. There was a slow swell of shoddy workmanship, a disinclination to revise, and a tendency to overwrite in order to fill up more signatures a month. As a whole, the level of craftsmanship in Soviet literature in the twenties—while high in comparison with later years—lies far below that of the nineteenth century.[39]

[39] This fact, which preoccupied and depressed Voronskii more and more, led him to wonder in 1928 whether the improvements in the writer's economic position, which he himself had always championed, might not actually be encouraging hack work. ("O khudozhestvennoi pravde," *Iskusstvo videt' mir* [Moscow, 1928], pp. 21-22.)

Another and more profound consequence of the economic crisis was a new relationship between writers and literary journals. The established journals began to discover, around 1925, that many of their old reliables had begun to share talent with competitors. Even the proletarian writers, who had harped on their untouchable superiority, were beginning to creep into some decidedly nonproletarian milieux—Artyom Vesyolyi, for instance, into *LEF*, and Fyodor Gladkov into *RVS*. The best writers could of course have their pick. Meanwhile, even a top-grade journal could no longer hope to hold anything like a permanent cadre; for it had to court variety, and therefore could not take everything a prolific writer turned out even if he had been willing to offer it. As a result, the writer peddled his wares as best he could, and the less prestigious journals happily took second best.

Something like an open market in literature had grown up. In theory, all the journals and publishing houses paid the same rates. In practice, savage honorarium wars raged. But more important, something had changed in the attitudes of writers and journals toward one another. Editors and critics complained of disloyalty. Vladimir Ermilov, for one, accused the writers of regarding journals merely as outlets for their manuscripts, and insisted that they must give their loyalties to a single journal and take a deep personal interest in its fortunes.[40] Writers in turn grumbled about impersonal editors, and thought it scandalous that publishing houses and journals apparently preferred making profits to promoting unknown poets.[41] Literature was no longer the clubby activity it had been in the early twen-

[40] "Put' 'Molodoi gvardii,' " *Molodaya gvardiya*, No. 5 (1927), p. 195.
[41] Cf. V. Mayakovskii, "Podozhdyom obvinyat' poetov," *KN*, No. 4 (1926); I. Sadof'ev, "Pobediteli i pobezhdyonnye," *KN*, No. 2 (1926).

ties, when all the writers knew one another and enjoyed close personal ties—for better or worse—with editors and critics. Literature had become a big business. Many of the practices and abuses in publishing to which Western writers have long since resigned themselves came as a shock to these young Russians. Pavel Yarovoi, for instance, submitted two manuscripts to Voronskii for the almanac *Our Days* (*Nashi dni*): "I went to him about twenty times," Yarovoi recalled, "he hadn't read them. Nine months passed —he hadn't read them and wouldn't even promise to." On offering a story to *The Searchlight*, Yarovoi was informed over the telephone that it was "well-written" and would be published. But more than a year had passed, and nothing had happened.[42] One wonders whether Voronskii would have let Babel' or Leonov sit it out quite that long. But writers in the West who are not Hemingways or Faulkners can tell of many similar experiences.

One of the most eloquent and anguished indictments of the estrangement between writer and journal was made by the proletarian-Futurist poet Nikolai Aseev. Everything, he lamented, had turned into a business arrangement, transacted in cold cash. And both parties had to share the blame. Writers sold to the highest bidder, and cared nothing about where their work appeared; editors took no interest in writers once the contract was signed. Journals had ceased to be creative centers, and now resembled vast employment agencies. The quality of literature must inevitably suffer. "The failure to take an interest in the physiognomy [*oblichie*] of a journal," he wrote, "in its distinctive literary personality, creates indifference in the first instance toward the quality of the work that is printed next to yours, and then, imperceptibly, toward the quality of your own material."[43] Aseev proposed that each journal

---

[42] P. Yarovoi, "Skvoz' stroi," *Rabochii zhurnal*, No. 3 (1925), p. 96.
[43] "Brodyachaya literatura," *Zhurnalist*, No. 10 (1926), p. 29.

reach into the diaspora and reassemble a cadre of writers who would then compete—not in fruitless polemic but for the sake of raising standards—with writers on other journals. Unfortunately, Aseev's vision was totally impractical, a nostalgic appeal to a past that could not return. His observations hit the mark, his bitterness was certainly justified; but the relationship between writers and thick journals had changed unalterably. *RVS* held out longer than its competitors; but with Voronskii's departure in 1928 it quickly turned, like them, into another haphazard assemblage of talents.

WITH THE decline of the thick journals, the literary organizations took on a new importance. For all the clatter they made, most remained relatively small until the middle of the decade. Four of the most prominent in 1924 were the VAPP, with 717 members; the Union of Peasant Writers (VSKP), with 214 members; the Union of Writers (VSP), which was made up chiefly of fellow travelers and numbered some 323 members; and the Smithy, with 49. But by October 1 of the following year—just when people began to complain about the journals—the membership of these organizations had shown marked growth: the VAPP recorded an impressive 2,898, and seemed well on its way to becoming the mass organization that the Octobrists envisaged; the Union of Peasant Writers had almost quadrupled in size, to 709; the Smithy had doubled to 100. Only the VSP hardly budged, adding a mere 37 members. Other groups—both old and new—were far smaller. The roster of *LEF* numbered between 15 and 25; the Constructivists, the Union of Dramatists of the Revolution (Soyuz Revolyutsionnykh Dramaturgov), the Neverov Collective of Worker-Peasant Writers (Kollektiv raboche-krest'yanskikh pisatelei imeni Neverova), and the Pass

(Pereval) came next in importance, each counting between 20 and 30 members.[44]

Membership in one of these organizations could offer advantages to the writer, especially the beginner. For one thing, he was less likely to starve than if he were completely on his own: friendship, connections, slush funds, and doles could help carry even the least productive. Furthermore, an organization, particularly one of the smaller ones, offered him a chance to rub shoulders with more mature writers. They in turn could try out works in progress on colleagues, who presumably would be both more perceptive and more sympathetic than the critics. In those uncertain times, the sense of fraternity undoubtedly boosted morale; few are the lonely geniuses in any age. Finally, the individual literary organization might well have been in a better position than any journal or any individual to prod the Party and government into making the necessary reforms in the system of compensation; precisely because it *was* organized, the bureaucracy—which thinks in terms of organizations rather than individuals—might have been more inclined to give it a hearing.

Throughout his career, Voronskii assailed the common tendency to make literary organizations synonymous with literature. In their very exclusiveness (probably few writers belonged to more than one) Voronskii saw great dangers to talent: a retirement from the literary world at large, a self-defensiveness that made constructive self-criticism

---

[44] All the figures are according to V. Narbut, "Khudozhestvennaya literatura v 1924 i 1925 gg.," *Zhurnalist*, No. 1 (1926), p. 16. Narbut also gives a breakdown, for five of the organizations, according to the number of Party and non-Party members, social origin, and sex. Two other large organizations he mentions are the Leningrad (Independent) Branch of the All-Russian Union of Writers, with 250 to 300 members as of October 1, 1925, and the Union of Poets, with 100 to 150 members; comparative figures for 1924 are not available. According to S. Gusev, the vsp had over 800 members as of the spring of 1927 ("Kakaya Federatsiya pisatelei nam nuzhna?" *Pravda*, April 30, 1927, p. 5).

impossible and, worst of all, complacency. Furthermore, he was convinced—at least from 1923 on—that the principles by which such organizations operated were more appropriate to political parties than to literature; the talk, particularly among the proletarians, swirled around ideologies and tactics, the activities pointed more to self-perpetuation than to the education of the writers. Voronskii thought the point was proved by the precipitous decline in the quality of those writers associated with the VAPP. He always regarded the journal as the real center of literature, not merely as a display case, but as a school that would draw promising writers out of the parochialism of literary groups, would bring them together in an amicable atmosphere that encouraged the exchange of enthusiasms and ideas, and would help perfect their craft by discussing their problems in print, rejecting the bad work, and publishing the good. This was idealistic, perhaps; but Voronskii tried hard to make it so in his own journal, and he hoped that others would follow the example.

But by the mid-twenties, Voronskii, like many others, had reluctantly begun to conclude that the literary organization might be a necessity after all. The economic problem had defeated the journals: since they had no resources beyond the honorariums, which were inadequate, they could not support a completely professional literature of high quality. Literature had grown too large to tolerate intimate societies of writers grouped around journals. The harsh laws of competition no longer made it practicable for a journal to carry along talented beginners while they learned their craft; the economics of survival naturally favored established writers who would attract subscribers. For a journal like *RVS* that still took seriously its mission of educating and training young writers through commerce with their elders, a separate literary organization might well have seemed the only answer.

The literary organizations were becoming powers by default. But almost no one was satisfied with them as they then stood. Somehow the Octobrists epitomized everything that had been worst about them, and, it was feared, everything that was inevitable if the organizations now gained too much power: strident self-promotion, below-the-belt fighting tactics, and intolerance of dissension. Although the Central Committee Resolution of 1925 had dampened polemic, people could remember Averbakh's dictum that writers did not appear spontaneously, but had to be developed out of a powerful, monolithic organization; in that sense, he said, the individual talent was meaningless.[45] Still fresh in mind too was the ridicule that he had heaped on Bukharin's supposedly self-contradictory idea that an autonomous proletarian literature and a freely competitive literary life could coexist.[46]

Most people conceded that some sort of organization was probably necessary, but they wanted one that would be immune to whatever had infected the old *On Guard.* There was a large play of ideas on just what form it should take. The Press Workers envisaged a kind of trade union: they had been shocked to learn that, of the writers who had replied to a questionnaire of theirs, more than half belonged to no organization, and none had ever gone on an "organized" vacation to a sanitarium or rest home.[47] A questionnaire sent out by the journal *The Life of Art* (*Zhizn' iskusstva*) revealed that the many prominent writers of every ideological persuasion who responded all wanted the benefits of an organization without any of the restraints, some-

[45] Speech at Meeting of Press Section of Central Committee, May 9-10, 1924, *K voprosu o politike RKP (b) v khudozhestvennoi literature* (Moscow, 1924), pp. 40-41.

[46] "O literaturnoi politike Partii," *Na postu,* No. 1 (1925), pp. 50-51.

[47] S. Ingulov, "Kak zhivyot i rabotaet sovetskii pisatel'," *Pravda,* September 30, 1925, p. 3.

thing like a loose federation of writers.[48] That was the position at which Voronskii reluctantly arrived as well. He had in mind an association of writers who would be bound not by regulations but by likemindedness, comradeship, and a devotion to excellence. And he expressed the hope that such an organization would at last succeed in bringing about a close, creative association between proletarians and fellow travelers, who had so long been kept apart by the insidious principle of "grouping." In effect, he was admitting that his journal had failed to realize one of its major objectives; but he laid the blame at the door of the proletarian organizations. Now the time had come "to raise, to gather together, to teach, to bring into literature young Communist and proletarian forces, link them with the finest achievements of our glorious literary past, overcome vulgar over-simplification [*uproshchenstvo*], Communist snobbery, naïve ethnographism. . . ." Fellow travelers, for their part, would profit from the ideological invigoration of contact with their proletarian brethren.[49] The old program for *RVS* was now being stretched upon the frame of the literary organization. No doubt Voronskii thought of such an organization as a floating reserve of talent on which his journal could draw at will. Yet by proposing it, he was actually reversing the relationship: *RVS*, in effect, would no longer be an organizing center in itself, but merely an outlet for one or more independent organizations. In this way, Voronskii implicitly conceded that the day of the thick journal had passed.

Voronskii never founded an organization of this kind himself. But circumstances made him the mentor of a group

---

[48] "Ko vsem pisatelyam SSSR," *Zhizn' iskusstva*, No. 43 (1926), p. 14. The questionnaire was repeated in Nos. 44 and 45. Among the writers who replied were Zamyatin, Aleksei Tolstoi, Fyodor Sologub, Fedin, and Mikhail Kazakov.

[49] "O Federatsii sovetskikh pisatelei," *KN*, No. 4 (1927), p. 217. See also his "O proletarskom iskusstve," *KN*, No. 7 (1923), p. 274.

which in many respects embodied his new views: the so-called "Pass" (Pereval). Of all the literary groups of the time, the Perevalists identified themselves most closely with *RVS*, while preserving their identity as a group. The relationship provides a case study of the interaction of the two competing principles of literary organization in the late twenties—the group and the journal.

THE PEREVAL began as a rebellion against authority. By late 1923, certain talented young writers within the "October" group—notably Golodnyi, Svetlov, Yasnyi, and Vesyolyi—had grown restive under a set of regulations that cramped their literary friendships and their literary methods. Most of them were poets, and the oldest was but twenty-five. In looking about for a new home, they were drawn to *RVS*, which served no particular group and seemed to care mainly for quality. They began to publish there, in defiance of October's ban on trucking in print with fellow travelers, and soon severed all ties with their stern parent. It was these Communist Youth (Komsomol) poets, as they were usually called, who formed the nucleus of the future Pereval group. One of the founding members has described how it happened:

> At the same time, several young writers from the revolutionary peasantry and the Communists, who belonged to no particular group, were beginning to gather informally around *Red Virgin Soil*, having already published some things in the journal. The young people became acquainted, found common interests, and at the beginning of 1924 decided to organize a group of worker-peasant poets under the name of "Pereval." About fifteen people, half of them Communists, soon joined the nucleus of Komsomols: Zarudin, Nasedkin, Kaurichev, Druzhinin, Akul'shin, Vetrov, E. Sergeeva, Yakhontova, and others. About once a week they would get together

for readings of their works. They would meet in the office of the "Circle" publishing house.[50]

The Perevalists were one of the most varied literary groups of the twenties. The founders were mainly poets, but within a year or so their ranks had swelled with prose writers like Boris Guber and Anna Karavaeva, and, somewhat later, with a number of critics and theorists—notably A. Lezhnev, Dmitrii Gorbov, Valentina Dynnik, and S. Pakentreiger—who had already won reputations in the world of letters, largely through their contributions to *RVS*. Most came from the working class or the peasantry, but there were some fellow travelers, a few representatives of the old intelligentsia, and even people who by origin would have to be classified as petty-bourgeois. No group operating under the rule of the Octobrists would have tolerated such mongrelization. But Voronskii must have been intrigued, for here was proof of his contention that writers of very different backgrounds could work together in harmony, while retaining their individualities.

The Perevalists contributed to most of the major journals of the time. The flower of their work, however, bloomed in the eight miscellanies (*sborniki*) bearing their name that appeared between 1924 and 1932. The first of them made an impressive appearance, with 261 pages and twenty-nine writers, but gave no clear picture of the group's aims; the opening editorial statement was too brief, modest, and vague to qualify as a platform. After identifying the contributors merely as "a group of young writers—prose writers and poets," the statement went on to invite other youths who supported the aims of the Revolution to submit their work, particularly if it had to do with "our worker's new way of life in the factory and the plant, in the recent past and the present, a way of life that is virtually untouched by

50 V. Nasedkin, "K dvukhletiyu 'Perevala,' " *Pereval*, IV (Moscow-Leningrad, 1926), 167.

contemporary literature."[51] Readers whose curiosity might have been pricked by the absence of that shrill self-promotion that usually accompanied the launching of new groups had to wait until the third volume for a more precise statement of aims and principles. By then, the group had gained some confidence.

They began with a ringing denunciation of parochial literary organizations—meaning, though not naming, the VAPP—disclaimed any intention of getting involved in the quarrels of the time, and offered themselves as a kind of centrist group by reaffirming, as an article of political and literary belief, the principle of comradely cooperation among all social classes. "The working class," they said, "can consolidate its power and create all the prerequisities for the development of its artistic culture only on condition of an intimate link with the peasantry and the toiling intelligentsia."[52] A special appeal went out to the young literary hopefuls in the provinces. Despite some ambitious talk, more or less *de rigueur* in those days, about "mass work," writing came first. The Pereval artist could create as he liked, bound only by a devotion to realism, stylistic excellence, and the desire to "give as full and creative a reflection of our reality as possible, the logic of old human attitudes and the building of new ones, the growth of a new social mind [*obshchestvennost'*] and of a new man."[53]

The ideas and often the wording of these statements carried a strong flavor of Voronskii and *RVS*. This is not surprising; for, despite professions of neutralism in the great literary dispute, the Perevalists made no secret of their admiration for Voronskii. They took their name from the title of one of his articles,[54] and used the editorial office

[51] "Ot redaktsii," *Pereval*, I (Moscow-Leningrad, 1924).
[52] "Pereval," *Pereval*, III (1925), 251.
[53] *Ibid.*, p. 254.
[54] Namely, "Na perevale," *KN*, No. 6 (1923). "Pereval" means "mountain pass" and symbolized the transition from old to new.

of *RVS* as their mailing address. In questions of literary theory and criticism, they were, as one of them put it, "wholly at one with the position of Comrade Voronskii."[55] The *RVS* critics looked in on the group's meetings occasionally; Voronskii's remarks on such occasions were considered "particularly valuable."[56] When the group finally did acquire its own critics, the most important of them, as we mentioned, had already made a name with their contributions to *RVS*. And in the fellow traveler writers associated with the journal, the Perevalist found his teachers. While deploring their political illiteracy, he considered them essential to that "first condition" that proletarian writers must observe: "intensified and deepened work to master the elements of the culture of the past and the technical achievements of the masters of our own time and of the past."[57] Leonov, Shishkov, Ivanov, Pil'nyak, and Esenin were among those who attended Pereval readings in 1925 and 1926.[58]

Voronskii went to considerable trouble to attract these young writers in the first place: Nasedkin reports that he was not at all shy about "propagandizing" the earliest defectors from the VAPP. And after the group had formed around *RVS*, he devoted a large and sympathetic article to them, mentioned them frequently in print, and let it be understood that they exemplified what honest Soviet writers should be: hard-working, sincere, individualistic, humble, properly appreciative of the fellow travelers, and actually writing instead of issuing manifestoes and aching for power. In that most of them were at the same time lyricists and Communists or Komsomols, they lent support to one of Voron-

---

Andrei Belyi had earlier used the term in a well-known essay on the crisis of Russian culture (*Na perevale* [Berlin, 1923]), but his influence in this case is very doubtful, to say the least.

[55] Nasedkin, "K dvukhletiyu 'Perevala,'" p. 170.
[56] *Ibid.*, p. 171.   [57] "Pereval," p. 251.
[58] Nasedkin, "K dvukhletiyu 'Perevala,'" p. 171.

skii's key ideas: that a writer could be both "artistic" and "contemporary."[59] Consequently, he drew heavily on them for his journal. The most distinguished contributions in poetry came from Aleksandrovskii, Svetlov, Altauzen, Druzhinin, Zarudin, Yasnyi, and Bagritskii; in prose, from Prishvin, Vesyolyi, Evdokimov, Zavadovskii, Ognyov, and Karavaeva.

The platform of 1927 should have dispelled any doubts that might have lingered in the public mind about the enormous debt the Perevalists owed to the thinking of *RVS*. It was actually printed in the journal, and the ideas were all familiar to loyal readers. There was strong disapproval of the notion that any one literary group, however distinguished, should enjoy "hegemony"; support for the principle of "free creative competition" in all the arts; a definition of literature's task as "the continual recording of the human personality in its inexhaustible variety"; a protest against "any attempts to schematize man, vulgar oversimplification of any kind, deadening standardization, any belittling of the writer's personality in the name of petty manners-and-mores painting" (an obvious dig at the radical proletarians); an insistence that literature must link itself to the classical heritage, not only of Russia but of the world; a concept of the work of art as a unique organic individuality "where elements of thought and feeling are recast esthetically"; an emphasis on high standards of literary craftsmanship; and a suggestion of the "sincerity" doctrine in the insistence on the "revolutionary conscience of each artist" which "does not permit him to conceal his inner world."[60]

One could not ask for a more concise refresher of the journal's main ideas about art. The Pereval group had be-

---

[59] "O 'Perevale' i pereval'tsakh," *Prozhektor*, No. 4 (1925), pp. 19-21. Nasedkin's remarks are in *ibid.* For another useful appraisal, cf. A. Lezhnev, "O 'Perevale,'" *Voprosy literatury i kritiki* (Moscow-Leningrad [1924]), pp. 165-76.

[60] "Deklaratsiya vsesoyuznogo ob''edineniya raboche-krest'yanskikh pisatelei 'Pereval,'" *KN*, No. 2 (1927), pp. 233-36.

come a satellite. But the satellite seemed to be exerting an appreciable pull on the tides of the parent body as well. Even though the Perevalists were a loose-knit group, with never a very stable membership, a recognizably Perevalist cast of writing had taken form by 1927. In fiction and poetry, it is marked by high lyricism, a fondness for peasant themes, and an emphasis on the universal and immediate human experiences such as love and compassion, which unite men, as against the class differences which divide them; in criticism, by the insistence that enthusiasm, freshness, sincerity, and competent craftsmanship carry far more weight than "content" and "ideology." Since all these ideas predominated in *RVS* itself after 1926, it is easy to understand the special attraction Voronskii felt for these young poets. One cannot be sure whether direct borrowing in either direction was at work here, or simply the natural development of coinciding ideas. The fact that many of the critics for *RVS* became Perevalists after 1924 neither proves nor disproves mutual influence; but it is unquestionably a symptom of the degree to which journal and group had come together.

These coincidences were not lost on readers—least of all on the Octobrists. Still smarting over the much-publicized defection of the VAPP's most promising young talents, they charged that the Perevalists were really shock troops organized "by Comrade Voronskii specially for the struggle with proletarian literature."[61] One's impulse, considering the source, is to dismiss the charge as nonsense—the more so as the Pereval itself contained a good many "proletarian" writers. Yet there is a certain logic here. Why should Voronskii not have used an eager young group as a weapon in the bitter fight against "proletarian literature" in Rodov's sense of the term: against the VAPP? Could he have been tempted?

[61] Resolution of Third Moscow Conference of Proletarian Writers, October 1924, as quoted in *Istoriya russkoi sovetskoi literatury* ("Khronika"), I (Moscow, 1958), 639.

It is highly unlikely, at least up to 1927. In wooing the
Perevalists, Voronskii probably had no intention of making
any change in the direction of his journal. Rather, he hoped,
or so we may assume, to reinforce his basic policy of bringing together writers of every social background. That
policy had never been realized to Voronskii's satisfaction,
largely because the proletarian writers did not contribute
as much to *RVS* as he had once anticipated. For that he
blamed their own indifference to craftsmanship as well as
intimidation from their self-appointed leaders, the Octobrists. Very likely he saw in the Pereval a way of overcoming both impediments: of bridging the chasm that gaped between proletarians and fellow travelers, and of helping to
raise the standards of proletarian literature. The special
effort the Perevalists made to court provincial writers also
laid a pipeline into an area that Voronskii by himself could
not watch closely. Finally, in the Pereval, *RVS* would have
a reserve of respectable talent right at hand.

But Voronskii's enthusiasm was tempered with caution.
While esteeming the "sincerity," "lyricism," and "health" of
the Perevalists, he considered them artistically immature,
certainly in comparison with the fellow travelers; and he
never made for them the expansive claims that the Octobrists made for the proletarian writers. Indeed, he was very
much disturbed by the undertow of "bohemianism" that he
detected in some of them. He was willing to attribute it to
circumstances, not wilfullness—the wretched poverty of the
writer's calling, the pall cast on the glories of the Civil War
by the drab realities of the NEP—but he reckoned it insidious to sound ideology and good literature.[62] He also ra-
tioned the amount of time and energy he gave to the group,
let himself be listed as an editor of the miscellany in the
first volume only, and limited his contributions to an article
or two. Once in a while he would turn up at the group's

[62] "O 'Perevale' i pereval'tsakh," pp. 19-21.

meetings, but only as a critic, never as an organizer. Though he lent them the prestige of his name and the facilities of his journal, he took no part, according to one of the members, in their internal affairs, and kept them at a perceptible and frequently cool distance from *RVS*.[63]

The Perevalists, of course, cherished the patronage of a famous and influential man of letters; yet they had no desire to become merely a training school for the literature section of *RVS*. They always upheld their right to publish where they pleased, even in journals that might be hostile to Voronskii. And they made a point of identifying themselves as a worker and peasant organization, three-fourths of whose members belonged to the Communist Party or the Komsomol. This could certainly not be said of *RVS*, which was dominated by fellow travelers. If Voronskii's enthusiasm for the Pereval was tempered by a keen awareness of their immaturity as artists, Perevalist enthusiasm for Voronskii was tempered by the knowledge that he represented writers who might easily taint them.

In any event, the Pereval was singularly ill equipped to function as a militant organization. The Moscow branch experienced all the privations of the typical small literary group in those years. Nasedkin reported in 1926 that "the majority of the members of 'Pereval,' not having any regular job, are dragging out a half-starving existence, living from hand to mouth." A mutual aid fund had been set up during the first year, but "the treasurer didn't have even enough money to give a dinner."[64] Nasedkin complained

[63] Gleb Glinka, *Pereval: The Withering of Literary Spontaneity in the USSR*, Research Program on the USSR (East European Fund, Inc.), Mimeograph Series No. 40 (New York, 1953), p. 18 (text in Russian). Still, he did appear at a meeting of the Northeast Organization of the Pereval in Vologda in November 1926, as a representative of the Moscow organization. Cf. his letter to Gor'kii, February 16, 1927, in *M. Gor'kii i sovetskaya pechat'. Arkhiv A. M. Gor'kogo*, x, Book 2 (Moscow, 1965), 46.

[64] "K dvukhletiyu 'Perevala,'" p. 171.

that the group felt like a "stepchild" because it got no encouragement or assistance from the government for carrying out "organizational" work. Assuming that the money had been forthcoming, one wonders just how aggressively the Perevalists would have used it. Their third miscellany, in 1925, carried an open letter addressed by the "Bureau of the Pereval" to "All provincial literary organizations and writers working alone," urging them to "form an organizational tie with the 'Pereval.'" Actually, this meant no more than "giving a detailed account of the membership of groups" and making reports on the conditions in which individual writers lived and worked, including "the attitudes of Soviet and Party organizations" toward them. All the parent body could promise in return was to "give provincial writers the opportunity to use the Moscow press"—a great deal in itself, of course, but hardly indicative of any serious ambition, at that time, of rivaling the VAPP.[65] The "mass" work they talked about seemed to reflect good intentions more than anything else; the glue that held them together was a sense of comradeship based on "productive and creative principles"—no more than that.

Over the years a good many writers came and went in the Pereval, so that the cumulative membership of the organization must have been rather large. At any one time, however, it stood at about the average for smaller literary groups in those days. Twenty-nine names had been appended to the first declaration; three years later, at the height of the Pereval's influence, fifty-six people signed the declaration printed in *RVS*. They called themselves the "Moscow branch," but in effect they were the whole organization.[66] The editorial boards of the earlier miscellanies

[65] "Vsem provintsial'nym organizatsiyam," *Pereval*, III (Moscow-Leningrad, 1925), 254-55.

[66] S. Gusev, writing in April 1927, estimated the membership of the Pereval at 250, but he did not say whether this represented just the Moscow organization (which seems doubtful), or the total mem-

reflect the same restless pattern of change, from one issue to the next. Not until 1926 was some stability achieved with the appointment of one "responsible editor," M. Barsukov; he remained on the job through the following year. Yet some orderly rules of procedure apparently operated: new candidates for membership underwent a screening, at least during the first year and a half of the organization's existence; and provisions were made for periodic reviews of the qualifications of old members as well. Nasedkin revealed that, at first, membership had been allowed to grow too rapidly; as a result, many writers were admitted who proved ideologically unstable and artistically unsound. Three purges had been carried out to remove the undesirables, among whom Nasedkin numbered "professional shouters"—writers, we may suppose, who wished to involve the Pereval in the polemics of the time.[67]

The evidence, then, indicates a desire to keep the group small and flexible. Revolutions have of course been made with far fewer numbers than the Pereval commanded; but there is no reason to suspect that they wished to cultivate anyone's garden except their own. At least, that was so up to 1927, when a change apparently occurred. Gleb Glinka, a member of the group who has left us valuable reminiscences of those years, asserts that Evdokimov and Pestyukhin, toward the end of the decade, aspired to turn the Pereval into a powerful, militant literary and political organization that could rival the VAPP's successor, RAPP.[68] What the other members of the Pereval thought of this project, and how far it actually got, Glinka does not say. But internal evidence indicates that change was in the air. The language of the 1927 resolution suggested new

---

bership including provincial groups. ("Kakaya Federatsiya pisatelei nam nuzhna?" *Pravda*, April 30, 1927, p. 5.)
    [67] "K dvukhletiyu 'Perevala,'" p. 171.
    [68] Glinka, *Pereval*, p. 19.

goals and tactics. While making the usual disclaimers of ambition and defenses of the artist's right to associate with whomever he wished, the signers insisted, in stronger terms than ever before, on the need to "create an artistic center" in order to "carry out the goals indicated by the declaration [i.e., the Central Committee Resolution of 1925]." They called on "all writers who share our views to unite around the 'Pereval' in their future creative work."[69] In addition, a broad appeal went out to "those writers who have not yet found their own path, are searching for it and are trying to bring themselves creatively closer to the Revolution."[70] No mention was made now of the provincial writers as such. The appeal was addressed to *all* writers in the Russian language. Nor, significantly, did this resolution (unlike its predecessor) segment the literary world into workers, peasants, fellow travelers, and decadents. The only criteria for membership now were those to which all good Soviet citizens should have been able to subscribe: "revolutionary contemporariness" and a concern for craftsmanship.[71] The Pereval seemed to be indicating a readiness to expand into a mass organization on an all-Union scale. Carefully avoiding the old divisive terms like "proletariat" and "fellow traveler," they reasserted their claim as a centrist group. It was not an unrealistic claim, considering their aloofness from the literary wars of the past; and the careful reference to the Central Committee Resolution, which epitomized the spirit of compromise, showed they were well aware of that.

The new role that Pereval announced for itself bore a striking resemblance to Voronskii's new concept of the ideal literary organization; and it may be significant that both changes occurred at about the same time. This still does not prove that Voronskii intended to use the Pereval to counter the VAPP, or that he approved of the increas-

[69] "Deklaratsiya . . . ," p. 236.
[70] *Ibid.*, p. 234.   [71] *Ibid.*, p. 235.

ingly militant attitude within the group. On the other hand, it is not enough to say that principle and tradition made such an intention unlikely; after all, he had changed his mind about literary organizations, and, as a Bolshevik, he would not have been above strong-arm methods for the good of the cause.

The question is moot. In any case, it was too late by 1927 for Voronskii or for Pereval, whatever their plans might have been. The VAPP had reached the same conclusions, by forced march, and moved, with admirable efficiency, to turn the talk about comradely cooperation to their own profit.

· I I I ·

We remember that the Central Committee Resolution of 1925 split the ranks of the Octobrists. One faction, the so-called "left," clung to the old slogans and tactics. The other, under Averbakh's leadership, gained control of the VAPP and revamped the Octobrist movement. To be sure, they continued to attack *RVS*, while stealing a good many of its ideas; yet they adopted a public attitude toward the fellow travelers that was more in the spirit of the Resolution's demands. In keeping with this new attitude, they proposed in 1926 to create an organization that would do what no proletarian organization had ever done before: bring men of the working class together under one roof with fellow travelers and members of the peasantry. This was quite a switch, since the Octobrists had always regarded any proposals for large heterogeneous bodies as plots to dilute and destroy proletarian solidarity. Permission was granted by the Press Section of the Central Committee; and in December 1926, the Federation of Organizations of Soviet Writers (FOSP) came into existence. Eventually all the major literary groups joined; but the most important, in size and power, were the three founding ones: the VAPP, the Union of Writers (VSP), and the Union of Peasant Writers (VSKP). Because all groups had grown steadily from the mid-twenties onward, the Federation was bound to be large; probably its membership would number around 5,000. Among other things, it would have a literary fund and a publishing house of its own, and perhaps most important, it promised to take "measures for improving the legal and material position of the Soviet writer."[72]

As vice-chairman of the VSP, Voronskii took part in the preliminary work of organizing the FOSP. When that work was done, he made a report, which apparently expressed satisfaction.[73] And well it might: the FOSP, though peddled as an Averbakh original, looked on paper very much like the kind of mass organization that Voronskii (and the Pereval) had come to accept as a necessity. But if there ever was any real consensus, it did not last long. Just three months after the organization had been formally declared alive, Fyodor Gladkov complained to Gor'kii: "The joint sessions of the delegates of the Federation of Writers are taking place in an atmosphere of implacable hatred, with bickering, brawls—a complete mess."[74] And by then it had become perfectly plain that Averbakh had no intention of giving the fellow travelers, let alone the peasant writers, an equal voice: the die-hard Octobrists, who opposed the FOSP as a compromise of proletarian principle, need not have worried. The VAPP quickly gained control through the simple expedient of rigging the votes in the executive. Voronskii spotted the plot, and devoted two indignant articles to it in RVS. In the first of them, he made a bitterly sarcas-

[72] According to S. Gusev, "Kakaya federatsiya pisatelei nam nuzhna?" *Pravda*, April 30, 1927, p. 5.

[73] "Apparently," because the only mention I have found of this report is by S. Gusev (*ibid.*), who quotes a few lines from it. He is attempting to show that Voronskii put his stamp of approval on the organization, and therefore had no cause to complain about it (see n. 75).

[74] Letter to Gor'kii, April 7, 1927, *Gor'kii i sovetskie pisateli. Literaturnoe nasledstvo*, LXX (Moscow, 1963), 93.

tic exposé of Averbakh's maneuvering (which that self-confident manipulator had scarcely troubled to conceal anyway), predicted its success and the consequent mockery of the very principle of federation, and contemptuously washed his hands of the whole business.[75] The second article, his final contribution to RVS, was written two months later and took a more moderate approach. Voronskii now asserted that he had no quarrel with the VAPP itself, and was even willing to grant it a leading role in the Federation. But he still insisted that with Averbakh in charge, no real federation was possible because it was not truly representative. What the VAPP should do was "decisively put the Averbakhs and Zonins in their more modest place"—that is, depose them—and confer with those Communists and proletarians who were not members of the VAPP and had hitherto been excluded from all serious deliberations: Gladkov and the Perevalists among them. If there were "another leadership," Voronskii concluded, then "we would enter VAPP and set to work there. . . ."[76] This attempt at a compromise was made in the form of an "open letter" to S. Gusev, who had replied to Voronskii's earlier article in a harsh and chiding manner.[77] But since Gusev was the head of the Press Section, which had acted favorably on the VAPP's petition to form the FOSP in the first place, had clearly been showing favor to Averbakh for the last year or so despite professions of neutrality, and even then was trying hard to get rid of Voronskii once and for all, Voronskii was simply wasting his breath. The FOSP went forward under VAPP auspices.

[75] "O Federatsii sovetskikh pisatelei," KN, No. 4 (1927), p. 216.
[76] "Ob uzhasnoi krokodile, o federatsii pisatelei i fal'shivykh frazakh (Otkrytoe pis'mo tov. Gusevu)," KN, No. 6 (1927), p. 242. According to Voronskii, the VAPP and its supporters would have two-thirds of all the votes in the Federation, the VSP one-third, and the others, none (p. 241). Cf. Averbakh's reply: "Literaturnye diskussii tekushchego goda," Na literaturnom postu, No. 13 (1927), p. 7.
[77] "Kakaya Federatsiya pisatelei nam nuzhna?"

The Pereval declaration of 1927 should also be read in the light of Averbakh's intrigues. It was published *after* plans for the FOSP had been announced; and though it never mentioned the new organization, the signatories must have had it very much in mind. For there is a long, savage thrust—behind which one can almost hear a cry of frustration—that warns writers about being taken in by the sight of the VAPP's eating humble pie. " 'Pereval' has always considered," they wrote, "that the ideological structure of VAPP's critical thought schematizes the artist, bullies his inner artistic independence, stifles in it any possibilities of giving this or that image an esthetic reworking that is close to the understanding and feeling of the writer." Against such intimidations they resolved to fight "for the original, distinctive writer, who participates in the creation of a new man—as a fighter and a builder."[78]

But now it was Averbakh who marched in step with the times. Voronskii's concept of the literary organization, as a kind of gentleman's club, was hopelessly outmoded. The crucial difference lay in the Party's attitude. Up to the middle twenties, the Party had implicitly disapproved of literary groups as disruptive, contentious, noisy, and fractious, and had refused to express a preference for any of them. As the Party's implement, Voronskii of course felt the same way. By the time he had come around to recognizing that some sort of organization might after all be desirable, the Party had developed a keen interest in literature, and had decided to move in. In supporting the VAPP's capture of the FOSP, the Party in fact was taking the first important step toward making literature official. From that moment on, any idea of a loose federation of writers was dead. Averbakh had maneuvered skillfully, combining the old Voronskii idea of federation with the VAPP idea of strong, centralized control. The result, the FOSP, suited the Party's palate admira-

[78] "Deklaratsiya . . . ," p. 235.

bly, and provided the prototype of the Union of Soviet Writers: the mass organization under tight Party control.[79]

In forming the FOSP, the VAPP had in effect chosen to disregard the old literary groupings based on class and ideology, which it had once defended so savagely. In this respect, it anticipated the Party's decision, in 1932, to abolish the designations "fellow travelers," "proletarian," and "peasant" for writers, making all writers "Soviet." But the same idea had been in the air—despite heavy fire from the Octobrists—long before the VAPP appropriated it. No one had argued for it more eloquently than Voronskii himself. Now it was taken up—but in a much different context than he could ever have imagined. In fact, something like the concept of a Soviet culture was beginning to form in the late twenties; and it was this which gave the final push to the tottering structure of the literary journals. For as this concept was interpreted—a set of norms and ideals that incarnated truth and therefore, to the Bolshevik mind (and, one might say, to the Russian as well), permitted no discussion—it made impossible the articulation and defense of the vigorous individual view that must inform any journal aspiring to be more than a mere compendium. The "line" now lay outside any one man or journal. A mass organization expressed it perfectly; the journals merely gave it voice.

WE MAY now make definite the tentative answer to the question posed earlier in this chapter: Shklovskii was right

[79] Understandably, Voronskii seems to have grown cool toward the idea of a mass organization after his experiences with the FOSP. In one of his last articles, we find him proposing the creation of a number of literary "schools," perhaps within existing groups, which would devote themselves to special problems: "Some might work out the problem of the conscious and unconscious, others—the psychology and dynamics of the perceptions, still others might undertake the task of 'opening up' the theme of labor, others might concentrate on the dialectic of art, etc." ("Iskusstvo videt' mir," *Iskusstvo videt' mir* [Moscow, 1928], p. 113.)

about the thick journals. Economic conditions, the growth of literature, political repression, and the rise of mass literary organizations had started their decline. Under Stalinism—when the concept of a unitary culture was made binding on all—the journals finally expired. But, strange as it may seem, no one could face the fact of death. As in the twenties, people continued to insist that the thick journal must stand at the center of literature, displaying a militant ideology in a large range of departments. Around 1929, many of the old departments were sandwiched back in; and for a while the journals seemed once again to flourish. But the litany of familiar sins—repetitiousness, timidity, triviality, tedium—soon droned forth anew. A Central Committee Resolution of August 1931, for example, complained that the journals lacked "firm work plans" and "cadres of writers," and could not be distinguished one from the other.[80] Gor'kii noted that they had no consistent line and no individuality: "they put in one or two articles that by nature are absolutely indistinguishable from identical articles in specialized publications."[81] And so it has gone, until very recently.

There was a curious formalism that kept the critics at work embalming the corpses of the journals. By 1927—thanks in no small measure to the successes of *RVS*—the thick journal had come to stand for literary stability, affluence, and quality; it was the talisman of a past that by now had been not merely dignified, but gilded and sentimentalized as well. Any suggestion of decline in the journal immediately called up visions of a decline in literature itself. It was as if the very form had the power to evoke literature worthy of filling it. But the nineteenth century has other lessons for those who will learn. One of the most compelling is that the thick journal flourishes only in a pluralistic

---

[80] "Ob izdatel'skoi rabote. Postanovlenie TsK VKP (b) ot 15 avg. 1931 g.," *O partiinoi i sovetskoi pechati* (Moscow, 1954), p. 422.

[81] "Chto dolzhen znat' nash massovyi chitatel'?" *Pravda*, July 3, 1933, p. 2.

society. A reviewer writing in *The Contemporary* in 1851 introduced his survey of literature for the previous year in the following words:

> The society of England and France is divided into a multitude of factions, each of which has a sphere of ideas all its own, strives to express them, and brings every effort to bear so that these particular ideas should triumph over other ideas that stand opposed to them. In the clash and constant struggle of these various interests lies a significant part of the activity, life and development of those societies, and consequently of their literatures....
>
> One may ask: is a phenomenon of this kind possible in our literature? Decidedly not. . . . The main reason why it is impossible lies, we think, in our characteristic tolerance, which restrains us from forming separate groups and therefore from making a one-sided pursuit of this or that idea. As a result of this characteristic of our society and of our literature, our journals themselves do not manifest any sharp differences among one another, and they can be distinguished only by a few, and for the most part extremely faint, nuances. The main difference among them consists not so much in the shape of their views on things, as in the greater or lesser degree of talent or learning that their contributors possess.[82]

"Tolerance," of course, is the writer's euphemism for "censorship," and his sweetly reasonable tone thinly veils a feeling of profound distress over the lack of variety. (He does not spell out what his readers knew: that there had been an abundant variety in society and the journals not too long before.) Other commentators of the time complained about writers who were breaking their ties with specific journals and publishing at random, literary criticism

[82] "Obozrenie russkoi literatury za 1850 g.," *Sovremennik*, xxv (St. Petersburg, 1851), Section III, 7-9.

that was turning into mere "bibliography," nit-picking that was passing for polemic—employing, in short, virtually the same glossary that critics drew upon in characterizing the defects of the thick journals some eighty years later.[83] These observations were made at a time when the severe censorship imposed in 1848 was still in force—a time, in other words, similar to Stalinism, though far less savage. The fact that both periods told adversely on the thick journal suggests that one law of the form is a need for controversy, so that strong positions, and therefore strong "lines," may be taken. This is not to say that thick journals had no useful function under Stalinism: they remained the major outlets for new writing, and served as primary organs of censorship. But they travestied a glorious tradition.

In the past fifteen years, however, things have changed. A pluralistic culture has slowly been growing up. Schools and factions have once more begun to appear in literary life. Polemic crackles; dispute swirls. Significantly, the thick journals have recovered their individuality and some of their old sparkle, as centers of this pulsating activity. Meanwhile, the one literary organization that exists, the Union of Soviet Writers, has fallen into utter disrepute in the eyes of many writers. It no longer seems to play an especially important role even in official literary life. Writers like Pasternak, who have been expelled from it, or who have refused to join, manage to survive. The "sections" are virtually moribund, for no longer do writers subject their works in progress to the scrutinies of the preliminary censorship. Paradoxically it may be that the specialized non-literary journals, of which more and more are appearing, are actually now giving vitality to the thick journals, in-

---

[83] Cf., e.g., N. G. Chernyshevskii, letter to N. I. Kostomarov, 1853, as cited in A. G. Dement'ev, *Ocherki po istorii russkoi zhurnalistiki 1840-1850 gg.* (Moscow, 1951), p. 105. This letter is not included in the Soviet edition of Chernyshevskii's complete works (*Polnoe sobranie sochinenii*, 16 vols. [Moscow, 1939-1953]).

stead of draining it as they did in the twenties. Certain disciplines, like science and economics, show far greater boldness and imagination than do the arts. Ultimately these qualities may infect the thick journals as well. In any event, their history has not yet closed.

CHAPTER X

Epilogue

VORONSKII was purged ostensibly for being a Trotskiite. "In 1925," the *Literary Encyclopedia* writes, "he sided with the [Trotskii] opposition in the Communist Party and carried on factional work."[1] During the trials of the 1930's, his name was mentioned frequently in connection with Trotskii and other so-called enemies of the people. V. Stavskii reported, for instance, that in 1928, the writer Ivan Kataev, together with a few colleagues from the Pereval group, had gone to Voronskii's place of banishment "for directives" and had "collected money to send to Trotskiites in exile."[2] Since 1956, with the "rehabilitation" of Voronskii, important qualifications have been made. We are now told that although he was "under the definite influence of Trotskiite views on literature," it has "become known" that he was "not connected with the Trotskii underground," and regrets are expressed for the "unjust" linkage.[3] But why was the linkage made in the first place?

Voronskii seems to have committed one serious overt political error: he was a signatory of the "Platform of the Forty-Six," that allegation of inefficiency and dictatorial exclusiveness on the part of the Party's leadership prepared at the height of the economic crisis of 1923. Though there is no evidence that Trotskii was directly responsible for the Platform, the signatories, as E. H. Carr has noted, "included most of those who, both earlier and later, were Trotskii's closest political associates"; and the language, tone, and substance of the Platform's objections closely re-

[1] "Voronskii," *Literaturnaya entsiklopediya*, II (1929), 313.

[2] "Sdelat' vse prakticheskie vyvody," *Literaturnaya gazeta*, August 27, 1936, p. 2.

[3] V. Ivanov, "O literaturnykh gruppirovkakh i techeniyakh 20-kh godov," *Znamya*, No. 5 (1958), p. 199.

sembled Trotskii's own. Collusion was immediately suspected and, at the Thirteenth Congress, openly charged.[4]

Apart from this, we have no other evidence that Voronskii took a direct hand in inner-Party politics on Trotskii's
side or on anyone's else's. The important thing, however, is
that the linkage of these two men was by no means im-
plausible: it was not simply another swoop of that great
brush labeled "Trotskiist" with which practically all "de-
viationist" tendencies were daubed after 1927. Voronskii
had little to say in public about administrative, economic,
or political matters; but Trotskii, with his facile, witty, and
often irreverent pen, was very much involved in the literary
discussions of the time. And on two of the crucial literary
issues, their views virtually coincided: on the policy appropriate to the fellow travelers, and, with some important
differences, on the question of proletarian culture. Since
literary criticism to the Marxist is but another branch of
politics, Trotskii, the politician, easily became the other
face of Voronskii, the literatus. Virtually from the moment
RVS was founded, people had thought of these two men as
blood brothers in matters of literature and culture. Why not
in politics as well? Understandably, Averbakh and his colleagues lost no opportunity to strengthen these associations, especially as word of Trotskii's increasingly precarious
position in the Party began to spread; for with Voronskii
gone, they might well succeed in realizing their long-frus-
trated ambition to be masters of literature.

[4] E. H. Carr, *The Interregnum, 1923-1924, A History of Soviet
Russia*, IV (London, 1954), esp. 297, 338. Various signatories appended comments to the text (reproduced in Carr's translation on pp.
367-73), expressing agreement or, more often, some reservations.
Voronskii's signature appears beside those of A. Bubnov and V.
Smirnov, both members of the editorial board of *RVS* at that time.
In his autobiography, Trotskii mentions Voronskii just once: "We
learned from the newspapers of new arrests of several hundred people,
including 150 of the so-called Trotskyist centre. The published names
included . . . Voronsky, our best literary critic . . ." (L. Trotskii,
My Life [New York, 1930], p. 564).

Those who knew what was going on within the Party might also have remarked a curious parallel rhythm in the fortunes of Trotskii and Voronskii. To review briefly Trotskii's position: throughout 1923, few people had any idea that dissension existed between Trotskii and the Politburo. The Party as a whole and the country at large still regarded him as a major source of policy. Yet by 1924, he stood virtually alone. The "literary debate" between him and his colleagues over matters of theory and practice had been going on throughout the fall and winter of 1924, and it came to a climax with his resignation from the Commissariat of War in January 1925. After a period of quiescence, the struggle resumed in March 1927, with Trotskii's attack on the Politburo's China policy. By June and July of that year, Stalin was pressing for a decision which would rid the Party of Trotskii; and finally in November, that decision was made.[5]

To these events let us juxtapose certain episodes in Voronskii's career as editor of *RVS*:

1924

Trotskii is virtually isolated in the Politburo. He loses influence in the Commissariat of War.	Voronskii's position is undermined by the appointment of an editorial board with Raskol'nikov, an On-Guardist, on it—and this after Voronskii's apparent triumph at the May 9-10 meeting of the Press Section of the Central Committee.

1925

January: Trotskii resigns from the Commissariat of War.	January: Voronskii leaves *RVS* (or is removed) and the On-Guardists take over.
February onward: the inner-Party struggle is becalmed.	February onward: Voronskii returns to *RVS* as editor, though Yaroslavskii, a Stalin man, now sits on the editorial board. The polemic with the On-Guardists virtually ceases for a time.

[5] Cf. Isaac Deutscher, *The Prophet Unarmed. Trotsky: 1921-1929* (London, 1959), *passim*.

1926

The inner-Party struggle resumes.	Voronskii openly expresses premonitions of personal political defeat at the hands of Averbakh.

1927

June-July: Stalin presses to remove Trotskii.	June-July: Voronskii is removed as chief editor, though he still remains on the editorial board.
November: Trotskii is expelled from the Party.	December: Voronskii is dismissed from *RVS* and *Searchlight,* and early in 1928 is expelled from the Party.

The coincidences are curious. But they point less to the collaboration of two men (for which no real evidence exists) than to the pull of two important new developments: literature, by 1924, was being drawn into internal Party politics, and *RVS*, as the leading journal, was being made a political football, even though the Party publicly maintained its original position of strict neutrality in literary matters; and the emerging faction in the inner-Party struggle was forming a new literary policy that pointed in a direction quite different from Voronskii's.

THE Party policy that had been in effect since 1917 rested upon a very important, though largely implicit distinction between two kinds of literature: political or official Party literature, on the one hand, and imaginative literature on the other. Over the first kind the Party always maintained a jealous, watchful, and complete control, not only censoring what was written, but prescribing what must be written. For the second, the Party had only one essential test—the test of loyalty—and its policy, from the very beginning of Bolshevik rule, had been designed to make as many writers as possible as loyal as possible to its aims. Beyond that, it

took no interest in the "imaginative" aspect of literature—
in "style," "form," "language," "imagery," and so on. The
fact that *RVS* was deliberately made an official organ of
the state and not of the Party reflected the sense of this distinction: the Party in effect was announcing its intention of
letting imaginative literature develop as it might, subject
only to a censorship that regulated "content"—in other
words, that which in a work of literature could be paraphrased. But even here, the Party did not hesitate to inter-
vene the moment it felt its own political interests were being threatened. Writers who ventured dissident political
opinions in their works quickly learned that. In the Party's
eyes, they transgressed neutral territory and entered the
political preserve, where they must be judged by the rules,
whose chief keeper was the Party. The Proletkul't leaders
were free to do as they liked until they stated that the cultural development of the proletariat must proceed independent of Party guidance, and foolishly challenged Lenin
on the matter. But since the Party alone could act in the
name of the proletariat, the cultural challenge immediately
translated itself into a political challenge; and Lenin
rammed a disclaimer down the throat of the Proletkul't in
1920.[6]

Gradually, however, the notion of two literatures began
to blur. For this the literary polemic of 1923-1925 was
largely responsible. From the outset the Octobrists made it
clear that they regarded all literature as a branch of politics. Their premises, their lines of argument, even their
vocabulary—literary "class struggle," writers of the "left"
and the "right," "deviations," "betrayals," and so on—came
straight from the agitation-propaganda manual. Voronskii
desperately tried to preserve the old distinction between
politics and literature; but in vain. He found himself compelled to fight according to the Octobrist rules if he was to

[6] Cf. V. V. Gorbunov, "Bor'ba V. I. Lenina s separatistskimi ustrem-
leniyami Proletkul'ta," *Voprosy istorii KPSS*, No. 1 (1958), p. 32.

fight at all. No profusion of inverted commas around words like "proletarian" and "fellow traveler" to distinguish the literary from the political variety could disguise the fact that the Octobrists had succeeded in confusing the two in everyone's mind.

Gradually the Party's pronouncements on literature began to reflect the confusion too. Early Party congresses had given space in their resolutions to commentaries on the press and to problems of propaganda and agitation, but never specifically to belles lettres. It is only in the resolution of the Twelfth Congress in 1923 that we find belles lettres mentioned for the first time:

> In view of the fact that during the last two years imaginative literature in Soviet Russia has grown into a major artistic force which is extending its influence chiefly to the masses of worker-peasant youth, it is essential that the Party should, in its practical work, place on the agenda the question of guiding [*rukovodstvo*] this form of social influence.[7]

A year later, the resolution of the Thirteenth Congress pushed matters perceptibly further. From the "agenda," imaginative literature moved to the worktable of the ideologue:

> Taking into account that no one literary current, school or group can or ought to speak in the name of the Party, the Congress emphasizes the need for regulating the question of literary criticism and for making, in the pages of the Party and Soviet press, the fullest possible Party interpretation of models of imaginative literature.[8]

By the following year, Vareikis, head of the Agitation-Propaganda Department of the Central Committee, was

---

[7] *O partiinoi i sovetskoi pechati. Sbornik dokumentov* (Moscow, 1954), p. 270.

[8] *Ibid.*, p. 311.

calling not merely for a Party interpretation of imaginative literature, but for a literature actually created according to Party prescription. A survey of readers' preferences made by the Press Department of the Central Committee had shown, not surprisingly, that imaginative literature ranked first, followed by sociological and economic tracts; and from this Vareikis concluded that the Party must

> prompt the creation of an imaginative literature which is suitable for the ideological education of the broad masses in the spirit of socialism, in the spirit of those historical revolutionary tasks on whose fulfillment the working class of the Soviet Union is now working in the sphere of politics and economics.[9]

By now the two-literatures distinction had been abandoned: a Party pronouncement on literature of *any* kind could be taken as a pronouncement on all other kinds as well. Voronskii did not grasp this vital point at the time. In fact, the Party still hesitated to spell it out. The first real public statement of Party policy, the famous Central Committee Resolution of June 18, 1925, was deliberately ambiguous. The crucial passage reads as follows:

> While capable of judging without error the social and class content of literary movements, the Party as a whole can in no way bind itself by adhering to any one movement *in the area of literary forms*. While guiding literature as a whole, the Party can hardly support any *one* literary faction (classifying these factions according to their different views of form and style), just as it cannot resolve, by means of resolutions, questions of the form of the family, though in general it does and doubtless should provide leadership in the construction of a new way of life. Everything indicates that a style suitable to

[9] "O nashei linii v khudozhestvennoi literature i o proletarskikh pisatelyakh," *Pravda*, February 18, 1925, p. 5.

EPILOGUE

the age will be created, but it will be created by different methods, and there is as yet no sign of a solution to this problem. Any attempts to bind the Party in this direction in the present phase of the country's cultural development must be rejected.[10]

This passage was open to two interpretations, depending on the reader's views of literature. For those who inclined toward the notion that literature's specific nature lies in "form," the statement might well have expressed the Party's disinclination to interfere in any way: if content, after all, was not pertinent to literature then it did not matter whether or not the Party controlled it; the important thing was that the Party had disclaimed competence in what really mattered—form. For those whose view of literature was chiefly content-centered, the statement could be read as an assertion of the Party's intention to supervise and prescribe the literary output: if form was not what mattered, then it made no difference whether or not the Party tried to regulate it; in any case, form was determined by content, which the Party *could* regulate.

Probably Voronskii proceeded on the first assumption. In language and in sentiment, the paragraph could have come from his own pen.[11] Read by itself, it indeed seemed to bestow the blessing of authority on his journal's new concern with defining the specificity of literature as something different from mere content, and to give latitude for further development in almost any direction the journal might choose to go. But in the context of the whole resolution, this statement means just the opposite. Everywhere else, literary factions are classified not "according to their different views of form and style," but according to their

10 "O politike partii v oblasti khudozhestvennoi literatury," *Pravda,* July 1, 1925, p. 6.
11 According to Herman Ermolaev, Bukharin "wrote the resolution." Cf. *Soviet Literary Theories, 1917-1934: The Genesis of Socialist Realism* (Berkeley and Los Angeles, 1963), pp. 45-46.

social, political, and class composition. That, in fact, was a natural habit of mind even of Party leaders as "literary" as Trotskii and Lunacharskii: Trotskii's famous definition of the fellow travelers, for instance, was a wholly "class" definition, which touched literature only incidentally.[12] The resolution itself made quite clear the connection between a specific class situation and a specific literary situation. Party policy toward the peasant and bourgeois writers, for example, simply restated the general Party policy toward the peasantry and the bourgeoisie as a whole:

> in the period of the proletarian dictatorship, the Party is confronted with the problem of how to get along with the peasantry while slowly reshaping it; how to allow a certain collaboration with the bourgeoisie while slowly forcing it out; how, finally, to put technicians and other segments of the intelligentsia at the service of the Revolution, while winning them away, ideologically, from the bourgeoisie.[13]

In short, the statement on literary groups, taken in the context of the whole resolution, makes no sense unless we assume that the mention of "form" is gratuitous. The Party, then, was stating its intention to direct literature and the arts. In fact, it soon moved to tighten its grip, with such measures as the reorganization of the book-publishing industry and the suppression of experimental theater.[14] Voronskii, in the meantime, was moving in just the opposite direction. By the time he realized this—probably late in 1926, when he publicly forecast his purge—it was too late.

[12] *Literatura i revolyutsiya* (2d ed., Moscow, 1924), pp. 44-86.
[13] "O politike partii . . . ," p. 6.
[14] Cf. "V Tsentral'nom komitete RKP(b)," *Pravda*, June 7, 1925, p. 5; L. Blyakhin, "O rukovodstve knigoizdatel'skoi deyatel'nost'yu," *Pravda*, May 21, 1925, p. 1; V. Knorin, "Teatr i sotsialisticheskoe stroitel'stvo," *Pravda*, May 22, 1927, p. 3; "Vsesoyuznoe soveshchanie po voprosam teatra pri agitprope TsK VKP (b)," *Pravda*, May 11, 1927, p. 4; May 13, 1927, p. 4.

He did nothing, apparently, to bridge the chasm that had opened—nothing, at any rate, that would have meant the sacrifice of principle to political expediency. He reacted to the campaign against him with incredulity and then disgust. He must also have mused bitterly on the irony of a situation that had transformed him from the Party's chief instrument to the Party's chief scapegoat—a situation that he himself had helped to create, in his insistence that the Party must render a *dixit* on literature to put an end to the long and disordering series of disputes. But whatever his private opinion, he never gave voice publicly to any disagreement with Party policy. Nor, on the other hand, did he ever make any public recantation of his own views.

VORONSKII would have been useless to the Party as events moved away from him. All his writings had made clear that he stood opposed to the "activist" or "dialectical" view of literature, especially as it involved the use of literature for direct political ends; but it was precisely this view that finally prevailed from 1928 on. The "mechanists" were branded heretics. Though Voronskii attempted to compromise between these two basic views of reality, he was lumped among the "mechanists" and thereby among the enemies of progress. Compromise had no place in the either-or atmosphere of the late twenties. But for Voronskii to have shifted ground now would have meant undoing five years of bitter struggle.

Even if he had shifted, it is unlikely that he could have escaped disgrace; for he had become an important and influential literary figure in his own right, and as such rivaled the Party's literary pretensions. Furthermore, he had evolved a theory of literature that went far beyond what the Party, and he himself, had envisioned in 1921 and 1922. He had shown, in effect, that the "imaginative" part of literature could not be as airily dismissed as the Party thought, that it was in fact even more important than anything which could be cut to the measure of "loyalty." It is significant that the central theme in all the officially inspired criticism of Voronskii's theory of literature—from 1927 until today—has been the same: his early writings (which make "contemporariness" the test of literary worth) are rated useful, but his later idea that literature constitutes a world independent of ideology, politics, and class struggle, a world beyond time, beyond change, is branded a dangerous and sad deviation. Sad because it is un-Marxist; dangerous because it flings a direct challenge at the Party on its own ground, by trying to remove an important area of experience from Party control.

It may also be that the Party decided to sacrifice Voronskii for the greater good of literature. The polemic had driven a wedge deep into literary society; fear, hostility, and contempt divided "proletarians" and "fellow travelers." Under the circumstances the Party would have found itself hard pressed (short of resorting to terror, which it was not yet prepared to do) to create the united literary front it considered necessary for bringing literature to bear on the practical tasks of socialist construction. The fellow travelers presented an especially ticklish problem: they were closely identified in the public mind with "Voronskiism"; but the Party needed them very badly. How could "Voronskiism" be eradicated without eradicating the fellow travelers and, with them, nearly all Russian literature of any quality? The answer lay in reminding everyone that "Voronskiism" was invented by a man named Voronskii, identifying it with "Trotskiism," the contrivance of a man named Trotskii, and then casting both out. It had worked, after all, with the Gadarene swine.

And it seemed to work now. The reputations of the leading fellow travelers survived the demise of *RVS*; many of them survived even the purges of the middle thirties. Voronskii became the focus of the noisy campaign against "deviations" of all kinds which the RAPP, under Averbakh, waged between 1928 and 1932. The appearance in 1928 of *The Art of Seeing the World* furnished a convenient handle. All the familiar old charges against Voronskii were wheeled out and fitted with new wings. Neglect of the proletarian writers, and the failure, described picturesquely as "tail-endism" (*khvostizm*), to provide vigorous Communist leadership for the fellow travelers formed the leitmotifs in the litany of invective. Vigorous efforts were made to destroy the reputation of Voronskii's theory of literature once and for all. Not only was it proclaimed alien, in all its parts, to the spirit of socialism, useful only as a "point of departure for speeches by all kinds of reactionaries in art," but utterly unoriginal as well: "he did not so much pursue 'his own' line as write cowardly 'critical' commentaries on someone else's [i.e., on Trotskii's]."[15] One critic summed up and dismissed Voronskii's entire career with the observation that he "began as a comrade, continued as a good citizen [*grazhdanin*: the term used, often scornfully, to refer to people who were not members of the Party] and ended as a Gracious Gentleman."[16]

Evidence of "Voronskiism" and even "neo-Voronskiism" —the literary equivalents of "Trotskiism"—was soon discovered everywhere. The terms were smeared on anyone who disagreed with the RAPP, and thus they lost any real meaning. But Voronskii had left a group of loyal disciples in the Pereval, and it was on them, as an object-lesson in the ways of "Voronskiism," that the full weight of the RAPP campaign fell.

After Voronskii's disgrace, Lezhnev, Gorbov, Zamoshkin, and Pakentreiger all wrote books which echoed most of the essential points their teacher had made in his

[15] "Litso nashikh protivnikov. A. Voronskii," *Na literaturnom postu*, No. 21-22 (1930). The first quote is on p. 4, the second on p. 3.

[16] I. Grossman-Roshchin, "Iskusstvo izmenyat' mir," *Na literaturnom postu*, No. 4-5 (1929), p. 33. Original italics omitted.

Art of Seeing the World. For them, too, art's purpose is to "see the world," the real world of disinterested beauty. This process, they thought, is intuitive—above reason or sheer craftsmanship—and it works through "immediate impressions," through the artist's forgetting himself in order to "reincarnate" himself in the object he is to depict. Art is a reality as real as any other, but it rises above everyday reality; this is its social function as well. This meant, for the Perevalists, that any artistic method in principle is valid, because all art has the same concern: the "objective" discovery of the world.[17]

Averbakh and his co-workers dismissed these new books as "vulgarized" and "primitivized" rehashings of ideas which even in Voronskii's version were outmoded, unoriginal, and baneful, and held them up as evidence that "Voronskiism" was still very much alive. Lezhnev, the best known of these critics, fell under especially close scrutiny as Voronskii's "trusty arms-bearer."[18] The RAPP critics went

[17] A. Lezhnev, *Razgovor v serdtsakh* (Moscow, 1930); D. Gorbov, *V poiskakh Galatei* (Moscow, 1928); N. Zamoshkin, *Literaturnye mezhi* (Moscow, 1930); S. Pakentreiger, *Zakaz na vdokhnovenie* (Moscow, 1930). Gorbov also developed the idea, exactly opposite to Plekhanov's, that the artist *must* be in disharmony with his class if he is to produce good art. In this, Gorbov departed from his Pereval colleagues, as well as from Voronskii (D. Gorbov, *Put' M. Gor'kogo*, quoted by L. Averbakh, "Doloi Plekhanova [Kuda rastyot shkola Voronskogo]," *Na literaturnom postu*, No. 20-21 [1928], p. 24). V. Friche, attacking this idea, pointed out that among other things it would make proletarian art quite impossible ("Otkroveniya mistera i missis Britling ob iskusstve," *Pechat' i revolyutsiya*, No. 4 [1929], pp. 8-17).

[18] M. Serebryanksii, "Epokha i eyo 'rovesniki,'" *Na literaturnom postu*, No. 5-6 (1930), p. 24. For a typically savage attack on Lezhnev, cf. V. Ermilov, "Garmonicheskii obyvatel'," *Na literaturnom postu*, No. 11-12 (1929), pp. 19-33.

For other attacks on the Pereval group by the RAPP leadership, cf.: "Protiv reaktsionnoi shkoly Voronskogo. Rezolyutsiya sektsii literatury, iskusstva i yazyka Kommunisticheskoi Akademii o sodruzhestve pisatelei 'Pereval,'" *Pechat' i revolyutsiya*, No. 5-6 (1930), p. 106; L. Averbakh, "Doloi Plekhanova," *ibid.*, pp. 15-30. For appraisals by

on to discover the "practical" consequences of these "Voronskiist" theories in the work of the Perevalist prose writers and poets: their predilection for nature writing merely disguised a "protest against socialist construction," an "estheticization of the past," a "Rousseauism," a "gypsy romanticism," which fled the real world of class conflict.[19] Sletov's story "Mastery" (Masterstvo)—an updated version of the Mozart-Salieri theme—was attacked for its celebration of intuition over craftsmanship and its "priestly aristocratic" view of the artist.[20] Ivan Kataev's story "Milk" (Moloko) was singled out as an illustration of the Perevalist "new humanism," which merely recast the pernicious notion that universal truths were more important than class-conditioned ones.[21]

The climax of the campaign against the Pereval came when the Communist Academy drew up a lengthy specification of grievances, which ended with an appeal to individual Pereval members to defect.[22] Actually, a slow attrition had been going on within the group since 1928, and

---

the Litfront, that short-lived (1930) coalition of Pereverzevites and members of the leftist opposition within RAPP, cf.: M. Bochacher, "Gal'vanizirovannaya voronshchina," *Pechat' i revolyutsiya*, No. 3 (1930), pp. 12-22; E. Blyum, "Burzhuazno-liberal'naya kritika za robotoi," *ibid.*, No. 5-6 (1930), pp. 18-29; M. Gel'fand, "Literaturnye zametki," *Pravda*, May 19, 1929, p. 5. For a compact discussion of Litfrontism, cf. Ermolaev, *ibid.*, pp. 102-04.

[19] The first quotation is from M. Grebeshchnikov, "Nepogrebyonnye mertvetsy (O 'Perevale' i pereval'tsakh)," *Komsomol'skaya pravda* (March 8, 1930), p. 3; the second from "Protiv reaktsionnoi shkoly Voronskogo . . . ," p. 106; the third from M. Bochacher, "Gal'vanizirovannaya voronshchina," p. 22. The stories referred to are P. Pavlenko's "Shematony," M. Prishvin's "Medvedi," and N. Zarudin's "Drevnost'."

[20] "Protiv reaktsionnoi shkoly Voronskogo . . . ," p. 106. In Sletov's story, Luigi, a master violinist, is blinded by Martino, a talentless pupil who wishes to learn rules for creating works of art. Sletov was accused of laboring his point by making his hero a revolutionary.

[21] M. Serebryanskii, "Epokha i eyo 'rovesniki,'" p. 23.

[22] "Protiv reaktsionnoi shkoly Voronskogo . . . ," p. 107.

only a hard core of ten or so now remained. Voronskii is said to have urged them to disavow him publicly in order to save themselves.[23] But they refused. And they continued to publish literature and criticism, and carry on vigorous counter-attacks against their critics up until the Central Committee's decree of 1932, which abolished all proletarian literature groups and, in effect, all others too. A few of the Perevalists, however, continued to meet privately until the final reckoning, which came during the trials of 1936-1938. Then the issue of "Voronskiism" once more swam to the surface, and many of his erstwhile disciples (as well as their former enemies) were arrested.[24]

WHAT HAD become of Voronskii in the meantime? The details of his life after his purge are still fragmentary. During most of 1928, the year he was expelled from the Party, he apparently lived in exile from Moscow. By November, however, he had returned to the capital and had begun to take a limited part in literary life again. We know that in November or December he participated in a discussion of Dmitrii Gorbov's highly controversial essay on art, *In Search of Galatea* (*V poiskakh Galatei*), at a joint session of the Moscow Association of Proletarian Writers (MAPP) and the Pereval group.[25] One of his major works, *The Art of Seeing the World*, also appeared that year; and the second volume of *Waters of Life and Death* came out the following year. Coincident with a massive purge in the ranks of Party and government that began in March 1929, he again dropped out of sight. But we know that in the summer of that year he was in or near Lipetsk. Isaak Babel' talked with him then, and reported his impressions in a letter:

[23] Gleb Glinka, *Pereval: The Withering of Literary Spontaneity in the USSR*, Research Program on the USSR, Mimeograph Series, No. 40 (New York, 1953), p. 67.

[24] Cf. *ibid.*, pp. 24-27.

[25] "Khronika," *Pechat' i revolyutsiya*, No. 1 (1929), p. 188.

A.[leksei] K.[onstantinovich] has changed a lot. He
has shrunk, grown quite wrinkled and, in general, is a
very sick man. It looks as if he is seriously ill, although
the doctors cannot agree on what it is. Some say that it is
a kidney inflammation, others that it is appendicitis. My
impression is that a serious disease is taking its toll inside him.

Babel' suggests a spiritual crisis (and no wonder!) yet
writes in terms of physical illness, perhaps with his eye on
the censor, for this was a letter sent abroad. In any case, he
found Voronskii the same in one essential way: "His conversation is, of course, unchanged. He is still as much in
love with literature as before, still ardent and naïve."[26]

This resiliency served him well. In 1930, he was brought
back to Moscow as the senior editor of Russian classical
literature in the State Publishing House. Although he had
no say in matters pertaining to contemporary writing, "by
dint of my Voronskiism," as he wryly observed in a letter
to Gor'kii, he apparently was given a free hand within his
own province.[27] It was a large and important province, too;
and Voronskii set about bringing it to order with his characteristic zeal. One of his major projects was an anthology
of "progressive" writing from the 1860's, about which he
corresponded at some length with Gor'kii. In 1930 or 1931,
he renounced his "Trotskiism" and was readmitted to the
Party.[28] But his final letter to Gor'kii, in April 1931—and the
last letter by him to anyone of which we have any record—

[26] Letter from Lipetsk, August 31, 1929, quoted in *Isaac Babel:
The Lonely Years 1925-1939*, ed. Nathalie Babel (New York, 1964),
p. 128.

[27] Letter to Gor'kii, January 25, 1931, *M. Gor'kii i sovetskaya
pechat'. Arkhiv A. M. Gor'kogo*, x, Book 2 (Moscow, 1965), 78.
Hereafter abbreviated as *Arkhiv*.

[28] The date given by I. Smirnov is 1930 ("Pis'mo A. K. Voronskogo
V. I. Leninu," *Novyi mir*, No. 12 [1964], p. 219); 1931 is given in
an editorial note in *Gor'kii i sovetskie pisateli. Literaturnoe nasledstvo*,
lxx (Moscow, 1963), 94.

hinted at impending trouble: "The conditions for work, to
tell the truth, are not very easy, partly on account of continual reductions in the supply of paper, partly on account
of an overwhelming mass of worrisome trifles, which a man
can't get away from."[29]
From that time until his arrest in 1937, his career is
shrouded in darkness. Yet whatever else may have happened, he did go on writing, and was free to publish. *Literary Portraits* (*Literaturnye portrety*), which appeared in
1929, was his last contribution to criticism, and consisted
of articles that had been written much earlier. Now, encouraged no doubt by Gor'kii's flattering comments about
Waters of Life and Death, he turned to fiction and biography. An autobiographical novel (*The Seminary [Bursa]*),
various short stories and tales, and *Zhelyabov*, a biography
of the revolutionary, all appeared in 1933 and 1934.[30] He
also completed a book on Gogol' for the "Life of Illustrious
People" series, which was printed but never distributed:
it was confiscated at the time of his final arrest and all but a
few copies were destroyed. One chapter has recently been
published in abridged form in the journal *New World*.[31]
Still in the archives is an unpublished manuscript entitled
"Meetings and Conversations with Maksim Gor'kii"
(*Vstrechi i besedy s Maksimom Gor'kim*).[32]

RVS WENT on until 1942. But in a real sense its life did not
outlast Voronskii's departure fifteen years previously.
Fyodor Raskol'nikov was the first of several men who took

[29] Letter to Gor'kii, April 2, 1931, *Arkhiv*, pp. 78-79.
[30] The tales and stories are collected in his *Rasskazy i povesti*
(Moscow, 1933). Three tales are published in Nos. 9 and 10 of
Novyi mir for 1934.
[31] "Iz knigi 'Gogol' " (K 80-letiyu so dnya rozhdeniya kritika),"
Novyi mir, No. 8 (1964), pp. 228-37. Cf. also the introductory remarks ("Predislovie") by Yu. Mann, pp. 228-30.
[32] Cf. *Arkhiv*, p. 371, for an editorial note that mentions this manuscript and quotes from it.

on the job of chief editor after 1927. He promised to correct the journal's "errors" and make it more "serious"[33]—which presumably meant flushing out all traces of Voronskii's influence and pumping in plasma from the RAPP theories of literature and from the writings of those "proletarians" whom *RVS* had been neglecting. Inasmuch as Raskol'nikov had long been active in the proletarian literature movement and was then sitting on the editorial board of *On Literary Guard*, there was every reason to suppose that he would succeed in accomplishing what he had pledged.

But murmurs of discontent soon filled the air. People began to complain that something was very much wrong with the "new" *RVS*. What sort of journal was it, after all, that would print works by Sergeev-Tsenskii, Aleksei Tolstoi, and Boris Pil'nyak, yet allow V. Friche, one of its co-editors, to rise in the Communist Academy and attack these very works as reactionary?[34] *RVS* became a prime target for those Octobrists who had broken with Averbakh and the VAPP in 1925 over the question of how to interpret the Central Committee's Resolution on literature, and who now continued to oppose the RAPP. For them, any suggestion of "compromise" with the fellow travelers meant treason. Their scrutiny of the journal's pages revealed that the literature section had failed to attract any significant number of proletarian writers, and still depended mainly on fellow travelers—"right-wing" ones at that—who filled it with pessimism, nostalgia, and hostility toward Soviet life. The appointment of Dmitrii Tal'nikov as chief critic in 1929 proved, as far as they were concerned, that *RVS* had become a vehicle of "right-opportunistic" propaganda; for Tal'nikov had argued that the campaign to involve the artist in socialist construction must move cautiously, lest it

[33] "Po literaturnym vecheram i konferentsiyam," *Na literaturnom postu*, No. 1 (1928), p. 94.
[34] N. N., review of *RVS*, No. 12 (1928), *Na literaturnom postu*, No. 1 (1929), p. 67.

frighten him off and drive him even further into an isolated world of art.[35] The cry for reform went up. And with the June issue of 1930, the Litfrontists took over the journal, with I. Bespalov as editor. They had little time to show what results their harsh regime might bring, for a year later, *RVS* became an organ of the Federation of Soviet Writers (FOSP) and added to its editorial board three prominent authors—Aleksandr Fadeev, the chief editor (a proletarian), and Vsevolod Ivanov and Leonid Leonov (both fellow travelers). Finally in 1932 it became an official publication of the Union of Soviet Writers.

The critics kept a close watch on *RVS* between 1928 and 1932 to see what all this shuffling would bring. They found, instead of the improvements that successive editors prom-

[35] "Literaturnye zametki," *KN*, No. 2 (1929), esp. pp. 189-95. This article was attacked by M. Gel'fand, "Zhurnal'noe obozrenie," *Pechat' i revolyutsiya*, No. 4 (1929), pp. 80-96. Cf. also G. Lominadze, "'Krasnaya nov'' v 1928 godu," *Molodaya gvardiya*, No. 10 (1928), pp. 215-23.

The leftist opposition within RAPP had long been insisting that the RAPP leaders were in the grip of "Voronskiism" (see the statements by S. Rodov and others in "Pis'ma v redaktsiyu," *Pechat' i revolyutsiya*, No. 3 [1928], pp. 196-222). All such distinctions were discarded when the Party came to assert complete control in literary matters. Voronskii, the Perevalists, the RAPP leaders, the Litfrontists, and "right" deviationists were all lumped together with breathtaking facility. For example, P. Yudin, one of the philosophers of the new "Leninist" (i.e., Stalinist) line, wrote in 1932:

> in the field of literary scholarship . . . there existed, besides the strong and long-term influence of Voronskiism and Pereverzevism —a combination essentially of mechanistic and idealistic views— the direct influence of the Deborinist [read: "idealistic"] methodology, which was most clearly represented by Bespalov, Zonin [both Litfrontists] and a number of other direct disciples of Deborin. Deborinism also strongly told on the works of Averbakh, Libedinskii, Ermilov and others [members of the RAPP leadership].

("Za dal'neishee razvyornutoe nastuplenie na teoreticheskom fronte," *Za marksistsko-leninskoe uchenie o pechati* [Moscow, 1932], p. 6.) For a good bibliography of the enormous polemical literature of the late 1920's, cf. *Literaturnye diskussii* (*Bibliograficheskii vypusk No. 1*) (Moscow, 1931).

ised, a relentless decline in quality. Literary criticism seemed trivial and timid, fiction "boring" and riddled with "hack work." The nonliterary departments had all but vanished. No one seemed willing to take stands or define issues. The journal lacked visible direction, goal, and personality. A. Lezhnev summed it up with the dry observation that "*Red Virgin Soil* is being presented to us as some grandiose palace of culture, built by Marxist architects," whereas in reality it was nothing but a "merchant's private house, decorated with all the tastelessness and lack of harmony we expect from that sort of building, where only on rare occasions do we find a really valuable piece which has gotten there by some happy coincidence of circumstances or because the owner happens to have a friend who knows something about art."[36]

These were the same points which critics were making about *Young Guard*, *New World*, *October*, and *The Star*. Generally speaking, the decline in *RVS* could not really be attributed to incompetence or malice on anyone's part, least of all Raskol'nikov's. Rather, it was a symptom of the sickness that afflicted all thick journals at the time. That sickness began somewhat later in *RVS* than elsewhere; but the symptoms had shown themselves early in 1927, even while Voronskii was still editor. The scope and quality of literary criticism fell off sharply; the silhouettes and surveys of contemporary literature ceased, as did discussions of literary theory; the poetry section gradually filled up with the tuneless mouthings of hacks; and fiction, while it could boast of Leonov and Olesha, could not rival the richness of the previous year. Raskol'nikov took over a patient that was

[36] " 'Krasnaya nov' " za 1928 god," *Pechat' i revolyutsiya*, No. 1 (1929), p. 119. Cf. also a letter that the head of the State Publishing House, A. V. Khalatov, wrote to Gor'kii in 1932 complaining that "the new profile of *RVS* is very weak and we are still very far from making this journal the leading one" (January 15, 1932, *Arkhiv*, Book 1 [Moscow, 1964], p. 258).

already dangerously ill. The wrangle between the RAPP and the Litfrontists for possession of the journal in 1930 only aggravated the illness; but even the restoration of something resembling decency and order, in the new editorial board of 1931, made no appreciable difference. *RVS* had lived its day.

Most of the old contributors left en masse shortly after Voronskii. Many gathered around *New World*. But this journal was only a pale shadow of what *RVS* had been. A good many people began to remember Voronskii, now disgraced and exiled, with nostalgia. Even some of his bitterest enemies admitted that *RVS* under his direction had at least been lively. One of the finest tributes to his work came from Fyodor Panfyorov, a staunch supporter of the RAPP, who wrote in 1928:

> Voronskii, when he was editor of *Red Virgin Soil*, knew how to catch artistic value. True, to make up for that, he would stumble over ideology. . . . But Voronskii's conversations with an author, his sensitive attitude toward a writer, were of immense benefit to the latter: these conversations compelled the writer to work on himself.[37]

· I I ·

The real work of *RVS* was accomplished by 1928. Nobody tried seriously to undo it, despite Voronskii's disgrace; it was too pervasive and too useful. The journal offered not only a consistent body of theory, but two other features which illustrated the theory, fed it, and gave it an authority that its competitors lacked: a vigorous criticism, and an impressive corpus of belles lettres. Left to themselves, the writers for *RVS*—most of them fellow travelers— might have had far less impact on the literature of the time, for they could have been hounded into silence, even dur-

[37] "Pisateli o 'tolstykh zhurnalakh,'" *Na literaturnom postu*, No. 24 (1928), p. 60.

ing the twenties, by the kind of tactics the Octobrists employed, or pushed into small organizations with strong public stands that could have turned on them later—as the Perevalists discovered—when all literary groups came to be regarded as political menaces. Within *RVS*, however, they partook, by association, of the respectability of Marxism; their assemblage created an impression which they could not have made if they had been scattered throughout a number of journals; and some of the best critics of the time were on hand to interpret their work to an eager public.

All three of the journal's major activities—theory, criticism, and belles lettres—have come down, in varying degrees, into Soviet literature. Most of the writers discovered and championed by *RVS* are now solidly lodged in literary history. Large areas of the work in theory and criticism have been absorbed too. Even in the twenties, the very men who cut *RVS* down with one hand often quietly picked it up with the other. The esthetic of RAPP, for instance, owed a heavy debt to Voronskii and *RVS* for such ideas as art as the cognition of life, the "living man" (that is, a man both rational and intuitive) as the proper hero, "immediate impressions" as art's chief product, a study of the classics as the basis of sound writing, and so on.[38]

Socialist realism has been more eclectic. Certainly it attaches great importance to the shaping role of classes on art; sees social activism as the final test of "infection"; makes art the servant more of practical political goals than of ideals; and regards art's purpose as overcoming physical reality, not reconciling man to a supra-reality through immediate impressions.[39] In these respects, it is hostile to the *RVS* es-

---

[38] For a good appraisal of RAPP's indebtedness to Voronskii, cf. Edward J. Brown, *The Proletarian Episode in Russian Literature* (New York, 1953), pp. 58-86.

[39] Cf., however, Georg Lukács, *The Meaning of Contemporary Realism* (London, 1963), esp. pp. 13-16, which suggests the struggle

thetic. At the same time, it echoes *RVS* in several crucial ways: it places the novel at the apex of literary achievement; reads literature in terms of strong central heroes; makes unobtrusiveness the mark of a superior style; considers grandeur and sublimity the reactions apposite to art; effaces the personality of the individual creator; and despecifies genres and language in the same ways as *RVS*. From socialist realism wafts a familiar aroma of neo-classicism too: in the canons of acceptable writers; the doctrine of imitation; the hierarchy of genres (though with prose supreme); the emphasis on the cognitive, not the affective, benefits of art; the leading role assigned to literary criticism; the lack of interest in nature and in lyricism; the tendency to emphasize universals at the expense of particulars, with a corresponding warp toward abstraction; the habit of attaching fixed meanings to words; the mind-body dualism as the basis of literary conflict (expressed in the well-known opposition of duty and passion in the socialist realist novel); and so on. This neo-classical drift has quickened under socialist realism, moved partly by its own momentum, but also by circumstances: one notes that the civic virtues of classicism are those preached by the Soviet state—obedience, order, right-mindedness, materialism—but without the tempering force of justice.

In effect, socialist realism has attempted to blend two very different views of the nature of art—the one, an "activist" view, represented by *LEF* and October; the other, a "contemplative" view, best represented by *RVS*. Frequently the result has been a paralyzing incompatibility. For example, the socialist realist esthetic, like *RVS*, makes the nineteenth-century novel the highest form of literary

for peace as a universal that transcends class (and nation). It will be interesting to see whether this idea, so firmly rooted now in the political life of Communism, and so reminiscent of Voronskii's view of a progressive ideal as basic to art, will make any inroads into the Soviet Marxist esthetic.

utterance, but, unlike *RVS*, it refuses to recognize that the novel thrives on complexity and ambiguity, and instead forcibly fits it to an "activist" concept of man and society which seems more appropriate to the romance, the allegory, the parable, or even the ode.[40] It is significant, however, that such a synthesis is considered desirable and possible: the past's relevance to the present, in all, or nearly all, its parts, is taken for granted. The socialist realist's attitudes toward that past, and even the techniques he employs to deal with it, are familiar to readers of *RVS*. The term "critical realism," which has been in vogue since the 1930's, merely renames the concept of objective value as it was developed in *RVS*; under its aegis, Voronskii's policy of progressively appropriating the past has continued, until now, practically any writer who is safely dead qualifies for consideration as a "classic." A recent Soviet anthology of twentieth-century literature shows that even the so-called "decadents" have achieved a certain eminence.[41] Although the theorists of socialist realism have displayed a tougher self-assurance in bending the past to suit their needs, the sentimental adulation of that past, so characteristic of *RVS*, lives on. And, having appropriated the past, the socialist realists use it in much the same way as did *RVS*: as a model for the contemporary writer, and sometimes as a club to beat him with.

But this attitude toward the past would not be possible without the assumption that a national culture exists, forms a unity, and continues in uninterrupted movement from the earliest times to the present. This idea is rather recent, at least in literature. Not until the middle of the nineteenth century could Russian men of letters contemplate the past without a sense of uneasiness: Belinskii's assertion in 1834

[40] The same point has been persuasively made by Abram Tertz, *On Socialist Realism* (New York, 1960).

[41] *Russkaya literatura XX veka (Dorevolyutsionnyi period). Khrestomatiya*, ed. M. A. Trifonov (Moscow, 1962).

that "we have no literature,"[42] expressed his contempt for what he regarded as a poverty-stricken and foreign-dominated ancestry; his chief concern, from that point on, was to stimulate the creation of a truly national Russian literature. But perhaps not until Dostoevskii's famous oration on Pushkin, and the Symbolists' discovery that Gogol' was a very "modern" writer, did the past become a vital and viable concept. *RVS* was largely responsible for bringing this concept down into the 1920's, whence it has passed into Soviet culture. But at the time, it was considered a radical piece of effrontery: most Marxists then talked of internationalism, and looked on expressions of nationalist sentiment as manifestations of bourgeois chauvinism.

Yet by now, the idea is a commonplace. And just as it operated in the twenties in *RVS*, to allow the absorption of much of the pre-Revolutionary heritage, so now it operates to allow Soviet writers to absorb that past most relevant and meaningful for them: the twenties. The cloud Stalinism threw over that decade has begun to lift. Within the past ten years, many writers have been "rehabilitated" in name, and many long-forgotten works have been republished. More recently, serious study and reappraisal of the twenties has gotten under way. Within the first five months of 1966, for example, one journal, *Problems of Literature* (*Voprosy literatury*), ran a long article on the literary polemic of 1922-1925, and another on the Formalists.[43] They are typical of the kind of reevaluations that are now being made—disappointing in that they offer little new information to the Western reader; encouraging in that they are resurrecting material that is completely unfamiliar to

---

[42] "Literaturnye mechtaniya," *Polnoe sobranie sochinenii*, i (Moscow, 1953), 22. Original italics omitted.

[43] L. Kishchinskaya, "Literaturnaya diskussiya 1922-1925 godov (K istorii stanovleniya ideino-esteticheskikh printsipov sovetskoi literaturnoi kritiki)," *Voprosy literatury*, No. 4 (1966), pp. 35-55; S. Mashinskii, "Puti i pereput'ya," *ibid.*, No. 5 (1966), pp. 70-90.

most Soviet readers and treating it as something still vital, fresh, and relevant to the problems which literature faces today. Typically, the first of these articles insists that the principals in the dispute were "sincere," despite their "errors," and emphasizes the experimental nature of much of their work—which is both a justification and, in Soviet conditions today, an effective piece of advertising.

Voronskii himself is undergoing a radical "rehabilitation." It has been possible to mention his name in print at least since 1954. He figured in the first fumbling reappraisals of the twenties that began shortly thereafter. Finally, in 1963 the publishing house "Soviet Writer" brought out a sizable anthology of his critical writings in a printing of 8,500, which is very respectable for a book of this kind. Perhaps the book's most interesting feature is the extensive critical introduction by A. G. Dement'ev. He recalls the time when "it was impossible to say one good word about Voronskii," and observes with disapproval that "notions about Voronskii as the evil genius of Soviet literature have implanted themselves to the same degree that his books have been completely forgotten." His avowed purpose is to restore Voronskii as a figure of first-rank importance in Russian literature. To be sure, it is only a partial restoration: he writes Voronskii off as a theorist, with a recital of familiar sins, running from neglect of the proletarian writers to exaggeration of the irrational element in man. But, with the embarrassing features disposed of, Dement'ev can insist all the more on Voronskii's achievement as a critic. And a sizable achievement it is too. The reader is shown a man endowed with

> a passionate love for literature, the ability to make a profound and comprehensive analysis of a work of art, to reveal a writer's view of life in organic oneness with his individual style . . . the capacity for detecting an artistic gift in a beginning writer, of bringing to public attention,

supporting and defending the talented Soviet "fellow traveler" writer, and the ability to beat an ideological enemy according to all the rules of polemic.

As an illustration of these merits, Dement'ev offers nineteen of Voronskii's articles, with the assurance that they are still fresh and insightful.[44] This article seems to have established a pattern. Subsequent assessments of Voronskii—including Gabriela Porębina's—emphasize the same strengths and the same weaknesses. If his work as a theorist remains unknown to the Soviet reader, his stature as a critic has continued to grow. For example, the publication in 1963 of Volume 70 of *Literary Heritage*, though devoted to Gor'kii's correspondence with young writers, contains numerous references to Voronskii and leaves no doubt that he was a central figure in the literary life of the twenties. His friendship with Gor'kii, which Dement'ev points up to support his case, was eloquently documented by the publication of their correspondence in 1965. More and more students of the twenties are quoting remarks from his articles as a matter of course.[45] There seems to be increasingly less hesitation about acknowledging his influence on even the saintliest figures in the Soviet literary shrine. In an article in Volume 74 of *Literary Heritage*, for example, L. K. Kuvanova analyzes the notes made by Dmitrii Furmanov for a discussion of Babel's *Red Cavalry* in 1924 and concludes: "If we compare these notes of Furmanov's with Voronskii's article on Babel', then we can see that most of Furmanov's main points coincide with the basic propositions of Voron-

[44] A. Voronskii. *Literaturno-kriticheskie stat'i*, compiled by G. A. Voronskaya and A. G. Dement'ev, ed. by L. Shubin (Moscow, 1963). Dement'ev's introduction, entitled "A. Voronskii—kritik," is on pp. 3-46. The first two quotes are on p. 34, the third one on p. 24.

[45] Cf., e.g., *Istoriya russkogo sovetskogo romana*, I (Moscow-Leningrad, 1965), where some of his opinions on Vsevolod Ivanov, Zamyatin, and Belyi are cited.

skii's article."[46] His book on Gogol' has been proclaimed a
landmark in Russian criticism: the first truly Marxist approach to the writer, accounting at once for sociology and
form, and in this respect providing a corrective to the earlier studies by Belyi (too formalistic) and Pereverzev (vul-
garly sociological).[47] And finally, the one thing without
which the efficacy of "rehabilitation" remains uncertain has
been supplied—an association with Lenin. Dement'ev's introduction mentions the close interest with which Lenin
followed the formation and the fortunes of RVS; but it was
left to an article in *New World*, at the end of 1964, to furnish a quotable saying and documents to back it up. Here
the existence of several letters from Voronskii to Lenin is
mentioned by way of demonstrating the "direct contacts"
between the two men; one of them is published in full;
and we are assured that "Lenin had a high opinion of Voronskii and considered him an old and reliable comrade."[48]

There is no way of predicting how far this sort of thing
may go. But it seems safe to say that until an honest attempt is made in Soviet Russia to grapple with the kind of
questions Voronskii raised, and go along with them where-
ever they may lead, Marxist theory and criticism can make
no substantial progress there. And until the kind of literature championed—and, to a large extent created—by RVS
is not only appreciated but studied in its own country, a
major part of the heritage that writers and critics today
are anxious to recover must remain obscure to them. Vo-

---

[46] "Furmanov i Babel'," *Iz tvorcheskogo naslediya sovetskikh
pisatelei. Literaturnoe nasledstvo*, LXXIV (Moscow, 1965), 501. The
point had already been made by Dement'ev ("A. Voronskii—kritik,"
ibid., p. 35), but Kuvanova follows it out in detail. She concludes
that there are some differences, and that Furmanov used only those
parts of Voronskii's article with which he agreed. The article in
question is "Literaturnye siluety," *KN*, No. 5 (1924).

[47] Yu. Mann, "Predislovie," *Novyi mir*, No. 8 (1964), pp. 228-30.

[48] I. Smirnov, "Pis'mo A. K. Voronskogo V. I. Leninu," *Novyi mir*,
No. 12 (1964), first quote on p. 213, second on p. 215.

ronskii himself often did not understand the literature he liked, nor was he always prepared to follow out (if he perceived) the consequences of his own ideas. Whether Soviet Marxism today can do so, without ceasing to be Marxist, is one of the questions it must, for the sake of its very vitality, answer. In the quest for a new esthetic—and so long as Marxism prevails, one must talk about a single esthetic—the ideas and ideals set in motion by *RVS* in the twenties may continue to live and to operate in the liberating spirit intended by their makers.

Selected Bibliography

THE WORKS cited below are meant to provide a general guide to readers, not an exhaustive listing of the sources consulted or quoted in this study. Two large categories have been omitted altogether, for lack of space: articles in *RVS* itself and belles lettres. Both are referred to in relevant parts of the text.

I. MEMOIRS AND LETTERS

Chukovskii, K. *Iz vospominanii.* Moscow, 1959.

Del'vig, A. I. *Moi vospominaniya.* Vols. 1-4. Moscow, 1912-1913.

Evgen'ev-Maksimov, V. and G. F. Tizengauzen (eds.). *Shestidesyatye gody. M. Antonovich, Vospominaniya. G. Z. Eliseev, Vospominaniya.* Moscow-Leningrad, 1933.

Fedin, K. *Gor'kii sredi nas.* 2 vols. Moscow, 1943-1944.

―――. *Pisatel', iskusstvo, vremya.* Moscow, 1957.

Furmanov, D. *Iz dnevnika pisatelya.* Moscow, 1934.

Ivanov, G. *Peterburgskie zimy.* New York, 1952.

Ivanov, Vsev. *Povesti, rasskazy, vospominaniya.* Moscow, 1952.

Karavaeva, A. *Po dorogam zhizni. Dnevniki, ocherki, vospominaniya.* Moscow, 1957.

Khodasevich, V. *Literaturnye stat'i i vospominaniya.* New York, 1954.

Litovskii, O. *Tak i bylo. Ocherki. Vospominaniya. Vstrechi.* Moscow, 1958.

Nikulin, L. *Lyudi i stranstviya. Vospominaniya i vstrechi.* Moscow, 1962.

Otsup, N. *Sovremenniki.* Paris, 1961.

Pod' 'yachev, S. *Moya zhizn'.* Moscow, 1934.

Rozhdestvenskii, Vs. *Stranitsy zhizni. Iz literaturnykh vospominanii.* Moscow-Leningrad, 1962.

Seifullina, L. *O literature.* Moscow, 1958.

Shaginyan, M. *Dnevniki. 1917-1931.* Leningrad, 1932.

Shklovskii, V. B. *Sentimental'noe puteshestvie, vospominaniya 1917-1922.* Moscow-Berlin, 1923.

Trotsky, Leon. *My Life.* New York, 1930.

Veresaev, V. V. *Vospominaniya.* 2d ed. Moscow, 1938.

Voronskii, A. *Waters of Life and Death.* Trans. by L. Zarine. London, 1936.

————. *Za zhivoi i myortvoi vodoi.* Book 1: Moscow, 1927. Book 2: Moscow, 1929.

Zaitsev, B. *Moskva.* Munich, 1960.

Zamyatin, E. *Litsa.* New York, 1951.

Zelinskii, K. *Na rubezhe dvukh epokh.* Moscow, 1959.

II. STUDIES OF JOURNALS, PROBLEMS OF THE PRESS

Bas, I. *Bol'shevistskaya pechat' v gody imperialisticheskoi voiny.* Moscow, 1939.

Buzlyakov, N. I. *Voprosy planirovaniya pechati v SSSR.* Moscow, 1957.

Clive, John L. *Scotch Reviewers: the Edinburgh Review, 1802-1815.* Cambridge, Mass., 1957.

Dement'ev, A. G. *Ocherki po istorii russkoi zhurnalistiki 1840-1850 gg.* Moscow, 1951.

————. (ed.). *Ocherki istorii russkoi sovetskoi zhurnalistiki, 1917-1932.* Moscow, 1966.

Evgen'ev-Maksimov, V. E. *Nekrasov i ego sovremenniki.* Moscow, 1930.

————. *Ocherki po istorii sotsialisticheskoi zhurnalistiki v Rossii XIX veka.* Moscow, 1927.

————. *"Sovremennik" pri Chernyshevskom i Dobrolyubove.* Leningrad, 1936.

Friedberg, Maurice. *Russian Classics in Soviet Jackets.* New York, 1962.

Hoffman, Frederick J., Charles Ellen, Carolyn F. Ulrich. *The Little Magazine: A History and a Bibliography.* Princeton, 1946.

Kuleshov, V. I. *"Otechestvennye zapiski" i literatura 40-kh godov XIX veka.* Moscow, 1959.

Kuz'michev, V. *Pechatnaya agitatsiya i propaganda*. Moscow, 1930.

Kuznetsov, F. *Zhurnal "Russkoe slovo."* Moscow, 1965.

Liwoff, G. *Michel Katkoff et son époque*. Paris, 1897.

Morino, Lina. *La Nouvelle Revue Française dans l'histoire des lettres*. 6th ed. Paris, 1939.

Mott, Frank L. *A History of American Magazines*. 4 vols. Cambridge, Mass., 1938-1957.

III. HISTORY, THEORY, CRITICISM

Aaron, Daniel. *Writers on the Left*. New York, 1965.

Abramovich, G. L., N. K. Gei, V. V. Ermilov, M. S. Kurginyan (eds.). *Teoriya literatury. Osnovnye problemy v istoricheskom osveshchenii. Obraz, metod, kharakter*. Moscow, 1962.

Abrams, M. H. *The Mirror and the Lamp: Romantic Theory and the Critical Tradition*. New York, 1958.

Albérès, R. M. *L'Aventure intellectuelle du XXᵉ siècle; panorama des littératures européenes, 1900-1959*. Paris, 1959.

Aronson, M. and S. Reiser. *Literaturnye kruzhki i salony*. Leningrad, 1929.

Arvatov, B. *Iskusstvo i klassy*. Moscow-Petrograd, 1923.

Averbakh, L. *Za proletarskuyu literaturu*. Leningrad, 1926.

Balukhatyi, S. *Teoriya literatury. Annotirovannaya bibliografiya. I. Obshchie voprosy*. Leningrad, 1929.

Bauer, Raymond. *The New Man in Soviet Psychology*. Cambridge, Mass., 1952.

Belinskii, V. G. *Polnoe sobranie sochinenii*. 13 vols. Moscow, 1953-1959.

Belinsky, V. *Selected Philosophical Works*. Moscow, 1956.

Bergson, Henri. *L'Évolution créatrice*. 52d ed. Paris, 1940.

Blok, Aleksandr. *The Spirit of Music*. Trans. by I. Freiman. London, 1946.

Bogdanov, A. *O proletarskoi kul'ture*. Moscow-Leningrad, 1924.

Brang, Peter. *Studien zur Theorie und Praxis der russischen Erzählung 1770-1811.* Wiesbaden, 1960.

Brodskii, N. L. (ed.). *Literaturnye salony i kruzhki. Pervaya polovina XIX veka.* Moscow-Leningrad, 1930.

Brown, Edward J. *The Proletarian Episode in Russian Literature.* New York, 1953.

———. *Russian Literature Since the Revolution.* New York, 1963.

Carr, E. H. *The Interregnum, 1923-1924 (A History of Soviet Russia).* Vol. iv. London, 1954.

Caudwell, C. *Illusion and Reality: A Study of the Sources of Poetry.* London, 1955.

Chernyshevskii, N. G. *Polnoe sobranie sochinenii.* 16 vols. Moscow, 1939-1953.

Chernyshevsky, N.G. *Selected Philosophical Essays.* Moscow, 1953.

Chukovskii, K. *Futuristy. Igor' Severyanin, Kruchonykh, Vl. Khlebnikov, Vas. Kamenskii, Vl. Mayakovskii.* Petrograd, 1922.

Comte, August. *Cours de philosophie positive.* 6 vols. Paris, 1835-1852.

Daniels, R. V. *The Conscience of the Revolution: Communist Opposition in Soviet Russia.* Cambridge, Mass., 1960.

Deutscher, I. *The Prophet Unarmed: Trotsky, 1921-1929,* 3 vols. London, 1959.

Dobrolyubov, N. A. *Sobranie sochinenii.* 9 vols. Moscow, 1961-1964.

———. *Selected Philosophical Essays.* Trans. by J. Fineberg. Moscow, 1948.

Druzhinin, A. V. *Sobranie sochinenii.* 8 vols. St. Petersburg, 1865-1867.

Eikhenbaum, B. "Literatura i pisatel'," *Zvezda,* No. 5, 1927, pp. 121-40.

Erlich, V. *Russian Formalism: History, Doctrine.* 's-Gravenhage, 1955.

Ermakov, I. D. *Ocherki po analizu tvorchestva N. V. Gogolya.* Moscow-Petrograd, n.d.

Ermolaev, Herman. *Soviet Literary Theories, 1917-1934: The Genesis of Socialist Realism.* Berkeley and Los Angeles, 1963.

Fischer, Ernst. *The Necessity of Art: A Marxist Approach.* Baltimore, 1963.

Fiziologiya Peterburga, sostavlennaya iz trudov russkikh literatorov. N. Nekrasov, ed. St. Petersburg, 1845.

Friche, V. F. *Problemy literaturovedeniya.* 2d ed. Moscow-Leningrad, 1931.

———. *Sotsiologiya iskusstva.* Moscow-Leningrad, 1926.

Glinka, G. *Na perevale.* New York, 1954.

———. *Pereval: The Withering of Literary Spontaneity in the USSR.* Research Program on the USSR. Mimeograph Series No. 40. New York, 1953.

Gorbachov, G. *Sovremennaya russkaya literatura.* 3d ed. Moscow-Leningrad, 1931.

Gorbov, D. *V poiskakh Galatei.* Moscow, 1928.

Gor'kii, M. *O literature. Stat'i i rechi, 1928-1936.* N. F. Bel'chikov, ed. 3d ed. Moscow, 1937.

Gor'kii, M., A. Serebrov, A. Chapygin (eds.). *Sbornik proletarskikh pisatelei.* Petrograd, 1918.

Gorky, M. *Culture and the People.* New York, 1939.

Gosplan literatury (Literaturnyi tsentr konstruktivistov—LTsK). Moscow, 1925.

Grits, T., V. Trenin, M. Nikitin. *Slovesnost' i kommertsiya (Knizhnaya lavka A. F. Smirdina).* V. B. Shklovskii and B. M. Eikhenbaum, eds. Moscow, 1929.

Holthusen, J. and D. Tschiževskij (eds.). *Versdichtung des russischen Symbolismus.* Heidelberger Slavische Texte, No. 5/6. Wiesbaden, 1959.

Howe, Irving. *Politics and the Novel.* New York, 1957.

Hyman, Stanley Edgar. *The Armed Vision.* rev. ed. New York, 1955.

Ingulov, S. "Kak zhivyot i rabotaet sovetskii pisatel'," *Pravda*, September 30, 1925, p. 3.

Intelligentsiya i revolyutsiya. Sbornik statei M. N. Pokrovskogo, N. L. Meshcheryakova, Vyach. Polonskogo i A. Voronskogo. Moscow, 1922.

Ivanov, Razumnik V. *Istoriya russkoi obshchestvennoi mysli.* 4th ed. St. Petersburg, 1914.

Ivanov, V. "O literaturnykh gruppirovkakh i techeniyakh 20-kh godov," *Znamya,* No. 5 (1958), pp. 190-209; No. 6, 1958, pp. 179-98.

K voprosu o politike RKP (b) v khudozhestvennoi literature. Moscow, 1924.

Kaverin, V. "Legenda o zhurnal'nom triumvirate," *Zvezda,* No. 1, 1929, pp. 160-92.

Knox, Israel. *The Aesthetic Theories of Kant, Hegel and Schopenhauer.* London, 1958.

Kogan, P. S. *Literatura velikogo desyatiletiya.* Moscow-Leningrad, 1927.

———. *Nashi literaturnye spory.* Moscow, 1927.

Lenin, V. I. *Ob intelligentsii.* Moscow, 1925.

Levidov, M. "Samoubiistvo literatury," *Zvezda,* No. 1, 1925, pp. 253-62.

Lewis, R.W.B. *The Picaresque Saint: Representative Figures in Contemporary Fiction.* Philadelphia and New York, 1961.

Lezhnev, A. *Razgovor v serdtsakh.* Moscow, 1930.

———. *Voprosy literatury i kritiki.* Moscow-Leningrad, n.d.

Lezhnev, A. and D. Gorbov. *Literatura revolyutsionnogo desyatiletiya.* Moscow, 1929.

Lidin, V. *Pisateli. Avtobiografii i portrety sovremennykh russkikh prozaikov.* Moscow, 1926.

Lifshits, M. *Lenin o kul'ture i iskusstve. Sbornik statei i otryvkov.* Moscow, 1938.

———. *The Philosophy of Art of Karl Marx.* Trans. by Ralph B. Winn. Angel Flores, ed. New York, 1938.

Literaturnye diskussii. Bibliograficheskii vypusk No. 1. Moscow, 1931.

Lossky, N. O. *History of Russian Philosophy.* New York, 1950.

Lukács, Georg. *Die Theorie des Romans. Ein geschichts-philosophischer Versuch über die Formen der grossen Epik.* 2d ed. Berlin-Spandau, 1963.

————. *The Meaning of Contemporary Realism.* London, 1963.

Lunacharskii, A. V. *Osnovy pozitivnoi estetiki.* Moscow, 1923.

————. *Stat'i o literature.* Moscow, 1957.

————. "Tezisy o zadachakh marksistskoi kritiki," *Novyi mir,* No. 6, 1928, pp. 188-96.

L'vov-Rogachevskii, V. *Noveishaya russkaya literatura.* 5th ed. Moscow, 1926.

Maritain, Jacques. *Art and Scholasticism and the Frontiers of Poetry.* New York, 1962.

Marks i Engel's ob iskusstve. A. V. Lunacharskii, ed. Compiled by F. P. Shiller and M. A. Lifshits. Moscow, 1933.

Marx, Karl and Friedrich Engels. *Literature and Art: Selections From Their Writings.* New York, 1947.

Mathewson, Rufus W., Jr. *The Positive Hero in Russian Literature.* New York, 1958.

Mehring, Franz. *Zur Literaturgeschichte von Hebbel bis Gorki, Gesammelte Schriften und Aufsätze, II.* Berlin, 1929.

Meyerhoff, Hans. *Time in Literature.* Berkeley and Los Angeles, 1960.

Mordovchenko, N. I. *Russkaya kritika pervoi chetverti XIX veka.* Moscow-Leningrad, 1959.

Oksionov, I. (ed.). *Sovremennaya russkaya kritika: 1918-1924.* Leningrad, 1925.

Ovsyaniko-Kulikovskii, D. N. *Istoriya russkoi intelligentsii. Itogi russkoi khudozhestvennoi literatury XIX veka.* 2 vols. Moscow, 1906.

454   BIBLIOGRAPHY

Pakentreiger, S. *Zakaz na vdokhnovenie*. Moscow, 1930.
Paul, Eden and Cedar. *Proletcult*. London, 1921.
Pereverzev, V. F. (ed.). *Literaturovedenie. Sbornik statei.* Moscow, 1928.
Phillips, William (ed.). *Art and Psychoanalysis.* Cleveland and New York, 1963.
Pisarev, D. I. *Sochineniya v chetyryokh tomakh.* Moscow, 1955-1956.
Pisateli-sibiryaki. Literaturno-kriticheskie ocherki. Novosibirsk, 1956.
Plekhanov, G. V. *Literatura i estetika.* 2 vols. Moscow, 1958.
———. *Unaddressed Letters: Art and Social Life.* Moscow, 1957.
Polonskii, V. *Ocherki literaturnogo dvizheniya revolyutsionnoi epokhi.* 2d ed. Moscow-Leningrad, 1930.
Porębina, Gabriela. *Aleksander Woronski. Poglądy estetyczne i krytycznoliterackie (1921-1928).* Wroclaw-Warsaw-Cracow, 1964.
Pospelov, G. *Teoriya literatury.* Moscow, 1940.
Poulet, Georges. *Studies in Human Time.* New York, 1959.
Pravdukhin, V. *Literaturnaya sovremennost', 1920-1924.* Moscow, n.d.
Problemy sotsialisticheskogo realizma. Moscow, 1961.
Proletariat i literatura. Sbornik statei. Leningrad, 1925.
Rodov, S. *V literaturnykh boyakh.* Moscow, 1926.
Rozanov, I. N. *Putevoditel' po sovremennoi russkoi literature.* Moscow, 1929.
Sarraute, Nathalie. *L'Ère du soupçon. Essais sur le roman.* Paris, 1956.
Sayanov, V. *Sovremennye literaturnye gruppirovki.* Leningrad, 1928.
Schücking, L. L. *Sociology of Literary Taste.* London, 1950.
Smena vekh. Sbornik statei. Prague, 1921.
Somerville, J. *Soviet Philosophy: A Study of Theory and Practice.* New York, 1946.

Spiritual Problems in Contemporary Literature. S. R. Hopper, ed. New York, 1957.

Stolyarov, A. *Dialekticheskii materializm i mekhanisty.* Leningrad, 1938.

Struve, Gleb. *Russkaya literatura v izgnanii.* New York, 1956.

Sud'by sovremennoi intelligentsii (Sbornik dokladov i rechei A. V. Lunacharskogo, P. N. Sakulina, N. I. Bukharina, Yu. V. Klyuchnikova). Moscow, 1925.

Taine, Hippolyte. *Philosophie de l'art.* 2 vols. 18th ed. Paris, 1921.

Tarsis, V. *Sovremennye russkie pisateli.* Leningrad, 1930.

Tertz, Abram. *On Socialist Realism.* New York, 1960.

Tolstoi, L. N. *Chto takoe iskusstvo?* in *Polnoe sobranie sochinenii.* xxx. Moscow, 1951.

———. *What is Art? and Essays on Art.* Trans. by Aylmer Maude. New York, 1962.

Trotskii, L. *Literatura i revolyutsiya.* 2d ed. Moscow, 1924.

Trotsky, Leon. *Literature and Revolution.* New York, 1957.

Tschiżewskij, D. (ed.). *Anfänge des russischen Futurismus.* Heidelberger Slavische Texte, No. 7. Wiesbaden, 1963.

Tynyanov, Yu. *Arkhaisty i novatory.* Leningrad, 1929.

Vitman, A. *Vosem' let russkoi khudozhestvennoi literatury (1917-1925).* Moscow, 1926.

Voprosy literatury i dramaturgii (Disput v Gosud. Akademicheskom Malom teatre v Moskve 26 maya 1924 pod predsedatel'stvom A. V. Lunacharskogo). Leningrad, 1924.

Voronskii, A. *Iskusstvo i zhizn'.* Moscow-Petrograd, 1924.

———. *Iskusstvo videt' mir.* Moscow, 1928.

———. *Literaturno-kriticheskie stat'i.* Compiled by G. A. Voronskaya and A. G. Dement'ev. L. A. Shubin, ed. Moscow, 1963.

———. *Literaturnye portrety.* 2 vols. Moscow, 1929.

———. *Literaturnye tipy.* Moscow, 1927.

———. *Literaturnye zapisi.* Moscow, 1926.

Voronskii, A. *Na styke*. Moscow, 1923.

———. *Ob iskusstve*. Moscow, 1925.

Voznesenskij, A. "Die Methodologie der russischen Literaturforschung in den Jahren 1910-1925," *Zeitschrift für slavische Philologie*, IV, 1927, 145-62; V, 1929, 175-99.

Watt, Ian. *The Rise of the Novel*. Berkeley and Los Angeles, 1959.

Wimsatt, W. K., Jr. and C. Brooks. *Literary Criticism: A Short History*. New York, 1957.

Wellek, R. *A History of Modern Criticism, 1750-1950*. 4 vols. New Haven, 1955-1965.

Zalkind, G. *G. P. Kamenev (1772-1803). Opyt imushchestvennoi kharakteristiki pervogo russkogo romantika*. Kazan', 1926.

Zamoshkin, N. *Literaturnye mezhi*. Moscow, 1930.

Zaworska, Helena. *O nową sztukę. Polskie programy artystyczne lat 1917-1922*. Warsaw, 1963.

Zenkovsky, V. V. *A History of Russian Philosophy*. 2 vols. New York, 1953.

Index

abstractness in art, 194, 195*n*, 229, 254, 260, 264, 354. *See also* concreteness; science
Acmeists, *RVS* on, 245
active vs. passive art, 255-56; Voronskii on, 79, 197-98, 202, 223-24, 226, 257; Futurists on, 151-52; *LEF* on, 190-91, 200; Aksel'rod on, 221-22; socialist realism on, 438-39
adventure tale, as genre, 98, 133, 137, 316
Aesop, 295
Agitation-Propaganda Department, *see under* Communist Party
Akhmatova, A., 131
Aksel'rod (Ortodoks), L., xi, 19, 187, 216, 220-22, 228-29, 252-53, 280-81, 284-85
Akul'shin, R., 397
album, literary, 58
Aldanov, M., 5, 246*n*, 250
Aleksandrovskii, V., 356, 368, 401
Alekseev, G., 317
allegory: Pil'nyak's use, 115, 120, 125, 128, 315; Belyi on, 120
almanac, literary, 56, 63, 376
Altauzen, D., 401
Al'tman, N., 151
Andreev, L., 95, 144, 266-67
anecdote, as genre, 97, 315
Anisimov, L., pseud. of A. Voronskii, 30*n*
Aranovich, D., 277, 278
architecture, 277, 278; in *LEF*, 154
Aronson, M., 63*n*
Arosev, A., 93, 232, 370; *Torment*, 10, 12, 318; "On the Earth Beneath the Sun," 318-19
art: place in new society, arguments about in 1920's,

72-73, 78-79, 199-200, 228-29; *RVS* makes synonymous with "literature," 193, 261; theme of, in literature of 1920's, 343-44; theories of, *see under* active vs. passive art; Aksel'rod; Belinskii; Bogdanov; Bukharin; change; character; class; cognition; Communist Party; concept; concreteness; contemporariness; continuity; creative process; culture; dialectic; dialectical; disinterestedness; Dobrolyubov; drama; emotion; form; formal-sociologism; Freud; Friche; Futurists; genre; general and particular; genesis; genius; Gor'kii; harmony; hero; history; idea; ideology; image; imagination; imitation; immediate impressions; infection; innovation; inspiration; intellect; intention; intuition; knowledge; language; *LEF*; Lelevich; Lezhnev; Lukács; lyricism; Marxism; mechanists; monumentalism; moral; novel; objective; Octobrists; organism; past; Pereval; Pereverzev; Plekhanov; proletarian culture; Proletkul't; RAPP; realism; reality; *RVS*; reflexology; science; sight; sincerity; socialist realism; sociography; specificity; Stanislavskii; style; subjective; Symbolism; theme; time; L. Tolstoi; truth; typicality; universality; Voronskii
artist: as hero in literature of 1920's, 94, 343-44; place in new society: *RVS* on, 72-79, 197-98, 219, 222-30, 386-87, 429*n*; *LEF* on, 153-55, 190;

195, 214, 221, 222, 224, 252, 276-77, 286, 294, 298, 305; *LEF* on, 222; socialist realism on, 438
Ingulov, S., 383, 385*n*
innovation in art, 300-01, 309
inspiration: Futurists, 151, 152; Lezhnev on, 205. *See also* intuition; creative process
instinct, *see* primitivism
intellect, role of in art, *RVS* on, 195-97, 206-07, 211. *See also* science; creative process
intelligentsia: in Revolution and Civil War, 3-5; Voronskii on, 73, 79-80; in literature of 1920's, 90, 316, 327, 328, 335-36, 338, 340-43; in Pil'nyak, 102-03, 107, 112, 116; on peasantry, 105*n*, 227*n*, 327; in Ivanov, 134-35, 145; Marxist view, 247; and proletariat, 327, 342
intention, in art, 211-12, 213*n*, 274
intuition, in art: *RVS* on, 205, 206, 208, 209-11, 214, 221, 233, 257, 258, 272, 275, 438; Octobrists on, 210; *LEF* on, 210, 237, 238; Proletkul't on, 225-26; Pereval on, 429; RAPP on, 430, 438. *See also* creative process
Irkutsk, 374
Ivanov, G., 105*n*
Ivanov, V., 417*n*
Ivanov, Vsevolod, 98, 118, 132, 316, 322, 379, 400; and *RVS*, 10, 12-13, 132, 312, 435; reception, 12-13, 79, 128-33, 138, 145-46; and Gor'kii, 21, 131-32; Voronskii on, 29*n*, 31*n*, 73, 75, 89, 130-33, 146-47, 232, 354, 443*n*; importance, 100, 146-47; and Pil'nyak, 128-31, 138, 145, 146; "joyfulness" of, 130-32;

and military fiction, 139, 143-44; and pre-Revolutionary literature, 146-47; after 1925, 146
works: Altaic Tales, 88-89; "a-psychological" stories, 326; *Armored Train 14-69*, 128, 130, 132, 133, 135-37, 140-41, 144-45, 146; *Azure Sands*, 97, 128, 130, 132, 133, 136-37, 142, 144; "Cotton," 345; "Duty," 345; "The God Matvei," 141-42; *The Guerrillas*, 10, 12-13, 21, 79, 128, 130, 132-37, 142, 145-46; "How Burial Mounds Are Made," 138-40; *Khabu*, 132, 314, 321*n*
characteristics: style, 88-89, 129; characters, 92, 130, 133-38, 144-45; view of world, 92, 129-33, 138-45; narrative technique, 129, 133-37; landscape, 129-30, 138; themes, 138-46, 345
Ivanov, Vyacheslav, 5
Ivanova, I., 357*n*
Ivanovo-Voznesensk, 20, 25, 26, 319

Jew, in literature of 1920's, 328, 337-40, 346, 347, 356
Johnson, Samuel, 300
Jones, Ernest, 205*n*
Journal:
precursors, 38-39
18th century: definition, 38; types and characteristics, 38-42; commercialism of, 39, 41, 49-50; *Both This and That*, 40*n*; *Drone*, 40*n*, 41; *Day's Labors*, 40*n*; *Free Hours*, 39; *Hellish Mail*, 40*n*; *Industrious Bee*, 39; *Innocent Exercise*, 39; *Miscellany*, 40*n*; *Monthly Compositions*, 38; *Monthly Fashion Publication*, 39*n*; *Moscow Journal*, 41; *Musical Entertainment*,

Guard, 148, 150, 159-60, 366, 368, 395; *On Literary Guard*, 175, 271, 368, 379, 434; *Press and Revolution*, 149; *Red Grainfield*, 163; *Red Pepper*, 378; *Searchlight*, 32, 378, 391; *Star*, 148, 370-72, 436; *Young Guard*, 148, 170, 178, 236, 365-68, 436

    private journals (1920's): 4, 21, 148, 372-75; *New Russia*, 247n, 372-73; *Russia*, 372-73; *Russian Contemporary*, 372-74 See also emigrés; *LEF*; Proletkul't; provinces; *RVS*; Smithy; Symbolism

Joyce, James, 18

Jung, Carl, 205n

K. T., 7n, 11n, 13n

Kamenskii, V., 151

Kant, Immanuel, 221, 284-85

Karakozov affair, 62

Karamzin, N., 40, 121

Karavaeva, A., 11, 227, 312, 375, 398, 401

Kasatkin, I., 81, 83, 263n, 314

Kataev, I., 345, 417, 430

Kataev, V., 312; *The Embezzlers*, 314, 330; "Rodion Zhukov," 325; "Fire," 329; *Time, Forward!*, 363

Kaurichev, N., 397

Kaverin, V., 52n, 98, 118, 373

Kazakov, M., 396n

Kazin, V., 158, 296, 356

Kerzhentsev, P., 169n, 178

Khalatov, A., 185n, 436n

Kheraskov Circle, 39

Khodasevich, V., 4n, 5, 245, 373

Kievan literature, 136

Kirillov, V., 158, 321, 356, 368

Kirshon, V., 365, 374

Kishchinskaya, L., 169n, 367n, 441n

Klimskii, A., pseud. of A. Voronskii, 27

Klychkov, S., 105n, 263n, 314, 356

Klyuev, N., 105n

Knorin, V., 425n

knowledge, art as, 193-98, 200, 207, 212-13, 215-17, 221-22, 224, 253. See also truth

Kogan, P., 86, 301; on Voronskii, 34, 364; on emigrés, 248-49

Kolomna, in literature, 269

Komarov, Matvei, 49

Komsomol poets, see Communist Youth poets

Korenev, G., 356

Korolenko, V., 40, 295

Kovalenko, D., 16n

Kozhevnikov, S., 375n

Kraevskii, A., 44-47, 60, 61

Krasnov, P., 249

Kruchonykh, A., 151

Krupskaya, N., 3, 8, 10, 15

Krylov, I., 41, 295

Kryuchkov, P., 185n

Kuleshov, V., 47n

Kuprin, A., 5, 115, 144

kuranty, 38

Kushner, B., 154

Kuvanova, L. K., 443, 444n

Kuz'minskaya, T. A., 214

labor theory of beauty, 199n

language: *RVS* on, 263-66, 268, 284, 288, 292, 315, 439; Marxism and, 309; Party on, 421; socialist realism on, 439

Lavrenyov, B., 370

Lawrence, D. H., 18

Lebedev, D., 6n

LEF (Left Front of Arts), 390; and *RVS*, 86, 150, 156, 189, 191-92, 203-04; explanation of name, 150n; origins, 152-53, 189; and Futurism, 152-53, 155, 189; program, 153-54; literary theory, 153-56, 159,

novella, 353; published in *RVS*, 314-15

Novikov, N., 40*n*

Novonikolaevsk (Novosibirsk), 374

Nurmin, pseud. of A. Voronskii, 25

objective: value in art, 233, 243, 245, 246, 258, 298, 429; describes creative process, 207, 230; describes reality appropriate to art, 214, 217, 229, 233, 246. *See also* reality

"Objectivism" in literature, 78

Oblomov, 230

Obradovich, S., 356

Octobrists, 149, 236, 365, 367, 368, 371, 387, 392, 395, 397, 398, 402, 403, 409, 412, 438; explanation of term, 160*n*; not synonymous with "proletarian literature," 168

history: origins and formation, 86, 159-60; journals controlled by, 148, 150, 159-60, 175, 271, 365-68, 371, 379, 395, 434; program, 159-62; split in, 174-75, 408; "right" (Averbakh) wing, 408-12, 438; "left" wing, 434-35; "right" wing captures VAPP and FOSP, 408-12

theory of literature, 160-63, 191, 195, 199, 201-04, 210, 222, 225-26, 229-31, 234, 237-39, 241, 243, 255, 257, 271, 273, 291, 345-46, 377-80, 421-22, 438; indebtedness to *RVS*, 408, 438; contribution to socialist realism, 439-40

polemic, with *RVS* and Voronskii, 150, 159-87, 203-04, 230-31, 233, 402, 421-22; allies in, 168-69

opinions: on Pil'nyak, 125-26, 161; on *LEF*, 155*n*; on Party policy toward literature, 159, 160-62, 166, 203-04; on literary organization, 159, 161-62, 395, 408-09; on proletarian literature, 160-64, 191, 202, 238, 371, 422; on fellow travelers, 160-62, 408-09; on Leonov, 161; on Babel', 162; on Pereval, 402

reception: Party on, 170, 173-74, 380, 411-12, 417-26; Gor'kii on, 172-73; Maiskii on, 371; Voronskii on, *see under* Voronskii

Octobrist poets, 296; defect to *RVS*, 163, 168, 367, 397, 402

Odoevskii, V., 42

Ognyov, N., 106*n*, 124, 312, 317*n*, 401; *The Diary of Kostya Ryabtsev*, 69, 316*n*

Olesha, Yu., 313, 314, 436; *Envy*, 338-46, 356*n*, 360-61

Ol'khovyi, B., 235*n*

Ol'minskii, M., 10

Omsk, 374

"On the Policy of the Party in the Area of Belles Lettres," *see* Communist Party

On-Guardists, explanation of term, 160*n*; *see also* Octobrists

Ordzhonikidze, G., 150

Oreshin, P., 356

organism: reality as, 201-02, 242-43, 251-52, 298; as effect of art, 218, 360; national literature as, 245, 252; criticism as, 302-03; art as: *RVS* on, 242-43, 245-46, 250-52, 267, 280, 282-83, 286, 287, 288, 298, 310, 361, 440-41; Pereval on, 401

organization, literary, xii, xiii; Party on, 20-21, 166-67, 380, 411-12, 423, 425; Proletkul't on, 157-58; Octobrists on, 159,

THIS BOOK forms part of the STUDIES OF THE HARRIMAN INSTITUTE, successor to:

STUDIES OF THE RUSSIAN INSTITUTE

ABRAM BERGSON, *Soviet National Income in 1937* (1953).

ERNEST J. SIMMONS, JR., ed., *Through the Glass of Soviet Literature: Views of Russian Society* (1953).

THAD PAUL ALTON, *Polish Postwar Economy* (1954).

DAVID GRANICK, *Management of the Industrial Firm in the USSR: A Study in Soviet Economic Planning* (1954).

ALLEN S. WHITING, *Soviet Policies in China, 1917–1924* (1954).

GEORGE S.N. LUCKYJ, *Literary Politics in the Soviet Ukraine, 1917–1934* (1956).

MICHAEL BORO PETROVICH, *The Emergence of Russian Panslavism, 1856–1870* (1956).

THOMAS TAYLOR HAMMOND, *Lenin on Trade Unions and Revolution, 1893–1917* (1956).

DAVID MARSHALL LANG, *The Last Years of the Georgian Monarchy, 1658–1832* (1957).

JAMES WILLIAM MORLEY, *The Japanese Thrust into Siberia, 1918* (1957).

ALEXANDER G. PARK, *Bolshevism in Turkestan, 1917–1927* (1957).

HERBERT MARCUSE, *Soviet Marxism: A Critical Analysis* (1958).

CHARLES B. MCLANE, *Soviet Policy and the Chinese Communists, 1931–1946* (1958).

OLIVER H. RADKEY, *The Agrarian Foes of Bolshevism: Promise and Defeat of the Russian Socialist Revolutionaries, February to October, 1917* (1958).

RALPH TALCOTT FISHER, JR., *Pattern for Soviet Youth: A Study of the Congresses of the Komsomol, 1918–1954* (1959).

ALFRED ERICH SENN, *The Emergence of Modern Lithuania* (1959).

ELLIOT R. GOODMAN, *The Soviet Design for a World State* (1960).

JOHN N. HAZARD, *Settling Disputes in Soviet Society: The Formative Years of Legal Institutions* (1960).

DAVID JORAVSKY, *Soviet Marxism and Natural Science, 1917–1932* (1961).

MAURICE FRIEDBERG, *Russian Classics in Soviet Jackets* (1962).

ALFRED J. RIEBER, *Stalin and the French Communist Party, 1941–1947* (1962).

THEODORE K. VON LAUE, *Sergei Witte and the Industrialization of Russia* (1962).

JOHN A. ARMSTRONG, *Ukrainian Nationalism* (1963).

OLIVER H. RADKEY, *The Sickle under the Hammer: The Russian Socialist Revolutionaries in the Early Months of Soviet Rule* (1963).

KERMIT E. MCKENZIE, *Comintern and World Revolution, 1928–1943: The Shaping of Doctrine* (1964).

HARVEY L. DYCK, *Weimar Germany and Soviet Russia, 1926–1933: A Study in Diplomatic Instability* (1966).

(Above titles published by Columbia University Press.)

HAROLD J. NOAH, *Financing Soviet Schools* (Teachers College, 1966).

JOHN M. THOMPSON, *Russia, Bolshevism, and the Versailles Peace* (Princeton, 1966).

PAUL AVRICH, *The Russian Anarchists* (Princeton, 1967).

LOREN R. GRAHAM, *The Soviet Academy of Sciences and the Communist Party, 1927–1932* (Princeton, 1967).

ROBERT A. MAGUIRE, *Red Virgin Soil: Soviet Literature in the 1920's* (Princeton, 1968).

T. H. RIGBY, *Communist Party Membership in the U.S.S.R., 1917–1967* (Princeton, 1968).

RICHARD T. DE GEORGE, *Soviet Ethics and Morality* (University of Michigan, 1969).

JONATHAN FRANKEL, *Vladimir Akimov on the Dilemmas of Russian Marxism, 1895–1903* (Cambridge, 1969).

WILLIAM ZIMMERMAN, *Soviet Perspectives on International Relations, 1956–1967* (Princeton, 1969).

PAUL AVRICH, *Kronstadt, 1921* (Princeton, 1970).

EZRA MENDELSOHN, *Class Struggle in the Pale: The Formative Years of the Jewish Workers' Movement in Tsarist Russia* (Cambridge, 1970).

EDWARD J. BROWN, *The Proletarian Episode in Russian Literature* (Columbia, 1971).

REGINALD E. ZELNIK, *Labor and Society in Tsarist Russia: The Factory Workers of St. Petersburg, 1855–1870* (Stanford, 1971).

PATRICIA K. GRIMSTED, *Archives and Manuscript Repositories in the USSR: Moscow and Leningrad* (Princeton, 1972).

RONALD G. SUNY, *The Baku Commune, 1917–1918* (Princeton, 1972).

EDWARD J. BROWN, *Mayakovsky: A Poet in the Revolution* (Princeton, 1973).

MILTON EHRE, *Oblomov and His Creator: The Life and Art of Ivan Goncharov* (Princeton, 1973).

HENRY KRISCH, *German Politics under Soviet Occupation* (Columbia, 1974).

HENRY W. MORTON and RUDOLPH L. TÖKÉS, eds., *Soviet Politics and Society in the 1970's* (Free Press, 1974).

WILLIAM G. ROSENBERG, *Liberals in the Russian Revolution* (Princeton, 1974).

RICHARD G. ROBBINS, JR., *Famine in Russia, 1891–1892* (Columbia, 1975).

VERA DUNHAM, *In Stalin's Time: Middleclass Values in Soviet Fiction* (Cambridge, 1976).

WALTER SABLINSKY, *The Road to Bloody Sunday* (Princeton, 1976).

WILLIAM MILLS TODD III, *The Familiar Letter as a Literary Genre in the Age of Pushkin* (Princeton, 1976).

ELIZABETH VALKENIER, *Russian Realist Art. The State and Society: The Peredvizhniki and Their Tradition* (Ardis, 1977).

SUSAN SOLOMON, *The Soviet Agrarian Debate* (Westview, 1978).

SHEILA FITZPATRICK, ed., *Cultural Revolution in Russia, 1928–1931* (Indiana, 1978).

PETER SOLOMON, *Soviet Criminologists and Criminal Policy: Specialists in Policy-Making* (Columbia, 1978).

KENDALL E. BAILES, *Technology and Society under Lenin and Stalin: Origins of the Soviet Technical Intelligentsia, 1917–1941* (Princeton, 1978).

LEOPOLD H. HAIMSON, ed., *The Politics of Rural Russia, 1905–1914* (Indiana, 1979).

THEODORE H. FRIEDGUT, *Political Participation in the USSR* (Princeton, 1979).

SHEILA FITZPATRICK, *Education and Social Mobility in the Soviet Union, 1921–1934* (Cambridge, 1979).

WESLEY ANDREW FISHER, *The Soviet Marriage Market: Mate-Selection in Russia and the USSR* (Praeger, 1980).

JONATHAN FRANKEL, *Prophecy and Politics: Socialism, Nationalism, and the Russian Jews, 1862–1917* (Cambridge, 1981).

ROBIN FEUER MILLER, *Dostoevsky and the Idiot: Author, Narrator, and Reader* (Harvard, 1981).

DIANE KOENKER, *Moscow Workers and the 1917 Revolution* (Princeton, 1981).

PATRICIA K. GRIMSTED, *Archives and Manuscript Repositories in the USSR: Estonia, Latvia, Lithuania, and Belorussia* (Princeton, 1981).

EZRA MENDELSOHN, *Zionism in Poland: The Formative Years, 1915–1926* (Yale, 1982).

HANNES ADOMEIT, *Soviet Risk-Taking and Crisis Behavior* (George Allen & Unwin, 1982).

SEWERYN BIALER and THANE GUSTAFSON, eds., *Russia at the Crossroads: The 26th Congress of the CPSU* (George Allen & Unwin, 1982).

ROBERTA THOMPSON MANNING, *The Crisis of the Old Order in Russia: Gentry and Government* (Princeton, 1983).

ANDREW A. DURKIN, *Sergei Aksakov and Russian Pastoral* (Rutgers, 1983).

BRUCE PARROTT, *Politics and Technology in the Soviet Union* (MIT Press, 1983).

SARAH PRATT, *Russian Metaphysical Romanticism: The Poetry of Tiutchev and Boratynskii* (Stanford, 1984).

STUDIES OF THE HARRIMAN INSTITUTE

ELIZABETH KRIDL VALKENIER, *The Soviet Union and the Third World: An Economic Bind* (Praeger, 1983).

JOHN LEDONNE, *Ruling Russia: Politics and Administration in the Age of Absolutism 1762–1796* (Princeton, 1984).

DIANE GREENE, *Insidious Intent: A Structural Analysis of Fedor Sologub's Petty Demon* (Slavica, 1986).
RICHARD F. GUSTAFSON, *Leo Tolstoy: Resident and Stranger* (Princeton, 1986).

Library of Congress Cataloging-in-Publication Data

Maguire, Robert A., 1930–
  Red virgin soil.

  (Studies of the Harriman Institute)
  Bibliography: p.
  Includes index.
  1. Russian literature—20th century—History and criticism. 2. Krasnaĭa nov´. I. Title. II. Series.
PG3022.M3   1987   891.7'09'0042   86-24391
ISBN 0-8014-9447-8 (pbk. : alk. paper)